ROADS TO THE PALACE
Jewish Texts and Teaching

**FAITH AND CULTURE IN
CONTEMPORARY EDUCATION**
General Editor: Jo Cairns, Director of the Centre for Research
and Development in Religion and Education (CREDERE) at the
Institute of Education, University of London

The aim of this new series is to identify major questions and issues
concerning the education of individuals and communities in a post-
modern world. Leading scholars from the main denominations,
together with humanist thinkers, examine the role of theological
and non-materialist concepts in inter-cultural and inter-faith
educational discourse. Their thinking challenges many existing
educational norms.

Volume 1:
ROADS TO THE PALACE
Jewish Texts and Teaching
Michael Rosenak

In preparation:

Volume 2:
HINDUISM AND HUMAN VALUES
A Model for Humanity
Dvijadas Bannerji, Jo Cairns and Amar Desai

Volume 3:
THE CATHOLIC SCHOOL NOW
A Culture of Faith in a Secular World
Jo Cairns and Paddy Walsh

ROADS TO THE PALACE

Jewish Texts and Teaching

Michael Rosenak

Berghahn Books
Providence • Oxford

First published in 1995 by

Berghahn Books

Editorial offices:
165 Taber Avenue, Providence, RI 02906, USA
Bush House, Merewood Avenue, Oxford, OX3 8EF, UK

© Michael Rosenak 1995

Library of Congress Cataloging-in-Publication Data
Rosenak, Michael.
    Roads to the palace : Jewish texts and teaching / Michael Rosenak.
        p.   cm. -- (Faith and culture in contemporary education : v. 1)
    Includes bibliographical references.
    ISBN 1-57181-058-7 (hardback : alk. paper)
    1. Judaism--Study and teaching.   2. Jewish religious education --
Philosophy.   I. Title.   II. Series.
BM70.R66   1995   95-17226
296.6'8--dc20   CIP

British Library Cataloguing in Publication Data

A catalogue record for this book is available from the British Library.

Printed on acid-free paper in the USA.

Cover Illustration: © 1995 David Moss
Courtesy of Bet Aplha Editions, Rochester, New York

To Geulah

A king is in his palace, and all his subjects are partly in the country and partly abroad. Of the former, some have their backs turned towards the king's palace and their faces in another direction; and some are desirous and zealous to go to the palace, seeking "to inquire in his temple" and to minister before him, but have not even seen the face of the wall of the house. Of those who desire to go to the palace, some reach it, and go round about in search of the entrance gate; others have passed through the gate, and walk about in the ante-chamber; and others have succeeded in entering into the inner part of the palace, and being in the same room with the king in the royal palace. But even the latter do not immediately upon entering the palace see the king, or speak to him; for after having entered the inner part of the palace, another effort is required before they can stand before the king—at a distance or close by—hear his words or speak to him.

Moses Maimonides

CONTENTS

PREFACE

*R*oads to the Palace reflects many years of study, conversation, and teaching. I am grateful to all who talked with me and taught me, but particularly so to those who knew that my inclination and vocation were to translate all learning into theology and educational philosophy—and who yet remained patient and even interested.

In my experience, there have been some who could not relate seriously to the palace of Jewish learning and living, and others who knew themselves to be walking on the one and only road to it. To be blessed with teachers, students, and colleagues who have empathy for the title and are willing to talk and argue about it is thus no small matter. At the Hebrew University's Melton Center for Jewish Education in the Diaspora, I am particularly fortunate in this respect. Happily, I have also enjoyed the constant encouragement of Alan Hoffmann and Dr. Ze'ev Mankowitz, the former and present directors of the center. Special thanks go to Ms. Carmen Sharon, deputy director of the Center, for her practical advice and help.

Some of the foundations of this work were laid in my earlier work, *Commandments and Concerns: Jewish Religious Education in Secular Society* (1987), and, as I shall explain, some of the major themes of that book are developed here. This development led through projects and courses, as well as papers written on several occasions. Thus, the discussion below on values (Chapters Nine and Ten) grew out of an earlier and less elaborate formulation in my theoretical guidebook, *Teaching Jewish Values: a Conceptual Guide* (1987), published by the Melton Center. An earlier treatment of Chapters Eleven and Twelve appeared in the Melton Center's *Studies in Jewish Education,* Vol. 6 (1993). The substance of Chapter Fifteen was presented with a somewhat different focus in a paper delivered at Jews' College in London in 1989, at a conference entitled "Traditional Alternatives: Orthodoxy and the Jewish Future." It was then published in *Orthodoxy Con-*

fronts Modernity, edited by Rabbi Jonathan Sacks in 1991. My thanks go to colleagues at the Melton Center and at Jews' College, particularly Chief Rabbi Sacks, for helping me to develop and initially formulate the themes of those chapters.

Those who have enriched this book through their comments include Professors Seymour Fox, Zev Harvey, and Dr. Jonathan Cohen of the Hebrew University and Dr. Beverly Gribetz of the Ramaz school in New York, each of whom read chapters relevant to their specific fields (educational theory, Maimonides, and teaching Talmud). Rabbi Dov Berkowits was kind enough to read the entire book carefully; I asked him to do so because I knew that he would read it with the eye of a profound scholar of Torah and a master of Jewish teaching. I am grateful also to my student and educational colleague, Rabbi Scot Berman, who read and commented on various sections, and to the doctoral students in Jewish education at Stanford University with whom I studied and to whom I taught an advanced draft of this book in February 1993. Professor Arnold Eisen at Stanford not only read and discussed the entire book with me, but made concrete and copious suggestions. He treated my book and myself with the genuine affection and honest critique that mark close friendship. I thank him, therefore, for both.

My friend and colleague, Professor Barry Holtz of the Jewish Theological Seminary, read carefully and commented thoughtfully. Also, he never failed to accord me helpful advice in practical as well as theoretical matters germane to this book. Among my readers, I should also like to mention my son, Avinoam, a sharp yet understanding commentator. We think alike on many things, so I always have his sympathy, but he thinks for himself, so I try to listen carefully.

To my editors at Berghahn Books, my warmest thanks. I have tried to be clear, but without them some of my good intentions would not have been translated into practice. I especially thank Dr. Marion Berghahn, my publisher, who devoted many hours to conversation and comment. Like many writers, and perhaps more than most, I need to be reminded that not every written word is sacred and that clarity is more precious than a clever but obtuse sentence. Even mine! I also express my gratitude to Mr. Udi Cohen, a Jerusalem educator and my graduate student in Jewish education, for preparing the index.

Professors Jo Cairns and Roy Gardner of the Institute of Education of the University of London have been particularly helpful. Jo and I have built a firm friendship and working relationship in recent years. And I am proud and happy to have this book initiate a new scholarly project of the institute, a series of volumes on the cultural and educational philosophies of living faith communities. Jo and

Roy worked diligently to make that happen. Roy was also kind enough to read the book in order to determine which Jewish-Hebrew terms required translation or explanation. In this very practical manner, he quite rightly pointed out that an exposition of educational philosophy from within a specific cultural or religious community need not be unnecessarily obscure to those outside it.

Roads to the Palace was begun early in 1990. In the fall of that year, a critical illness led me to assume, at least for several weeks, that it would never be written. Though thanksgiving to God "Who heals the sick" is reserved for prayer and is wildly inappropriate in prefaces, I would be remiss if I did not gratefully mention His talented and dedicated emissaries, specifically, the medical staff at the community hospital at Ellenville, New York City, and most especially Professors Richard Popp of the Stanford University Hospital and Jonathan Halperin of the Mt. Sinai Department of Cardiology. They are embodiments of the medical person as *mensch*. Nor may I neglect to mention and thank Professor Moshe Sokolow of Yeshiva University who got me there in time. I also thank my son, Dr. Daniel Rosenak, who devotedly helped shepherd me back to health. Finally, my loving appreciation to my wife, Geulah, who was there with me, in every way, at the right time.

To her, and not only for that, I dedicate this book.

INTRODUCTION

*I*n recent years, there has been a spate of books that explicate "what Judaism says." There have also been significant study books designed for use at evening seminars or summer retreats. My present work is not intended as a contribution to either of these categories. It is, rather, an attempt to glean directions for philosophy of Jewish education from the sources of the Jewish literary tradition. There are inherent difficulties in such a venture.

To begin with, teachers and other people frequently conceive of educational philosophy as little more than a medley of edifying ideas, raw material for after-dinner speeches by well-meaning community leaders, consisting of no more than exhortation and perhaps enrichment. At times teachers find themselves vaguely uplifted by it; they also experience philosophy to be quite useless in the actual practice of their trade. Since they learn nothing practical from it, educators tend to think they can manage quite well without it.

Educational-philosophical discourse that is focused on religious conceptions of the good life and of the righteous person is especially vulnerable; it seems tailor-made for a rhetoric of self-righteousness. And yet, from philosophy of education as from all philosophical discourse, we have the right to expect reasoned positions: on what is worthy, why certain cultural goods ought to be transmitted, and why it is difficult to do so with integrity and effectiveness. Religious educational thought that sounds like no more than a cluster of dogmatic pronouncements gives the field a bad name.

Jewish educational philosophy faces additional difficulties.

The first of these is that the Jewish tradition is *midrashic* (interpretative) rather than philosophical in nature. This means that it thinks in terms of events, experiences, paradigms, concrete social ideals, *halakhot* (laws), personal and covenantal relationships, and stories. It is fundamentally different from the Greek philosophical tradition, where logic and abstract notions of the good and the true invite the wise to speculate before acting. Is it necessary for this tradition of concreteness to translate itself into the seemingly alien mode of philosophy to achieve a contemporary self-understanding and communicability? And if so, how can this be done without a reductionism that makes it redundant?

Secondly, this tradition, when reaching out into universal educational discourse to argue on behalf of its internal idea of *Paideia,* of education and culture,[1] is likely to descend to apologetics. The widespread bias that Judaism has no *Paideia,* but only social conventions, tribal loyalties, and narrow theological notions may well create a fortress mentality among defenders of the Jewish cognitive minority, making them, alternatively, abrasive or self-effacing. That is hardly helpful to educators, who justifiably wish to cultivate in their pupils clear identities of convictions that are both realistic about the world, yet, at the same time, not burdened by superfluous enmities or by undue defensiveness.

Finally, Jewish educational philosophy, while bound to a sacred literature which is religious to the core, must take account of the fact that it addresses school people, parents, policymakers and curriculum writers who have very varying conceptions of how this literature is to be studied, understood and used to shape contemporary Jewish life. Though Judaism is a religious heritage, it is not a culturally disembodied confession. It resides within a concrete and historical people. Therefore, religious Jews belong to the Jewish people which includes, in modern times, explicitly secular members. And a secular Jew is culturally bound to the Jewish religious tradition in a way that, say, the secular Englishman is not likely to be bound to the Anglican Church.

Given the contemporary diversity among Jews as to how their religious and national identities are to function and interrelate, there can today be no single Jewish philosophy of education. And while the enterprise of shaping any Jewish educational philosophy must build on some understanding and acknowledgment of the Jewish tradition's religious foundations, it cannot evade, even in the case of religious Jews, general cultural and even civilizational issues.

To counter the tendency of educational thought to wax poetic and overly polemical, the analytic and critical functions of educational

1. See Werner Jaeger, *Paideia: The Ideals of Greek Culture,* translated by Gilbert Highet from second German edition (Oxford: Basil Blackwell, 1954).

philosophy must be consciously and appropriately used. These have been beautifully described by Dearden[2] to include the making of "necessary distinctions to clarify meaning, explor(ing) conceptual possibilities and try(ing) to identify what is necessary and what is contingent." Dearden urges us to:

> expose question-begging, misleading claims and inconsistency ... draw implications, show the full extent of someone's commitments, reveal absurd consequences, highlight by parallel arguments, draw attention to unnoticed alternatives and test assumptions ... probe the validity of justifications, draw attention to areas of undeserved neglect, redress serious imbalances and assemble pertinent reminders.

Dearden insists that philosophy of education should be enabled to "expose narrow conceptions, probe presuppositions and reveal hidden connections or expose spurious unity .... clarify ideals and articulate imaginative new conceptions. It should redescribe to bring into different focus, show how certain notions will not do the work expected of them, show how one thing prevents the recognition of another, identify misplaced emphases or misdirected attention and set things in a wider illuminating context ..."

These are worthy goals and worthwhile tasks, and may not be neglected. Yet religious, possibly all, educational philosophy requires an explicitly normative dimension as well. To show the full extent of someone's commitments, if they are your own, involves spelling out what you consider true and good and consequently which goods you wish to impart to others. In philosophizing about education, you will have to explain on some grounds shared with others why these commitments are persuasive to you and how they may be made at least plausible to others.

Moreover, educational thought must show how thinking may be related to doing. Philosophy of education should not be narrowly practical, yet it must intimate how one can move from ideas to children and from principles to concrete situations in which they are to be applied. Less than that cannot be called educational except in the most stipulative and scholastic sense.

The specific problems of Jewish educational philosophy demand special attention to the issue of translation, which Berger[3] has described, in the context of religious traditions, as the reformulation of traditions "in terms appropriate to (a) ... new frame of reference." Berger describes such translation as cognitive surrender, as a largely futile attempt at rehabilitating religious traditions and salvaging

2. R. F. Dearden, *Theory and Practice in Education* (London: Routledge and Kegan Paul, 1984), pp. 31–32.
3. Peter L. Berger, *A Rumour of Angels: Modern Society and the Rediscovery of the Supernatural* (Harmondsworth, England: Pelican Books, 1971), pp. 34-35.

their relevance. But there ought to be, and I believe, have always been, modes of partial translation. The practitioner of partial translation insists that such a reflective yet deeply embedded cultural-religious world-view as the Jewish one can be expressed in varied literary or philosophical modes without sacrificing its character and authenticity. S/he holds that without such partial translation, authenticity and relevance cannot be brought together in education. Much of this book therefore deals with the arts of partial translation, as represented by the homiletic *(midrashic)* tradition of Judaism. It is this *midrashic* mode that the educational philosopher is invited to use in redescribing (Jewish education in order) to bring (it) into different focus.

In this process, a crucial role is assigned to what I believe to be useful conceptions of *language* and *literature.* I utilize these terms to suggest the distinction between source and commentary respectively; between sacred tradition and interpretation, and between the foundations of the good life and the ways it may actually be lived. These ways, I hope to show, must be diverse, especially in our pluralistic age, but philosophical-educational criteria may be established for what is valid and justifiable and what suffers, in one direction or another, from serious imbalance.

In my previous study of Jewish educational philosophy, *Commandments and Concerns,* I was primarily concerned with delineating and examining two focuses of religious tradition and life and describing their encounter with modernity. There I posited that Jewish religious life has both an institutional, imposed, and normative dimension, which I termed explicit, and a personal, spontaneous, and inward dimension, which I called implicit. The general thrust in that book was to show that philosophy of religious Jewish education is concerned to link and partially integrate these dimensions in the lives of educated Jews, and how it sees education promoting this end. In the present work, my intention is to locate philosophy of Jewish education in its subject matter, the textual tradition. Language, in this book, is parallel to what I previously called the explicit aspect; literature, to the implicit one. I intend to demonstrate that out of the textual tradition of Judaism, philosophy of education may be mined. My thesis is that the *midrashic* mode need not relinquish its *midrashic* character to reveal its philosophic riches, if only appropriate conceptual tools are used to mine it, or, in more traditional terms, to learn it. We shall, therefore, learn Torah in this book. This will be done in a fragmentary and merely illustrative way, of course, but not, I hope, haphazardly.

To clarify the presenting problem, I begin with an examination of how philosophy of education works and how a religious-literary tradition may encounter it. To do this, it is necessary to indicate how the language of Judaism, i.e., Torah, thinks, and how literature is made within it. This examination is followed by a survey of some views of the relationship between the substance of the language itself (Torah) and wisdom *(hokhmah)*. Wisdom is a store of experience and thought. It generally is formulated in a specific language but supplies building blocks for new literature in many languages, thereby enriching them. Though it is not to be shoddily or even casually appropriated by the masters of any language, all languages, the Jewish one included, would become narrow and inert without replenishment by wisdom. At the same time, we shall insist that while wisdom from anywhere replenishes language, it can never replace it.

An outstanding literature project in the Jewish tradition, of interpreting the language of Torah, is that of the medieval scholar, philosopher and teacher, Moses Maimonides. I have chosen to explore Maimonides rather than a modern Jewish thinker as a potential source of educational philosophy because he seems paradigmatic for translation. Both his admirers and critics admit that he considers it both appropriate and commanded to uphold the norms of the tradition and also that it is to be understood through the prism of hokhmah (wisdom). Because he is a model of translating the nonphilosophical language of Torah into philosophical categories, we may justifiably address questions of educational philosophy to him; he can help us see what educational discourse that is both Jewish and philosophical looks like.

Once having seen how translation works and how philosophical wisdom can coax communicable theories out of Torah, we then move to an explicitly normative character ideal of the Jewish-rabbinic tradition, that of fear of Heaven, *Yirat Shamayim.* I partially translate it into moral and existential philosophy in order to clarify this value concept[4] and to make its character ideal more generally comprehensible, more philosophical. This is necessary not only because the educational teachings of Judaism are of interest and perhaps of value to non-Jewish educators as well, but also because Jewish educators, as noted above, do not automatically share assumptions, convictions, and educational ends.

To illustrate how such a normative educational issue may be clarified philosophically through a joint study of Torah and how philosophy of education may foster commonalties without deviously blurring distinctive viewpoints, we assemble a roundtable of arche-

---

4. This term has been developed by and is generally identified with Max Kaddushin. See Max Kadushin, *The Rabbinic Mind,* 3rd ed. (New York: Bloch Publishing Co., 1972).

typal Jewish educators who learn Torah together. These educators explore whether *Yirat Shamayim* speaks to them in some common fashion as a result of their study and whether they can philosophically reconceptualize this concept in order to gain a common educational approach to it.

Our next exploration is primarily a *halakhic* (legal) and *aggadic* (homiletic-narrative) study that exposes to view two distinct tiers of value in the language. We find that value talk is readily coaxed out of the world of the Talmudic sages once conceptual hokhmah is mobilized to give us congenial uses of the term value itself. Here we discover internal Jewish criteria for what may be considered doctrinal as well as the place of value clarification within this doctrine—and its limits.

Our final text study is designed to examine how initiation and commitment, as done and taught by the Talmudic sage Hillel, may be better understood for educational purposes through a contemporary philosophical discussion of practice.

In the concluding chapters, I address the need to tie together thinking and doing in education. I here seek to locate a lexicon of Jewish teaching, to examine whether norms, even for secular-minded people, are still viable. Then I suggest some curricular guidelines, on the basis of the proposed lexicon, for the educated Jew.

I believe that these guidelines, as well as the deliberations that precede them, have something to say to educators of other faiths as well. This is not because these guidelines are not rooted in the particular tradition of Judaism, but because this particular teaching, as will be shown, has an explicitly universal aspect that addresses all created in God's image. Furthermore, the mode of philosophy of education, as a form of hokhmah (wisdom) is specifically designed to create a broad community of discourse. I hope that this book enhances such discourse, helps clarify how Judaism thinks educationally, what it expects Jews to diligently teach their children—and why. I assume that some readers of this book will be primarily interested in its philosophical-educational thesis while others will be more interested in its suggested uses of texts for education. To the latter I suggest that they might consider beginning their reading with Section III-V. Then, before proceeding to Section VI, I should advise them to return to Section I, for the key to the final chapters. Those most concerned with the philosophical-educational aspect of the book will probably begin at the beginning.[5]

And now, to avoid the "serious imbalance" caused by overly long introductions, we should begin.

---

5. For this suggestion, I am indebted to Mr. Udi Cohen.

Section I

EDUCATION,
LANGUAGE, AND LITERATURE

1

LARGE QUESTIONS,
ANCIENT TEXTS

*I*n Section Two of this book, a significant role is assigned to the following *mishnah:*

> All Israelites have a share in the world to come, as it is written, 'Your people also shall be all righteous, they shall inherit the land forever; the branch of My planting, the work of My hands wherein I glory' (Is. 60:21). But these have no share in the world to come: one who says that the resurrection of the dead is not taught in the Torah; one who says that the Torah is not from Heaven; and the atheist ...
>
> *Sanhedrin* 10:1

The reader may well ask what this *mishnah* has to do with the alleged subject of this volume, education. Which educational issues does it suggest? How is it related to deliberations or prescriptions about teaching? What does it have to do with the interests and capacities of pupils? With the cultivation of human potentialities, or methods of instruction?

The reader surely deserves an explanation, especially since in our discussion of that *mishnah*, we shall not really be concerned with it itself, but with what Maimonides does with it in the Introduction to Chapter *Helek* of his *Commentary to the Mishnah.* S/he was promised a book on Jewish educational thought garnered from the literature of Torah. Is medieval commentary on *Mishnah* in that category?

Let us state all this somewhat differently, from the writer's perspective: what are we actually looking for and where are we looking for it? What is the educational thought we wish to locate and clarify through an illustrative study of selected sources? What do we mean by a source?

Education and Educational Thought

First, we should say something about the terms education and educational thought. Education has been succinctly defined by Frankena[1] as "the activity of fostering or transmitting excellences," generally in children and young people. The term "excellences," he tells us, includes abilities, traits, and skills. Moral dispositions too are excellences, no less than competence in comprehending and/or using various worthwhile bodies of knowledge. The underlying assumptions are: (a) that we don't have all these dispositions innately, (b) that they must, at least in part, be acquired, and (c) that such acquisition is both possible and may, at least to a degree, be acquired through what is called education.

An educated person possesses excellent dispositions. He or she has been given, or helped to develop, what is considered a worthy outlook and a sound understanding of reality and life. Such a person can think and act well, and has the desire to do so. Ultimately, education makes it possible for human beings to live good social and individual lives, however defined.

The phrase that creates so much difficulty for educational philosophy, is, of course, "however defined." It is not enough to say that we ought to educate young people to be fine individuals and good citizens, possessed of such exemplary traits as honesty and courage; to make them knowledgeable in all branches of wisdom, and skilled in solving all problems that come their way. We have to know, or perhaps decide, how good traits work, what we mean by wisdom, and whether all problems are equally worth our attention. Actually, we don't even know what attention implies. Are all the most important problems of life invitations to solving them or are many of them in principle insoluble and only to be nobly endured? Or ignored?

And that's not all. It is not enough to determine which dispositions, competences, and bodies of knowledge are worthwhile, helping to make people excellent. There is obviously no time in anyone's education for learning everything that someone, somewhere, considers important or indispensable. We have to decide on priorities for there are things we may consider supremely worthwhile that others will call trivial. For example, most people in the world do not view either Talmud (the Rabbinic texts that constitute the core of the Oral Torah) or modern Hebrew literature as significant or interesting

---

1. William Frankena, *Three Historical Philosophies of Education* (New York: Scott, Foresman and Co., 1965), p. 8, and see my discussion of this: Michael Rosenak, *Commandments and Concerns: Jewish Religious Education in Secular Society* (Philadelphia: The Jewish Publication Society, 5747/1987), p. 27.

enough to burden children with; there are too many other, "really important" things to learn. So why do some people, specifically, many Jewish educators, nevertheless insist on one or both of these "subjects" as crucial for the curriculum? Why do some people think that a knowledge of "how to do" Talmud, or physics or gymnastics, contribute to a person's ability to live "a good life" while others are happy to do without one or all of them? And if one thinks that Talmud is interesting but Hebrew literacy or a great "Israel experience" is more important, how did s/he decide that?

Because of this cluster of questions, any philosophy or education requires close attention to the question: Why are some dispositions or "excellences" to be regarded as worthy and worthwhile? On the basis of which principles do we know that these, rather than other excellences should be encouraged, cultivated, taught? Is it because "reason" teaches us how to distinguish between what is worthy and what is not? Is it because "revelation" makes clear distinctions for us between the sacred and the profane? Or because "experience" demonstrates what has been found useful or what is needful for a fulfilled life in a particular generation or in particular circumstances?[2]

What – Why – How

When we think educationally, we ask ourselves which ideals of attitude, morality, knowledgeability, and general competence we should foster; we also ask why. We seek justifications, in terms of what we believe about reality, humankind, wisdom, and goodness, for having chosen these particular ideals.

Therefore, in looking at Jewish sources, we shall wish to see whether we can find a Jewish world of principle (basic assumptions and beliefs) in them and what they tell us about visions and prescriptions concerning the good life that flow from these assumptions and beliefs for individuals and communities/societies. Philosophy of education is predicated on the axiom that only where there are ideals of human behavior, aspiration, morality, and understanding is it possible to establish what the content of education should be. The philosopher of education is one who insists that educational decisions ought to be made and defended in terms of what we believe about reality, knowledge, and value. For only when we consider what we believe and how we should therefore act, can we answer Frankena's question: why are these dispositions (rather than others)

---

2. The "reason," "revalation" and "experience" terms are placed in quotation marks because their precise meanings are the subject of much discussion and controversy.

to be regarded as excellences and cultivated? Only after dealing with that question is it appropriate to ask: how shall we go about educating toward these excellences? To what extent can they be transmitted? For whom? And by which means?

As a matter of fact, we do not generally think about "why questions" like these in educational discussions. Rather, we tend to move directly to the educational ventures that concern us and ask ourselves how best to implement them. For example, we wish to know what should be done in this classroom, or in that summer camp activity. As practical educators, we wish to know how to teach a particular subject matter, how to interest children, train teachers, or win the support of parents and schools systems for specific programs. Generally, our concern is not with the grounds of what we do, not with the kinds of human beings our institutions of education ought to produce but with the methods of carrying on the teaching-learning process despite such stark facts as pupils' boredom and teachers' fatigue.

In other words, most talk about education concerns itself with the theory of education and not the philosophy of education.[3] In theory-of-education discourse, we ask how to do education. This means, for example, that we deal with subject matter (like Talmud or physics or scouting) and decide how to relate it to other areas of study, to simplify it or make it more attractive for educational use. Or, we are concerned with teachers, and how they may best teach; or we ask how pupils, given their present stage of cognitive and emotional development, their prior experiences and perceived interests, will adequately learn. We also look at the environment in which education takes place; we wish to know whether it supports or sabotages what teachers, armed with subject matter, intend to foster in their pupils. And, of course, educational discourse usually attempts to set plausible proximate objectives: what we should like to achieve in a given time frame and setting, and how we may evaluate success in achieving it. To give just one example: we usually think that children should learn to read right at the beginning of their school careers and we discuss how best to accomplish that goal, and what would constitute the achievement of it, and how to evaluate it.

Theories of education are extremely complex because they require input from various disciplines, and they involve many inter-

3. For further discussion on the distinction between theory and philosophy of education, see Elizabeth Steiner Maccia, "The Separation of Philosophy from Theory of Education," *Readings in the Philosophy of Education,* edited by John Martin Rich (Belmont, CA., Wadsworth Publishing Co., Inc., 1968), pp. 383–93. For citations in the text, pp. 387, 389.

actions. For example, we routinely solicit the aid of psychological theories to explain how children learn, and our understanding of the child as learner cannot be seen in isolation from our notions about the teacher as socializing agent and of the society that commissions him or her. And yet, paradoxically, theory of education is often identified with aphorisms and pithy prescriptions of what to do.

Thus, to the extent that Jewish educators have investigated the sources of Jewish tradition for educational wisdom, it has often been to locate Biblical, Talmudic or *midrashic* comments on good teaching, laudable pupils, good or bad environments or developmental timetables for the introduction of diverse subjects for study.[4] Sometimes these Biblical or rabbinic sayings are treated with respect in the educational discussion; at other times they are discounted for their disagreement with modern (mainly psychological) axioms of educational theory.

For example, the *mishnaic* tractate *Avot,* also known as *Ethics of the Fathers,* tells us that an overly stringent teacher cannot successfully teach (2:6); our experience as well as our modern conceptions of morally acceptable relationships to children lead us to nod appreciatively at that sentiment. On the other hand, when we read in Proverbs (13:24) that "One who spares the rod spoils his child" we are likely to be infuriated or amused. Who considers adult aggressiveness a valid educational practice?[5] Most modern people will agree with the sage Raba *(B.T. Baba Batra 21b)* that "a teacher of young children (like a vine-dresser, a ritual slaughterer, a blood-letter and a town scribe) is to be dismissed immediately" (if inefficient) according to the general principle that "anyone whose mistakes cannot be rectified should be dismissed immediately." Raba, they feel, apparently understood how teachers can permanently affect pupils,

---

4. For far-ranging studies on these, see Joseph Safran, *Pirkai Iyun b'Toldot Hahinukh Hayehudi I (Studies in the History of Jewish Education I)* (Jerusalem: Mosad Harav Kook, 1983), Chap. 1–2; Moshe Aberbach, *Hahinukh Hayehudi B'Tkufat Hamishnah V'hatalmud (Jewish Education in the Mishnaic and Talmudic Period)* (Jerusalem: Rubin Mass Ltd., 1982).

5. The *Haredi* (ultra-Orthodox) community, however, does not generally allow itself such latitude in evaluating the theory of Biblical and Talmudic teaching. Thus, for example, a twentieth-century educational and religious mentor of *Haredi* Judaism, Rabbi Eliyahu Dessler, sees this prescription, to hit children, as part and parcel of an eternally true world view, though he does not sanction doing so cruelly or arbitrarily. R. Eliyahu L. Dessler, *Mikhtav Eliyahu III,* edited by A. Carmel and A. Halperin (Bnei Brak, Israel: Committee for the Publication of the Writings of Rabbi E.L. Dessler, 1964), pp. 360–62. It is an interesting characteristic of *Haredi* (ultra-traditional) educational writings in general that traditional theoretical ("how to") statements are considered no less binding than philosophical statements. See, for example, S. Wagschal, *Successful Hinukh: a Guide for Parents and Teachers* (Jerusalem and New York: Feldheim, 1988) in which each educational prescription is given rabbinic (Talmudic, *midrashic,* etc.) authorization.

for better or worse. Our sources are rich in educational sayings or even prescriptions of this kind.

However, in this book we are only peripherally interested in explicit educational statements or suggestions to be found in the classic writings of Judaism. Our point of departure is that the theoretical statements (telling us how to educate) are subservient to the philosophical questions: Which excellences shall we cultivate? Why are these excellences to be considered worthy? In other words, we are concerned, first and foremost, with ideals of human existence that education is responsible for cultivating if possible and for the fundamental beliefs that justify adhering to these ideals and transmitting them to the young generation that is destined to replace us.

Consequently, we find a text such as the following educationally provocative:

> S/he who sheds the blood of a person, by humans shall his/her blood be shed, for in the image of God He made the human being (Genesis 9:7).

In this verse, which the Talmudic sages categorized as one of the seven *Noahide* commandments binding on all humanity,[6] there is both the statement of a prescription for ideal human behavior and its justifying principle. In the ideal (commanded) society, persons are not to kill one another and society is responsible for punishing those who disrupt the ideal (commanded) state. And the reason: "for" human beings are created in God's image. The Torah here gives us a belief stated (as such beliefs generally are!) as both fiat and fact, without which there would be no good reason to desist from murder or for society to interfere. Without the phrase, "for in the image of God He made the human being," killing might be conceived as a private matter between two people, one of whom was, fortunately, strong and the other, regrettably, weak.

From this verse we learn that children should be taught to honor the dignity of others, for these others, like themselves, are created in God's image. Educators who believe this text to be normative will affirm that those who shun violence out of respect for God's commandment have acquired an excellence. This excellence of course conflicts with some other conceptions of the good and the worthy. For example in a Nazi society, doing what the Torah demands is taken to be a shameful weakness "for" the world is a jungle and the only significance achievable in an absurd cosmos comes through gaining power and inflicting pain. Conversely, those who accept the principle that the Torah conveys the will of God to us and thus gives us access to what is good and worthy, know the Nazi principles to be

---

6. *Sanhedrin* 56a–b. Here and throughout the book, Talmudic citations are from the Babylonian Talmud. Therefore I omit the abbreviation "B.T." in citing the Talmud.

mistaken and the ideals of human action and existence that flow from them to be evil, idolatrous.

However, it is not sufficient to declare given principles good and to simply assert that certain human excellences naturally derive from them. In an environment in which there is competition between bodies of principle, the educational thinker will wish to examine why some beliefs are more worthy of assent and loyalty than others. S/he will investigate whether given ideals, such as conferring dignity on people by virtue of their humanity, can be justified only by theological principles (such as that of our verse) or also by others that build on funds of human discernment, such as humanistic ones. Also, s/he will ask how the ideal not to kill human beings, "created in the image of God," can be reconciled with the commandment, that is, the theologically founded ideal, to kill those who murder.

To these philosophical questions, the educator will wish to add such theory-of-education questions as: how can one develop in young people an abhorrence of killing that is packaged with the commandment of execution? Is this package congenial to the norms of the society in which our children live or antithetical to them? In which ways is it congenial or antithetical? How shall such an ideal be actually cultivated in young people, in light of what we think we know about the aggressive and self-centered features of human nature?

Interestingly, we cannot reflectively deal with these questions without being referred back to some philosophical ones: is educating for this package (of considering human beings as created in God's image and therefore executing killers) to be seen as a normative given or should one seek to interpret the commandment of execution so that it becomes virtually inoperative (as renowned sages in our tradition have done), thereby eliminating the friction between two different and conflicting ideals?[7] Or, perhaps, should the trait fostered in children be not abhorrence or empathy for specific acts but a religious orientation, say, of obedience to authority? Or, conversely, should we cultivate spiritual autonomy, which locates God's will in conscience, perhaps informed by texts but never coerced by them?

It is now clearer, we hope, how educational thought will be explored in this book. We shall be looking, through a limited number of illustrative texts of the Jewish tradition, for discussions of philosophical issues in education, namely passages that provide guidelines for identifying excellences and for legitimating them. At the same time, we shall be looking for theory-of-education discourse in the tradition, which relates to methods of educating. However, given the dependence of educational theory upon educational phi-

---

7. See *Makkot* 1:10 and our discussion in Section III, Chapter 2.

losophy, (that is of *how* questions upon *what* and *why* ones) we shall
be concerned with theory-of-education matters within a context of
philosophical issues.

What is a Jewish Source?

What illustrative texts of the Jewish tradition are, and what is meant
by a Jewish source, turns out, upon cursory examination, to be a
rather complex question. Is a treatise by the twelfth century Moses
Maimonides, taking off from a theme he finds in a *mishnah* that was
codified and canonized as Oral Torah in the third century C.E. to be
considered a source?

The question of what is a source in Judaism, what is to be considered Torah, is the subject of much *midrashic* discussion. Torah, the Talmudic sages agree, is the revealed word of God, but there are
exegetes and theologians who insist that God Himself spoke only the
first two of the Ten Commandments and all the rest were spoken by
His servant Moses, who, in speaking, was perhaps also mediating,
stating God's will in a language that could be understood (heard) by
the hearers.[8] On the other hand, one *midrashic* tradition maintains
that even that which will be taught by a student of Torah in the last
generation of human existence was already revealed at Mount Sinai.[9]

Clearly, we have two different ideas here. And this situation of
controversy is one we should expect to encounter frequently. The
Jewish tradition, while reflective, always reflects on concrete, sometimes even disorderly, matters. Unlike the Greek philosophical tradition, it shuns abstractions. It is not even friendly to consistency, when
this consistency ignores the particular details of *halakhah* (law) and the
remembered stories and experiences with and about the self, the
world, other people and God. And these laws, stories and experiences are varied, seemingly inconsistent, often paradoxical.

And so, we have a variety of ideas and directions, all of them in
our sources. The doyen of medieval commentators is Rabbi Shlomo
Yitzchaki, generally known by the acronymic name of Rashi. In his
commentary on Exodus 21:1, Rashi cites the Tannaic (early Talmu-

---

8. See for example, *Exodus Rabbah* 34:1, where the verse, "The voice of the Lord comes
   with strength" (Psalms 29:4) is interpreted to mean "According to the strength of each
   individual (to receive it)" and compare Maimonides, *Guide to the Perplexed* II: 33.
9. For example, *Midrash Tanhuma* II 60:1. See the discussion in David Weiss-Halivni,
   Pshat and Drash; Plain and Applied Meaning in Rabbinic Exegesis (New York and
   Oxford: Oxford University Press, 1991), pp. 112–19.

dic) *midrash, Mekhilta,* to the effect that God told Moses to order the
Divine laws clearly, like a set table, so that people could learn God's
will in a straightforward and simple manner. Yet we also find another
Talmudic sage declaring that the words of Torah as taught by the
wise are riddled with contradictions and disagreements which per-
plex the student, who has no way of knowing which of the conflicting opinions to accept. The only pedagogical advice given the
learner here is to listen carefully to the various conflicting views in
order to ascertain the truth; the only theological comfort is that scripture authorizes many views, including disagreements. And the proof-
text for this: the verse introducing the Ten Commandments that
states that "God spoke *all* these words ..."[10]

When we think of the source, the authoritative text of Judaism, we
naturally think of the Torah, comprising the five books of Moses. But,
of course, the entire Bible, the *Tanakh,* is, by the rabbinic act of can-
onization, given the status of source; it too is viewed as an expression
of God's will, wisdom, revelation. And then, of course, there is the
Oral Torah, codified in the *Mishnah,* continued in the discussions of
the *Gemara,* later to be elaborated in commentary, *halakhic* responsa,
and constantly mined for new (historical, moral, political) significance
by *aggadic midrash* and afterward, by more systematic philosophical
and mystical exegesis.

How can the Oral Torah, the record of human discussions, dialectics and decision making, be Torah, when it is the Bible in which
God utters commandments in fire and cloud? The Talmud relates
that this question raised difficulties even in the time of Hillel and
Shammai, shortly before the Common Era. One of the famous three
heathens who appeared before them, wishing to be converted,[11] stip-
ulated that he wished to accept only the Written, not the Oral Torah,
presumably because it made no sense to him to have "two *torot,*" one
of which endowed ongoing human conversation with the status of
revelation. Hillel, as we shall see, answered that question with
hermeneutic finesse, but the heathen did have a point. He may have
been particularly startled to hear that the Written Torah is supremely
holy but that the specific norms it teaches depend on the masters of
the Oral Torah; if they say that "an eye for an eye" means monetary
compensation, then that's what, as Torah, it does mean. Not even a
heavenly voice, unequivocally expressing God's opinion in an
halakhic controversy, can overcome the rabbinic masters who may
cite scripture against its author—and overrule Him.[12]

10. *Hagigah* 3b.
11. *Shabbat* 25 and see discussion below, Section V.
12. *Babba Meziah* 59. But this episode is often quoted out of context and its humanistic message is not as unequivocal as some interpreters would have it. On this, see

So, the Oral Torah is certainly a source: after all, it is Torah.[13] But sometimes, sooner or later, the Oral Torah, already written down and studied with a view to further and ongoing commentary, must also be canonized, closed. Otherwise, revelation never stops: in the flow of changing circumstances and perpetual commentary, it is in danger, because of overwhelming richness, of losing all specific content.[14]

In a sense, that is what always threatens to happen. Gershom Scholem has pointed out that revelation is not only kept accessible and meaningful by commentary, but that commentary tends to become traditional, that is, an aspect of Torah itself, sharing its sanctity and authority, a constantly expanding Oral Torah.[15] Scholem demonstrates this specifically through the mystic texts of medieval Judaism, which cannot abide the cessation of tradition-become-revelation. Because of the infinitude of God's Word, Torah continues to "gush forth."[16] Conversely, commentary can step within the bounds of the Bible itself where some texts explicate other ones. Yet the Oral Torah is the locus of commentary even if the rabbis "found" its *halakhot* in the words of revelation spoken by God at Mount Sinai.

In light of the above, can clear distinctions between sources and commentary actually be made? Indeed, there are Jews and Jewish educators who refuse to make the distinction. They claim that everything in the Jewish tradition should be treated with the reverence and authority due to sources. Conversely, there are those who consider everything that has come down to us as no more than a contextual and non-authoritative commentary on previous and, ultimately, primordial commentaries. In the first case, an educated Jew must apparently know everything or accept the authority of those who allegedly do; in the second case, the entire tradition is a storehouse of culture from which each person selects as much or as little as s/he wishes.

Walter Kaufmann, *Critique of Philosophy and Religion* (Garden City, N.Y.: Anchor Books, 1961), pp. 335–38.

13. The Talmudic rabbis often reiterate that the meaning of the Written Torah is established by the rabbinic readers. For example, the statement of R. Yohanan: "God made a covenant with Israel only for the sake of what was transmitted orally" *Gittin* 60b. For a scholarly and now classic discussion of this, see Gershom Scholem, "Revelation and Tradition as Religious Categories in Judaism," in *The Messianic Idea in Judaism* (New York: Schocken Books, 1971), pp. 282–303.

14. On this, see Michael Fishbane, "The Notion of a Sacred Text," in *The Garments of Torah: Essays in Biblical Hermeneutics* (Bloomington and Indianapolis: Indiana University Press, 1992).

15. Scholem, "Revelation and Tradition," pp. 284–92.

16. We, therefore, in the blessing recited upon reading the Torah, thank God not for having given us the Torah but thank Him for constantly giving it. See lengthy citation (from *Avodat Ha-Kodesh* by Meir ben Gabbai) explaining the infinite meanings of the Torah which "gushes forth" out of its infinite (Divine) source, in Scholem, "Revelation and Tradition," pp. 298–300.

In most Jewish educational frameworks, we do not find this all-or-nothing approach. Rather, teachers and pupils assume that sources are to be treated differently than commentaries. Teachers treat some books with more reverence than others, and they are more overtly critical of some than of others. For example, with regard to what are considered sacred texts, it is customary, at least in principle, to read the text more closely and to speak of understanding and resolving "difficulties" within it. The rhetoric of resolving difficulties of course puts the onus upon the reader, who must struggle to understand the text more adequately. On the other hand, other books are presented to pupils as important, for they help resolve difficulties in the first group of books, but the difficulties in them pose no existential threat to Jewish faith or cultural identity, nor is the reader required to resolve these difficulties. Rather, these latter books constitute a culture of footnotes to the former ones. Moreover, one may (except in ultra-traditionist schools) choose from among them, as one naturally chooses from among the resources of a cultural heritage.

Studying Torah for most teachers is fathoming the depths of the sources with the aid of diverse commentaries that may readily be placed historically and contextually, and that constitute the history of Torah study. This history is the bridge of the contemporary student to the Torah; it makes the Torah accessible, but it is not the Torah itself. One cannot invest it with the authority of the Torah and one may, perhaps must, choose from among its treasures. As Ben-Yaakov, a prominent Israeli educator has argued, it makes no theological or cultural sense for students to disparage a Talmudic passage with the claim that Rashi, the medieval commentator, explicitly says something else.[17] Similarly, while one may suggest, say, an anti-Maimonidean interpretation of Judaism, or one that finds little inspiration in the mystical tradition,[18] one could hardly imagine an anti-Biblical or even anti-Talmudic interpretation that would not be seen as a radical revision of what tens of generations have meant by Judaism. Nor would it be considered plausible to say that one who does not understand a Biblical or Talmudic passage through the eyes of, for instance, Martin Buber, has read him/her-

17. Yohanan ben-Yaakov, "HaNoar Hadati V'darkai Hinukho" ("Religious Youth and the Manner of its Education"), Amudim (Journal of the Religious Kibbutz Movement) 467 (Heshvan 5745/Nov. 1985), pp. 80–83.
18. See, for example, Michael Wyschograd, *The Body of Faith: Judaism as Corporeal Election* (New York: Seabury Press, 1983) for a contemporary anti-Maimonidean theology. Today arguing for a non-mystical Jewish tradition is less common, largely due to the work and influence of G. Scholem. Yet it obviously has been done and in much modern liberal Jewish theology was standard. It also was found in modern neo-Orthodox thought. See Scholem's critique of German neo-Orthodoxy in this regard, "The Politics of Mysticism: Isaac Breuer's *New Kuzari*," in *The Messianic Idea in Judaism* pp. 325–34.

self out of the tradition. Buber's admirers may claim that his theology and exegesis offer not merely a possible, but to them, a persuasive way of seeing the Bible, but it would make no cultural sense to demand of the Bible that it explain and agree with Buber. And, while *halakhic* compendia have usually been considered more authoritative the later they are, their authority derives from the Talmud, which these codes and responsa make operative and accessible in their given historical epochs.

Paradoxically, the very fact that one can argue with commentary serves to protect what is viewed as the sacred tradition. Witness, for instance, how Nehama Leibowitz, the great Bible teacher of our generation, teaches the Torah. In the study sheets and books that sum up her work of half a century, she confronts her students with various commentators, and gets them to understand how these exegetes understood the source. Harvey has described it well:

> If, for example, there is a difference of opinion between two commentators like Rashi and Nachmanides on how to interpret a verse, Leibowitz will force the student to ask himself why Rashi favors one interpretation and why Nachmanides favors the other. What was the textual problem which led Rashi to interpret the verse as he did? Was Nachmanides bothered by the same problem? What did Nachmanides see (or not see) which led him to reject Rashi's interpretation? Is the issue at stake merely linguistic? Perhaps there is also a theological or philosophic issue at stake? Why, ultimately, do Rashi and Nachmanides disagree, and what is at stake in their disagreement?[19]

Again, however paradoxical it may seem, Leibowitz, in urging students to both understand the differences of opinion between commentators and the issues behind their disagreements and even sometimes offering reasons for supporting one view over the other is actually maintaining the invulnerability of the sacred texts. For the question raised vis-à-vis the text is invariably: who understands it correctly? The question is not: is the text itself worthy of support? The question whether the text itself is perhaps unacceptable rather than just "difficult" is never raised. Because of its difficulty, myriads of wise students have commented upon it, intent on discovering its meaning, disagreeing about how to understand it.

Two Metaphors

The Midrashic tradition makes many metaphors available to the student engaged in the study of Torah to describe the blending of tradi-

---

19. Warren Z'ev Harvey, "Professor Nehama Leibowitz: Israel's Teacher of Teachers," *The Canadian Zionist*, 50, no. 4 (1981), p. 11.

tion and commentary, of loyalty and interpretation. Let us look at two of them.

In one, Ben Bag Bag[20] tells us that one should "turn it (the Torah) over and turn it over again for everything is in it." He advises the student of Torah to "grow gray and old in it, and turn not away from it, for there is no better rule for you than it" (*Avot* 5:25). In another, on the basis of Jeremiah 23:29, "Is not My Word like fire? says the Lord; and like a hammer that breaks the rock in pieces?" the sages comment: "As the hammer splits the rock into many splinters, so will a scriptural verse yield many meanings" (*Sanhedrin* 34a).

The first metaphor, Ben Bag Bag's, reminds one of a treasure of infinite worth, or perhaps a sack of endless depth and unsuspected niches and pockets. If you have a problem or question, the place to look is always in the Torah. If you haven't found what you're looking for, you obviously haven't turned it over sufficiently, haven't plunged its depth and explored its corners, haven't grown "gray and old in it." Keep on looking, don't give up, for what you are tempted to seek elsewhere is right here, if only you know how to search and if only you persist. Indeed, what you are looking for may reflect your specific situation, your sensibilities and needs alone; perhaps others never felt impelled to look in that particular corner, they didn't have your problem. If you turn it over and over again, you will eventually find even that which no one but you has ever sought. Perhaps it will never be sought, or found, again. For everything is in it.

The second metaphor, of the hammer breaking the rock, seems bolder, certainly if we imagine the rock to be not only the verse itself but also those being hit (encountered) by their reading of Torah in their particular situation. These readers experience both that the hammer has changed them, and that through their reading of Torah, many sides of it never before seen and heard, have come into view and, as it were, come into being. While the hammer itself does not break, for "God's word endures forever" (Isaiah 40:7), the recipient and his or her world, as a microcosm of meaning, is split, and the many dimensions of that world are exposed. This happens through a verse being studied. Its many potentialities previously hidden by layers of mass, are revealed; a verse yields (lays bare) many meanings. The fiery sparks fly between the rock (the here-and-now person

---

20. R. Adin Steinsaltz, in his glossary on *Hagigah* 9b, (Tractate *Hagigah*, explained and translated by Rabbi Adin Steinsaltz, [Jerusalem: Israel Institute for Talmudic Publications, 1984], p. 40) cites the view that Ben Bag Bag (and Ben Heh Heh, who may have been the same person) were among those converted by Hillel, according to the story in *Shabbat* 25, which we analyze in Section V. When we come to that story, we shall see both the humor in and the plausibility of that nickname.

and the presently addressed verse) and the hammer (God's over-flowing and perhaps inexhaustible intention).

The idea of Torah and commentary we have examined combines bold innovation with radical conservatism. Because the text being commented upon is "The Torah of the Lord (which) is perfect" (Psalms 19:8) and promises "that everything is in it," it demands absolute loyalty and commitment. And yet, new circumstances and sensibilities create, as Rawidowicz explains,[21] a sense of alienation from the text. We are bound to believe it or culturally to rely on it, but it no longer rings true. It has become difficult and it threatens to become absurd. And the awkward meeting of allegiance and alienation engender the need for interpretation, for a new understanding that will nourish the loyalty and overcome the alienation.

A good and graphic illustration of allegiance to the sources and how the reality of new circumstances threatens that allegiance is any page of a learned edition of the Pentateuch (Five Books of Moses), such as the well-known *Mikraot Gedolot,* where the Biblical text, sometimes only a verse or two of it on a page, is surrounded by voluminous commentary, from various lands and times. The commentators, with their exegeses, their sometimes conflicting understandings, literally hover over the precious verses. They stand guard over the pristine text, protecting it against all attackers, those who might, God forbid, misunderstand moral, legal or narrative difficulties as absurdities. Conversely, they seek to educate the reader who might not read the text seriously enough to perceive that there are problems to be addressed. For the commentators are fully aware of the difficulties in the verses under discussion; hence their commentaries. Their enterprise is to resolve them. Thus they will maintain the Torah as perfect, yet yielding often unsuspected meanings.

Let us now return to our previous discussion. Are these commentaries themselves, like the Oral Torah itself, texts, sources?

What would happen if we viewed all of these commentaries as sources? If they were all "revelation that never stops" the logic of Jewish tradition would require that they too all be protected by commentary, which would, as commentary proceeds through the generations, have more and more sources to cover. But that must make doctrinal and normative continuity illusionary and make even the specific identity of the tradition elusive. For all of these sources (i.e., the commentaries) would need their own *Mikraot Gedolot.* All of them, too, would have to be not only carefully studied and considered in Torah study but justified in order to protect Judaism. But

21. Simon Rawidowicz, "On Interpretation," in *Studies in Jewish Thought,* edited by N.N. Glatzer (Philadelphia: The Jewish Publication Society of America, 1974), pp. 45–80, and particularly, pp. 47–48.

that must be, to all but the most authority-bound reader, an impossible task. For, if anything said by a pupil (reader) in any later generation was already said at Sinai in the sense that it is part of the very faith that must be zealously guarded by all legitimate theologies, then contemporary interpretation based on contemporary circumstances and consciousness becomes, at best, scholastic, at worst, dishonest. It will be difficult for the modern reader to conceive of the Torah as perfect if its study demands subtle or blatant dishonesty. Most contemporary pupils, whom we should like to see interacting with the splintered "rocks" of texts whose new meaning is revealed through their reading, will shun the blows of such a fearsome and unwieldy "hammer."

But if there is no hammer, no rocks and no sparks, there cannot be meaningful Jewish education. If we wish to answer the question of what excellent dispositions are, and to understand our sources as providing guidelines for answering that question, we require a clearer conception of what such sources are. The two alternatives are to deprive all the books of Judaism of their foundational and authoritative status, and thus of our inclination to interpret them; or, conversely, to see them as all equally holy and thus meaningless to us and our students—for they pose no challenge to the teacher and pupil, but only a demand for absolute loyalty. And such a demand is likely to be perceived by most as personally threatening and/or collectively dogmatic and dull.

How can we distinguish in principle between what we should like children to consider their religious and cultural home and what we think they should be at home with? The distinction is important: it is between their heritage itself and the history of that heritage. The former, if Jewish education will be successful, reflects who they are; the latter reflects what they have discovered about their collective identity, and which options for cultural appropriation and creativity their Judaism makes available to them.

In the following chapter we shall suggest a theoretical conception that may serve as a ground for Jewish education that distinguishes between home and feeling at home. We shall suggest that Jewish education gains its *raison d'etre* from a legitimate desire or even a commandment to teach a Jewish language and to cultivate learners who not only understand it, but who live within it and who are capable of appreciating a Jewish literature that is articulated in that language.

According to this view, the philosophy of Jewish education rests upon the grounds of the Jewish language. The assumptions and aspirations of the language are capable of answering Frankena's questions: what shall be learned and why? And, in the theory and practice of Jewish education, the language exposes to view the staples of subject matter as well as standards for innovative cultural discourse.

What do we mean by language and how is it different from literature? And what are the relationships of this language to other languages, for example, the Western philosophical one? In the following chapter, we turn to these issues.

2

TORAH AND WISDOM

Language and Literature

A way of looking at the relationship between sources and commentary is suggested by the distinction made by Oakeshott and
thereafter by Peters between language and literature.[1] The *language*
of a culture sets down its basic assumptions, problems, aspirations,
and understandings. It establishes its forms of rhetoric, its methods of
inquiry, its patterns of community, its symbolic expressions, its paradigms of order, coherence, and norm.

Let us expand on these concepts and suggest that *language* gives us
our collective identity, our stores of what is self-understood among us,
our forms of articulation and communication. Only those who know
the *language* are capable of using it for cultural expression, commu-

---

1. Michael Oakeshott, "The Study of 'Politics' in a University," in *Rationalism in Politics and Other Essays* (London: Methuen and Co. Ltd., 1962) refers to language as "a
manner of thinking" and literature or text as "what has been said from time to time
in a language." (The difference suggested is that between the poetic imagination, for
example, and a specific novel, though Oakeshott does say that languages are appropriately studied in conjunction with some literatures that are paradigmatic. [p. 313])
While I have learned much from Oakeshott's conceptions here, especially in the
development of my own conception of sacred literature, I have expanded the
notion of language to include much of what Oakeshott calls civilization, which
includes "a stock of emotions, beliefs, images, ideas, manners of thinking and manners of activity." (pp. 303–4). I have also been much helped by Peters's use of language and literature in R.S. Peters, "Reason and Habit: The Paradox of Moral
Education," in Peters, *Moral Development and Moral Education* (London: George Allen
and Unwin, 1981), pp. 45-60, and specifically, pp. 51–52.

nion, and enhancement; they alone can make literature within it. In *literature,* they show the power of their language to shape reality[2] and to provide a home within reality for those who speak it. As ever new *literature* is created in the language, its funds of meaning are explored and broadened; simultaneously, those who speak are expressing themselves, revealing sides or splinters of themselves that they can or wish to bring to light only in that *language.*[3]

Of course, the creation of a *language* and its presentation as a datum in the cultural world can be accomplished only through *literature.* That is, language-as-culture is never presented, certainly not to the infant being initiated into it, by grammatical tables or treatises (in another language!) on its beauty or worth. Rather, a *language* is learned through sentences spoken, circumstances negotiated, assumptions stated and tested in the crucible of human life. *Language* appears on the scene when there is *literature* in it, when it is first spoken. When a new *language* makes its appearance in foundational *literature,* it may seem, if it is a startling novelty, to come upon the scene with the force of a revelation. Indeed, for those who believe in the supreme worth of the *language* of Judaism, it is a revelation brought down from Heaven, a *language* taught by God.[4]

Let us carry this train of thought further. The language of Judaism appears on the stage of history as high drama—as God teaching Torah, i.e., the divine language expressed in God's own language-

2. In saying this, I suggest that language is reminiscent of what Peter L. Berger calls "plausibility structure," as this concept is discussed, for example, in his *The Sacred Canopy; Elements of a Sociological Theory of Religion* (Garden City, N.Y.: Doubleday and Co., Inc., 1967).

3. In this and the following paragraph I have italicized the terms *language* and *literature* to indicate the specific connotation these terms have here. Unless otherwise noted, this is the way these terms are used throughout the book.

4. This point is powerfully and poetically made by Abraham J. Heschel, *"Shamayim min Hatorah"* ("Torah from Heaven") in his *Torah Min Hashamayim B'Aspaklariyah Shel Hadorot (Theology of Ancient Judaism)* III (Jerusalem: The Jewish Theological Seminary of America, 1990), pp. 30–32. This feature of Jewish adherence to Jewish language, namely that it has traditionally been believed to be from Heaven, protects the language from the subjective and sometimes irrational features of philosophies of culture that consider the languages of convention and custom of particular groups immune to moral and rational critique. As revealed language, it is neither arbitrary nor simply conventional. Therefore, truth-talk or truth claims are not irrelevant to it. Furthermore, this language, through the seven *Noahide* commandments, claims to be universal truth though it is, in other respects, only the truth for Israel (e.g., laws of *kashrut* and *Shabbat*). That the relationship between a tradition and reason need not be one of blind irreconcilability is well expressed by Hans-Georg Gadamer; he demands that we distinguish between "streams of conceptions" within which we stand and which supply us with fruitful presuppositions and those presuppositions that imprison and prevent us from thinking and seeing. See Richard E. Palmer, *Interpretation Theory in Schleiermacher, Dilthey, Heidegger and Gadamer* (Evanston: Northwestern University Press, 1969), p. 183.

teaching literature, to the elected people, Israel. The books which present and teach this language through the pedagogic literature that exemplifies the language and sets rules for its use are *holy;* one cannot eradicate or even, in principle, ignore any part of the sacred (i.e., language creating and presenting) literature without diminishing future possibilities of literature-making in that language. Thus, the treasure house of language, the holy literature, must indeed be defended at all costs. Furthermore, the wealth of the language and its potentialities is testified to by the scope, diversity, and depth of the literature it makes possible. Those who create this literature feel privileged to be using this language. They consider that they owe it to the language to use it in a manner that testifies to its perfection, thus, in our case, "to enlarge Torah and to glorify it" (*Avot* 6:11). And in the process, they often borrow from other languages and adapt foreign literature when it is felt to be necessary or appropriate.[5]

As we have already noted, there are, not unexpectedly, differing opinions about the point at which sources end and interpretations begin: what the language is and where the literature that keeps it alive and accessible enters the picture. What are the outer limits of holy literature, which constitutes and teaches the language, and where does commentary, literature that exemplifies the language and demonstrates its power, begin? For example, a significant number of pious and/or learned Jews believe that kabbalistic (mystical) writings, especially the Zohar, are themselves part and parcel of the language, and that neither Bible nor Talmud can be understood without it. Conversely, there are those who are no longer comfortable with the demand to protect the norms, rhetoric, and even beliefs of Talmudic sages. They locate the language presenting literature in the Bible alone, and perhaps limit it to certain portions of the Bible. Some contemporary Jews declare that only the *halakhla*, as a body of norms, is really the language-as-literature of Judaism; others find prophetic ideas and their pristine translations into (ethical) practice to be the sum of holy writ. Conversely, as we have already noted, there are ultra-traditionist Jewish communities that refuse to make the source-tradition distinction; everything said by an acknowledged authority, in every generation, is a source. For these communities all literature is indistinguishable from what the language means and has always meant.[6]

5. Whether the material being appropriated is considered foreign or inherent in the language itself is itself an important part of the cultural and educational discussion. See Section II. That in situations of cultural crisis cultures will have recourse to other languages in order to help them with their own rehabilitation is cogently argued by Alisdair MacIntyre in *Whose Justice? Which Rationality?* (London: Gerald Duckworth and Co., Ltd., 1988), Chap. XVIII–XIX.

6. For an illustration of this, see R. Aaron Kotler, *How To Teach Torah* (Lakewood, N.J.: Beth Medrash Govoha, Rabbi Aaron Kotler Institute for Advanced Learning, 1972).

Each of these approaches suggests or mandates a specific philosophy of Jewish education. *For education, as a cultural activity, is the teaching of a language and helping learners to see it as their home. It is, at the same time, cultivating an appreciation of its literature and enabling the next generation to make literature in the language.*

Two Hermeneutic Approaches

In the following chapters, our search for educational thought will direct us to both sources (language) and to the ongoing cultural conversation upon it (literature). We shall not explicitly determine where the one ends and the other begins. For a book attempting to set guidelines for philosophy of Jewish education in general, such a determination would be unnecessarily divisive with regard to differently believing Jews. It is, furthermore, a task for which we claim no scholarly or theological qualifications. However, there is a distinction and we cannot evade drawing it, intuitively and roughly. This is the distinction between different hermeneutic approaches that we shall call upon, for sources and commentary, respectively.

The first approach, suitable for literatures, is the one usually identified with E.D. Hirsch.[7] Hirsch maintains that the most ethical way of ascertaining the meaning of a text is to respect the author's intention and to seek it out; the original meaning, what he or she said to a particular group of readers and listeners, is the best meaning. However, Hirsch makes the distinction between meaning, which is that which the text is taken to represent, and significance, which is meaning as related to something else. The meaning of the text is its "thereness," its self-identity that does not change from one moment to the next. Meaning represents a principle of stability, while significance or meaningfulness for a particular reader can change with the changing contexts in which meaning is applied.[8]

A second approach, of which Gadamer is an important representative[9] may be called the existential-historical view. According to this conception, the distinction between meaning and meaningfulness (significance) is impossible to maintain since we cannot hope to understand the past except from within our own historical situation, which itself supplies us with a pre-understanding of the past, which

---

7. E.D. Hirsch, *Validity in Interpretation* (New Haven: Yale University Press, 1967); *The Aims of Interpretation* (Chicago and London: University of Chicago Press, 1976).
8. Hirsch, *The Aims of Interpretation*, pp. 79–80.
9. Hans-Georg Gadamer, *Truth and Method* (New York: Seaburg Press, 1973); Georgia Warnke, *Gadamer: Hermeneutics, Tradition and Reason* (Stanford, CA: Stanford University Press, 1987).

is already there before we start thinking. This pre-understanding of the past and its cultural goods is itself part of the historical baggage of our situation. Our pre-understanding does not bar us from hoping to understand the past, but we must realize that it is our sole means of access to it.

There is, then, a gap that must be bridged between the past (of the text) and the present (of the reader), and this gap can only be partially bridged. Yet this does not mean that one can do whatever one wishes with the past; it has meanings that the reader is endeavoring to "catch." The reader, even though he or she is in a different set of circumstances and in a different historical-cultural setting, must conduct a faithful, receptive activity of listening to it. This is especially required when the past is embodied in a text still seen as holy. For in that case the text is still the reader's language.[10]

Such an historicist hermeneutic assumes that the past and present are situated in different historical situations but that they are also part of one continuous history. The relationship between the reader and the text is dialogical. Through the dialogue, the text's meaning is always being rediscovered, even though comprehension of it is always incomplete.

Now, our first metaphor of learning, "Turn it over and turn it over again …" suggests to us that traditional Jewish educators will find it difficult to existentially maintain Hirsch's distinction between meaning and significance with regard to those texts they consider holy, that is, those that pristinely present the language itself. If what they hold to be Torah is given[11] for every possible context to all genera-

---

10. For a summation of this orientation and its theological ramifications, see Emil L. Fackenheim, *To Mend the World; Foundations of Post-Holocaust Jewish Thought* (New York: Schocken Books, 1989), pp. 256–59. See also Rudolph Bultmann, "Is Exegesis Without Presuppositions Possible?" in *The Hermeneutics Reader: Texts of the German Tradition from the Enlightenment to the Present,* edited with an introduction by Kurt Mueller-Vollmer (New York: Continuum, 1985), pp. 242–55.

11. The concept of the "givenness" of the Torah has traditionally been understood to point to its divine authorship. In this regard, of course, modern Jewish educators will hardly reach a consensus. Three points of view are found among those who insist on maintaining the concept of Torah as language, and therefore holy: (a) the cultural view that the Jewish tradition, like any other, has formative literature that created a national and religious self-image and focus; (b) the traditionalist view that God conveyed the Torah to Moses, who transcribed it through an act or acts of prophecy; and (c) the liberal-traditional view that the divine Author entrusted the transcription and editing to prophets, scribes, and sages, or, in the ineffable divine revelation, evoked the Torah. In contemporary Jewish thought, the first is often associated with Ahad Ha'am (Asher Ginzberg). See, for example, "Sacred and Profane," in *Selected Essays of Ahad Ha'am,* translated from the Hebrew, edited, and with an introduction by Leon Simon (Cleveland, New York and Philadelphia: Meridian Books, 1962), pp. 41–45. The second approach is elaborated by such modern Orthodox scholars as Emanuel Rackman, *One Man's Judaism* (New York: Philosophical Library, 1970). The third approach is most often associ-

tions, then the various forms of significance-finding, in the Bible and/or rabbinic literature,[12] are part of the language, part of the meaning itself. If this is the case, these texts demand for education, midrashic dialogue rather than detached investigation of the original meaning.[13] This means that we see ourselves as historically remote from the original context in which the words were spoken, but still directly addressed by them. Therefore we may, in many cases, require a new idiom, a new *midrash,* that makes the text and its teaching comprehensible in our situation too.[14] For sources, then, "everything is in it"–even for you.

On the other hand, the literature that articulates options of articulation and response within the language makes most sense, even educationally, when its contexts are kept in mind, when they are seen as part of a conversation, of an ongoing cultural enterprise in which sources are protected and kept accessible. Here, the Hirschian model does seem appropriate. True, a literature of tradition, i.e., commentary on Torah, has crucial significance for the contemporary student, for it marks road signs on a path that is continuous with the rest of Jewish covenant-language history. But what the authors meant in a particular moment in history need not necessarily be present to the contemporary reader. For example, some medieval Jewish philosophy may seem dated to even devoted contemporary Jews. So, when we deal with historical literature in Jewish tradition, an appropriate metaphor might well be "the hammer on the rock." In literature sparks do indeed fly. But even when they fade, as they are prone to do, the hammer is still poised to

---

ated with Franz Rosenzweig. See, for example, *Franz Rosenzweig: His Life and Thought,* presented by Nahum Glatzer (New York: Schocken Books, 1953), for example, p. 158, pp. 242–47.

12. The question which parts of the tradition are Torah, thus holy, belongs to a different controversy. Thus, one may consider only a small part of traditional literature sacred, say, only the Ten Commandments in the Bible, and still accept the second of the three positions noted above (n. 11).

13. In the dialogical mode, the student of Torah will not understand the historical distance and circumstantial dissonance between him/herself and the text as an occasion for debunking (e.g., "The rabbis, like all primitive religionists, thought that ... which we now recognize as a pre-scientific mode ...") combined, perhaps with a homily of contemporary meaningfulness and insight ("The rabbis believed that ... but we know ... However perhaps we can still learn from this text that ..."). Rather, the historical distance will be viewed as requiring that we re-mythologize. I stress that this approach is indicated for education, in which the language is being transmitted. It is not suggested that this would be an acceptable orientation for academic scholarship in which the sacred literature is being investigated. That this distinction requires reflection and study with regard to possible relationships between commitment and openness should be obvious.

14. Emil L. Fackenheim, "Demythologizing and Remythologizing in Jewish Experience; Reflections Inspired by Hegel's Philosophy," Proceedings of the American-Catholic Philosophical Association XLV (1971), pp. 16–27.

strike. It is always about to create new sparks, new ways of seeing the verses of foundational (holy) literature.

Stating this more prosaically: bodies of literature, of commentary, must indeed speak, but they do not have the last word. Every generation must make some literature, lest the language be forgotten, or become incomprehensible.

Torah and *Hokhmah*

Up to this point in our chapter, we have tried to distinguish between language and literature by drawing on two traditional metaphors. But even our use of such terms as language and literature and our reference to schools of hermeneutics are based on the assumption that Jewish educational thought, if it is to be communicable, must be closely related to educational thought as such! It must learn from other educational experiences and discover ways to use other educational conceptions. To be enriched, and to share its own riches with others, it must be cognizant of philosophies and theories of education that are not in the language of Judaism.

Yet, some will maintain that such communicativeness with non-Jewish education and educational thought is useless or even corrosive. Therefore, the question whether the *hokhmah* of general educational thought is relevant and legitimate when applied to Jewish education must be forthrightly addressed. For some certainly are convinced that Jews should strive for educational thought unalloyed with Gentile wisdom. They believe that the Jewish tradition not only has but unambiguously states what good Jewish education is.

So, one point of view is that *hokhmah,* understood in any sense that is not Torah, is really worthless, dealing at best with accommodation to this world, and at worse propagating false conceptions of value and reality. A second, more moderate approach suggests that wisdom, the fruit of reason and experience, is legitimate for others, but, for bearers of the Sinaitic revelation, superfluous; after all, Torah contains all wisdom for those fortunate enough to have it. According to a third view, wisdom and Torah are twin sources of truth, perhaps even parallel avenues of revelation. Thus one can understand Torah best through recourse to wisdom and reflection upon it; at the same time, it is Torah, the more direct revelation, that gives instruction with regard to wisdom's parameters and its proper uses.[15]

15. See Shalom Rosenberg, *Torah Umada B'hagut Hayehudit Hahadashah (Torah and Science in Modern Jewish Thought)* (Jerusalem: Ministry of Education and Culture, 5748) Part I for discussion of these diverse approaches; also, Harry A. Wolfson, "Maimonides and Halevi: a study in typical Jewish attitudes towards Greek philosophy

Rappel has examined possible responses to general wisdom by surveying commentaries on the *mishnah* in *Avot (Ethics of the Fathers).*[16] This *mishnah* demands, in the name of Rabbi Elazar ben Arach, to be "diligent in the study of Torah and (to) know what to answer the heretic" (Z–19). Some commentators understand the *mishnah* to prohibit general studies, while others give grudging permission to deal in philosophy and other external wisdom for the precise reason that one must know it in order to refute its claims to truth. But Rappel also cites commentators who consider the study of general wisdom not merely permissible but even laudable, and not simply in order to rebut atheists. Thus, R. Yaakov Anatuli (Anatollio), a thirteenth-century thinker and exegete, declares that it is worthy for a person to study speculative wisdom. Though such wisdom is not autonomous and not capable of giving principled foundations for the ideal life, it is analogous to the implements of the artisan, without which he cannot carry out his design.

Susser's political-philosophical exploration[17] into the differences between the sacred tradition of Judaism and the Western Greek-Christian one well describes what is at stake in the argument among those who deny the value of *hokhmah,* those who grudgingly permit it, and those who consider it useful or even necessary, respectively. The tradition of Judaism, he argues, lacks the abstractness of Greek-Christian thought. It does not state philosophical principles and then invite the jurist, moralist or educator to apply these principles to concrete cases. It is not even a system of law or a systematically formulated world view but a road to walk *(halakhah),* memories and stories *(aggadah).* In its legal aspect, it begins with teeth and eyes, sunsets, fields, and oxen; "halakhah is a total way of living, a religio-legal constitution of existence that legislates with such exhaustiveness and thoroughness that it constitutes a non-philosophical but densely real portrait of the good life."[18] This "densely real portrait," we may add, characterizes Judaism's theological, as well as its legal-political dimension. The things that God wants and that people do for good or for ill are "like a king of flesh and blood

in the Middle Ages," Jewish Quarterly Review, 2 (1912), pp. 120–60, and Harry A. Wolfson, "The Double Faith Theory in Clement, Saadia, Averroes and St. Thomas and its Origin in Aristotle and the Stoics," *Jewish Quarterly Review,* 33 (1942–1943), pp. 213–64; Also, Rabbi Isaac Bar Sheshet's "Responsum Concerning the Study of Greek Philosophy," introduced and edited by Menachem Marc Kellner, *Tradition,* 15, no. 3 (Fall 1975), pp. 110–18.

16. Dov Rappel, *"Have Shakud L'Imod ... Ma Shetashiv L'apikorus"* ("Be Alert to Learn Torah and Know What Answer to Give a Heretic"), *Tehumim* III (Tzemet Publishers, Alon Shvut, 5742), pp. 477–85.

17. Bernard Susser, "On the Reconstruction of Jewish Political Theory," *Forum,* no. 45 Jerusalem: World Zionist Organization, (Summer 1982).

18. *Ibid.,* p. 75.

who said to his servants ..." or "the son who said to his father ..."
In theology as in law, the fundamental question appears to be "how
is this done" or "how did this happen" rather than what abstract
principle, such as justice or truth, is to be applied in particular cases.
Thus, while the Western tradition begins with such questions as
"What is it to be human?"

> The Jewish tradition grasps the issue from the other end. It begins with the
> palpable existence of the various actors in particular instances. Rights are
> not abstractly postulated and then translated by jurists and legislators into
> the language of positive law but rather, first and foremost, fleshed out in all
> their existential variety without a view to subsequent philosophical
> abstraction. The philosopher's task, insofar as there is one at all, is to erect
> an intellectual scaffolding to the legal edifice–keeping in mind that scaf-
> folding is an external construct which has no existence without the edifice.
> It is only in the pervasive quality of its culture, in its ubiquitous ethos and
> behavioral totality that the tradition can be approached as a living whole.[19]

This does not signify that the Jewish tradition is unreflective and
that it has no theory. It means only that it cannot be studied as disembodied ideas, for it is always an embodied theory. One must learn
manifold particulars in order to reflect usefully. In Susser's words,
"... the Jewish tradition of political discourse ... (in) an important
sense ... overcomes the chasm between theory and practice that is
the source of such perennial concern in Western thought. Practice is
the medium through which the theory operates."[20]

If we assume, with Susser, that the Jewish tradition cannot simply
be translated into Western cultural modes without losing its content,
then certain educational consequences need to be considered.

(a) A tradition that reveals its reflective-theoretical dimensions
only through its particulars cannot be expected to readily declare
its principles and doctrines. The existential variety must be experienced by the learner. That being the case, the educated Jew
empowered to think reflectively about Judaism and Jewish education must be armed not with definitions (What is it?) but with paradigms (How does it work and how do you do it?). Therefore, this
tradition has been traditionally appropriated by learning Torah
rather than by inculcating truths. And yet, since the Jewish tradition
is reflective, has principles, and teaches truths, the young person
must eventually learn to see the ideas that permeate the practice if
s/he is to be truly educated.[21]

19. *Ibid.,* p. 76
20. *Ibid.,* p. 75.
21. On paradigms as against definitions, see Hubert L. Dreyfus, "Knowledge and
    Human Values; a Geneology of Nihilism," *Teachers College Record,* 82, no. 3
    (Spring 1981), pp. 507–20. For a discussion of the story-philosophy dichotomy in

(b) Since education is essentially concerned with communication, it makes sense to assume that pupils surrounded by a Western culture that starts spiritual discourse with the enumeration of first principles and regards definitions very highly, will have difficulty comprehending a Jewish culture that bids them simply to "go and learn." They will be neither motivated to study Torah nor will they understand what they are doing unless they are, for all intents and purposes, removed from their Western non-Jewish environment. But that is often impossible and, to most Jews, undesirable. As a result, Judaism, to become accessible to students, must be partially translated into a Western idiom.

(c) However, this is not merely an educational tactic, made necessary by such sad circumstances as *Galut* (exile) and assimilation. It is part of the historical reality of the Jewish people and of Judaism itself. The tradition has, at least since the second commonwealth, been in continuous contact with Western Hellenic culture, has learned from it and absorbed aspects of it, as well as contributed to it. From the Talmudic sage, Shammai, who posited that "the heavens were created before the earth" since "a person does not first build a house and then made a blueprint,"[22] through the great medieval philosophers such as Maimonides and Gersonides, Judaism has become accessible to Jews in various cultures by judiciously appropriating some of the cultural language of the surroundings. Furthermore, the use of this Western language made possible an ongoing process not only of Jewish self-understanding but also of legitimation. The Jewish tradition and its bearers, coming into contact with foreign societies that made valuative and cultural claims, had to justify and explain what Judaism said, and why it continued to deserve the loyalty of Jews. And this could only be done in a language that the listeners, Jewish and Gentile, understood. As a result, when historic Judaism is presented to pupils today, it itself constitutes a record of partial translation. Maimonides, one of the greatest teachers of Judaism of all times, is to be found both in his encyclopedic compendium of *halakhah*, the *Mishneh Torah* and his philosophical *Guide to the Perplexed*. Moreover, the meticulous subject classification in the *Mishneh Torah* owes much to Greek ways of thinking, while the philosophy in the *Guide* may be seen as a bold *midrashic* enterprise, a continuation of previous exegesis and *aggadah*.

Jewish education, see Garet Mathews and Howard Deitcher, "Doing Philosophical Theology in the Seventh Grade at Halevy School," *Religious Education*, 88, no. 2 (Spring 1993), pp. 294–304.
22. *Genesis Rabbah* I: 15.

Let us now return to the problem of Torah and *hokhmah*. We may assume that all the sages and exegetes who have addressed the problem of their relationship, are aware that Judaism and Western culture think and function differently. We may also take it for granted that they all consider Torah, as Jewish teaching-for-life, to be supremely worthy and capable of answering the question: What makes something an excellence that should be transmitted to the young? All are also aware of the fact that, in Jewish history, there have apparently been numerous translations from the world of Torah to the world of the Greeks, the world of *hokhmah*.

Some of those who comment on this problem are afraid of translation. They see it as a road to cultural and religious assimilation. And to the question of how the tradition can be made communicable to the young, their answer is that it will be understood only if the learners are strictly segregated from the alien and hostile world surrounding them. Naturally, they do not agree that authentic Judaism has borrowed or learned from others. They believe that what great Jews like Maimonides seemed to take from others were originally aspects of Torah and simply misplaced until great scholars reclaimed them, or that the sorry circumstances of their time forced them to temporarily make use of foreign notions.

Here we come to those who are ready to make use of *hokhmah* in order to explain Judaism to the heretic. They say that *hokhmah* is suitable and legitimate under certain circumstances, when unfortunate conditions prevail. In an ideal situtation, it would not be needed, for Judaism has an internal body of theory that it will reveal to the faithful student of the Torah. Yet they realize that this ideal situation does not correspond to the external reality. Most of those we wish to educate are already far on the road to heresy; if the only way to answer them is with *hokhmah*, so be it.

This group is not far removed from those who are in favor of *hokhmah* but only because people require motivation for learning. They admit that Judaism, in the world in which we live, requires not only communicably formulated explication, but also plausible justification. Those in this group may admit that this was always the case; it is legitimate, they say, to formulate Judaism in the idioms of those who must speak its language in any given generation.

And this brings us to those, like Anatuli, who perceive of the truths of the Torah as hidden treasure, to be drawn out of its hiding place by speculative wisdom. In this view, it is considered impossible that the Torah has no philosophy because it is a totality of truth. But that philosophy must be coaxed out of the Torah. This means that *hokhmah*, too, is a hammer, striking upon the rock of Jewish tradition, exposing its often hidden layers of meaning. Conversely, we may argue that *hokhmah*, Western philosophy and consequent bodies of theoretical knowledge, including the wisdom contained in educational thought in this and previous generations, are also rocks. When these educational-philosophical rocks are struck by Jewish conceptions of culture and education, unanticipated dimensions of meaning come into view. In this book on Jewish philosophy of education, we shall have to "learn Torah" even before we formulate theories. We shall have to demonstrate that there are Jewish conceptions of culture and education.

Our assumption is that the Jewish tradition is a reflective one and thus is rich in theory. Conversely, we shall maintain that it has not, except in historical situations of cultural siege, disdained to learn wisdom wherever it might be found, and that this wisdom, because of its systematic nature, has helped clarify the truths found in the language of Torah. This means that non-Jewish philosophy has often been useful and, at times, indispensable in making Jewish literature.

And now, having made these clarifications, we may return to the beginning. What we hope to do is look at selected sentences of the language educationally, that is, in a way that helps us answer Frankena's questions: (a) What are excellences, and (b) how do we know what they are. We will also look at some of the literature that re-examines and restates the language in circumstances where it threatens to become incomprehensible or alien. Finally, we shall endeavor to do some educational literature, or commentary, of our own on the basis of what we have discovered from learning Torah. This we shall do with the aid of some relevant *hokhmah* about what is meant by the language and its proper expression and transmission.

And so, we can now begin, not at the beginning, but somewhere in the domain between language and literature, with Maimonides on *inter alia*, a *mishnah*.[23] There, as throughout, we shall attempt to learn-teach but we shall also try to explain, in the hope that *hokhmah* will make learning Torah clearer and help us to focus it on our specific educational concern. This concern, as we have said, is the transmission of Jewish language, protected and kept accessible by ever-new literature.

This literature will help teachers remain relevant without loss of authenticity; it will also encourage the young to do their own thing, in the holy language of those who first heard and spoke it.

---

23. We have indicated why Maimonides as a philosopher is not exactly in the category of language. Namely, one can do philosophy of Judaism from an anti-Maimonidean viewpoint. On the other hand, many Jewish scholars, especially *halakhists,* will insist that Maimonides is an authority who cannot be ignored and whose difficult passages must be explained. In other words, they will use the rhetoric designed for dealing with language when discussing Maimonides.

Section II

A PHILOSOPHER OF JUDAISM
FOR JEWISH EDUCATION

3

THE ROAD
TO THE PALACE

*W*e have chosen to begin our explorations on the Jewish text and philosophy of education with Moses Maimonides, generally known to his Jewish readers and students acronymically as "the RaMBaM." (Rabbainu Moshe ben Maimon). The reason is that this medieval prince of Jewish learning and teaching, of *halakhah* and theology, was a philosopher of Judaism, one who built bridges between Torah (the language of Judaism) and *hokhmah*, wisdom. Consequently, we may expect to find him dealing more explicitly than many other spokesmen of the text tradition, with the questions that agitate reflective educators looking for a philosophy of Jewish education.

And so, it makes good sense to turn to him with the questions that are generally addressed to educational thinkers, and to request that he relate to them as a philosopher and as an outstanding teacher-interpreter of Judaism. Besides the very general ones with which Frankena supplied us,[1] these questions include the following:

(a) Who is the ideal Jewish human being? What is an ideal education that cultivates such Jewish human beings?

(b) Are all ideal Jewish persons alike in their achievement of ideal goals? Or are there different ways of being educated and excellent Jewish human beings? Or, given the unequal endowments of human beings, should one admit that some people are simply not capable of reaching true excellence?

1. See Chapter 1, p. 4.

(c) Assuming that children, as children, cannot be expected to understand or appreciate their own human potential as defined by the Jewish educational philosopher, what might be considered legitimate and even educationally necessary compromises designed to move children in the direction of that intellectual, moral, etc. potential? In other words, what kind of educational theory is congruent with what the particular philosopher defines as Judaism?

(d) To which extent is education to be seen as the socialization of the young person into his or her culture? Is there a conflict between socialization and acculturation, on the one hand, and individuation on the other? What can educators do to negotiate or resolve this conflict so that socialization will contribute to the self-realization of the person as an individual rather than hinder it? Or are either socialization or individuation to be viewed as suspect—even undesirable—for some or all people? And even if they are both considered good in principle, are there children who do not require such negotiation because of their great talents or, conversely, do not deserve them because of their innate deficiencies?

(e) What are criteria for teachers who can achieve these ends and adequately employ suitable means for reaching them?

(f) Whence our certainty about who the ideal Jewish person is? What are appropriate and legitimate theories of education at different ages and for different people? What is the correct relationship between the individual and society, and who is a good teacher? What authorizes and justifies our normative positions on these questions?

Philosophy of Judaism and Philosophy of Education

We do not often look to Jewish thinkers to examine such questions. We think of them as stating religious doctrines, exhorting to loyalty, and giving homiletic rationales for the commandments of Judaism. We tend to assume that they cannot be expected to have a total vision of human life, of the relationship between faith and inquiry, of society and individual self-realization. This is largely due to the fact that we think of Jewish tradition as being somehow supplementary to "general" culture, which, due to its presumed generality, is alone trusted to have worthy visions, comprehensive views, and rational policies. Judaism is often assumed to be the weaker albeit older sister of our Judeo-Christian-Hellenic historical heritage. Partly, this is because we have unreflectively accepted the bias, still widespread in Western civilization, that Judaism represents an early and unrefined form of human culture and that, as such, it lacks the power to reflect on spirit and culture sufficiently to shape a true philosophy of education.[2]

Yet neither our own emancipated prejudices nor those of some in the non-Jewish community are justified. Jewish thinkers, following in the footsteps of poets, prophets, and sages of *aggadah* and *halakhah* are intensely concerned with such issues, at times explicitly and at times implicitly, that is, sometimes they mention education and sometimes they don't. And some, of whom Maimonides is perhaps the outstanding spokesman, sought to demonstrate that Biblical and rabbinic ideals of culture and education could—in fact, should, be wedded to the reflective mode of philosophy. Maimonides held that this mode is part and parcel of the divine revelation to Israel, a crucial component of the Oral Torah, Talmudically termed, *Pardes*.[3]

Hence, it may be justifiable to expect that, within the philosophy of Judaism in Maimonides's writings, one can find a philosophy of education.

2. E.g., E.B. Castle, *Ancient Education and Today* (Harmondsworth, Middlesex: Penguin Books Ltd., 1961), Chapter 5. This opinion, that there is no ideal of *Paideia* in Hebrew thinking, has been explicitly and derogatorily developed by Jaeger in his classic study of Greek culture and education, *Paideia*: "We are accustomed to use the word culture, not to describe the ideal which only the Hellenocentric world possesses, but in a more trivial and general sense, to denote something inherent in every nation of the world, even the most primitive. We use it for the entire complex of all the ways and expressions of life which characterize any one nation. Thus the word has sunk to mean a simple anthropological concept, not a concept of value, a consciously pursued ideal. In this vague analogical sense it is permissible to speak of Chinese, Indian, Babylonian, Jewish or Egyptian culture, although none of these nations has a word or an ideal which corresponds to real culture." (Jaeger, *Paideia*, 1, pp. xvii.) Jaeger adds that, while "every highly organized nation has an educational system ... the law and the prophets of the Israelites, the Confucian system of the Chinese, the Dharma of the Indians are in their whole intellectual structure fundamentally and essentially different from the Greek ideal of culture." Several pages thereafter, Jaeger tells us that the Greeks "were the first to recognize that education means deliberately moulding human character in accordance with an ideal ... Other nations made gods, kings, spirits; the Greeks alone made men." *Ibid.*, p. xxii–xxiii. One can only suppose that he never read the Bible. For the bias that ignores or maliciously dismisses Jewish civilization and its goods, see Harvey Shulman, "The Bible and Political Thought; Daniel Elazar's Contribution to the Jewish Political Tradition," *Judaism*, 41, no. 1 (Winter 1992), pp. 18–20.

3. With the Talmudic prescription (*Kiddushin* 30a) as a source, Maimonides states that the time "allotted to study should be divided into three parts. A third should be devoted to the Written Law, a third to the Oral Law and a third should be spent in reflection, deducing conclusions from premises, developing implications from statements, comparing dicta, studying the hermeneutical premises by which the Torah is interpreted, till one knows the essence of these principles, and how to deduce what is permitted and what is forbidden from what one has learned traditionally. This is termed Talmud." Part of what is here called Talmud consists of the esoteric studies termed *Pardes*; this is philosophy. Maimonides, *Mishneh Torah*, "*Hilkhot Talmud Torah*" ("Laws of Torah Study") I: 11–12; "*Yesodai Hatorah*" ("Foundations of the Torah") IV:13, and see discussion in Isadore Twersky, "Philosophy as an Integral Part of Talmud," in *Introduction to the Code of Maimonides (Mishneh Torah)* (New Haven and London: Yale University Press, 1980), p. 488–500.

We have not set ourselves the task of spelling it out in a detailed and comprehensive manner. But even for the purposes of a merely illustrative exploration of an aspect of Jewish *Paideia*, centering on Maimonides, one must address the problem of where one may look for it. The Rambam, as a towering *talmid hakham* (scholar of Judaism), did not only write treatises on philosophical matters. He codified the entire corpus of Talmudic *halakhic* teaching, a stupendous undertaking which has been called "a quantum jump in the development of rabbinic literature as a whole and the history of codification in particular."[4] He enumerated and explicated all the commandments of the Torah. Maimonides wrote a daring and profound philosophical work, to guide the perplexed of his generation. He wrote epistles on various subjects, as well as legal *responsa* on *halakhic* questions addressed to him. Scholars differ about what he considered most important, and to what extent he meant to say different things to different audiences, to accommodate their varying religious and intellectual requirements. And, as is the case with every voluminous, complex, and careful writer, there are scholarly arguments about what the Rambam really meant and even, what he really believed.[5]

We shall not dwell on these controversies except where they directly affect educational philosophy and we are certainly not qualified to make sweeping pronouncements upon them. Rather, we shall read several passages which, upon careful examination, seem to state or clearly suggest ways of dealing with the questions that educational philosophy asks. Especially, we shall look thoughtfully at a section of one of the Rambam's earlier writings, his *Introduction to the Mishnah*, specifically his "Introduction to Chapter *Helek*," in which he enumerates the doctrines of Judaism but also sets forth theo-political and educational principles that are to re-occur, as a persistent theme, in later writings.

But before coming to that, we might attempt to learn something about the way Maimonides thinks and the assumptions he makes. To do so, we shall look briefly at other, seemingly unrelated works.

Religion and Rationality

Let us begin with the parable that gives our book its name. It appears near the end of Maimonides's explicitly philosophical work, *A Guide to the Perplexed*:

4. Twersky, "Philosophy as an Integral Part of Talmud," p. 515.
5. Twersky remarks that "To a great extent the study of Maimonides is a story of 'self-mirroring'." *Ibid.*, p. 358. See note 6 on that page for a survey of different opinions about Maimonides and his teachings. See also, Aviezer Ravitsky, "*Sitrai Torato Shel Moreh Nevukhim; Haparshanut B'dorotov U'bdorainu*" ("The Esoteric Aspect of the Guide for the Perplexed; Exegesis in his Times and in Ours"), in *Al Da'at Hamakom (Studies in the History of Jewish Philosophy)* (Jerusalem: Maxwell-Macmillan-Keter Publishing House, 1991), pp. 142–81.

A king is in his palace, and all his subjects are partly in the country and partly abroad. Of the former, some have their backs turned towards the king's palace and their faces in another direction; and some are desirous and zealous to go to the palace, seeking "to inquire in his temple" and to minister before him, but have not even seen the face of the wall of the house. Of those who desire to go to the palace, some reach it, and go round about in search of the entrance gate; others have passed through the gate, and walk about in the ante-chamber; and others have succeeded in entering into the inner part of the palace, and being in the same room with the king in the royal palace. But even the latter do not immediately upon entering the palace see the king, or speak to him; for after having entered the inner part of the palace, another effort is required before they can stand before the king—at a distance or close by—hear his words or speak to him.[6]

We have more than an inkling as to who the king is and who his subjects are. From this passage alone, it is clear that there are those who have no interest in reaching the palace, while our attention is directed to those who do, and to the difficulties involved in actually reaching it. There is also an intimation that the highest ideal is not reached by most. It requires, at the very least, great effort to stand before—and speak to—the king.

As the Rambam himself explains his parable: those abroad have no religion; Maimonides sees them as irrational beings. Those whose backs are turned to the palace hold false doctrines either adopted in consequence of great mistakes made in their own speculations or received from others who misled them. These people, the Rambam believes, are dangerous, worse than the irrational ones; it may at times be necessary "to slay them and to extirpate their doctrines, in order that others should not be misled." We note that the menace posed by these people derives from their doctrinal errors and we shall not be surprised to find those approaching and entering the palace to be judged primarily by thought and truth rather than by deeds or even intentions. Indeed,

> Those who desire to arrive at the palace, and to enter it, but have never yet seen it, are the mass of religious people; the multitude that observe the divine commandments, but are ignorant. Those who arrive at the palace, but go around it, are those who devote themselves exclusively to the study of the practical law; they believe traditionally in true principles of faith, and learn the practical worship of God, but are not trained in philosophical treatment of the principles of the Law, and do not endeavor to establish the truth of their faith by proof.[7]

We see that the Rambam has little respect for those who don't investigate the principles of religion. In fact, he bars entrance to the palace even to Talmudic scholars who are unreflectively satisfied with the doctrines that have been transmitted to them. Lacking

6. Maimonides, *Guide to the Perplexed,* III: 51.
7. *Ibid.*

philosophical reflection, even such learned people merely "go around the palace." However,

> Those who undertake to investigate the principles of religion have come into the ante-chamber ... But those who have succeeded in finding a proof for everything that can be proved, who have a true knowledge of God, so far as a true knowledge can be attained, and are near the truth, wherever an approach to the truth is possible, they have reached the goal, and are in the palace in which the king lives.[8]

For Maimonides, then, the highest worship of God is only possible after correct notions of Him have previously been achieved.[9] Believing that religion is ultimately concerned with intellect and the striving for truth, he can surprise the modern reader by referring to "people without religion" as irrational beings, and anger conventional traditionalists, who do not understand the Torah and its commandments as designed to teach truths and to spur people to strive for truth.

As we shall see, Maimonides shows how the Torah makes it possible for simple people to act in morally acceptable ways even if they are not yet ready for—or simply incapable of—intellectual understanding. Yet the morality that arises from understanding is most praiseworthy and unshakable. This is nicely illustrated in two letters. In an epistle to Obadiah the Proselyte, who had asked him whether he, as a proselyte, could refer in his prayers to "the God of our fathers ..." "Who has brought us out of the land of Egypt," Maimonides reassures him that indeed he should, for Abraham is the father of all who accept his teaching, in all generations:

> Abraham our Father taught the people, opened their minds, and revealed to them the true faith and the unity of God ... Ever since then whoever adopts Judaism and confesses the Unity of the Divine Name, is counted among the disciples of Abraham our Father, peace be with him. These men are Abraham's household ...[10]

And, in a letter to Hasdai Halevi, Maimonides explains the Talmudic adage that "the pious among the Gentiles have a share in the world to come" (*Sanhedrin* 105a) to mean: "if they have acquired what can be acquired of the knowledge of God, and if they ennoble their souls with worthy qualities."

> "There is no doubt that everyone who enables his soul with excellent morals and wisdom based on faith in God, certainly belongs to the men of the world to come."[11]

8. *Ibid.*
9. "I have shown you that the intellect that emanates from God unto us is the link that joins us to God." *Ibid.*
10. Isadore Twersky, "Letter to Obadiah the Proselyte," in *A Maimonides Reader,* edited with introduction and notes by Isadore Twersky (New York: Behrman House, Inc., 1972), p. 475.
11. Twersky, "Letter to Hasdai Halevi," *A Maimonides Reader,* pp. 477–78.

The emphasis on good actions based on understanding and wisdom is given literary and structural expression even in the *Mishneh Torah,* the Rambam's *halakhic* code, which begins with *"Hilkhot Daot,"* laws of true opinions, and ends with what the Rambam, based on his interpretation of Talmudic doctrine, considers the appropriate and correct way to conceive of the Messiah and the Messianic age.[12]

Two Perfections

What, for Jews, does the Torah consider a social and individual ideal? What does it say about the ideals of good conduct and correct understanding?

In *The Guide to the Perplexed,* Maimonides tells us that the Torah "as a whole aims at two things: the welfare of the soul and the welfare of the body." Most of the Torah's commandments deal with the welfare of the body, namely, with social order and morality. This is achieved "by the abolition of wrongdoing" among people and "the acquisition by every human individual of moral qualities that are useful for life in society." The welfare of the soul, however, is "indubitably greater in nobility." It consists, in the first instance

> of the multitude's acquiring correct opinions corresponding to their respective capacity. Therefore some of them (namely, the opinions) are set forth explicitly and some of them are set forth in parables. For it is not in the nature of the common multitude that its capacity should suffice for apprehending that subject matter as it is.[13]

The Torah intends to create the society in which there is "perfection of the body." For such a society, the Torah prescribes a common language of religious action and sentiment, and a moral code. Therein individuals may climb ever higher on the ladder of "perfection of the soul"–from correct opinions, incumbent on everyone, to the highest humanly possible knowledge of the truth, to which only a few may aspire and which only prophets, and Moses more than any, have reached.[14] There is some intellectual mobility in society and the wise should try to draw those who are far from wisdom and true love of God closer by proper instruction.[15] But it is no simple matter for "the

---

12. For a careful study of this structure see Ravitsky, "Sitrai Torato Shel Moreh Nevukhim," pp. 74–104.
13. *Guide to the Perplexed,* III:27.
14. *Mishneh Torah: "Hilkhot Yesodai Hatorah"* ("Laws of the Foundations of the Torah") VII:6; *Guide to the Perplexed* II:35.
15. Z'ev (Warren) Harvey has pointed out to me that Maimonides, who in his early work (specifically, the *Introduction to the Mishnah*) conceived of the multitude as incapable of intellectual and spiritual advancement, did envision them as able to gain "knowledge of God" in his later works–that is, in the *Mishneh Torah* and *The*

multitude" to scale these heights and even the wise person, indeed more than anyone, knows what the limits of human understanding are.

For a person's understanding is limited and not everyone's understanding can attain to the clear truth. And if a person will follow the thoughts of his heart, he will destroy the world because of his limited understanding ...[16]

The "multitude," and indeed every person has "been commanded not to exercise freedom of thought to the point of holding views opposed to those expressed in the Torah; rather we must limit our thought by setting up a boundary where it must stop and that boundary is the commandments and the injunctions of the Torah."[17] Nevertheless, those who know how to correctly engage in intellectual inquiry, having made the proper preparations in piety and preliminary studies, that is, in the knowledge and practice of *halakhah*, and training in mathematics and natural science[18] must do so, despite their spiritual apprehension of the limits of human understanding, "for the intellect is the honor of God." The prophets and sages who warned against investigating "what is above, what is below, what is before and what is after" did so "not to deprive the intellect of the apprehension of things that it is possible to apprehend—as is thought

---

Guide to the Perplexed. See, the end of "*Hilkhot Melachim*" ("Laws of Kings") in the *Mishneh Torah,* where the Rambam envisions Messianic times as characterized by a comprehensive "knowledge of God" and also *The Guide to the Perplexed* III:11, which expressed the same idea. Hence, in *Mishneh Torah, "Hilkhot Teshuvah"* ("Laws of Repentence") X:5 we find the Rambam ruling that "... when instructing the young, women, or the illiterate generally, we teach them to serve God out of fear or for the sake of reward, till their knowledge increases and they have attained a large measure of wisdom. Then we reveal to them this secret truth, little by little, and train them by easy stages till they have grasped and comprehended it, and serve God out of love." (See further discussion of this, Chapter 4, pp 63–66) On Rambam's attitude towards Torah study by women, see Warren Zev Harvey, "The Obligation of Talmud on Women According to Maimonides," *Tradition,* 19, no. 2 (Summer 1981), pp. 122–30. Harvey maintains that while the Rambam's decision to rule according to the individual opinion of R. Eliezer in the Talmud that women should not be taught Torah has had a detrimental effect on the study of Torah by women throughout the generations it is reasonable to deduce that he only referred in his stricture to Oral Torah but not to Written Torah or to Talmud. That is, he did not release women from knowledge of the commandments or of philosophical study *(Pardes),* but did not wish to see them as judges who determined specific points of law as community leaders.

16. *Mishneh Torah, "Hilkhot Avodat Kokhavim"* ("Laws of Idolatry") II:3.

17. *Maimonides, Sefer Hamitzvot* (The Book of Commandments) Negative commandment no. 47.

18. In explaining why instruction should not begin with metaphysics or "obtuse and difficult subjects," Maimonides states that, according to one Biblical simile, wisdom is compared to water. On this a particular interpretation of the Sages is the following: "He who can swim may bring up pearls from the bottom of the sea (but) he who is unable to swim will be drowned; therefore only such persons as have had proper instruction should expose themselves to the risk." *Guide,* I:34. This of course does not refer to "bread and meat," that is, "the essentials of what is prohibited and what is permitted," which must be taught to all.

by the ignorant and neglectful.[19] Far from it! For "perfection of the soul" does consist in one "becoming an actually intelligent being," learning to know "about the things in existence all that a person fully developed is capable of knowing."

Nevertheless, the larger society and its welfare constitutes an absolute necessity even for those of the spiritually endowed who do make unflagging and strenuous efforts to achieve knowledge. Maimonides insists that individuals in isolation from society cannot hope to attain intellectual and spiritual perfection and the primary aim (perfection of the soul) can only be achieved after attaining the secondary one (perfection of the body). For human beings are social by nature and require that their basic needs be supplied. This can only be achieved in society, in which there is division of labor. Therefore, both perfections, that of the group and of the individual, are necessary. As Maimonides sums it up: "the true Law ... namely, that of Moses our teacher–has come to bring us both perfections."[20]

Maimonides, here as elsewhere in the *Guide*, describes the ideal individual. It is a person who serves God by loyal participation in the commanded life of the *mitzvot*, which ensures "perfection of the body," i.e., a just society, and who has achieved the highest possible "perfection of the soul," the greatest degree of which s/he is capable of intellectual understanding. It is the latter that corresponds to true "love of God."[21]

However these normative statements do not explicitly tell us how that ideal is related to the formative tasks of education. For that, we could turn to Maimonides's code, the aforementioned *Mishneh Torah*, specifically to his *Hilkhot Talmud Torah* (Laws of Torah Study), where the laws regarding the initiation of the individual into the community and the parameters of study that are required of the individual are detailed.

If we choose, nevertheless, to take a close look at the Rambam's *Commentary on the Mishnah*, it is because there the relationship between culture and education seems sufficiently spelled out for us to read it as a piece of educational-philosophical literature. We shall

19. "These are pleased to regard their own deficiency and stupidity as perfection and wisdom, and the perfection of others as a deficiency and a defection from (the) Law (of the Torah) and (they) ... thus 'regard darkness as light and light as darkness.'" (Isaiah 5:20). *Guide*, I:32. On this issue, see Lawrence Kaplan and David Berger, "On Freedom of Inquiry in the Rambam–and Today," in *The Torah U-Madda Journal*, edited by Jacob J. Schechter (New York, Yeshiva University, 1990), 2, pp. 37–50.
20. *Guide*, III: 27.
21. "But the truths which the Law teaches–the knowledge of God's Existence and the Unity–creates in us love of God, as we have shown repeatedly ... .The two objects, love and fear of God, are acquired by two different means. The love is the result of the truth taught in the Law ... while fear of God is produced by the practices prescribed in the Law." *Guide*, III: 52.

see, as we read part of this treatise carefully, that it is all about the need to transmit funds of wisdom to children, and about the immense difficulties adults encounter when they attempt to do so.

We are not primarily interested here in the theological storms that swirl around specific features of the Rambam's position, for example, his rationalistic explanations of the commandments and the intellectualism underlying his brand of piety. It would, of course, distort our discussion not to relate to these matters, and ultimately, we shall have to point to possible limitations of intellectualism for Jewish educational philosophy. Nevertheless, our task here is not to defend his particular philosophical literature of Judaism or to take issue with it. Rather it is to observe the Rambam using *hokhmah*, wisdom, to coax guidelines for learning and teaching out of Torah. It is to see him doing philosophy of education.

And now, for some study.

Education and the "World-to-Come"

As we already mentioned at the beginning of Chapter One, the Rambam's discussion takes off from the first *mishnah* in the tenth chapter of the Tractate *Sanhedrin*:

> All Israelites have a share in the world to come, as it is said, "Your people also shall be all righteous, they shall inherit the land forever; the branch of My planting, the work of My hands wherein I glory" (Is. 60:21). But these have no share in the world to come: one who says that the resurrection of the dead is not taught in the Torah; one who says that the Torah is not from Heaven, and the atheist. Rabbi Akiva adds: one who reads the apocryphal books or who utters charms over a wound saying, "I will put none of the diseases upon you which I have put upon the Egyptians, for I am the Lord that heals you" (Ex. 15:26). Abba Saul adds: the one who pronounces the letters of the Tetragrammaton.

The Rambam begins his treatise on this *mishnah* with the statement: "I must speak now of the great fundamental principles of our faith," and he concludes it with his well-known thirteen principles of Jewish faith.[22]

A careful reading reveals why this particular *mishnah* is so congenial to Maimonides, who intends to buttress his view that having and understanding fundamental principles are the highest goal of Judaism, for they lead to what he will in later years, in the *Guide for*

---

22. The English text for *Introduction to Perek Halek* used here is that of Twersky, *A Maimonides Reader*, pp. 401–423.

the Perplexed, refer to as perfection of the soul. While the Torah requires strict adherence to the commandments and to the details of the *halakhah,* (thereby making perfection of the body feasible) the end-aim of Judaism is to bring one to the truth about God, the created world, the divine communication with Israel and humankind, and the revealed blueprint for Jewish and human perfection. As we have already seen, simply doing the right thing and maintaining social order, without some degree of perfection of the soul is not enough for a direct link with God. The most sublime commandment, "to love the Lord your God," directs people's hearts to that.

The *mishnah,* we repeat, seems congenial to this view. It says that all Israelites have a share in the world-to-come and that certain persons who do not believe specific doctrines (to which particular heretical actions testify) have no share in the world-to-come. This appears to mean, as Schweid has pointed out,[23] that these heretical persons are in fact not Israelites (i.e., Jewish) at all, for all Israelites as such have a share in the world-to-come! They are thus in a different category than ordinary sinners, such as Sabbath desecrators, consumers of non-kosher food, thieves or adulterers. Those who commit sundry sins that are a consequence of their appetites rather than of their convictions are still Israelites, and as such, do have a share in the world-to-come; all Israelites have this. Therefore, only those who entertain false principles and act on these false beliefs have read themselves out of Israel. For example, reading apocryphal books in the mistaken belief that they are holy and norm-giving marks one as not being Jewish. Membership in the Jewish people is determined by belief in fundamental principles.

The substantive discussion begins with a description of the varying views to be found with regard to the term of the *mishnah,* "the world to come," which Maimonides terms "the expected good" or "the good for which we hope." He states that "the masters of the Torah hold differing opinions concerning the good which comes to a person as a result of carrying out the commandments which God commanded us through Moses our teacher."

---

23. Eliezer Schweid, *"Tzidukon Hahinukhi Umedini Shel Mitzvot Ha'Emunah Lefi Mishnat Harambam"* ("The Educational and Political Justification of the Commandments of Belief in the Rambam's System"), in *Ta'am V'Hakashah (Feeling and Speculation)* (Ramat Gan: Massada Ltd., 1970), p. 101. I am extremely indebted to Professor Schweid for his analysis of this work of Maimonides. In his *Commentary to the Mishnah,* (on *Sanhedrin* 10:2) the Rambam notes that with regard to those listed there as having no share in the world-to-come, kings and commoners, the foundations of faith were disrupted *(hitkalkilu)* in them and they had doubts about some of them. On the other hand, those who sin and deserve the death penalty for their sins have a share in the world-to-come. On the educational ramifications of "for its own sake" in the realm of individual self-knowledge and self-actualization, see Chapter 13, pp. 231–34.

The Rambam summarizes five such views. Since he tells us that "much confusion has invaded the opinions" of even "the masters of the Torah" in this matter so that it is almost impossible to find a view "uncontaminated by error," we are prepared for the possibility that these views will, in toto or partially, be unacceptable or even implausible to him. (Yet it is surprising to find the Rambam admitting to confusion among masters of the Torah. Aren't these masters the guardians of the language of Torah? How can a master of the Torah have an incorrect understanding of the beliefs of Judaism, if correct beliefs are the key to what he will later call "entering the palace"? We shall see how he resolves the issue.)

The first view is that "the expected good" is the Garden of Eden, where all material things are found in luscious abundance, where rivers flow with wine and fragrant oils "and many other things of that sort." In this view, evil persons go to *Gehennom,* "a place of raging fire and agony." A second view entertains hopes for "the days of the Messiah, in whose time all men will be angels, living forever and enjoying such miraculous delights as garments brought forth from the earth fully woven ..." and many other "impossible things." Evil men, declare the partisans of this view, will not merit to see those wonderful days and happenings.

According to a third view "the good for which we hope" is the resurrection of the dead. Each person will "return to his dear ones and eat and drink and never die again." A fourth view has it that there will be "bodily peace and mundane success," with material abundance for all. A Jewish king will rule over "those that oppressed us." (Conversely, if we do evil we can anticipate a situation of subjugation and poverty, like "our present exile.") The fifth group combines the opinions of the others. "They assert that the ultimate hope is that the Messiah will come, that he will resurrect the dead, who will enter the Garden of Eden, where they will eat and drink in perfect health forever."

Before mentioning Maimonides's explicit evaluation of these diverse opinions we recall that he has noted "confusion" within them. More specifically, he is impatient with the details of the wondrous things awaiting us in the Garden of Eden: "... beds of silk ... and many things of that sort." More blatant is his scorn for the expectations of the second group, which believes "many impossible things." In fact, with reference to all five views, he speaks of "this strange world to come" and expresses distress that people busy themselves with such matters as whether the dead will arise fully dressed or naked. The preoccupation with such questions signifies that people do not distinguish between the trivial and the significant, nor, and perhaps consequently, "between the ultimate good itself and the means which lead to the ultimate good."

This distinction, as we shall see, is crucial to the difference between philosophy of education, which spells out the final ends of the educative enterprise, and the theory of education, which deals with the means of reaching these ends.[24] The difference between the two is spelled out in the parable that follows Maimonides's description of the five views of the world-to-come.

> Imagine a small child who has been brought to his teacher so that he may be taught the Torah which is his ultimate good because it will bring him to perfection. However, because he is only a child and because his understanding is deficient, he does not grasp the true value of that good, nor does he understand the perfection which he can achieve by means of Torah. Of necessity, therefore, his teacher, who has acquired greater perfection than the child, must bribe him to study by means which the child loves in a childish way. Thus the teacher may say, 'Read, (i.e., study) and I will give you some nuts or figs; I will give you a bit of honey.' With this stimulation, the child tries to read. He does not work hard for the sake of reading (i.e., studying) itself, since he does not understand its value. He reads in order to obtain the food. Eating these delicacies is far more important to him than reading, and a greater good to him.

As the child grows up, other things become manifestly desirable. At various stages in the child's maturation the teacher will "bribe" him with beautiful shoes or nice clothes; this will drive him to study for he "wants the garment more than the Torah." Eventually, as the child grows, motivation will be produced by monetary reward and, at a still later stage:

> ... his teacher may say to him ... "Study so that you may become the president of a court, a judge, so that people will honor you and rise before you as they honor So-and-So." He will then try hard to read in order to attain his new goal. His final end will then be to achieve the honor, the exaltation and the praise which others might confer upon him.

Maimonides's parable describes a process of learning which is "maneuvered" by progressive levels of extrinsic reward. And his conclusion: "Now, all this is deplorable." Whether the student is given figs or an exalted position (at a later stage of development), he still has deplorably not grasped that one should study Torah because it is "the ultimate good," designed to bring the learner "to perfection."

We have now been brought to see that the various schools of thought about the expected good are analogous to the various gifts children are promised as extrinsic rewards for being good. They do not comprehend that the Torah and its commandments are themselves the goal of study and observance; the knowledge of Torah and its practice are their own intrinsic goals. Yet Maimonides does not denounce, in its proper context, this "deplorable" state of affairs. He

24. See Chapter 1, pp. 5–10.

agrees that it "is unavoidable because of man's limited insight, as a result of which he makes the goal of wisdom something other than wisdom itself, which makes a mockery of truth. Our sages called this learning not for its own sake." Those who have not reached the high level at which they can serve God out of love (i.e., possessed of real intellectual understanding) will remain faithful and observant; one may hope "that they ... would ultimately grasp the truth and the way toward perfection, just like the child in the analogy."

Here, then, we find the Rambam reiterating the Talmudic adage: "A man ought always to labor in the Torah, even if not for its own sake. For, doing it not for its own sake, he may come to do it for its own sake (*Pesahim* 50b). He interprets this to mean that study for extrinsic reward is permissible because the Torah takes cognizance of the way children develop and of childishness in people in general, their "limited insight." This helps us to understand the startling fact that those having only childish understandings of "the expected good" can cite Scripture and the sages in support of their "deplorable" views. God's Torah and its inspired interpreters, the sages, teach us not only what ought to be and what education aims for, but how to teach, given human character and human limitations.

But what is necessary for the immature may never be viewed an an ideal, an "ought." It is not a philosophy, but only a theory of education, albeit a theory sanctioned by the Torah and the sages. God, through the medium of divinely inspired prophets and sages, is a pedagogue, teaching us in the Torah how to move people from ignorance to understanding! But the wise, the educated person is beyond that.

> A good man must not wonder. 'If I perform these commandments, which are virtues, and if I refrain from these transgression, which are vices which God commanded us not to do, what will I get out of it?' This is precisely what the child does when he asks, 'If I read (study), what will you give me?' The child is answered in some such way because, when we know his limited understanding and his desire for something other than a real goal, we answer him on the level of folly, as it is said in Proverbs 26:5: "Answer the fool according to his folly."'

The ultimate objective of education for Maimonides is that the learner should become a person who studies the Torah for its own sake, that is, in order to be a Torah-studying person, who knows it and whose knowledge and philosophical understanding is interlinked with doing it, i.e., carrying out its commandments.[25]

And this brings Maimonides to a classification of three groups of people, two of which obviously do not understand this distinction

25. See Maimonides's Introduction to the Tractate *Avot, Shmone Perakim*. On the relationship between character, thought, and action, see also Twersky, *Introduction to the Code of Maimonides,* pp. 510–13.

between what we today categorize as philosophy and theory of education and would never agree that the language of Judaism makes this distinction.

These groups, says the Rambam, have different understandings of the teachings of the sages. The first and largest group accepts these teachings in their literal sense, "in spite of the fact that some of their teachings, when taken literally, seem so fantastic and irrational that if one were to repeat them literally, even to the uneducated, let alone to sophisticated scholars, their amazement would prompt them to ask how anyone in the world could believe such things true, much less edifying." These people think that what the sages said in order to make the Torah understandable to those still in childish stages of development is what mature people are required to believe as dogma. What the sages, according to Maimonides, looked upon as a translation of the truth for the benefit of children, they foolishly see as the pristine teaching itself.

Rambam intimates that the members of this group are not only or necessarily the inarticulate and simple. "I have observed them, read their books and heard about them." These people "believe that all sorts of impossible things must be"; they have not understood science nor acquired knowledge. The outstanding quality of this group is folly, and their inability to penetrate to the inner meaning of the sages' teachings "destroys the glory of the Torah ... for they make the Torah of God say the opposite of what it intended."

> For He said in His perfect Torah, "The nations who hear of these statutes shall say: Surely this great nation is a wise and understanding people" (Deut. 4:6). But this group expounds the laws and teachings of our sages in such a way that when the other peoples hear them, they say that this little (i.e., not great) people is foolish and ignoble.

The worst offenders, states Maimonides, are the preachers who expound what they themselves do not understand. "If only they would be utterly silent, it would be accounted to them as wisdom" (Job 13:5). Unhappily, however, they think they understand "and they vigorously expound to the people what they think rather than what the sages really said."

The second group, also numerous, likewise takes the sayings of the sages literally, but declares them false. On the basis of their literal reading and understanding, they "slander the sages, declaring them to be fools." "They imagine that their own intelligence is of a higher order than that of the sages" while, in fact, "they are more stupid than the first group." Moreover, while the first group are fools, whose opinions and preachments are deplorable folly, the second group is not only ignorant but also "accursed." Clearly these people, like the former group, cannot make the distinction of the

sages between Torah for its own sake (philosophy) and Torah not
for its own sake (theory).

Then there is a third, alas, minute, group:

> The members of this group understand that the sages knew as clearly as
> we do the difference between the impossibility of the impossible and the
> existence of that which must exist. They know that the sages did not
> speak nonsense, and it is clear to them that the words of the sages contain
> both an obvious and a hidden meaning.

Wise people (i.e. those in the third group) know that our sages had
to speak in riddles and analogies "and employ such figures of speech
as are easily understood by the masses"; indeed Solomon, the wisest of
men, did exactly that in Proverbs, the Song of Songs and parts of Ecclesiastes. In fact, says Maimonides, the sages themselves understood
many things in the Bible in metaphoric terms, instructing us thereby
how to relate to metaphoric statements and hidden meanings.

In the remainder of his commentary on this *mishnah*, the Rambam explains how we should understand the world-to-come. The
world-to-come described here may be said to represent an ideal
state of human development and an ideally congenial environment
for such development.

Thus, in "the world-to-come," which as a historical reality is synonymous with Messianic times, there will be a genuine intention on
the part of all people to "know the Lord" and Scripture promises that
the world will in those days indeed be filled with the knowledge of
God, e.g., "I will put My Torah in their inward parts and I will write
it in their heart" (Jer. 31:34).

> The world-to-come is the ultimate end toward which all our effort ought
> to be devoted. Therefore the sage who firmly grasped the knowledge of
> the truth and who envisioned the final end, forsaking everything else,
> taught: All Israelites have a share in the world-to-come.

Nevertheless, the righteous person should not serve God even to
attain the historical world-to-come, but to cultivate virtue and avoid
vice. S/he will thus become fully human, acquiring the nature of the
perfect human being. "His soul thus attains the eternal life it has
come to know, which is the world-to-come, as we have explained."
In other words, it is possible to attain "the world to come" even without, or before, the historical Messianic development that will create
the optimal social conditions for the knowledge of God and human
perfectibility. While not all can reach such perfection, all "can
acquire correct opinions according to their respective capacities."

In conclusion Maimonides explains the thirteen principles "upon
which our religion is based."

> When a man believes in all these fundamental principles and his faith is
> thus clarified, he is then part of that 'Israel' whom we are to love, pity and

treat, as God commanded, with love and fellowship. Even if a Jew should commit every possible sin, out of lust or mastery by his lower nature, he will be punished for his sins but will still have a share in the world to come. He is one of the 'sinners of Israel.' But if a man gives up one of these fundamental principles, he has removed himself from the Jewish community. He is an atheist, a heretic, an unbeliever who 'cuts among the plantings.' We are commanded to hate him and destroy him. Of him it is said: 'Shall I not hate those who hate You, O Lord?' (Ps. 139:21).

Maimonides presents an educational ideal. He has, even in the few passages that we have cited in our discussion, related (at least!) to all the questions mentioned at the beginning of our chapter. We have an educational-philosophical conception of the ideal person; we have authorization for an educational theory that cultivates such persons. We have more than a hint of what a good teacher is like and what a harmful one might be. We have touched upon Maimonides's view of how the good society makes possible a good individual. And we have been clearly told that the Torah, understood philosophically, is both the ideal subject matter of education, and its blueprint. Education is designed to cultivate people whose highest aspiration will be the world-to-come, which is the ultimate end towards which all our efforts ought to be directed and to do so with due regard for man's limited insight so that they will have to study not for its own sake before they can reach the level of Torah for its own (intrinsic) sake. As for the educated person, he or she partakes personally and consciously in the world-to-come and anticipates the historical situation in which the conditions for universal perfectibility will be realized, i.e., the Messianic days.

The modern educator is likely to find aspects of Maimonides's doctrine problematic. S/he may consider it bound to outworn metaphysical conceptions and elitistic. Moreover, some may find the stringent *halakhic* regimen which cements the social "perfection of the body" overly conservative for modern people and even arbitrary. They may say that it demands too much socialization and perhaps the wrong kind. Even those who wish to learn Jewish educational philosophy from this medieval master will want a clearer view of what is theologically and philosophically intimated in his outlook for the educator and how aspects of it can be translated into educational practice.

How may the contemporary educator understand and perhaps use the Maimonidean model in his or her work? How can contemporary, and even classic, educational thought illuminate aspects of the Rambam's teaching for this educator?

Let us now turn to these questions.

4

RAMSEY
MEETS THE
RAMBAM

*I*n the passages of Maimonides we have read, we may locate a number of central educational issues. Each of them raises diverse questions, and invites further clarification. In this and the following chapter, we shall examine three of these issues, clarify their underlying assumptions and point to some theoretical and practical educational ramifications. In doing so, we shall draw upon the work of several theologians and educational philosophers.

Issues and Questions

(1) *Principles, Action and ... Education? Or Indoctrination?*
The Rambam declares, in diverse theological and *halakhic* contexts, that the highest expression of Jewish faith and existence is to accept and eventually gain optimal understanding of the truth. This philosophical truth is the inner content of the Torah, its ultimate demand and its redemptive promise. While all Jews must observe the commandments, and while the revealed norms of morality as found in the seven *Noahide* laws ideally oblige all human beings, only knowledge of God and perfection of the soul will give Jews and the righteous of the nations of the world a grasp of the real meaning of the commandments bestowed upon Israel and mankind, respectively. Only knowledge makes possible love of God. The ideally actualized

Torah is a synthesis of religious and moral action and an understanding of its principles.[1]

Clearly, then, the commandments as specific actions or behaviors do not exhaust the realm of knowable reality or set limits to the religiously commanded life. Yet, in a sense, they set the agenda, both for the investigation of the divine truth and for the limits to what simple people are qualified and permitted to investigate. In fact, they teach humility even to the wise. For though some practical commandments seem to be beyond human comprehension they are nevertheless binding on all, whether wise or simple. At the same time, perfection of the soul through knowledge remains humankind's highest good, and is required even by the multitude to the greatest extent possible. The knowledge they can acquire, largely through parable and metaphor, gives them too a share in the world of truth, in the world-to-come.

Obviously, the educated person understands the truth differently than the ignorant one and thus has a larger share in the world-to-come. Such a person consciously knows his or her religious life to be comprised of action and thought. Wishing to enter the palace of the king, s/he understands that neither simple piety nor transmitted and unreflectively accepted doctrine suffice. S/he has been educated to accept principles that lie behind the commandments, to examine them, and, upon better understanding them, to raise the level of action to a more profound spiritual level.

A number of educational questions arise in this context of education into the world of principle.

(a) The educated Jew, according to Maimonides, has to accept these principles both before and after inquiry, since rejection, as we have seen in Maimonides's interpretation of the *mishnah* in *Sanhedrin*, is tantamount to ceasing to be an Israelite. But doesn't this expectation and demand deal a mortal blow to honest inquiry?

(b) When do children begin learning principles in a more than rote manner, given that in their early stages of development they cannot understand but only accept them? Why, indeed, should they accept them? And how does learning for understanding differ from the inculcation of childish acceptance, of pure and simple indoctrination?

(c) If commitment to the way of life of Judaism ("perfection of the body") is a prerequisite for wisdom, and is a social demand made by

---

1. "Now we have made it clear several times that love is proportionate to apprehension." Maimonides, *Guide to the Perplexed* III: 51, On this, see David Hartman, *Maimonides: Torah and Philosophic Quest* (Philadelphia: Jewish Publication Society, 1976), Chap. 5. For the Maimonidean approach to the relationship between the commandments and reason, see Twersky, *Introduction to the Code of Maimonides*, Chap. 6.

the Torah on everyone, why not simply teach that, and leave wisdom to the wise, assuming that they will get to it through their own volition and the personal cultivation of inner power? After all, one cannot assume a deep understanding of the truth of Judaism for most people in any case. Will not any attempt at perfection of the soul in education lead the multitude to the kinds of distortions decried by the Rambam (in the *Introduction to Perek Helek*)? Recall how he bemoans the first group, those who take the words of the Sages literally and thereby defame Judaism!

(2) Development, Intrinsic Ideals, and the Teacher

The Rambam presents, in his *Introduction to Perek Helek*, what we may call a theological as well as a psychological conception of human development. He describes children's inability to appropriately understand the Torah and allows the teacher, on the authority of the Torah itself and the sages, to offer them extrinsic goals of learning.[2] When and if a particular learner reaches intellectual and thus, religious, maturity, s/he understands that his/her previous motivations for study were unworthy of the Torah, that the only meaningful reward for learning it is intrinsic.

Here, two central questions deserve our attention:

(a) What exactly is meant by an intrinsic ideal in education and why is it seen as the only worthy end-product of education? Is it not the fact that most of what we do in education is, justifiably, concerned with making us function more adequately, socially and personally? To help us achieve with greater ease and satisfaction what we want to do, and get out of life?

(b) If lower stages represent not only levels of childhood cognition, but foolish conceptions of the truth (recall the five views concerning the world-to-come!) of all too many adults, what will happen if Judaism is presented by teachers who do not belong to the philosophically understanding group? After all, the Rambam has informed us that the latter constitutes such a small group!

(3) Philosophy, Elitism and Piety

Maimonides seems to be presenting us with one exclusive aim of education: the educated Jew as philosopher. Does this not imply that most people, despite pious hopes for their eventual improvement, are inferior and may be taught Platonic lies? That authentic education is

---

2. This stage theory is primarily theological, because it overtly assigns religious value to the movement of the largest number of people possible towards an adult (i.e., normative) level of comprehension. (Were it basically psychological, it would simply describe this movement, with alleged neutrality.)

only for the elite? But in that case, how can the Torah's command-ment to "diligently teach your sons," all of them, be accommodated? Isn't it possible for those who lack philosophical understanding to come to piety and love of God through other ways, in line with their specific temperaments and talents? Is moral fervor always inferior and suspect when it is not imbued with intellectual sophistication?

In this chapter we shall take up the first of these issues and explore how norms and principles are related in what may be called the Rambam's educational philosophy.

Principles and Reasoning: Maimonides and a Modern Educator

At first glance, it seems to make eminent and deceptively simple sense to understand the Rambam as one would a modern and open educator who educates children to really understand their commit-ments. Like such an educator, the Rambam is easily imagined dis-missing religious commitments that are no more than conformism and blind loyalty.

This modern educator may declare that a way of life has to have a rationale in order to meaningfully survive. It must deserve the assent of intelligence, for one cannot wholeheartedly and responsi-bly maintain attitudes and practices that are not related to defensible ideas. S/he will note that if this was generally true in all times, this must be particularly so in an open society where loyalties, especially those of minority faith communities, are constantly being called into question. Children, in other words, should learn a religious culture for which there are reasons, which can be justified within the major-ity culture in which they live.

Such a stance is not necessarily apologetic. It can, in fact, be pre-sented as a proud national-cultural argument. Our modern educator may be saying that the wrong view, that Judaism has a way of life but no firm principles of its own, was invented by Jews who wished to belong to other cultures that had their own philosophies of life.

Maimonides might go along with some of this contemporary and open educator's reasoning. He would certainly agree that learning to withstand criticism of Judaism is important. He would also agree that the practices of Judaism can be carried out with proper intention and real conviction only by those who understand what they are, in ideational terms, actually doing.[3]

---

3. Twersky, *Introduction to the Code of Maimonides,* p. 513.

Yet, while our modern and progressive educator might be gratified to have the Rambam as predecessor and ally, even a brief theoretical investigation will cast doubt on the alleged meeting of minds between them.

To begin with, our contemporary educator who stresses ideas, reasoning, and Jewish value clarification would not necessarily insist that the reasons, the ideas, and the principles talked about in schools, community centers, and camps derive from knowledge of God, i.e., a metaphysical truth. He or she might well consider moral reasoning as adequate and appropriate even without theological grounds, or perhaps even the better for not being cluttered up with such metaphysical and unverifiable considerations. The Rambam, on the other hand, would insist that secularized moral reasoning that scorns the highest perfection (of an intellectual knowledge of God) lacks all religious status. He might also suspect that our modern educator is more preoccupied with the process of looking for principles and reasons, than with finding and understanding what is, for the Rambam, at least, the truth.

To state this in more general terms: Maimonides would agree with the contemporary philosopher of education, Richard L. Peters, that one not only needs reasons for adhering to codes and their rules, but good ones. It is these good reasons to which children are to be introduced and the rightness of which, hopefully, they will eventually understand. Like Peters, Maimonides wants the pupils to sense "what there is in the cherished pursuit ... to feel from the inside the rightness of a course of action." He would agree that if this "sense of rightness," based on good reasoning, is not achieved, nothing has been accomplished. Peters gives the following, obviously absurd example of what might be wrong reasoning:

> Suppose it is said that one ought not to slash people with razors, which is to suggest that there are reasons for not doing that. We inquire what the reasons are and are told that people bleed as a result and blood is red and that is why we should not do it.[4]

Now this reasoning, consciously comical in considering more than absolutely necessary redness as the reason for not injuring people, is obviously not one that will induce a sense of rightness. Or as Maimonides, our no-nonsense medieval personage, might say more sternly, it is not the true one. Maimonides would certainly admit that our modern educator who believes in basing Jewish education on reasons and principles is not likely to descend to such absurdities. Yet, he might say, such reasons as contributing to Western civilization, surviving as a recognizable cultural group, or expressing our

4. Richard L. Peters, "Reason and Habit," p. 47.

deepest intuitions symbolically are also not good reasons for they are simply—not true.

The Rambam has another problem with the modern ideational approach that our hypothetical educator, as modern and open, affirms. The latter assumes that reasons and principles allow the reflective person not only to find a key to understanding faith and faith actions, but ultimately, to either justify or reject them. Through reasoning and inquiry we are often enabled to reaffirm, but speculation and investigation also give grounds to question and refute. Maimonides, as we have seen, places the blame for rejection of the Torah on the frailties and misuse of the human intellect. It is a *mitzvah* to think, to prove, and to know through inquiry, but it is doubly sinful to reject on the basis of thought; first, because a person who thoughtfully rejects will refrain from carrying out the commandments of the Torah; second, because this person has thought fallaciously and thus exhibited stupidity, hubris, and rebellion.

"Thinking fallaciously" is an expression that our modern and progressive educator is likely to shy away from, or to reserve for scientific matters; s/he certainly does not like to apply it to normative or religious questions. We cannot, therefore, expect him or her to sympathize with the Rambam's stricture on independent thought for those who are not ready for it. For the modern approach is based on the assumption that it is not terribly important which principles or doctrines are used to explain or buttress agreed-upon ideals in theory. After all, one person may be plugged into and practice democracy because he thinks that human beings should impose a free and dignified existence onto an absurd cosmos, while another bases her adherence on the belief that all human beings are created in God's image and thus are divinely endowed with worth. The principles of cosmic absurdity and of divine order are certainly very different; nevertheless most moderns will assume that their respective adherents can serenely practice democracy together. Neither generally looks upon the other as fundamentally dangerous, and at least one of the two takes no interest in whether his opponent is facing away from or moving toward some allegorical palace in which true opinions and real experience with transcendence reside. For this reason, in the modern school everybody is deemed ready for independent thought. Even if it does not produce truth, it is good training.

"Seeing and Hearing":
Discernments and Commitments

How, then, may we clarify and illuminate Maimonides's doctrine of normative religion, a doctrine that is grounded in true ideas and urges its adherents to reach for an understanding of them? To what can it be usefully compared, in order to make it more approachable for contemporary educational thought and to bring it fruitfully into the conversation of educational practice? How can it be presented so as to sharpen focuses of controversy between itself and rival conceptions?

We suggest that the Rambam's educational thinking about norms and principles can be made educationally more lucid through a comparison with the concepts of discernment and commitment developed by Ian Ramsey in his work, *Religious Language.*[5]

In a chapter entitled, "What Kinds of Situations Are Religious?" Ramsey describes discernment as an experience in which there is, in a flash, or as a result of cumulative factors, a breakthrough in understanding. Something that was not known to us, even if we knew a great deal about it, suddenly becomes clear, is appropriated, takes on the character of knowledge. In Ramsey's phrase, "The penny drops; the ice breaks." If the situation that is suddenly transformed has an intense personal dimension, and/or is seen as especially significant, it has taken on depth; there is something akin to religious insight, discernment, vision in it. One might also say, the gestalt is formed; the pieces come together.

Ramsey gives a pithy example of how discernment sometimes happens at the moment we are told someone's name. He describes a situation of a person, perhaps himself, who meets and then frequently encounters another man.

> We may first have known him as the man in the bowler hat who came to sit next to us in the train. He then appears opposite us at lunch, and we begin to see him regularly. We now know him as the man who invariably orders 'Double Diamond,' the man who does the Times crossword in fifteen minutes; and as the weeks pass we come to know him as the man who has a wife and three children ... But one day he says, offering his hand: "Look here—I'm Nigel Short." At that moment there is a 'disclosure,' an individual becomes a 'person,' the ice does not continue to melt, it breaks. We have not discovered just one more fact to be added to those we have been collecting day by day. There has now been some significant 'encounter' which is not just a moving of palm on palm, no mere correlation of mouth noises, not just heads moving in some kind of mutual harmony.[6]

If Nigel Short were to ask our narrator to lend him some money, even the very next day, we would probably expect him to consider the request seriously, and even to agree. After all, we would say, he knows

5. Ian Ramsey, *Religious Language: An Empirical Placing of Theological Phrases* (New York: The Macmillan Co., 1963).
6. *Ibid.*, pp. 28–29.

the man! The discernment, Ramsey asks us to assume, brings a commitment in its wake. Just as a captain who knows his ship, will proverbially go down with it, just as one will do anything for a beloved person, and just as one who has discerned what it is to be a human being, can be expected to jump into the water to save a drowning person, so will any serious discernment bring a commitment with it.

Discernments are waiting for us at every juncture of our experience, and we never know when we will have one. We don't know exactly what may occasion them, or how they come to us but we know that discernments allow us to really know things, people, ourselves. And, discernments evoke commitments. Discernments without commitments, one might say, are empty and irresponsible.

According to Ramsey, those discernments that are of crucial importance in our lives such as discovering who we are or realizing what it means to be human should be recognized as having crucial religious significance; they are, actually, revelations. And what they reveal are also concommitant commitments. So, if I have had a discernment of what it means to be human, it becomes irresponsible to stand by while others cry out for help. If I have a discernment of goodness I find myself committed to protecting it and fighting evil. The "religious attitude (is) a discernment-commitment."[7]

The religious texts of Judaism, Bible, *Midrash,* and Talmud deal incessantly with what people realize and understand on the one hand, and what they are called upon to do on the other. In the Bible, we are shown scenes of seeing and hearing that remind us of discernment and commitment, respectively, and of the relationship between them.[8] The former, seeing, describes the great event or the outstanding moment when, for example, Israelites saw the great hand of God saving them at the Red Sea (Exodus 14:31) or, "saw" (i.e., experienced as a supremely important discernment) the sounds spoken at Mount Sinai (Exodus 20:125). The voice that is heard speaks the ensuing commitment demanded of those who saw. The People of Israel, having seen God utter the commandments, understand that they are being asked to hearken to His voice.

Were Maimonides to adopt the terminology of Ramsey, he might utilize it to explain why the discernments of the less than wise are not

---

7. *Ibid.,* pp. 18–19.
8. For a similar but not identical distinction between seeing and hearing in the Bible, see I. Jacobson, "*Al Neumai HaShem B'Sefer Iyyov*" ("On God's Speeches in the Book of Job") in *L'Baayat Hag'mul Bamikra (On the Problem of Retribution in the Bible)* (Tel Aviv: Sinai Pub., 5719), pp. 51–53. On discernment and commitment as a major theme in the first chapters of Exodus, examined on the basis of Emanuel Levinas's anthropology, see J. Schoneveld, "The Hebrew Bible–Common Sources for Jews and Christians in an Age Beyond Tradition and Modernity," *Face to Face–An Inter-Religious Bulletin* 10 (New York: Anti-Defamation League of Bnai Brith, 1982), pp. 38–42.

to be trusted. After all, their foolish discernments are going to suggest wrong, or even dangerous commitments! We might find him reminding us that the most exalted discernments, with the outstanding (partial and qualified) exceptions of the revelation at Sinai and at the Red Sea, are experienced only by prophets, and it is only the greatest of these, Moses, who discerns God's truth for Israel face-to-face. Thus only he brought us the Torah, with its consequent commitments, the *mitzvot*.[9]

Let us note how the Rambam explains the origins of idolatry, at the very beginning of the section in the *Mishneh Torah* that deals with this problem:

> In the days of Enosh, the people fell into gross error and the counsel of the wise men of the generation became foolish. Their error was as follows: 'Since God,' they said, 'created these stars and spheres to guide the world, set them on high and allotted them honor ... they deserve to be praised and honored ... and it is the will of God, blessed be He, that men should ... honor those whom He ... honored, just as a king desires that respect be shown to the officers who stand before him and this honor is (actually) shown to the king. When this idea arose in their minds they began to erect temples to the stars, offered up sacrifices to them ... prostrated themselves before them–their purpose, according to their perverse notions, being to obtain the Creator's favor ...
> As time gradually passed, the honored and revered Name of God was forgotten ... The world moved on in this fashion until that pillar of the world, the patriarch Abraham was born.

Maimonides explains that Abraham taught his true doctrine, as did his sons after him, thereby morally strengthening his adherents. And when there was a danger that the truth would be forgotten, replaced by the universally prevalent errors and perversities, then God, because of His love for us (discernment!) "and because He kept the oath made to our ancestor Abraham," (commitment!)

> appointed Moses to be our teacher ... After Moses had begun to exercise his prophetic functions and Israel had been chosen by the Almighty as His heritage, He crowned them with precepts and showed them the way to worship Him and how to deal with idolatry and with those who go astray after it.
>
> *Hilkhot Avodah Zarah* (Laws of Idolatry) I:1-2

Clearly then, the person with wrong understandings (faulty discernments) leads the world into sin. The righteous person, who discerns correctly, is the archetype of the ideal teacher, leading people upon the proper path–of commitment. Everything, then, depends on the right discernment, for this is what makes the difference between potential perfection and perdition.

9. As explained in the seventh and eighth fundamental principle of Jewish faith in "Introduction to *Perek Helek.*"

We suggest that Ramsey's terms may clarify for the educator both the teaching of true ideas, and the perfections which Maimonides considers to be the dual aim of the Torah and from which we derive the proper objectives of the educating community.

But one important qualification is necessary. Ramsey appears to assume that discernment precedes commitment.[10] We see and then we hear, to use the Biblical phraseology. We cannot be committed to something we have not truly discerned; that would be an empty and meaningless commitment. Would a Maimonidean teacher consider this an ironclad rule? Would he or she not suggest that commitments may function to create discernments? That saving a life would create an understanding of what is meant by the neighbor? Or that lending someone money may lead to really and finally knowing that person?

Indeed, Maimonides's description of "the wise men in the days of Enosh" (the grandson of Adam in the Biblical genealogy) follows the same sequence that we find in Ramsey. First, there is a wrong discernment by the seemingly wise, leading people to wrongly discern that it would be proper to serve the sun and stars; hence, and thereafter, their foolish commitment to idolatry. For Abraham, who began to reflect while still an infant, the discernment also came first; he grasped the truth. At the age of forty, he recognized his Creator. He then taught his family and those who joined his household to acknowledge the truth and to accept the way of God.

And yet, isn't it the educator's experience that in many cases we begin with commitment that we believe or hope will lead to discernment? Putting fundamental commitments before discernments certainly makes sense if we think of education as a purposeful adult activity, designed to lead children toward end-aims which they, in their present youthful stages of development, cannot comprehend. And this is, indeed, what any developmental conception of education that has a normative thrust demands. Those who have a normative philosophical conception of the educated person will not trust the most important discernments (those that Ramsey calls religious) of children to lead them to the correct (moral) commitments. To cite Peters again, "inculcated habit must precede the achievement of Reason."[11]

Socialization and the Two Perfections

We have seen that this appears to be the Rambam's position as well, but with an important proviso: he insists that children be taught and

10. Ramsey, *Religious Language,* pp. 15–16
11. Peters, "Reason and Habit," pp. 51–52.

be expected to accept (i.e., become committed to) certain wise but simplified discernments. To understand how and why this is so, let us return to his description of the aims of the Torah.

We recall that the perfection of the body, which requires that people be taught to refrain from evil and to engage in good actions so that society may be moral and well ordered, precedes the perfection of the soul. Stated differently: ever since the giving of the Torah, which is itself the product of the highest prophetic discernment, commitment precedes discernment. The rule now becomes *Na'aseh v'Nishma*, "to do and to hear" even before there is seeing. The community, which knows that commitment can (and ideally will) lead to discernment, must acquire the child's commitment, even by bribes, before the young person understands it so that s/he may (perhaps!) eventually understand it. For obviously, if and when the young person discerns what the Torah, in all its facets—moral, philosophical, theological—means, and that it is truth, he or she requires no more extrinsic motivations. He or she will then understand that "the intellect which emanates from God unto us is the link that joins us to God."[12]

The Rambam insists, then, on this (un-Ramseyian) sequence. We begin with commitment that leads to discernment creating, in turn, a more principled commitment. The insistence on this sequence follows from the fact that the perfection of the body, i.e., the socialization of people into morally and socially desirable patterns of behavior, is a simpler undertaking than perfection of the soul. The latter is at best a difficult and lengthy process. Though the actual discernment, the "ice breaking," may come in an instant, it often requires arduous preparation. It cannot be inadvertent that the Rambam portrays Abraham, a veritable knight of divine discernments, beginning, precociously, to reflect while still an infant; though it was only at forty that Abraham knew his Creator. It is also a process that is never completed, for there are limits to human understanding.[13]

This puts those who desire to arrive at the palace and to enter it but have never yet seen it in a different, more developmental light. This multitude that observes the divine commandments but is ignorant may, hopefully, in time, through the power of the social commitments imposed upon them (perfection of the body) become wise, gain discernments, enter the palace. Maimonides states in his code that it is possible for men and women of the multitude to move from fear to love of God. As he makes this point in the *Mishneh Torah*, we are reminded of his "Introduction to *Perek Helek*":

---

12. Maimonides, *Guide*, III:51.
13. Maimonides, *Mishneh Torah, Hilkhot Avodat Kokhavim* (Laws of Idolatry), I: 2.

Whoever engages in the study of the Torah in order to receive a reward or avoid calamities is not studying the Torah for its own sake. Whoever occupies himself with the Torah, neither out of fear not for the sake of recompense, but solely out of love for the Lord of the whole earth who enjoined us to do so, is occupied with the Torah for its own sake. The sages, however, said, 'One should always engage in the study of Torah, even if not for its own sake, for he who begins thus will end by studying it for its own sake.' Hence, when instructing the young, women, or the illiterate generally, we teach them to serve God out of fear or for the sake of reward, till their knowledge increases and they have attained a large measure of wisdom. Then we reveal to them this secret truth, little by little, and train them by easy stages till they have grasped and comprehended it, and serve God out of love.[14]

Yet, it is impossible simply to dictate commitments. To do so would testify to a disregard of the very process of human development that made the normative educator insist on giving priority to commitments (over discernments) in the first place. Maimonides himself notes this when he explains that the ignorant and childish study Torah to receive a reward or avoid calamities: These hopes and fears are surely themselves based on discernments, however childish. For the happy fact is that people do have discernments from their earliest days. Children miraculously learn our language,[15] they grasp nuances of culture, they discover what is unique and what can be classified. They do say, and not only upon being prodded by educators, "Oh, I get it," or "wow!," meaning, "I see." They are constantly comprehending things, they are learning, and, of course, education would be impossible without this innate gift. Moreover, what they see does shape their motives and commitments. And since so many of these discernments take place outside the purposive realm of education, socialization is (fortunately!) never complete.

Therefore, if there are commitments we want children to have so that they may come upon what we consider true or desirable discernments, we must link up these desirable (and for Maimonides, normative) discernments to their already existing ones. That is, we must give them motives for adopting good commitments in a manner that makes sense to them. Also, we must let them in on the discernments that we of the adult community see as the basis of our commitments, yet on their own level. In other words, just as we must give them goodies for the study of Torah, so must we supply basic, however childish, formulations of what perfection of the soul means to those wise persons who "have a share in the world to come." For otherwise why would children, or for that matter, the ignorant mul-

---

14. In *Mishneh Torah, Hilkhot Teshuvah* (Laws of Repentence), X:5.
15. R. David Kimchi (RaDaK), a twelfth-thirteenth century exegete, thus interprets Psalms 8:3 ("Out of the mouths of babes and sucklings have You founded strength")–the ability of babies to acquire speech demonstrates God's power.

titude, take on a commitment to the practiced Torah of the welfare of the body? In Maimonidean terminology: Where will they get the necessary *fear* that makes them accept the norms of the Torah even before they have *love*, i.e., understanding?[16]

This problem has, in what we have examined above of Maimonides's writings, a two-fold resolution:

(a) The Torah and the sages, in their theory of education, authorize the community, through its teachers, to impart childish (imaginative and far-fetched) formulations of true discernments. Teachers may not teach what is in principle false, for example, that there is no connection between Torah and the world-to-come, but they are allowed to portray the world-to-come in "strange" ways and to present it as an extrinsic reward for observing the Torah and studying it. That this is legitimate we know from the fact that such childish conceptions can rely on statements of the sages themselves who, in Maimonides's view, obviously did not themselves see matters childishly.

(b) Children are taught a fundamental formulation of correct opinions. In other words, they are given intimations of true religious (i.e., most important!) discernments. These they must accept in order to be Israelites. It is upon these foundations that the spiritually endowed and diligent may eventually build a genuine perfection of the soul.

This fundamental formulation is transmitted together with the social-religious commitments, with the *halakhot* of the perfection of the body. In a sense, these correct opinions are transmitted as though they referred to the "welfare of the body"; they are part of the process of belonging rather than of understanding. Note that it is at the very beginning of his discussion of the aims of the Torah, immediately prior to his delineation of the characteristics and norms related to the welfare of the body, that the Rambam informs us that "the well-being of the soul is promoted by correct opinions communicated to the people according to their capacity ... (either) in plain form ... (or) allegorically, because certain opinions are in their plain form too strong for the capacity of the common people."[17]

If there is a degree of philosophical mobility, and some people can move from fear to love of God, and the young person's initiation into the world of Torah study is also one of movement, from crass extrinsic rewards to, perhaps, an understanding of its intrinsic worth, then we may draw two conclusions:

16. See above, n. 14.
17. *Guide* III:27.

(a) The multitude that is not yet capable of knowledge should be moved in the right direction through transmitted and adapted discernments, and

(b) All children, because of the innate limitations imposed upon them by the given reality of gradual human development, should, in this regard, be counted among the multitude.

In both cases, teachers, working on behalf of the community of discernment and commitment, give an inkling of true opinion in a suitable form for children and others who are still on a childish level of understanding, and they socialize them into the norms related to welfare of the body, namely, the practical commandments. In other words, the community has the duty to teach those beliefs, (correct opinions), without which the commitments will seem empty, and therefore arbitrary even to the young and the others who are ignorant. The process of education therefore begins with socialization that includes rote and rudimentary instruction in the discernments of Judaism. It instructs the young in the life of the *mitzvot* and *halakhah* and proceeds, in the wake of commitments accepted but only vaguely understood, to the vistas of independently discovered discernment–the love of God.

Those who reach this stage know they themselves are required to return to the community, as leaders and mentors, as participants in its norms and their interpreters. For while in the perfection of the soul "there do not belong either actions or moral qualities ... (but) only ... opinions towards which speculation has led and that investigation has rendered compulsory,"[18] this seemingly Aristotelian aloofness is quickly qualified out of existence by the Rambam. The God who is known by the person of true religious discernment, by the lover of God, is far removed from the self-contained and morally detached and religiously indifferent thinking machine of Aristotle. The God of Israel does justice, loves mercy, and demands of those who cleave to the divine that they walk in His ways. Thus, the student of the Torah, who has learned that the study of Torah is its own intellectual reward, immediately discovers that the knowledge that is intrinsically valuable brings him or her not to the knowledge of an abstract deity but of the God Who is known by His acts, and that these ought to serve as a guide for our actions.[19]

18. *Ibid.*
19. On this, see Daniel H. Frank, "The End of the Guide: Maimonides on the Best Life for Man," *Judaism*, 34 (Fall, 1985), pp. 485–95; also, Alexander Altmann, "Maimonides's 'Four Perfections,'" *Essays in Jewish Intellectual History* (Hanover, N.H.: 1981), pp. 65–76. An important conclusion drawn by Hartman, *Maimonides and Philosophic Quest*: "By distinguishing between morality before and after knowledge of God, Maimonides is expressing a key theme of his philosophy: theoretical knowledge of God affects practice," p. 205.

It is clear that the perfection of man that may be truly gloried in is the one acquired by him who has achieved, in a measure corresponding to his capacity, apprehension of Him, may He be exalted, and who knows His providence extending over His creatures ... The way of life of such an individual, after he has achieved this apprehension, will always have in mind loving-kindness, righteousness and judgment, through assimilation to His actions, may He be exalted.[20]

Therefore, our student, coming out of the childhood of extrinsically motivated study and principles-by-rote finds him/herself faced with what seems like a paradox. As it is expressed in the "Introduction to *Perek Helek*"

... (The sages) hinted at what I have just explained to you, that the end of wisdom is neither to acquire honor from other men not to earn more money. One ought not to busy oneself with God's Torah in order to earn one's living by it; nor should the end of studying wisdom be anything but knowing it. The truth has no other purpose than knowing that it is truth. Since the Torah is truth, the purpose of knowing it is to do it.

We see, therefore, that Maimonides's educational philosophy is not very congenial to that of the modern and progressive educator with whom we began our discussion. The latter, like the Rambam, insisted that the individual understand the principles of Judaism so that Judaism could be lived rationally and plausibly and could be defended—but s/he had to admit that principled reflection and understanding might also lead to rejection. For him or her, it is the individual who is sovereign and must decide, for authentic religiosity wells out of the individual soul, is anchored in it and is responsible to it. This is the orientation that we have elsewhere described as "implicit religiosity" in which

discrete religions are illustrative of universal insights ('truths') and may—indeed, must—be justified before the bar of universal experience, including the child's. Truth is discovered by delving into experience; by eliciting the child's questions, and not the a-priori 'right' ones.[21]

If our analysis is correct, Maimonides's approach, on the fundamental educational plane in which children are socialized into the perfection of the body, is what we have called the "explicit religious" one. In this mode

one is born into the community that was 'chosen' for God's message and that sought and found God in a particular experience, that dictated a nor-

20. *Guide*, III: 54.
21. Michael Rosenak, *Commandments and Concerns*, p. 114.

mative mode of 'standing before' Him. The norms of the community provide the avenue to ultimate understanding.[22]

For those destined never to grow up spiritually and intellectually, this explicit religiosity is indeed the last word; unable to reach the king's palace, these loyal and obedient Jews yet have a share in the world-to-come. They desire to reach the palace and are facing in the right direction. This explicit religiosity is also, as already noted, the educational ground-laying for all, since children, like the multitude are not yet mature.

But, as we have seen, the ultimate purpose of religious life, the real link with God, is an individual achievement; it is what a particular person gains and has for him/herself, though it is constructed on the basis of the explicit religiosity which s/he has been taught, into which s/he has been initiated. The path of true religion, for Maimonides, is explicitly religious, for the fundamental discernments and commitments are given, imposed. But the goal and the character ideal is, what explicit religiosity promises the spiritually aspiring individual to achieve through its norms: ultimate understanding. The person who loves God has reached an individually gained discernment and devotion that transcends the norms of explicit religion, but, rooted in explicit religiosity, it stays with it. According to the explicitly religious mode, the truly righteous individual knows that the highest discernments go together with intensive commitments, that love, understanding, and reflection are not simply more mature than obedience and fear, but are transfigurations of them.

And here the educational enterprise as seen through the spectrum of a Maimonidean philosophy of education faces a formidable challenge, focused on the teacher. How can teachers give explicit religious education, including correct opinions for the multitude, while preparing learners to outgrow a childish orientation to the study and practice of Torah, an orientation which is not "for its own sake"? If most loyal Jews belong to that deplorable first group of those who take the words of the Bible and the sages literally and "possess no perfection which would arouse them to insight from within," ("Introduction to *Perek Helek*") who then will teach the spiritually gifted child? Can such teachers transmit the meaning of Torah for its own sake?

We turn now to this question, once again with the aid of a contemporary educational thinker.

---

22. *Ibid.*

5

LEARNING,
TRUTH, AND IRONY

*I*n this chapter, we shall examine the issue of development in a normative philosophy of Jewish education, and the consequent dilemma of the teacher whose duty it is to move pupils in the direction of what this educational philosophy construes to be wisdom. But first, let us recapitulate several points raised by Maimonides and the problems that they raise.

We have seen Maimonides portray the uncertain progression of children towards a worthy understanding of the Torah. The prospects of the multitude to catch a glimpse of all that it is in the power of men to know are even more dubious. And yet, it is such knowledge alone that brings people to love of God, to true religious self-realization.

Thus, in the educational conception of Maimonides, despite the patent differences between people, there can be only one and exclusive ideal goal of the educational enterprise: it is that all should be philosophically wise and therefore walk in … (God's) ways. There is a clear hierarchy of human achievement and self-realization. Only they are in the palace with the king who "have a true knowledge of God so far as a true knowledge can be attained and are near the truth …" (*Guide* III:51)

Maimonides and the Rambam

It is sometimes maintained that this conception of the genuinely educated Jew arises out of a dissonance between two facets of our writer, between what may be called "Maimonides the philosopher," on the one hand, and "Rambam the faithful Jew," on the other. It has been claimed that Maimonides the philosopher believes that only a small circle of people "who can be called a group in the sense that the (singular) sun is called a member of a group" ("Introduction to *Perek Helek*") can achieve the end-aim of Judaism. This viewpoint seems to lead inevitably to the position that the truth is not for everyone; only the select few deserve an education, while for the others training for specific social tasks should be sufficient. This, of course, was the path taken by Plato when he proposed the myth that the gods made some human beings out of more and others out of less precious materials and that it is therefore natural and just for people to be differently placed in society and consequently, given different educational preparations for their place in life. Is such a position possible for Rambam the faithful Jew? After all, the covenant of the Torah was made between God and all Israelites, all of whom have a share in the world-to-come! Must this not necessarily include the unsophisticated and the intellectually unendowed?[1]

This thesis of the Jewish philosophical dilemma and dissonance has been succinctly stated by the modern educational writer, Blumenfeld:

> Due to the influence of Greek philosophy, the Rambam understood the ideal student as a philosopher, intellectually superior, standing head and shoulders above the masses, and deserving of a special relationship and superior status. But at the same time, the Rambam was too deeply rooted in the spirit of Judaism not to know that the Torah is the inheritance of the whole House of Israel and that 'Moses commanded us (all) the Torah, the inheritance of the community of Jacob,' and therefore we are commanded to teach it (the Torah) to all ...[2]

Those who posit the Maimonides-Rambam dissonance may consider the theory of education which we found in the "Introduction to *Perek Helek*" as a proposed resolution of it. The theory of education, let us recall, was that, given the reality of man's limited insight, the Torah authorizes and even instructs us to offer extrinsic rewards to the child, to ease his or her initiation into Jewish society and the good life of the commandments that leads some to philosophical investigation and a few to philosophical understanding of the Torah's principles.

That this *theory* of education is inherent in the Torah is said to follow from the indisputable fact that the Torah promises rewards and

---

1. For Plato's "mythic lie," *The Republic* III, in *The Portable Plato* (New York: The Viking Press, Inc., 1948), pp. 409–10. As Harvey has pointed out to me, the Rambam did lean in this direction in his *Introduction to the Mishnah*, "Introduction to the Order of Seeds." See his *Hakdamot l'Parush Hamishnah (Introductions to the Commentary on the Mishnah)*, edited by Mordecai Dov Rabinowitz (Jerusalem: Mosad Harav Kook, 5721), pp. 79–81.
2. Shmuel M. Blumenfeld, *"L'mishnat Hahinukh shel Harambam"* ("On the Rambam's Educational Doctrine") in *Hahinukh* Shvat 5737 (1956), no. 2, p. 148.

punishments that are extrinsic to the good life. Surely the sages, the wisest of men, cannot be thought to actually adhere to views that even the moderately wise know to be foolish! Therefore, these views and the offer of extrinsic rewards to learners cannot possibly reflect Judaism's *philosophy* of education, what the Torah really views as desirable end goals, for it is impossible that Judaism's end goals should be what the wise consider foolish. Indeed, the wise know the opposite to be true: the Torah and the sages intend for Jews to be philosophically wise, and yet to walk in the ways of God and to remain loyal to the Torah's social legislation. For it is this legislation that facilitates the achievement of wisdom for some and makes bodily perfection possible for all. That is the ought of Jewish education, its ultimate objective!

But the above description, stressing the inherent differences between people and the supposed dissonance in Maimonides-Rambam, pays insufficient attention to a crucial element in the theory, namely that the Torah intended by its unsophisticated descriptions and extrinsic rewards to move people beyond their limited insight and get them to serve God out of love, as Abraham did.

It is true, says Maimonides, that our sages knew this to be a very difficult goal to achieve and that not everyone could achieve it.

> Therefore, in order that the masses remain faithful and do the commandments it was permitted to tell them that they might hope for a reward and to warn them against transgressions out of fear of punishment. It was hoped that they might be urged to strengthen their intentions so that they would ultimately grasp the truth and the way toward perfection, just like the child in the analogy which I cited above.[3]

Those who are unable to study for its (the Torah's) own sake because of their immaturity and perhaps insurmountable lack of spiritual endowment are obliged to study it even though not for its own sake. But it is possible that this will bring them to a stage in which they can become truly wise and serve God out of love. In the meantime, of course, all Israelites have a share in the world-to-come, through those aspects of the perfection of the soul that are given them and that they are bidden, as loyal Jews, to accept and believe.

The aim, in principle, is to move learners in the direction of wisdom, in recognition of the fact that less than that is deplorable but necessary. For all, therefore, the less is at least a foothold in the world-to-come, but for the spiritual energetic and endowed, it is only a first step. For them, the aim is *Torah lishmah,* Torah for its own sake. For them, Torah not for its own sake *(lo lishmah),* is only a marker on the way.

---

3. "Introduction to *Perek Helek,*" Twersky, *A Maimonides Reader,* p. 406.

Prescriptions of Educational Theory

Now, if indeed all Israelites have a share in the world-to-come of knowledge and service of God that is more than mindless observance, and we do not know who among our pupils will move towards perfection of the soul, then two educational prescriptions become evident. Otherwise the theory of education that prescribes how to educate towards Torah in line with the realities of human nature and development may sabotage the philosophy of education and the ideal educational outcome it anticipates.

First, even when teaching less than the truth, the teacher may never teach blatant falsehoods; every Jew must affirm certain principles that point towards the truth, whether s/he understands them or not.[4] These, for example, are the doctrines taught in the *mishnah* that opens the tenth chapter of *Sanhedrin*. To teach that the Torah is not from heaven would be false doctrine. However, what a child understands by "from Heaven" and, for that matter, by Torah cannot possibly correspond to what a mature and wise adult means by these terms, and it would be a waste of time to explain. Rather, the Torah directs us to teach religious-philosophical truths through stories and parables so that even the unsophisticated will grasp them and perhaps, through them, eventually come to a higher understanding.

But again, great care must be taken not to tell stories or parables that inculcate false ideas, i.e., those that cannot lead the child in the direction of the truth. Thus, one should teach that the righteous have a share in the world-to-come, a world that can be depicted in unsophisticated as well as sublime ways. For even the unsophisticated ways help the learner to apprehend the truth that learning Torah and practicing commandments is good and bears a reward, even if s/he still has a childish understanding and imagines the reward to be an extrinsic one.

The second prescription is that the teacher, if she is to move the pupil to higher stages and, hopefully, beyond the stages of "not for its own sake" will have to be a mature spiritual personality. Teachers who are themselves childish and cannot grasp the educational philosophy of Judaism should on no account be permitted to teach. Clearly, the great problem with the first group of those who misunderstand the words of the sages is not that, regrettably, there are such people, but that there are writers, preachers, and teachers among them. It is these whom Maimonides wishes to have keep

---

4. On how this universal requirement is articulated in Maimonides's *Sefer Hamitzvot (Book of Commandments)*, see Hannah Kasher, "*Ha'im M'clal Chayav Ata Shomeah Yachol B'mishnat Harambam*" ("Does the Category of 'Required' Imply 'Able' in the Rambam's Teaching?"), in *Iyyun* XXXVI:1, pp. 13–34.

silent. It is these, he says, who make the Torah, the source of wisdom, seem and sound like foolishness.

Why are they so dangerous? Let us assume, with Maimonides, that learners indeed proceed through stages and that some, no matter how few, have the possibility of reaching maturity, of learning Torah for its own sake. Yet, the Torah and sages, when understood literally, seem to support the views of those at early stages of development!

We do not have to posit dissonance between Maimonides the philosopher and Rambam the pious Jew and perhaps unmatched *talmid hakham* (Torah scholar), to understand the educational dilemma that the development conception, linked to idea of "the covenant with all Israel" creates for our thinker. On the one hand, the primitive and thus deplorable understandings of true doctrines enables all Israelites to have some share in the world-to-come. At the same time, however, these very understandings create difficulties for those at higher stages of development! The latter will think that the Torah and the words of the sages are themselves childish unless they learn to understand why the Torah spoke thus, namely to give a share to the unsophisticated and to provide guidelines for the "how," the methods and processes of education.

But imagine teachers who are themselves unsophisticated, who preach that these childish ideas correspond to what the Torah meant to say, not as an educational device, but as the truth itself. Such teachers will either thwart the progress towards maturity of those of greater ability or at already higher stages of development or they will undermine their commitment to Judaism! For these educators will insist in their instruction that the teachings of the sages must be taken literally, even when they say impossible things. Though a few sophisticated pupils will forego intellectual honesty for the sake of loyalty, the majority will deduce that the Torah and the sages hold extrinsic views of goodness and ridiculous views of reality. To these views they, the best students, cannot accede. Consequently, they will ridicule the ridiculous Torah they have been taught and thereby profane God's name.

So, teachers belonging to the first group of those who interpret the word of the sages will push bright and spiritually mature students into the second group. The teacher, who is her/himself no more than foolish and pitiable, may create pupils who are accursed, are to be hated, and, as principled deniers of the truth of Judaism, have no share in the world-to-come. Their education has blocked their path to truth and they have been denied the human actualization that comes to a person through knowledge of the truth.

The problem of the Rambam is perhaps more with the incongruities and tensions arising among the elements of educational situations (i.e., subject-matter, pupils, teachers, environment) than with dissonance within his soul: a subject-matter (Torah) that is the only way to truth but is philosophical in essence and extremely difficult; pupils who must be taught from early childhood but, as children, understand the truth "childishly"; and childish teachers who drive away the intelligent and therefore not only deprive the community of intellectually endowed leadership but deny their pupils a share in the world-to-come.

What are the educational prescriptions that Maimonides gives us on the basis of what we may call his theory?

(a) With regard to content or subject matter, he insists on teaching basic doctrines, i.e., the socially required perfection of the soul. However, he permits teaching these doctrines in a manner that the sophisticated person will consider primitive and unreasonable. He forbids teaching esoteric studies except to select students. He insists on teaching the norms of social-religious life, i.e., the *halakhah*, the observance of which as a public pattern of norms does not depend on sophistication.

(b) With regard to teachers, he wants teachers to offer appropriate rewards for study. What is appropriate depends on what will motivate the learner at a particular stage of development. He wishes that the members of the first group, those teachers who understand the sages literally, hence childishly, would be silent; their teaching leads to a defamation of Torah, among Jews and Gentiles alike.

(c) With regard to learners, he encourages them to "strengthen their intentions so that they might ultimately grasp the truth and the way to perfection." Yet he does not permit them to engage in speculative studies that they are not ready for; these might undermine their loyalty to the commandments of the Torah or lead them to heresy—i.e., the renunciation of the doctrines they have been taught as the minimal "perfection of the soul" for "the multitude."

The Uses of Contemporary Theory

Nevertheless, the contemporary teacher who wishes to learn from Maimonides's educational approach may well find these prescriptions inadequate. S/he requires a more detailed theory than the Rambam provides because circumstances have changed and the theoretical apparatus at our disposal has been immensely enlarged by almost a millennium of thought, conversation, and investigation. Let us briefly look at each of these developments.

Changes in circumstances: At present, and since the beginning of the modern era, the particulars of Jewish subject matter and curriculum are themselves subject to much controversy and the subject matter carries little or no a-priori authority for most learners. As for the environment, it is no longer wholeheartedly supportive of education for religious commitment and discernment. There are still teachers who are irrational (by Maimonides's standards) in their religiosity, but there are also many, even in nominally religious schools, who consider themselves irreligious rationalists. Moreover, contemporary learners can and do read and watch on television and video whatever they wish.

Consequences of Inquiry: As a result of diverse investigations, modern Jews can claim to have much more knowledge about the elements of education (i.e., subject matter, teachers, learners, and environments) than was previously available to educational thinkers and theorists.

With regard to knowledge: The subject matter of Judaism, Torah, has come under philosophical attack that is unprecedented in scope and in dissemination. Both its status as a single and unified corpus of truth and its moral-religious authority have been questioned–and undermined. As a result, there have arisen new theologies that seek to understand and confront modern inquiry into the historical, literary, and comparative-religious setting of Judaism's sacred literature. Among the consequences and products of such inquiries and confrontations are new approaches to organizing, understanding, and teaching the sources of Judaism and its ongoing literature.

We also have a growing literature about teachers and teaching, even wide-ranging theories of instruction that examine what teachers actually do and what they ought to do. And, without a doubt, we know more about the process of learning. In the wake of what we study and put forward as new knowledge, we concomitantly have more controversies about cognitive, moral, and religious development than in the past. Therefore, there is not only more data about the development of the child but also more discussion about what constitutes valuable data and what constitute valid ways of interpreting data.

In order to both flesh out and re-examine the consequences of the Rambam's educational teaching in the light of new circumstances, conceptions, and funds of knowledge, it seems sensible to look at a contemporary educational theory that is congenial to his thought. Doing so is likely to enrich our educational discussion in at least the following ways:

(a) It may give us not only a theory of what is childish understanding, but suggest curricular guidelines that build on such understanding. Maimonides does indicate what the content of this childish understanding is, and why it is prevalent and even unavoidable. But he does not supply a comprehensive curricular theory of subject matter that gives instructional guidelines concerning what to teach, not only to further the aims of the educating community, but also to address intrinsic interests of "childish" children by way of what the subject matter says to them and does for them. In Maimonides's theory, subject matter selection in terms of the pupil's interests is neither a self-evident need nor, perhaps, even a desirable one. In the highly organized and cohesive medieval community, it was thought that children's main interest ought to be preparation for adult communal life, which included study "till the day of one's death" and one was to get them there in any plausible way, e.g., with goodies or fine garments, as we have seen–or, for that matter, corporeal punishment.[5] We may also assume that the principles of subject matter selection that grow out of our interest in–and theories about–religious growth, the literary structures of text, and the relationship of these structures to what and how they teach were not available to Maimonides. Nor could he have been familiar with contemporary conceptions of psychological development and with their philosophical ramifications. Therefore Maimonides could limit his concern to children's motivation, which he knew, was extrinsic to the subject matter and thus very different from that of the educated adult.

(b) It may help us to draw out aspects and problems in Maimonides's educational conceptions that we are likely to overlook or not consider seriously enough in the absence of the general theory introduced for purposes of comparison.

(c) A general theory can help to highlight the specific contribution made by Maimonides as a thinker rooted in the tradition of Judaism and an interpreter of that tradition. For let us note: the reason for the mobilization of a general theory is not to suggest that Jewish thinkers already knew some of what we all know now, but to elicit and compare theories that draw upon the Jewish textual tradition and those that do not. Through such a comparison, our theoretical resources may be enriched and our practical possibilities enlarged. If we can indicate how our Jewish theory would evaluate our general theory, and vice versa, we shall expand our capacity for critique and for perceiving nuances. This enhanced capacity can, in turn, enable us to create a richer literature in the language of Judaism.

The theory that we turn to is that of the contemporary educational scholar, Kieran Egan.

---

5. Maimonides, *Mishneh Torah, Hilkhot Talmud Torah* (Laws of Torah Study) I:5; I:10; II:2.

Egan's Four Stages

A citation from Egan's discussion of teachers and pupils will help us establish the congeniality of his thinking to that of Maimonides:

> Educational development is a process. We reach an advanced stage only by passing through prior and prerequisite stages. This seems obvious enough, but it is frequently ignored. Many well-meaning teachers see creativity or freedom or disciplined scholarship as ideals of education, and, ignoring the fact that these represent the most sophisticated achievement of the best educated, they try to impose them on children … Teachers should be mostly concerned with helping people through stages of immaturity, enabling them eventually to achieve maturity. There is nothing wrong or shameful about being immature when young. If one has a distaste for the immature and their various modes of expression and kinds of interest, then there is no point trying to teach. Such teachers will be at constant odds with what the child needs most. (Conversely) If one delights in the expressions and interests of the immature, finding them most congenial, then there is no point trying to teach. Such teachers, who are usually immature themselves, will be concerned to keep children immature and will not help them—even if they could—to achieve greater maturity. We might wisely be equally wary of those who seem ashamed of having been young and those who see childhood as the best life has to offer.[6]

In this passage Kieran Egan offers us implicit philosophical conceptions of education and explicit theoretical ones. Philosophically, he tells us that advanced stages of development are synonymous with maturity, which, in turn, is the best life has to offer and is reachable only after childhood. The theoretical thrust of his remarks: that good teachers are aware of these stages, and they know that working towards maturity requires patience with the realities of human development. Good teachers neither identify with childish immaturity nor find it distasteful in the young. Since theory of education not only describes what is, but also prescribes what to do, we are led, by Egan's conception, to make subject matter congruent with stage of development, to choose certain types of teachers, and to train them to understand children even while they maintain a vision of maturity towards which they guide their pupils.

There are, of course, many educational issues germane to this passage that are not touched upon here. For example, is there one exclusive pinnacle of what is mature and the height of human achievement, or are there several from which persons may choose? Can everyone reach maturity by receiving the best education, or is

6. Kieran Egan, *Individual Development and Curriculum* (Hawthorne, Australia: Hutchinson, 1986), pp. 155–56.

the best education wasted on those of inferior intelligence, imagination or other innate disposition? What are these stages of development? And, perhaps most important, what is the content of "the best life has to offer"? Why?

The reader, I assume, has noted that Egan and Maimonides seem to grapple with similar issues and problems. One very crucial such problem is that children, due to immaturity, cannot appreciate the best life has to offer. Another problem is that some teachers are themselves immature; yet another that some teachers have no patience with immaturity. They also share a concern with how best to help people through the stages of immaturity.

Egan seeks a theory of development that is specifically educational in nature. He tells us that, in contradistinction to psychological theories, such a theory "focuses on the educational aspects of development, learning and motivation, and ... directly yields principles for engaging children in learning, for unit and lesson planning and for curriculum organizing, at each stage of a typical person's development."[7] It is geared to bringing about good transitions from stage to stage on the way to the mature, i.e., the normative stage.

The four stages Egan posits are the mythic, the romantic, the philosophical, and the ironic. Each refers to a particular way to make best sense of the world and experience, in stories, games, ways of conceptualizing, of imagining, comprehending, assigning worth. In earlier stages, the story is especially important because it "reflects fundamental categories of young children's thinking ... (and) it seems reasonable ... (to) use it in organizing knowledge so that children might best learn."[8]

In the mythic stage, children's stories are populated by strange monsters and humanized animals; they tend to be based on binary opposites most important in their own lives like love/hate, big/little or good/bad. This is the stuff fairy tales are made of. Binary opposites are eventually elaborated by ideas that mediate between the binary poles. Thus, hot/cold are negotiated by "quite warm," "quite cold;" death and life are negotiated by intermediaries such as ghosts, "things that are both alive and dead, as things warm are both hot and

---

7. Kieran Egan, "Towards a Theory of Educational Development," *Educational Philosophy and Theory,* 11 (2) (November, 1979) pp. 17–36. Though Egan has expanded on his stages of development in subsequent writings, we have chosen to use this succinct article for our outline of his approach. For a more detailed discussion on the difference between psychological and educational theories, see Egan, *Individual Development and Curriculum,* pp. 160–69, and Egan, *Education and Psychology: Plato, Piaget and Scientific Psychology* (New York: Teachers College, Columbia University, 1983). Here we merely note that one of the central features of an educational theory is that "it will have as a central component normative claims. That is, it will involve a concept of an ideally, or desirably educated person." *Individual Development,* p. 165.

8. Egan, "Towards a Theory," pp. 20–21.

cold." To make something really meaningful at this stage it should be built upon, and elaborated from, clear binary opposites.

Mythic thinking also features a lack of a sense of otherness. For example, differences in historical time or geographical location tend to be "obliterated." Nothing has changed "from the sacred beginning." Children have no experience with otherness and the world is adapted to their lack of experience.

This absence of otherness also disallows for a sense of the world as autonomous and objective. It is "absorbed into the child's vivid mental life." Everything thinks, feels, and acts as the child does–or would. So the world is full of entities that hate, love, and fear. "… children's imaginative life colors and charges their environment with a meaning derived from within."

If the mythic stage involves "making sense of the unknown world 'without' in terms of the known world 'within'," then the process of meaningful learning and its organization here involves "projecting these known things onto the outside world and as it were, absorbing the world to them."[9]

As the child develops serviceable concepts of otherness (thus of historical time, geographical space, causality, etc.) the romantic stage begins. "… The passage from the mythic stage coincides with the perception that the world is autonomous, is separate, and fundamentally different from the child." S/he must then forge a new relationship with (outside) reality and find ways to deal with its alienness. At the same time, in the midst of all this otherness, the child needs to establish a distinct identity.

In romantic stories, therefore, heroes or nations, etc., struggle and achieve glory against odds, against threatening nature, villains or sinister ideas. The plots are more complex and more realistic than in mythic stories, but their meanings are, perhaps unrealistically, clear. One knows what one should feel about the persons and forces involved and how matters should turn out. The child, identifying with the good people and forces, learns to overcome fear of the vast and mysterious world opening up before him or her by linking up with those who embody "qualities that best transcend the challenges posed by daily living in the real world … like courage, nobility, fortitude … ."[10] It now becomes quite obvious that the stuff of adolescent adventures, from Superman to Jack London stories and beyond to soap operas and series, is tailored to the romantic temperament, and judging by the popularity of television programs like *Dallas* and *Dynasty*, not only of adolescence. We seem to have made contact once again with Maimonides's "multitude."

9. For the mythic stage and the citations above, *Ibid.*, pp. 19–23.
10. *Ibid.*, p. 24.

Having to be concerned now with what the world is really like, the romantic child, teenager, or, alas, adult, begins by seeking binary opposites, now not within but without the self. There is an interest in extremes in the real world; hence the popularity of *The Guiness Book of World Records*. This goes together with a passion for details: who had the best batting average in baseball and what it was, who was most often divorced in Hollywood and how many times, etc. "... romance is, as it were, myth confined to the real world, but constantly beating against its limits." Since the romantic stage involves curiosity about the other in its very otherness the child wishes to know what it was like then, what it's like in exotic countries, how what is distant is different. In learning what things beyond the limits of their experience are like, children can better define what they are like. They want to try out limit situations: to collect all the baseball cards there are, to have pictures about everything in the life of their favorite player or movie star. "By exhaustively knowing *something*, one gets a sense of the scale of everything."[11]

Egan will have us note that the romantic perception sees the world in bits and pieces, bizarre facts, vivid true stories, but is little concerned with putting the pieces together. And those who manage to reach the next, the philosophic stage, are most engaged in that, in making the world into one unit that has interconnected parts. In seeing that they belong to this interconnected reality, they lose freedom but gain some security.

"The major defining characteristic of the philosophic stage, then, is the search for the truth about human psychology, for the laws of historical development, for the truth about how societies function ... the general laws whereby the world works. By knowing them the students will know their own proper place and roles, and so they will securely know themselves." All mere facts or bits of information must be organized into a general scheme. An attempt is therefore made to "establish a sense of the main features and their relationships and locate the particulars within the general context." Thus, students in the philosophic stage value abstract and generalized concepts such as society, culture, human nature, and so on. "Ideologies and metaphysical constructions represent the boldest lines that give order to the students' mental map of the world." Correspondingly, hierarchies are imposed upon data; things and people are ranked in line with some general ideas or categories. Thus, Bach (or Mozart, etc.) is the greatest composer who ever lived and Cadillac (or whatever) is the best automobile. "Frequently this leads to the imposition of single-criterion hierarchies where they are inappropriate, where

11. *Ibid.*, p. 27.

multiple-criteria should be applied." The ideology has, as it were, identified the truth about processes; it is said of people at this stage that "they think they know everything." And while people in the philosophic stage seem to have outgrown stories, they actually insist that history, as life, have a plot; "conceptualizing a process requires the imposition of some beginning and end."[12]

In the fourth, the ironic stage, one learns to appreciate that "no general scheme can adequately reflect the richness and complexity of reality ... it (the ironic stage) represents a clear appreciation of where we end and the world begins ... (whereas) at each of the previous stages there is some confusion about this, in which things that are a product of our modes of perception or manner of organizing knowledge are assumed to be part of the world."[13]

The ironic person, being presented with a dogmatic view of things, is likely to say "but it isn't that simple." The reason is that there are too many facts, too many diverse experiences with reality to bring under one philosophic umbrella.

Egan's educational theory assumes that stages are things we grow with and on rather than *out* of. There are genuine continuities between childish and adult thinking as well as discontinuities. In the philosophic or ironic stages we cannot learn anything from romantic or mythic stories but we do continue to enjoy them.[14] This explains professors who relish television thrillers, and ironic individuals who relax with philosophic-stage novels of ideas despite their largely wooden characters. For we have learned from each stage and what we have learned stays with us. Thus, from the mythic stage, Egan suggests, we learn the ability to derive meaning from the inhuman world. And those who have learned nothing from the romantic stage are either ignorant and dull, or knowledgeable pedants. As for the philosophic stage, we learn to organize knowledge into meaningful schemes. For the ironic person, these schemes have become not dogmatic lords of knowledge, but rather flexible servants. At each stage, a person uses what previous stages have taught him or her for new, more mature purposes.[15]

Egan candidly states the premises of his educational theory. Rather than starting from "the child and everyday experience" and

12. For a description of the "philosophic" stage and the citations above, *Ibid.*, pp. 27–32.
13. *Ibid.*, p. 32. (This key ironic perception is philosophically just as objectivistic about facts, apparently to be reached largely through scientific inquiry, as Maimonides's metaphysic is about the world. Both agree that learning truth is learning about things as they really are, and not as they appear to us because of our immaturity or ignorance.
14. Egan, *Individual Development*, p. 93.
15. Egan, "Towards a Theory," pp. 32–33.

"gradually working outward to the rest of the world along the lines of content associations," Egan suggests working "from outward limits inward." That is: the problem facing the human being who is growing into the world is to know reality and to find oneself within it or in relationship to various facets of it.

The mythic child cannot yet make the differentiation but the romantic one does move in the direction of exploring an autonomous world. In the philosophic stage the general features of reality are charted, and in the ironic stage, particulars are explored for their own sake. The goal of the educator, ultimately, is to make that possible. Why? Because knowing the truth gives joy "that both motivates and justifies the search." The similarity to the Rambam in intent, if not in terminology, is striking.[16]

Illuminations and Comparisons

We should not think that a comparison of congenial educational theories suggests that they are or should be identical. The differences are clear: irony comes close to representing the sensibility of the scientist. The joy Egan speaks of is aesthetic, not religious. And while Maimonides might well think that Egan's irony threatens, ultimately, to become a celebration of heroic and heuristic but anchorless existence, Egan might retort that the Rambam is in some ways stuck in the philosophic stage. Perhaps, he might say, Maimonides had no choice: in the chaotic vulnerability of life in the Middle Ages, only a humanly imposed sense on reality, romantic or philosophic, saved people from madness.

Yet the congeniality is there, illuminating educational issues and policies for students of the Rambam. Reading Egan, we understand better why Maimonides can legitimate the "deplorable" views of the various groups who so "impossibly" describe the world-to-come. In fact, when we look at these views again, we wonder whether they are not arranged in a kind of developmental order!

16. Compare, *Guide* III:27 on the perfection of the soul, which involves "knowing everything concerning all that it is within the capacity of man to know ..." Maimonides here may also be compared to Degenhardt and the concept of "knowledge for its own sake" that he develops. See M.A.B. Degenhardt, *Education and the Value of Knowledge* (London: George Allen and Unwin, 1982), especially Chapter 3, wherein the author draws the conclusion, similarly to Maimonides and Egan, that inherently valuable knowledge, while not serving any proximate goal, is what renders life meaningful.

Let us look at these groups again. Aren't those who think the world-to-come is the Garden of Eden actually describing a kind of fairy tale setting ("there houses are made of precious stone ... rivers flow with wine and fragrant oils," etc.)? The second view is also primarily mythic ("the earth will bring forth garments woven ..."). But isn't the third strongly romantic, depicting the triumph of humanity over the most obstinate and threatening feature of alien and autonomous reality, death? For the resurrection defeats death: "... a man will live after his death and return to his family and dear ones and eat and drink and never die again ..." The fourth group appears to have an ideology of how what is now sometimes called a "Torah-true life" will assure happy individuals and a good society. As for the fifth group, it puts all these deplorable (i.e., immature) views together into one general, hence philosophical, scheme.

These views, we may say, represent the stages that the Torah permits, for God knows the soul of the human being. He not only commands, but also educates. The Torah, to be a guide for life, must teach through myth, romance, and philosophy before it presents the mature human being with the ironic fact that the truth can never be completely known and that the greatest joy is to continue to learn towards it. This learning is not for the sake of finally arriving at the completed system of "what Judaism says," which, with adolescent finality, explains everything, but *l'shmah,* for its own sake. It is for knowing, in the confusing complexity of things, and in the ultimate incomprehensibility of God and His unity those matters that can be known and doing what can be done, that is, "walking in His ways."

If we look briefly at one passage of Torah, the Creation story, we can observe how "the Torah speaks in the language of people," all of them, at all stages.

No one can doubt that this story has its share of mythic descriptions: of magic trees, serpents that walk and talk, a man put to sleep so that God can produce a mate, even God walking in the midst of the magical garden. This story is also a romantic tale: of God, Adam and Eve, at first friends, but very soon apparent enemies. We also remember that Adam and Eve were the very first people in a distant and strange world. We recall that they had to decide whether to stand up to God by eating of the fruit of the tree or submissively to obey Him. Was their transgression an act of heroism, of asserting identity in the face of the other who commands but has no right to? Or did Adam and Eve fail to understand that the other here, God, is a Presence that stands with them against the world, that "He is with them in sorrow," the "force" that helps them to victory and identity?[17]

17. The reader may here have been reminded of the series of *Star Wars* films, and that was indeed my intention.

This is also a story for the philosophical stage, a story of ideas. It teaches that the idyllic life is one devoid of self-consciousness, a life of simplicity, of relationship, of obedience. The seemingly mythic and romantic features make philosophic sense. The tree isn't magical at all, but only a symbol of God's relationship with humans through commandment; in fact, it could have been any tree. "The idea is" that only disobedient humanity is barred from the Tree of Life (i.e., power through science), for immoral (disobedient) people will use science for immoral and therefore destructive purposes. Here then, is a philosophical *midrash* that explains it "the way it really is."

The ironic person looks at the story and finds the facts or things to consider too overwhelming for such simplicity. His or her comment, following the exegetical tradition, might well be: *Zarikh Iyyun,* this requires further study, it's complicated. True, the story is about obedience, but is that always a good thing? Didn't Moses sometimes argue with God, Who, on occasion allowed Himself to be convinced by His servant? (e.g., Numbers 14:19–20 and *Berakhot* 32a). Didn't he respond considerately to Abraham's demand that God not destroy Sodom if he found ten good people within it lest, *halilah,* God forbid, the "judge of the whole earth do injustice?" (Genesis 18:25).

But, that too may become a philosophy, making premature sense of everything within a scheme of ethical monotheism. For there are other facts to consider. For example, Abraham didn't talk back when told to sacrifice his son. There the moral argument is conspicuous by its absence, and God praised Abraham for that silence and readiness to carry out the inexplicable command, calling it "fear of God." Indeed, the ironic student of the Torah insists that the plenitude of conceptions and situations in Jewish language makes it difficult to make do with facile philosophical generalizations about Judaism. Therefore, *Zarikh Iyyun,* the matter requires further investigation. But, in the meantime, the Rambam would say, even while we investigate and may never reach a satisfactory answer, the life of community, of morality leading to knowledge, goes on. With regard to specific situations and cases, the question we ask is: what is the *halakhah*?

This way of understanding the study and life of Torah is contrary to what modern secularism conveys to our consciousness. We are supposed to be embarrassed by primitive elements in the textual tradition, indeed, to reject this tradition for its fairy tale myths, its romantic simplicity, its philosophic dogmatism. Yet the true state of affairs for the educated Jewish reader, studying the Creation story, or listening to it on the Sabbath on which it is read in the synagogue as the portion of the week is more like what Maimonides might say after consulting with Egan.

Namely, it is deplorable when seemingly mature people actually take the apparent fairy tale element literally, but even our sages permit seeing things that way for those who have to. As for the others, their reading has grown on the foundations of that mythic tale. They remember when it taught them the first important things they ever learned about listening to God, and they still enjoy the story. It rings true, brings back memories and it has led to other ways of looking at it. And when the small child at the synagogue or in school asks how the serpent in the Garden of Eden could actually talk, the true but "childish" answer is in the text: God made him that way. It is hardly the time to suggest that the serpent God made that way is perhaps the evil impulse within us, more puzzling a creation than a talking snake and an even greater chatterbox of temptation. Children don't know about the evil impulse yet, or rather, they cannot distinguish between what happens within and without.

And so, the Torah constitutes teaching, for everyone. Why should that be embarrassing? And given that the content of the Torah can be taught that way, Maimonides, were he with us today, might agree that one need not bribe children with nuts, golden stars, or other extrinsic rewards. Maimonides, reading Egan, might admit that *lo lishmah* could be interpreted as not yet "the best life has to offer," but offering something that is significant to the child in his or her present stage of development.

And this brings us to the danger posed by the teacher of the first group, who takes the words of the sages literally. This person seems to be none other than Egan's teacher who does think that childhood is the best life has to offer. Situated in the mythic or romantic stage, perhaps philosophically having put these stages all together, like the fifth group of those who misunderstand the world-to-come, ("Introduction to *Perek Helek*") this teacher does not understand that these stages at best prepare children and endow them with existential riches for the ironic stage. For it is in that stage that they seek truth, realize the complexity and unmanageability of it, and yet take joy in the search for it. The good teacher must realize what these early-stage riches are, that the stages themselves are inevitable, but that education looks beyond them.

To know this, of course, the teacher must him/herself be an ironic person. Are there enough such people? After all, even Egan admits that many people do not reach high levels of education, many do not even reach the philosophic stage. And it is hardly the case that every educator is fully mature or that most mature persons have a consuming ambition to be educators. The inevitable consequence must be classrooms in which romantic or philosophic souls teach. There, many bright persons will become spiritually stuck, living in an adolescent dream world or becoming philosophic fools, articulate dogmatists. And others will liberate themselves from their education. They will deny the terminal value of the early stages of their development and proclaim that educators are simpletons, that education is no profession for intelligent people. In Maimonidean terms, the religious frame of reference make the results sound even more catastrophic. As already noted, children being taught by fools (of the first group) may be turned, by their education, into those of the second group, heretics.

It seems to me that while this issue perturbs the Rambam, he does have an answer for the educational establishment, namely, that the Torah does not expect all Israelites, despite their share in the world-to-come, to reach the higher stages. What the Rambam finds the Torah to demand in the education of all Jews is their socialization into the norms of the community. These norms are of two kinds: there are the moral ones and there are those that symbolize the collective life of the covenantal community. All of these are in the domain of perfection of the body, which requires the educator to teach the actions making the pupil a *halakhah*-abiding individual. There are also, as we recall, the correct opinions incumbent upon everyone. These must be taught as the language of the community. Here we have "perfection of the soul" for "the multitude" and a first step towards the envisioned perfect development of the child. For it is hoped that gifted individuals will eventually become capable of making great literature in the language.

In short, not every teacher need be a model of knowledge of love of God. Each teacher must be God fearing,[18] instilling acceptance of what s/he accepts as correct practice for members of the community, buttressed by correct opinions which, however understood, are the basis of moral and religious behavior. Maimonides would say, therefore, that the Torah commands community before it demands individual perfection, and that what happens in the educational situation is first and foremost about community. And so, the plea of Maimonides that those who misunderstand the sages keep quiet, can be understood, for the teacher in that category, in a minimalistic sense: would that s/he be quiet about the theoretical truth that s/he doesn't comprehend! Not the romantic or even philosophical conceptions should be the subject of instruction, for these are imperfect perfections of the soul, but the Jewish way of life.

Nevertheless, this is only a partial solution of the problem. For Egan's point is that selection of subject matter should be guided by

---

18. In Maimonides's sense, i.e., loyally accepting Jewish belief, observing the commandments and conscious of reward and punishment for his or her behavior. See for example, *Mishneh Torah, Hilkhot teshuva* (Laws of Repentance) X:5.

how children understand the world and what they have to know about it and about themselves within it. In the contemporary situation, the insistence that the religiously foolish not teach what the understanding of children at particular stages suggests and demands is to leave real cognitive and spiritual development in the hands of the teachers who teach general subjects. These may, indeed, suffer from the same lack of sophistication as some Jewish ones, but, in the elementary school at least, they know that their primary concern is with development and children rather than a particular subject matter that makes the normative demands that Torah does. So, while the thesis of teach them *mitzvot* (commandments) and not philosophy might be a plausible Maimonidean educational thesis in an environment in which there are no real general studies, it is much less plausible in the society where there is both Torah and general culture. There, it sounds like abdication, an invitation to compartmentalization wherein the life of practice and the life of the mind and spirit are conducted in separate drawers of the personality. That is certainly not what the Rambam envisions![19]

And so, under contemporary conditions there seem to be only two alternatives for a Maimonidean educational philosophy. The first is disallowing secular education for the multitude, placing it in the category of what is spiritually injurious to the religiously ignorant.[20] The second is to invest heavily in the education of teachers who understand children yet understand life as adults do. Obviously, they need not be of the select few who have reached the highest levels of divine truth, but they must be encouraged to gain an ironic understanding and to be on the way towards it. In our context this means that they are humble about what they don't know and what they therefore cannot teach. And they, like all good teachers, are eager to learn more.

We have found the Rambam hypothetically criticizing Egan for the fact-mindedness of the ironic stage. For him the general philosophical scheme of things is, of course, not what people illicitly impose on reality, but what is revealed by God to His prophets. The innumerable facts, about the world and the Torah, do fit together for those of the highest discernment. And where Egan might criticize the Rambam for himself being too philosophical, he might well reply that the system does explain the facts. Yet since one never fully comprehends

19. Such compartmentalization does not seem congenial to the "perfection of the soul" which is a requirement of the Torah. *Guide* III:27.
20. It might also be argued that Maimonides would disallow religious education conducted by members of the first group: i.e., those who misunderstand the sages and teach wrong discernments and doctrines.

and one must always deal with the complexity of facts (*halakhic* and other) with integrity, the loyal and mature Jew is not fixated in the philosophical stage. Such a person clearly and admittedly doesn't think s/he knows everything.

Wisdom of the Heart

But there is one point with regard to the philosophical stage where criticism might be apt. The Rambam, we saw, has a hierarchy of value that is built on and around a single criterion. The palace is where the religious intellect is. Yet, multiple criteria for determining who the educated person is are equally plausible and certainly for a covenant people much more feasible. Ranking Jews and Gentiles in a way that makes the intellect the exclusive key to being in the king's palace is certainly not the only possible reading of the tradition of Torah. Are nobility of character and spiritual achievement, certainly end-aims of all educational thought, necessarily associated with mental endowments? Is the only way of being truly pious—to be a philosopher? True, we wish for something that genuinely educated Jews can have in common, but does it have to be a quality that is inaccessible to so many? It seems strange that God would make a covenant with a people for that!

Because Maimonides is a philosopher of Judaism and also a faithful and loyal Jew,[21] we have found him to be extremely helpful in locating philosophical-educational issues within the Jewish tradition. But, as already noted, the Rambam's insistence that Jewish commitment be unmistakably ideational and spiritual achievement be unequivocally philosophical represents only one approach in this tradition. It is noteworthy that the profound authority Maimonides enjoys in Jewish life flows from his *halakhic* code and responsa. In this sphere, Maimonides's writings are almost sacred; halakhically, he comes close to being *language*. But his philosophical approach, which we have found so useful for moving into Jewish educational thought, is just one of several Jewish *literatures*.

A prime example of a different approach is that of the medieval poet and thinker, Yehudah Halevi, who insists that existential attachment is superior to speculation. In his famous dialogue, *The Kuzari*,

---

21. On the status of Maimonides as one who pursued philosophy as a Jewish teacher of Jews, in contradistinction to Spinoza, for whom philosophy replaces revelation as a source of truth and invalidates it, see Leo Strauss, *Spinoza's Critique of Religion* (New York: Schocken Books, 1965), pp. 163–165.

he fervently insists on the distinction between the God of Abraham, Who is loved, and the God of Aristotle, who is merely admired for his unfeeling perfection. The common person, says Halevi, does not follow the instructions of the philosophers "because the human soul has a presentiment of the truth, as it is said: 'The words of truth will be recognized'."[22] In the modern era, Shmuel David Luzzatto, a nineteenth-century Jewish thinker and scholar, well represents the literature that distrusts philosophy, and that finds the true spirit of scripture and tradition to lie in moral sympathies and compassionate and upright character. Speaking of the medieval philosophers, he charges them with having relegated the majority of mankind to an almost subhuman status for their inability to understand metaphysical subtleties. What is required of us is to recognize the Almighty as the God of righteousness and mercy so "that these qualities may guide our ways."[23] The place of ultimate piety, he seems to be saying, is in the heart.

The expression "wisdom of the heart" is associated by the Bible with the building of the Tabernacle and the weaving of garments for the High Priest. The Torah demands that these very practical projects be executed with a religious intention as well as skill and intelligence, that they be carried out by "the wise of heart." (Exodus 28:3). On these words, Rabbi Naftali Zvi Berlin, the renowned nineteenth-century head of the Lithuanian Yeshiva of Volozhin, comments,

> The place of wisdom is not in the heart but in the brain. But (understand the verse thus:) every place where it is written, 'the wise of heart,' the meaning is the fear of Heaven, which is the beginning of wisdom, and its place, as is known, is in the heart.[24]

What is this fear of Heaven whose place is in the heart? We have already come across the concept of the fear of Heaven. We have seen that, for the Rambam, it is a stage below the love of God; it is less than wisdom. Fear of God (or Heaven) constitutes merely a social ideal, reflected in the proper conduct of citizens of the theo-political community. Yet in many sources it appears as a comprehensive character ideal, signifying the educated Jew. Indeed, it may be the dominant end-aim of rabbinic educational reflection.

22. Judah Halevi, *The Kuzari; An Argument for the Faith of Israel* (New York: Schocken Books, 1964), IV:17.
23. Shmuel David Luzzatto, "Lessons in Jewish Moral Theology," in Luzzatto, *Ketavim (Selected Writings),* edited with introduction and notes by M.E. Artom (Jerusalem: Bialik Institute, 1976), pp. 104–5.
24. R. Naftali Zvi Berlin, *Ha'amek Davar* (Jerusalem: El Hamikorot Pub., 5726), on Exodus 28:3.

In the following section, we shall discuss how rabbinic sources understand this value concept. We shall see that its place is indeed in the heart but that it moves quickly to a panoramic view of personality and moral perfection. Is fear of Heaven, *Yirat Shamayim,* perhaps the high road to the palace of ideal human existence and self-realization? May it be that this road can be more widely traveled than the one on the map of *The Guide to the Perplexed* because the road signs can be understood by the intellectually simple as well as the philosophically gifted?

And yet, Maimonides might justly ask: how can a comprehensive character ideal be simple? How can reflection be divorced from intelligence? How can educational philosophy not be philosophy?

Let us now move to an examination of this issue.

THE FEAR OF HEAVEN:
GOD'S TREASURE

6

A GLOOMY TALE
OF THE HUMAN SOUL

Rabbi Hanina said: Everything is in the hands of Heaven except for the fear of Heaven, as it is written, 'And now, Israel what does the Lord your God ask of you but to fear ... (Deut. 10:12) Is then Fear of Heaven a small thing (i.e., why does He ask for nothing 'but', as though it were not much)? For R. Haninah said in the same of R. Shimon ben Yochai: The Holy One, Blessed be He has naught in His storehouse but the treasure of Fear of Heaven, as it is said, 'The Fear of God is His treasure.'

Berakhot 33b

The Travail of the Human Soul

A well-known *midrash (Tanhuma, "Pekudai")*[1] tells us what happens in Heaven before a child is born, what adventures the soul undergoes before seeing the light of day, and how his or her destiny is determined. When a man "approaches his wife," this *midrash* informs us, the Holy One, blessed be He, tells the angel who is guardian over pregnancy to "watch over the seed" and to bring it before Him. Then the Holy One determines at once everything about the person-to-be: whether that soul will be strong or weak, tall or short, male or female, foolish or wise, rich or poor. And yet,

---

1. There are several versions of this tale. In addition to the *Tanhuma* aggadah, cited above, see *Niddah* 17b and Seder Yizirat Hav'lad (The Midrash of the Creation of the Child). For the latter, see *Bet Ha-Midrasch–Sammlung* I, published by Adolph Jellinek, 2nd ed. (Jerusalem: Bamberger and Wahrmann, 1938) pp. 153–55.

whether it is to be just or wicked He does not determine, for as we say: "Heaven ordains all, save the fear of Heaven."[2]

We are told that the soul which is bidden to "enter that seed," protests vehemently, professing complete satisfaction with its angelic status, which is "holy and pure." But the Holy One tells it in no uncertain terms that "the world into which I would have you enter is better than the world in which you find yourself now. It was for this seed that you were meant on the day I made you." And "He bids the soul enter that seed, though against its will."

The cryptic nature of the divine decree and promise becomes even more blatant when the soul is planted in the womb of its mother. For no sooner is it settled there but the angel supervising the passage of the soul from its heavenly to an earthly state conducts the soul on two excursions. In one it is shown all that will transpire in its temporal life: where the soul will die, how it will live, and everything that lies in store for it (in that order!). One can suppose that after that excursion many souls are even more convinced than they were before that it would be better not to be born. For all is already decided and much of it, if we may judge by our own experience and what we know of others, is less than bliss. If the soul is really shown everything, then it may anticipate some future pleasures, but also much pain and humiliation. Perhaps it learns that some honor awaits him or her, but also most likely some shame and perhaps disgrace. So why, the soul may wonder, did God say that the world it is about to enter is better than the heavenly and pristinely spiritual existence known and enjoyed thus far? After all, the world is a harsh place, even for those who are not shown sundry horrors, tortures, holocausts on this prenatal trip. And alas, there are millions who are shown that.

The second excursion is very different but hardly more soothing. This time, the soul is conducted to heaven and hell, to see the righteous being rewarded for observing God's commandments and the wicked punished for not keeping the laws of the Torah. Now the soul is shaken out of its passive observer status. It is warned to be like the righteous in order to attain their reward and to shun the evil ways of those now suffering the torments of hell. We may imagine it slowly dawning on the soul what God meant about the goodness of this world. What it seems to be good for is testing the soul and determining its future destiny.

By the time the soul leaves the womb, it is a fully human creature, encased in its temporal body. When the angel comes to take it out

2. Thus in *Sefer Yizirat Hav'lad*. This is the version translated into English in *The Judaic Tradition*, texts edited and introduced by Nahum N. Glatzer (New York: Behrman House, Inc., 1969) pp. 332–35.

the creature again complains and protests, and cries. "And why does it cry? Because it must leave the world it has dwelt in."

At that moment, the angel "strikes the creature under the nose and extinguishes the light that shone over its head throughout its sojourn in the womb and bids it step forth, unwilling, and the creature forgets all it has ever seen." And comes out crying, for at that moment it sees seven worlds through which it will pass, from the frolicking world of childhood through the careladen years of adulthood, and the humiliating world of extreme old age. Nevertheless, when at the end the angel comes to take the soul from this world, it cries again: "Did you not lead me out of two worlds (i.e., Heaven and the womb) and set me down in this world in which I dwell now?" The angel replies, as ever patient but somber:

> "Have I not told you long ago that against your will you were fashioned and born, and so you are destined to die, and at last will give account and reckoning before the King of kings, the Holy One, blessed be He?"

The *midrashic* passage we are considering is elaborate and rich, and there is much of interest to educators.[3] But what most concerns us here is the underlying teaching of the passage. It is that on the one hand, we have no choice about being here and there is nothing we can do to change our fortunes in this world. On the other hand, our ultimate well-being depends only on us. We have in fact been sent into this world to exercise the choice of being righteous or wicked; for this is the only place that choice can be made. Everything is in the hand of Heaven, except the fear of Heaven.

A Problematic Educational Ideal

One can hardly imagine anything more contrary to the dominant ethos in contemporary education that this pietistic *midrash*. The modern educator sees him/herself working to change personal and communal fortunes, while our *midrash,* when translated into an educational idiom, informs him or her that all who enter this world should abandon hope of controlling it, of changing their destinies, of intelligently planning for a better and happier life. The poor are pathetically wasting their time in learning the skills that vainly

3. For example, we note that the *midrashic* writer adheres to the notion that learning is recall, for the soul learns everything before birth and is made to forget it. Also, the educational theorist and practitioner will be sensitive to the *midrash's* assumption that people are always happiest with the situation they happen to be in and that every new challenge evokes anxiety and is perceived as a threat.

promise to make them richer or more successful; the foolish will not
be made wise through improved syllabuses or sophisticated curricu-
lums. In these matters, everything is in the hands of Heaven. The
child should be constantly reminded of what he already once knew,
that this world is an arena of moral-religious choice and we cannot
really make it anything else. The *midrashic* writer evidently does not
believe that this world will be rendered more delightful or meaningful by educators who cultivate creativity, aesthetic appreciation or
technological proficiency. These pursuits are trivial—and useless.

One may, of course, make this pietistic gloom more palatable by
calling it starkly existential, but that doesn't bring it any closer to the
hopes that parents and teachers generally have for the educational
enterprise. Our *midrash* assumes that this world is only an ante-
chamber to the true world-to-come where each has, if s/he deserves
it, the appropriate reward. It even makes sense to suggest, as some
moralists have, that the righteous poor and the pious infirm, because
they suffer more in this world, have more to look forward to in the
next. For obviously they were given no rewards in this world.[4]

It is a somber view and, in fact, many voices in the Jewish tradition
take issue with it or qualify it, on philosophical, cultural, and historical
grounds. Maimonides, commenting upon the version of this *midrash*
that appears in Tractate *Niddah* moderates the teaching of the Talmudic
sage; he insists that people do have choices with regard to the shaping
of their lives.[5] In the world of the *Midrash* itself, we also find differences
of opinion. While one known *midrash* compares the commandments to
a rope being thrown to a drowning swimmer (very much in the spirit of
our aggadic tale) another *midrash* compares the commandments to
"chaplets of grace" upon the head of the faithful, merely adorning their
lives and making them beautiful.[6] The historic and ideational context of

4. See, for example, R. Elchanan Bunim Wasserman, *"Maamar al Bitahon"* ("An Essay
   of Trust"), in *Kometz Maamarim (Collection of Essays),* (Tel Aviv: published by his son,
   no date), p. 22. The idea that the person who suffers in this world is amply
   rewarded in the next is given classic literary expression in I. L. Peretz's well-known
   story, "Bontzye Shweig" ("Bontzye, the Silent"). For a translation of this from the
   Yiddish, Isaac Loeb Peretz, *Stories and Pictures,* translated by Helena Frank
   (Philadelphia: The Jewish Publication Society of America, 5707–1947), pp. 171–81.
5. Maimonides, *Shmoneh Perakim,* Chap. 8, severely qualifies this and limits it to dispositions and matters that are caused by physical laws of nature. Shaviv notes that R.
   Meir Hameiri in his commentary *Bet Habihirah* (on the Tractate *Niddah*) also qualifies this deterministic world view. See Yehuda Shaviv, *"Innyanai Hinukh, Horaah
   V'lemida Bemasechet Niddah"* ("Issues of Education, Instruction and Learning in the
   Tractate *Nidda*"), in *Iyyunim B'Hinukh* 15 Tammuz 5737 (July 1977), pp. 113–126.
6. In *Deuteronomy Rabbah* 6:3, R. Pinchas bar Hama states that the commandments
   always accompany a person as "chaplets of grace," even when s/he has no intention
   of performing a *mitzvah,* as, for example, when "a bird's nest chance before you."
   (Deut. 22:6) In *Numbers Rabbah* 17:5, the mitzvot are also said to accompany a person but the tone and the message are distinctly different. There the *midrashist*
   states that the fact that one is always accompanied by commandments "may be

our *midrash* is also explored in the world of contemporary Judaic scholarship, which places it in cultural context and perspective. For example, Urbach, though he insists that this story is distinctly Jewish and markedly different from the Platonic idea of "the previous world of souls," notes that the concept of souls pre-existing is found in our sources only from the third century C.E. onwards. Glatzer states that it may well have been influenced by Platonic and Stoic models of reality.[7]

Nevertheless, even if this particular cluster of *midrashic* tales states the case for fear of Heaven *(Yirat Shamayim)* very polemically and radically, and seems to define it rather one-dimensionally as obeying God's commandments, it is not really idiosyncratic. And its central value concept, *Yirat Shamayim,* has indeed been deeply embedded in Jewish tradition as an educational ideal. So much so that it would have been impossible or at least ludicrous to say of a Jewish person before the advent of modernity that he or she was well educated though happening to lack *Yirat Shamayim!*

In fact, the fear of Heaven and the acceptance of the yoke of Heaven was the fundamental end in itself of Jewish education, that which required no extrinsic justification. It pointed towards who the educated person was rather than what he/she did or knew.[8] As Rabbi Yehudah Loew, the Maharal of Prague, expressed it:

> The matter which is the purpose of everything is *Yirat Shamayim.* And because of this, Solomon concluded his book (Ecclesiastes 12) (with): 'The end of the matter, everything having been heard (is): Fear God and keep His commandments, for this is the whole of Man.'[9]

---

illustrated by one who has been thrown into the water. The captain stretches out a rope and says to him, 'Take hold of the rope with your hand and do not let go, for if you do, you will lose your life.'" See discussion in Nehama Leibowitz, *Studies in the Weekly Sidra (Ki Tetse),* translated and adapted by Aryeh Newman (Jerusalem: World Zionist Organization, Dept. for Torah Education and Culture 5719–1958), first series. We shall discuss this *midrash* more extensively below.

7. Ephraim E. Urbach, *The Sages: Their Concepts and Beliefs,* (Jerusalem: Magnes Press, 1975), pp. 245–48; Glatzer, *The Judaic Tradition,* p. 332.

8. Ends in themselves, or intrinsic aims as educational goals that require no further justifications, are similar to those goods that a person pursues *l'shmam,* for their own sakes. We have seen Maimonides focus such ends in themselves on intellectual comprehension, but it has been more common to see them within the matrix of *Yirat Shamayim.* See, for example, the late medieval philosopher of Judaism, Joseph Albo, in his Sefer Ha-Ikkarim (Book of Principles) 3:7: "And if you shall ask how the fear (of God) will bring a person to this high level of achieving eternal life–after all it (seems) more worthy that intellectual comprehension will do this!–Solomon in Ecclesiastes has already explained this and said that only Fear (of God) is the cause of immortality and that this matter depends on the wisdom of the Lord, may He be blessed who decreed it thus and it is unworthy to ask what the reason is." For a Hebrew-English version, *Sefer Ha-Ikkarim* III, critically edited by Isaac Husik (Philadelphia: The Jewish Publication Society of America, 5706–1946), Chap. 31, pp. 291–92. See discussion, Chap. 13.

9. R. Yehudah Loew ("Maharal of Prague"), "Netiv Yirat HaShem" ("The Path of the Fear of God"), *Netivot Olam (Paths of Eternity)* II (Bnei Brak: Yahadut Pub., 1980), p. 37.

It was a complex aim. For while it had to do with one's duties, ("keep His commandments") it was also, and perhaps first of all, a comprehensive image of character, virtue, and goodness. In the Jewish context, therefore, while it did mean observance of the commandments (as it does in our *midrash*) and study of the Torah, it also preceded them, and it meant carrying them out with a certain pious intention.

Therefore, while one was required to study Torah and to have a knowledge of it in all its particulars in order to live a life of *Yirat Shamayim*, for one could hardly fulfill the obligations imposed by the Torah without knowing the Torah,[10] yet without *Yirat Shamayim* knowledge was a castle built on sand. Of "one whose knowledge exceeds his fear," it was said that "his knowledge will not persevere." Having wisdom without fear of Heaven was considered analogous to "having wheat but failing to protect it against worms."[11]

> Said Rabba: At the time they bring in a person for judgment (after death) they say: Have you carried on commerce honestly, have you set aside times for the study of Torah, have you engaged in bringing children into the world, have you anticipated redemption, have you wisely deliberated and understood (deduced) one thing from another? And even in that case, If 'The fear of God is his treasure-house,' then yes, (all) this is worthy, if not, then it is worthless.
>
> Rabba, son of Rav Huna, said: Every person who has (knowledge of) Torah but has no *Yirat Shamayim,* is like the caretaker who has been given the inner keys to the treasure house but not the outer ones. How will he enter? Rabbi Yannai said: Woe to him who has no courtyard (Fear of Heaven) but makes a gate to the courtyard (study of Torah).
>
> *Shabbat* 31 a-b

Yirat Shamayim was, therefore, the hallmark of a fine Jewish character, but every decent human being, Jew or Gentile, was in some sense expected to have it. The real or apparent lack of it in others created dilemmas for the righteous. Abraham, for example, fearing that Avimelech, king of Grar would slay him for his wife, said of Sarah that she was his sister. When Avimelech becomes aware of the deception and calls Abraham to him for an explanation, the patriarch replies:

> Because I thought, surely the fear of God is not in this place and they will slay me for my wife's sake ... (Genesis 20:11).

---

10. Maimonides, for example, notes in his commentary on *Avot* 3:11, "He whose fear of sin precedes his knowledge (will find that) his knowledge will remain," to refer to one's orientation rather than to a sequence of attainment. "For how can fear of sin come before knowledge? Have they not said above (*Avot* 2:6) 'An ignorant man cannot fear sin'?" On fear of sin and fear of Heaven, see Chap. 7.
11. *Shabbat* 31a.

An Educational Forum on *Yirat Shamayim*

Despite the extreme gloom of our *midrash,* it does raise the questions whether one might still formulate Jewish educational ideals with due regard to *Yirat Shamayim.*

To us, it also suggests a focal topic for an educational discussion across the spectrum of Jewish belief and education. What does, or can, the educational-philosophic message of our *midrash* mean to the diverse communities of contemporary Jewish teachers? What can they do with it? Can they find a common ground to discuss a text whose normative thrust is that the purpose of being here is to obey God's commandments with "fear" in order to become a person who deserves the world-to-come? That the decision to fear Heaven is the only important one in life? And that it is independent of material circumstances?

We should assume that such a discussion, if held among teachers who represent the entire spectrum of Jewish world view and educational ideology, will begin in an atmosphere of deep suspicion. For reasons already mentioned, *Yirat Shamayim* is not really germane to the way modern educational thinkers and planners, Jewish ones included, generally formulate their assumptions and aims. The only place where we may find professed end aims identical with those suggested by our *midrash* is among ultra-Orthodox *(haredi)* educators. True, most modern Orthodox educators also believe that *Yirat Shamayim* is desirable, but for them it seems to refer more to a certain standard of religious observance than to a comprehensive ideal of character that requires the ideal student to accept his/her material circumstances with equanimity and to expend no energy on improving them. For many other Jewish educators, even that distinction seems like a mere nuance.

In secular schools in Israel and in some diaspora communities, the term and the idea have lost their plausibility in the eyes of most teachers. They no longer believe that there is a "Heaven" that determines human destiny, setting moral standards and rewarding the good. They place human fear in more naturalistic contexts; unlike the *midrashist,* they are likely to ascribe it to unpleasant (but reasonable) anticipations or to neurotic ones. Generally, they prefer to examine moral issues through the arts of deliberation independent of religion, and they have little use for concepts such as destiny. Therefore the aim of cultivating young people who have *Yirat Shamayim* has become unacceptable to them; they identify this educational ideal with outworn metaphysical and normative beliefs and/or with benighted communities. Consequently, their social-educational ideal is not to cultivate persons who embody *Yirat Shamayim* such as Torah scholars, devout artisans, and pious housewives. Rather, they have developed new models of self-actualization, such as the pioneer, the scientific scholar, the creative artist, and other modern heroic types of virtue and competence.

In fact, many modern Jewish educators, even among those who are not blatantly secular, are unlikely to use the rhetoric of *Yirat Shamayim* when they seek a principled foundation for their policies and pedagogy. They ask different questions from the ones implicit in our *midrash.* For example, are there absolute values and is it meaningful and helpful to speak of absolutes in character education? What remains relatively constant or even perennial in culture and what necessarily, even beneficially, changes? How are permanence and change to be reflected in Jewish education so that our children will be rooted but challenged too? Are spiritual matters concerned with socialization and initiation, as was so largely the case in the Talmudic and medieval Jewish tradition, or does the realm of value primarily address the individual? Given the need for some socialization, how can it be effected with decency, and without regimentation? What does a child need to know: which bodies of knowledge, skills, and modes of thought are called for in order to properly locate, confront, and solve the problems that characterize (and, in a sense, constitute) personal and collective life in our era?

If these are the questions around which, for most Jewish educators, Jewish life and education actually revolve, we can expect not only diverse approaches to *Yirat Shamayim,* but also some annoyance with those who bring it into the educational conversation. Nevertheless, if one views our *midrash* and the entire *Yirat Shamayim* literature of which it is a part to be a significant component of a classic philosophy of Jewish education, it does belong in educational discourse, certainly as a source, and perhaps as an issue. What did *Yirat Shamayim* mean in the Jewish tradition? Can it still be a formative idea or principle? Is it, at least, a resource for a modern ideal of Jewish character education? What happens to the religious-theological concept of *Yirat Shamayim* when educators attempt to translate it into moral and philosophical educational language?

Translation

Let us expand here on the issue of translation, since it will be so central to making sense of things for the educators who shall be discussing *Yirat Shamayim* in this section of our book.

When we observe what pedagogues do with subject matter that they are transmitting to pupils we see that translation is a staple of most educational activities and situations. For example, when teachers take pupils for an overnight hike to teach them scouting, they tell the youngsters that "we are going to have a great time." This is a didactically based translation of an exercise in social training and the inculcation of skills. When physicists assist in translating the substance of their subject matter into teaching models, or Biblical scholars help educators move scholarship into teaching Torah, they are likewise translating from scholarship to the classroom.[12] Thus, any translation is an attempt, usually by an expert, to render a concept located in a mode of discourse that is incomprehensible to particular hearers, because they don't know it or don't take it seriously, into an idiom that does make sense to them and evokes interest in them, so that they are enabled to learn something from the (original) concept.

The conceptual or contextual lexicon being translated may be initially incomprehensible or alien for diverse reasons. Perhaps the audience is not cognitively ready to understand. Perhaps the potential learners are simply ignorant and must have matters explained to them. Perhaps they do think that they know something about the subject but are hostile or indifferent to it; in that case, the expert may try not only to explicate his or her subject but to "sell" it, to demonstrate its importance. Possibly, because they lack experience with the field, the listeners are both ignorant and indifferent. They must then be helped to approach the subject by way of a learning model that makes them curious about the subject , comfortable with it, and ultimately knowledgeable about it.[13]

For example, religious concepts may, for religiously ignorant or indifferent listeners, be translated into moral and philosophical ones that, at the very least, capture something essential about the field as the person who is at home in it understands it. The listener gets to see what the theological-religious concept looks like when the theological significance and terminology are put aside or "bracketed." Thus, translators often introduce their translating activity by asking their listeners to look at it this way, i.e., in a way that is familiar to them, and more or less acceptable to them.[14]

12. *From Scholarship to the Classroom: Translating Jewish Tradition into Curriculum,* (edited by Seymour Fox and Geraldine Rosenfield (New York: Melton Research Center for Jewish Education, The Jewish Theological Seminary of America, 1977). See especially the essay by Joseph J. Schwab, "Translating Scholarship into Curriculum," pp. 1–30. Our deliberation does not follow his model, which insists that all four commonplaces of education (subject matter, teacher, learner, and environment) be kept equally and simultaneously in mind in deliberation and that experts on each participate in the discussion.

13. On education as the enterprise of locating adequate models through which to communicate knowledge to those who do not yet understand what we hope to transmit to them see Marc Belth, *Education as a Discipline: a Study of the Role of Models in Thinking* (Boston: Allyn and Bacon, Inc., 1965).

14. Teachers of young children are not likely to do this very much, and for good reasons. To paraphrase Peters, children require the stability and certainty of habit

When is such a translation helpful in making things clear and when does it become banal or overly apologetic? When does it become blatantly reductionistic, that is, claiming that the translation captures comprehensively all that the original conception means, so that the home language of the original conception becomes redundant? We shall return to this issue in due course.

Five Schools in Jewish Education

Before we examine what a translation of *Yirat Shamayim* for the purposes of a deliberation about this classic ideal may look like we shall introduce the participants in our projected discussion, five teachers who represent five basic approaches to Jewish education. Each of these educators has his or her own notion of an ideal environment or community, of fine and effective teachers, of ideal learners and graduates, and of a good curriculum. Several of our discussants will claim to be loyally continuing the Jewish tradition; others will admit to their discomfort with traditional ideals and even defend a partial or a thoroughgoing rejection of them. However, our rebels claim Jewish legitimacy and admit that this claim may oblige them to carry on a conversation, no matter how heated, with traditional ideals and virtues. Even when they insist on philosophical innovation and/or rejection of tradition, they agree that, as Jewish educators, they ought to explain what they are doing. Likewise, they think that traditionalists have the responsibility to defend those of their loyalties and convictions that seem to fly in the face of modern sensibilities, assumptions, and funds of knowledge.

Of the five in our group, Nehemyah is the unswerving traditionalist. Nehemyah believes that Jewish existence and education are founded exclusively on absolute and all-embracing norms, divinely revealed and, in principle, totally unchanging. From his mentors he has learned that one must strive, in a hostile world, to approximate past religious perfections. These may all be summed up by *Yirat Shamayim* as a comprehensive objective. *Yirat Shamayim* includes learning of Torah, reverence for Torah scholars, deeply ingrained piety, diligent observance of the commandments, and unabashed fear of divine wrath. Also, given the nature of modern pagan society, *Yirat Shamayim* mandates actual fear of the outside world and an emphatic and thorough-going separation from it.

Nehemyah has no problem with our *midrash;* he finds in the instructions and admonitions of the supervising angel a clear manifesto

---

rather than the ambiguities and ironies of reason. See Peters, "Reason and Habit," pp. 51–52.

of good Jewish education. Nehemyah fully concurs with the view that what counts is the kind of obedient and religiously reliable person you are, not what you achieve in the glittering world of falsehood. As a matter of fact, he accepts completely what the spiritual mentors of his community teach, that it is better not to achieve too much in this world.[15] Torah, based on the fear of Heaven, is the divinely bestowed—and imposed—blueprint for becoming a righteous person who is deserving of reward in the world-to-come.

Our second participant, Esther, also represents and defends a tradition-oriented and religious educational world view. She, however, is aware of the tensions between what her school of thought considers perennial and what it sees as transient or fluctuating features of culture and history. Esther has no doubt that the eternal, which is the locus of the religious, should mold character. This should be done, now as in the past, through the medium of the *halakhah*, which gives concrete form to the perennial and divine truth. The general cultural world is admittedly valuable, useful, and even exciting. Yet she maintains that it is not overtly value-teaching or even necessarily relevant to inherently religious concerns.

By this Esther does not mean to suggest that cultural matters concerned with achievement and aesthetic appreciation be disregarded or even played down in the curriculum. She and her colleagues provide it a very respectable, though compartmentalized, place alongside religious learning. And yet despite this ambivalent approach to general culture, which she both takes very seriously and yet somehow neutralizes, *Yirat Shamayim* is for her, in fact if not in theory, confined to matters that can be classified as religious.

Because she agrees that *Yirat Shamayim* should be a comprehensive ideal, that it should reflect character as well as ritual observance, she often finds herself making attempts to broaden the category of religion beyond its conventional parameters. She insists, therefore, that ethical behavior, simple decency, and nobility of character are in fact religious concerns and not secular ones. Nevertheless, Esther admits that success in inculcating *Yirat Shamayim* does tend to be measured by the continued religiosity of graduates. Religiosity, she knows, is usually considered synonymous with adherence to *halakhah*, specifically in such socially recognizable areas as Sabbath and *kashrut* (dietary law) observance. Furthermore, her experience shows that this success is expected to co-exist with achievement in those studies which our *midrashist* apparently considered meaningless: the secular ones focused on understanding, using, and enjoying this world.

---

15. R. Eliyahu E. Dessler, *Mikhtav Me-Eliyahu,* for example, *"Haosher V'hasakhar B'olam Hazeh"* ("Happiness and Reward in this World"), pp. 1–5.

Esther will therefore be of two minds about our *midrash*. She will express formal agreement with it but consider it too extreme in formulation. The *midrash*, she might say, tells us what is most important, but ignores goods and possibilities that modern people, including religious Jews, should take seriously.

A third approach is represented in our forum by Daniel, a liberal-religious educator. He, like the two teachers already introduced, views Judaism as a religious phenomenon and thinks of Jewish education as religious. However, he is uncomfortable with the rhetoric of absolute norms, especially when they are particular to one specific group. He cordially dislikes the compartmentalization of religious and secular concerns, a matter which does not overtly trouble Esther. To him, Judaism is a treasure house of spiritual insight which, through its various texts and text-people, addresses or encounters the individual, making him/her sensitive and responsive to the problems and wonders of existence. If pupils are taught to confront these problems and wonders authentically, they will learn religious commitment and find meaning in their lives.

Yet he insists that this should never to be done fanatically. Fanaticism he takes to signify narrow allegiance to collective memory at the expense of modern insight and inquiry or of the modern learner's individuality. Judaism at its best stands in relationship to the divine, which calls upon human beings in community for response and responsibility. This Judaism, he believes, is in its details a humanly constructed fabric of faith and fellowship and it reflects many experiences and many historical contexts. Daniel likes to make the analogy between religion and a mansion with many rooms, replete with diverse and often secluded corners in which individuals may find themselves and make themselves comfortable. Moreover, the windows are always open and doors are to be left ajar. God is everywhere.

The term *Yirat Shamayim* is not one that Daniel often uses. He feels that members of Nehemyah's ultra-traditionalist and Esther's modern Orthodox groups use it too much and too demonstratively and dogmatically. But he admits that there is no philosophical reason for him to shun it. It may, after all, be understood as a comprehensive term for inner piety, openness to the divine, and an all-encompassing reverence.

Daniel values our *midrash* for its power in reaching down into the existential fundamentals of human destiny. In the final analysis, he may declare, nothing is important but the kind of person you are. In saying this, Daniel is echoing our text. But, he somewhat defensively reminds us, that is also taught by spiritual people of all faiths.

In fact, Daniel has constructed an integrative program that deals with basic issues of life. He is now thinking about integrating our *midrash* and the medieval Christian morality play, *Everyman,* into his program. Yet he resents the suggestion that his sympathy for integration indicates a lack of Jewish loyalty and commitment.

Nehemyah, Esther, and Daniel have much to argue about but they all speak in the language of religious identity and aspiration. Though they don't perceive and prescribe religion in the same way, all assume that Jewish education strives to foster religious personalities.

However, as noted, these do not exhaust modern Jewish options. A fourth person at our roundtable, Carmela, though conservative in orientation (like Esther) is philosophically non-religious. To her mind Jewish education is, first and foremost, socialization into Jewish culture and into the community that is its historical bearer. This culture, she reminds us, has been lived and developed by scores of Jewish generations; we are now learning to more lucidly understand it through historical research. For Jews, it is this culture which should naturally focus their valuative and social life.

From her teachers and her own wide reading, Carmela has learned to take it for granted that every human being is born into a tradition within which s/he is led to discover his/her own identify and his/her own group's idiom for the articulation of universal concerns, experience, and values. Believing that every well-developed culture functions as a medium for the expression of individuality, she views the alleged conflict or dichotomy between persons and their groups to be, in principle, unjustified. Where it is found, it testifies to social malfunctioning and cultural deterioration and/or individual alienation. She readily admits that the individual, living in a world of change, has to select from tradition. But because this is a cultural privilege rather than an innate right, s/he must first, before doing so, learn the culture and understand it. Only then can s/he sense what is fundamental and what transient within it.

Carmela appreciates the *midrash* but insists on translating it into secular categories. The message of the tale of the soul is that character is more important than acquisitions or the achievement of material goals; it also teaches that we cannot always control our lives. Thus, we are warned against hubris and directed to the virtues, here called, in the language of Jewish culture, the commandments of the Torah. She is aware of the fact that translating the *midrash* into a non-religious idiom may involve some modifications in the message. Cultural appropriation, self-knowledge, and consequent self-actualization have become for her the meaning of obeying God's commandments. She expects the good teacher of Judaism to be cognizant of this; such a teacher will make a clear distinction between what the author intended and what we may learn from the traditional texts.

In her educational approach, *Yirat Shamayim* sounds out of place, for Carmela is suspicious of religious rhetoric. Religion, she believes, at least in its present state of fossilization and decay, undermines the cultural, hence human, character of spirituality and value. It also militates against the right and responsibility of persons to choose from among cultural goods at their disposal. This choice Carmela sees as absolutely necessary, not only to allow for individual authenticity but also to assure the development and health of the culture as a whole. For cultures, her own Jewish one included, she finds perpetually threatened: from the right, by historical fixations, from the left, by ignorant anarchy.

Finally, we come to the fifth person at our table, Amir. Amir is outspokenly secular and impatient with educators who coercively fetter the young with chains of tradition, whether religious or merely cultural. In Amir's community of educators, real education invites children to cultivate and fully utilize their natural and individual endowments for self-expression. They are to be empowered and encouraged to make intelligent use of the natural and human environment for their own rational ends and to search imaginatively for their own meanings in the world. Education is not to be enwrapped in tradition; that will only choke it to death. Nor is it primarily oriented to enculturation for, ultimately, educated persons are those who unfold, grow, and develop in their own unique ways. Good teachers, environments and subject matter will make it possible for children to realize their potential as individuals, yet also enable them to live with similar and dissimilar others in cooperation and mutual respect.

Though a radical secularist, Amir admits that tradition sometimes helps to solve certain problems. But he thinks that all too often it constitutes a major problem in itself. Religious faith, he finds, usually blinds believers to new circumstances, challenges, and opportunities, and to the potential in every human life for autonomy and self-making. Therefore, for him, good Jewish education is simply the appropriate education of Jews, that is, those who choose to live and cope within communities of Jews or who are forced to do so by circumstances beyond their control. Amir states uninhibitedly that he has little interest in *Yirat Shamayim* except as an historical datum.

For Amir, therefore, our *midrash* is no more than a pseudo-solution to exilic circumstances and to the problem of Jewish powerlessness. By no stretch of the imagination may it be seen as depicting any objective or metaphysical reality, or as suggesting a prescriptive lesson for our pupils. On the contrary, those Jews who lived in the world of the *midrashist* have too often gone passively to their own destruction. They neither solved their problems nor even recognized them.

For this, he admits, they are not to be condemned. Amir has no patience with the smugness of some of his colleagues and pupils on this score. Yet he cannot praise the victims either. For he truly believes that they were miseducated and thus rendered tragically powerless. What modern Jews need, and to what they must educate, is not fear of Heaven, but responsibility and reasonable self-confidence based on relevant competencies.

Some Ground Rules for the Deliberation About *Yirat Shamayim*

Our paradigmatic guests at the educational round table represent a situation of such principled controversy that consensus of any kind seems unfeasible. Under these circumstances, what can possibly be done to rehabilitate an ideal of *Yirat Shamayim*? How can an ideal so rooted in the tradition speak to the sensibilities of those contemporary Jews who have been alienated from it? For as we have seen, secularly oriented Jews claim that they don't need this ideal (our conservative-secular Carmela) or that they emphatically dislike it (Amir, our radical secularist). How, furthermore, can it even become the basis of a common conversation between different schools of contemporary Jewish education? Not only do even some religionists, such as Daniel, manage without it, but those who continue to speak about *Yirat Shamayim,* like Nehemyah and Esther, seem to use the concept as a slogan that threatens to exclude everyone outside the "faithful" community from being significant other Jews.

Nevertheless, those who maintain that *Yirat Shamayim* is a central conception for Jewish education need not write off those who disagree or those who feel that they already have it and know all about it. Their very willingness to engage in the conversation suggest that, perhaps, all our five educators entertain vague expectations of learning something from the others about faith in the modern world, and about the difficulties some contemporary Jews have with Jewish religious faith and its focal character ideal. Both the religious and the secular teachers may consider opposing views to their own as grossly mistaken and yet learn to discern in them ways to address problems and dilemmas that they have never considered or even acknowledged. This won't necessarily happen, but it may.

To make it possible, we must aim for common study of the sources, followed by maximal clarifications of diverse positions. Only then may we hope for at least the partial reconstruction of a common language between diverse schools of educational thought, a language that takes note of *Yirat Shamayim* as an educational ideal. It goes without saying that we must take the various philosophic and cultural positions of our discussants as each worthy of consideration, as all addressing themselves to inherent characteristics of our situation.

Let us set down several ground rules for study, translation, and discussion at our "round table" of educators:

(1) The discussion, like all contemporary Jewish educational discourse, should not shy away from philosophy as a medium that will enable Jews to share insights and commitments. There are at least three good reasons for this: (a) many modern Jews will not wish to seriously consider classic ideals in their traditional-religious language; (b) Jewish educational discourse in the contemporary world is likely to be enriched by categories learned from others; and (c) it is generally useful, in an open society, for such a Jewish-educational conversation to be as comprehensible to non-Jewish educators as possible.

Traditional ideals, therefore, must be at least partially translated into an idiom that makes sense to people who do not consider themselves bound by *halakhah* and/or religious doctrine. This is an insight suggested by the conservative-secular approach, which has tried to salvage theology and tradition by placing it in the context of culture and history. Yet, in the common universe of discourse that philosophy provides for Jewish education, we may expect some non-religious Jews, specifically those of the radically secular school of thought, to stubbornly raise the question whether the aims proposed for Jewish education require the use of the traditional term *Yirat Shamayim.* They may voice the fear that partial translation is simply a ploy for religious apologetics and manipulation and that traditionalist colleagues use it for theological sleight-of-hand, for attempted conversions to religious thinking. They will advise their religious colleagues to desist from such tactics "for their own good," so as not to corrupt religious concepts by conscious or unconscious reductionism.[16]

Conversely, religious Jews, even in the midst of the philosophical conversation, will legitimately continue to see the concept of *Yirat Shamayim* as anchored within the commandments of the Torah and

16. The difference between conscious and unconscious reductionism has been well defined by Phillips in his discussion of philosophical attempts to explain or explain away religious doctrines: the former claims religion is an illusion and seeks to reduce it to its proper status. The latter wants to present an account of religious belief, believes he has given such an account but has, in fact, reduced religion to something which lacks some of the fundamental characteristics of religious belief." D.Z. Phillips, *Religion Without Explanation* (Oxford: Basil Blackwell, 1976), p. 140. What I am calling partial translation is designed to prevent such unconscious reductionism while maintaining the largest feasible measure of communication and comprehensibility.

faith in their revealed or divinely inspired (i.e., not simply cultural) character. Religious participants in the discussion will be wary lest philosophical discourse become a tool for prying religious Jews away from religious convictions.

This means that, despite the need for translation of the concept of *Yirat Shamayim* into an idiom that might make it philosophically and educationally comprehensible and perhaps even feasible for teachers and communities that do not define their Jewish loyalties in religious terms, the concept's religious integrity must be protected. Neither Jewish unity nor educational consensus will be well served by semantic slickness or cultural corruptions. And yet when the religious character of the ideal is clearly delineated, there may well emerge non-religious ideals that are very close to it, which secular educators will plausibly see as historical outgrowths and innovative continuations of it.

(2) All discussions of *Yirat Shamayim* in Jewish education will have to be cognizant of the theological difficulties evoked for most contemporary Jews by reference to reward and punishment as a motivation for it. To be very concrete: if education for prayer is relatively easy in *haredi* education because children are readily taught that they are rewarded (or punished) for the way they pray, this can hardly be the dominant motivating factor for other, including most halakhically religious Jews.[17] Yet the discussion of the concept of *Yirat Shamayim* must be enriched by its various elements, including that of retribution; moreover, it must come to grips with the experience of the *haredi* community and the comprehensiveness of its educational ideal.

(3) Given the general commitment to competence in problem-solving and the view that optimal control of our environment is endowed with moral value, we may assume that *Yirat Shamayim* cannot, for the vast majority, be interpreted as negating all other educational ideals. At the same time, any examination of the ideal in its diverse formulations that guards against distortions will show that it cannot be viewed as simply one ideal among others. Whether such a notion can be acceptable to non-*haredi* educators, and in which sense, will constitute part of the discussion.

And now we are ready for study and conversation.

17. I am indebted for this insight to my student, Yeshayahu Bar-Yehudah, the Jerusalem educator.

7

FIVE EDUCATORS
EXPLORE
YIRAT SHAMAYIM

Our Educators Study Torah

Our educational forum is now going to explore the concept of *Yirat Shamayim* for the purpose of education.

This requires that they engage in two activities:

(a) First, they must carefully study texts which deal with *Yirat Shamayim* or are relevant to it, and discuss how specific character ideals flow from them or are suggested by them. As they study Torah, they will ask themselves what the selected texts are saying to them as educators who wish to cultivate "excellent dispositions" in their pupils.

(b) Then, they must examine the theological conceptions underlying the character ideal of *Yirat Shamayim* they have discovered. They will ask whether this religious and theological conception can be understood in some more generally philosophical manner that permits even educators who are not comfortable with religious doctrine to use it or to learn from it.

For their study and exploration, our five educators have invited M., a teacher of educational philosophy, to join their group for the first round of study sessions and discussions. He has suggested that the character ideal of *Yirat Shamayim* be partially translated from the language of commandment into the language of morality and existential thought. This will hopefully reduce defensiveness and maximize communicability. By engaging in this kind of translation, our educators will be able to "bracket" such theological issues as (1) the source of the character ideal; (2) the specific religious meanings assigned by the texts to the character ideal; and (3) the religious consciousness these texts demand or even assume.

The "bracketing" is intended only to remove obstacles to dialogue. This, however, is not to be understood as implying that these issues are unimportant per se or irrelevant. In fact, these issues will remain on the scene and will eventually be brought back to help our teachers determine where they have departed from the ideal and where they have introduced a new but related ideal. They will also have to recall the religious character of *Yirat Shamayim* to examine whether they have deliberately or unconsciously distorted this ideal.

As for the theology underlying the concept, especially in our original, blatantly theological *midrash,* we have said that the *midrash* is to be translated philosophically to make it more comprehensible and perhaps educationally useful. But here, too, the specific rules and assumptions of the religious belief language will be bracketed but not discarded. This means that the participants will be encouraged to suggest their own ways and idioms of understanding the texts, but will keep in mind that their ways of seeing them do not exhaust the religious possibilities within them.

The following is a summary of the notes taken by members of our roundtable on their initial discussions, background lectures, and study. The composite summary has, with the consent of the entire group, been edited by M., who has also supplemented the text study with a lecture on the concept of situation (Chapter 8) as well as requisite footnotes on texts studied or alluded to. He has commented on the responses of the participants and made closing comments on the sessions described below.

Summary of Learning Sessions

We have discovered that the classical sources on *Yirat Shamayim* are numerous and diverse. They constitute an ongoing conversation about character, value, and aspiration. We saw the term *Yirat Shamayim* much expanded and then subdivided in the course of this historically extended conversation. Thus, closely related concepts such as *Yirat Chet* (the fear of sin) and *Ahavat Shamayim* (the love of Heaven) are drawn into this value-ideal, supplementing and enriching it. Likewise, we came upon some sources that refer to a lower form of fear that involves retribution, and a higher one that is based on awe and reverence. For example, while *Yirat Shamayim* is often termed the highest ideal of a refined human existence, it is sometimes divided into fear of retribution and fear of the exalted Presence. Also, love of Heaven, *Ahavat Shamayim,* is sometimes described not only as the complement of fear, but its highest expression.[1]

In the course of the historical interplay between text and commentary, diverse valuative questions and dilemmas arise: is it more noble to love or to fear God? And if to fear, what kind of fear is most exemplary? If human nature is fundamentally base, should not love be collapsed into fear so that human beings will be able to restrain their innate bestiality? Conversely, if human nature has a natural tendency towards refinement and perfection, should fear of Heaven not be harmoniously linked to the innate moral sense with which people are endowed?[2] In the latter case, should not fear of retribution be considered as a mere early stage, of character development, to be replaced at maturity with *yirat hahitromemut,* reverence alone?

What is assumed by all is that one who fears Heaven, the *Yire Shamayim,* has a keenly developed sense of being in the Presence of God or of being called upon to be in His Presence. And while this Presence is normatively found in the Torah, *Yirat Shamayim,* we discovered, cannot be reduced to norms, even if they are those of the Torah.

1. The sense of Presence, of God who knows and sees everything, is often called "fear of sin." This, Urbach states, is sometimes considered the operative aspect of fear of Heaven; it connotes "being repelled by transgression." (Urbach, *The Sages,* pp. 366–67.) (On fear of Sin as fear of retribution, see also Moses Hayim Luzzatto, *Mesillat Yesharim,* Chap. 24. For a Hebrew-English edition, *Mesillat Yesharim (The Path of the Upright),* a critical edition provided with a translation and notes by Mordecai M. Kaplan (Philadelphia: The Jewish Publication Society of America, 5708-1948). On the interlocking of fear of Heaven and love of Heaven, see Urbach, *The Sages,* Chap. 14, pp. 400–19. An interesting distinction between the two is made by the medieval commentator-scholar, Moses ben Nachman (Nachmanides–Ramban). In his view all positive commandments stem from love, and all negative commandments from fear of God. See Shimon Kerner, "Teaching *Yirat Shamayim,"* *Ten Daat,* (publication of Jewish day school educators) Heshvan 5750, p. 13.

2. For example, Rabbi Elchanan E. Wasserman, "*Yirat Shamayim,"* posits that when God created mankind he told all creatures already in existence that he would create man in our image (i.e., His and theirs) so that humans would have, in addition to knowledge and speech, all bestial qualities "making him (man) worse than any animal (being both bestial and intelligent). Therefore He provided man with the strongest iron chain to permit him self-control "so that he would not destroy the world. And what is this chain? This is *Yirat Shamayim* for without it, even the wisdom of an Aristotle will not help him when he is attacked by his evil impulse." Wasserman, *Kometz Maamarim,* p. 40. Conversely, R. Abraham Isaac Kook, mystic thinker and first Chief Rabbi of modern Israel, states categorically that *Yirat Shamayim* may not push aside "the natural morality of man, because then it is no longer pure *Yirat Shamayim.* It must be blended with simple faith and natural morality in order for a person to be able to build all his/her highest spiritual traits." A. I. Kook, *Orot Hakodesh (Lights of Holiness)* III (Jerusalem: Mosad Harav Kook, 5724), p. 27.

One should recite the (first paragraph of the) *Shema* (Deut. 6:4-9) before (the second paragraph) *vehaya im shamoa* (Deut. 11:13-21) ... so as to first accept the yoke of the Kingdom of Heaven and after that, accept the yoke of the commandments ...

Berakhot 14 b

That the basis of fear of Heaven is to know oneself to be living before God and accountable to God alone is given classic expression in a story very reminiscent of our *aggadic* tale of the hapless soul, thrown into the world and facing Heavenly judgment and perhaps divine wrath and retribution for its shortcomings.[3] It is about Rabban Yohanan ben Zakkai, the great Tannaic (early Talmudic) teacher of the generation of the Destruction. When he took ill, we are told, his students came to visit him, whereupon he began to weep. When they asked him why he was weeping, he said to them:

(even) if I were being taken before a human king, who is here today and tomorrow in the grave, whose anger ... and confinement are time-bound, and whose death penalty is not eternal death, and I can appease him with words and bribe him with money, I would still weep ... And now that I am being taken before the King of kings, the Holy One, blessed be He, Who lives forever and Whose confinement is eternal, and if He kills me it is eternal death, and I cannot appease or bribe Him, and furthermore; when there are two roads before me, one leading to *Gan Eden* (Paradise) and one to *Gehennom* (Hell) and I don't know by which path I shall be taken—shall I then not weep?

They said to him, Master, bless us. He said to them: May it be God's will that the fear of Heaven shall be upon you like the fear of flesh and blood. They said to him: Master, is that all? He said to them: If only it were that much! Know that when a person commits a transgression he says, (I hope) that no person will see me ...

At the moment of his departure, he said to them: remove the vessels (from the room) so that they not become ritually impure (due to a dead person in the room) and prepare a seat for King Hezekiah of Judah who is coming.

Brakhot 28b

Yirat Shamayim for Rabban Yohanan ben Zakkai involves the sense of Presence, of being seen, both in public and in concealment. There is a focus on moral choice, the requirement to do well and not evil and, like in the *midrash* with which we began, on divine judgement. One can no more be free of God's commandments than one can escape death. Being so dependent and limited is sobering and, in critical existential moments, frightening. Yet, Rabban Yohanan, who

3. According to Urbach, this emphasis on retribution engendered a distinction between fear and love that is not an innate characteristic of the *Yirat Shamayim* tradition. Urbach, *The Sages*, pp. 356–57. Thus Antiginus, of Soho, teaches that one should serve God without hope of reward "and may the fear of Heaven be upon you." (*Avot* 1:3)

fears Heaven, knows how to put other fears in proper perspective. Paradoxically, because he fears God he has nothing else to fear.[4] And this fearlessness creates in him the confidence that gives him control and makes him responsible.

Rabban Yohanan has confidence in two senses. He maintains the ability to remain within the world of the *halakhah* and to teach it; thus he instructs his disciples to remove vessels to guard them from the ritual impurity of a place of death; he can give these instructions with equanimity even when it happens to be his own death. Second, he has confidence in his own deeds and judgment. Note that he tells his disciples to prepare a seat for King Hezekiah. According to Rashi's commentary on this passage, Hezekiah is coming to accompany him to the next world. Hezekiah, the very symbol of sovereignty and national pride, acted very differently from the way Rabban Yohanan did, when he compromised with Rome, collaborating to obtain Yavne and its sages. Yet, by accompanying him to the next world, Hezekiah may be seen to vindicate him, to agree that a responsible person must act in terms of his understanding of his specific circumstances. Rabban Yohanan was not inhibited at moments of leadership and decision-making by what Hezekiah might say. He knows that being in the Presence of God and being required to serve only the Holy One is a release from false servitudes and that the natural fear of inadequacy that accompanies every reflective human life and death provides no release from responsibility.[5] Just as Hezekiah did what he had to do, so Rabban Yohanan acted in accordance with what he felt to be required by the needs and circumstances of his times. He does not apologize for that.

Thus, while he fears and cries, he also has the stature to bless. He is enslaved to no one, not even to himself or to his fear. The moment of truth alienates Rabban Yohanan neither from his role as halakhic mentor nor from his inner truth as a leader. "The person who fears Heaven speaks with authority."[6]

---

4. This point is well made by *Tanna Debe Eliyahu*, Chap. 25: "It was fear of the Holy One that preceded all his (Abraham's) subsequent acts. (Because he feared Him) the Holy One said to him: 'Fear not Abram' (Gen. 15:1). 'Fear not' is said only to a man who genuinely fears Heaven." For an English version of this early medieval *midrashic* work, see *Tanna Debe Eliyahu (The Lore of the School of Elijah)*, translated from the Hebrew by William G. Braude and Israel J. Kapstein (Philadelphia: The Jewish Publication Society of America, 5741, 1981).

5. This view, that Rabban Yohanan ben Zakkai is vindicated by the appearance of King Hezekiah, is suggested by Rabbi Isaac Halevi Herzog, prolific scholar and former Chief rabbi of Israel. R. Herzog's approach is cited by Adin Steinsaltz in his edition of the Talmud, *Berakhot*, p. 125 (Jerusalem: Israel Institute for Talmudic Publications, 1967). That Hezekiah has come to accompany him is, as noted, the comment of Rashi on the passage.

6. *Berakhot* 6b. Literally, "the words of the *Yire Shamayim* are heard."

The *Yire Shamayim*: In God's Presence

From the sense of Presence flows many dispositions and character traits that, in the texts we have examined, are attributed to one who fears Heaven. Below are notes on some of the traits and paradoxes we discussed.

Many sources emphasize that the fearer of God, the *Yire Shamayim*, is obedient: he or she is faithful to the commandments because they are God's decree. Abraham was told by God that "now I know you to be a God-fearing person" after his readiness to sacrifice his son (Genesis 22:12). Because fear of sin is understood by the sages as fear of not obeying the commandments even before they are understood,[7] *Yirat Shamayim* signifies self-control and self-discipline, an innocent and pre-reflective acceptance of what is permitted, required, and forbidden. Though in the case of Abraham, this innocent acceptance follows a singular and excruciatingly problematic command, that is not what generally confronts persons within the historical-communal tradition. For them, the commandments are embodied within the corpus of the *halakhah.* It is the halakhic norm to which they are to be obedient, which they are to do even before they "hear," i.e., understand.[8]

It is intrinsic to the *halakhah* as a normative network which makes God's Presence accessible that it has something to say about–and seems to mandate a particular response–to every possible situation: how to safeguard one's health, how to commemorate such traumatic events as the destruction of the Temple, how to eat and how to regulate sexual relations. This *halakhic* ethos has been described by Simon as "limited asceticism."[9] Without turning his or her back on the world, the *Yire Shamayim,* living within the domain of the *halakhah,* will exercise partial self-denial: s/he will not eat everything edible, not feel deprived if certain experiences are out of bounds for him/her. A per-

---

7. *Avot* 3:9
8. The most prominent contemporary expositor of the *halakhah* as a total religious conception is undoubtedly Rabbi Joseph B. Soloveitchik (d. 1993). See his *Halakhic Man,* translated from the Hebrew by Lawrence Kaplan (Philadelphia: The Jewish Publication Society of America, 1983) and J.B. Soloveitchik, *The Halakhic Mind: an Essay on Jewish Tradition and Jewish Thought* (London: Seth Press, 1986). For a kindred yet distinct view, see R. Aharon Lichtenstein, "Does Jewish Tradition Recognize an Ethic Independent of Halakha?" in *Contemporary Jewish Ethics,* edited by Menachem Marc Kellner (New York: Sanhedrin Press, 1978), pp. 102–23. Another thinker who has insisted on *halakhah* as the cultural and religious language of Judaism and who has suggested some educational translations of this is Isaiah Leibowitz, *Yahadut, Am Yehudi U'Medinat Yisrael (Judaism, the Jewish People and the State of Israel)* (Tel Aviv: Schocken, 1975), especially pp. 13–84.
9. On *halakhah* as "partial asceticism," see Ernst A. Simon, "Law and Observance in Jewish Experience," in *Tradition and Contemporary Experience: Essays in Jewish Thought and Life,* edited by Alfred Jospe (New York: Schocken Books for Bnai Brith Hillel Foundation, 1970), especially pp. 226–28.

son who fears Heaven within the halakhic regimen of Presence will not conceive of self-realization as limited only by what appears to be possible; s/he must consider, first and foremost, what is permissible. The possibilities are restricted by religious (ethical and sacral) norms. Just as there are positive actions that are self-understood for the one who fears sin, so are certain actions out of the question. To do them would remove the offending person from his or her world of the Torah and thus from his/her locus of commitment and identity.[10]

However, our study of a crucial proof text for *Yirat Shamayim* seemed to make the point that this ideal requires much more than self-limitation, self-control, and subservience.

> And now O Israel, what does the lord your God ask of you but that you fear the Lord your God, to walk in all His ways, to love Him and to serve the Lord your God with all your heart and all your soul. To keep the commandments of the Lord and His statutes which I command you this day, for your good (Deut. 10:12).

Talmudic sages deduce from the first of these verses the doctrine with which our chapter begins, that all is in the hands of Heaven but for the fear of Heaven for the Torah states that nothing is required of us but fear, love, and service through faithful observance of God's commandments. But this interpretation, intimating that doing all these things isn't much because it leaves most things out of human control, in the hands of Heaven, is only one perspective. The passage has also, very plausibly, been understood to say that what God is only demanding is—everything. What more can be demanded of a person than fear, love, walking in His ways, and obeying all God's commandments "with all your heart and all your soul?" This maximalistic way of seeing this commandment is adopted by a *midrashic* writer on the book of Psalms:

> (David said:) One thing did I ask of the Lord, that was my request: that I may dwell in the House of the Lord all the days of my life, to behold the graciousness of the Lord and to visit in His sanctuary (Psalms: 27:4).
>
> The Holy One, blessed be He said to David: You said, 'one thing did I ask' and yet you ask for very much. He (David) said to him: (I am merely following in your footsteps for) You also said, "What does the Lord ask of you but ...' and yet requested much ...
>
> *Midrash Tehillim Shohar Tov* 27:5

This is a fascinating exchange between David, who seems to be asking for only "one thing" but in fact wants no less than to be con-

---

10. In this sense, we may "translate" the statement of Rabin bar Rav Adda in the name of Rabbi Yitzhak: "Everyone who regularly comes to the synagogue and fails to come on a particular day—the Holy One, blessed be He inquires about him (to ask, as it were, what happened to him?") and whether he has absented himself to perform a *mitzvah* or not. *Berakhot* 6b.

tinually in God's presence, and God who asks for everything that can be demanded of human beings. It is reminiscent of Paul Tillich's description of faith as requiring no less than ultimate commitment and granting no less than the hope of ultimate salvation. Within a non-idolatrous faith, human beings know that the Ultimate alone is justified in demanding everything and that it alone can promise everything. All else is relative.[11]

It is clear that in this context self-control and obedience, while indispensible, are insufficient, and by themselves seriously distort the ideal. An educated or simply well-trained obedience, staying within the parameters of permitted and forbidden, may, by denying the tensions within the ideal of *Yirat Shamayim,* undermine its comprehensiveness. Where both love and fear are demanded together and absolutely, and one is permitted to anticipate the fulfillment of the heart's greatest desires, self-control alone may imply a holding back, not giving everything, and, concomitantly, not really daring or deserving to hope for much. In this spirit a medieval aggadist teaches that awe without love, giving up without giving, is not enough:

> ... consider the parable of a mortal king who had to go away to a city far across the sea. He had two servants: one both loved the king and was in awe of him; the other was in awe of him but did not love him. He who loved the king and was in awe of him went and planted gardens and orchards of all kinds of fruits, every variety of each. But he who was only in awe of him did nothing at all.

Eventually the king came home and was delighted with what the first servant had prepared for him, and this gave great pleasure to the servant as well.

> But the servant who was only in awe of the king had provided scarcely anything at all for him, so that when the king entered the second servant's house and saw nothing but dried up stuff set out, he arranged it, the dried-up stuff, in such a way (as to make plain his displeasure). (When the second servant entered), he trembled as he realized the consequences of the king's displeasure.[12]

Carmela made the point that if to fear and love only God means that one must bring oneself to the Ultimate, then the ways we do so and the ways we distinguish between what God wants and what is trivial can be guided by the transmitted and codified texts but cannot be confined to them alone. The Ultimate is approached from within tradition and community; these are the raw materials that the king has put in our safekeeping. But each person and each generation has to do something with it; each of us plants trees and orchards in his/her own

---

11. Paul Tillich, *Dynamics of Faith* (New York: Harper and Row, 1957), pp. 1-3.
12. *Tanna Debe Eliyahu,* Chap. 28, pp. 347–48.

way. This, Carmela insisted in our discussion, must eventually affect our understanding of norm, tradition, and community.

Esther objected that the texts we were studying never permitted utilizing the concept of *Yirat Shamayim* to legitimate antinomian positions that make light of the commandments. She reminded us that the sages considered fear of Heaven to include reverence for the sages.[13] Likewise, one who sought to become a fearer of God in order not to obey the commandments was seen as not serving God in purity.

She and Nehemyah insisted that it is the halakhic tradition itself that classically sets guidelines with regard to what is most important and what is less so, and therefore what constitutes fear, love, and service. Her illustration was based on a *midrash* on the Song of Songs.[14] A person may be doing something very close to his/her heart, even something that seems crucially important, such as working out a scientific formula or writing a poem that may get lost if the concentration and writing and thinking are interrupted. And yet, looking at his/her watch, our creatively absorbed individual discovers that the Sabbath is about to begin, requiring that writing implements be put away, for work must be put aside within several short minutes. What will happen to the formula or poem? Yet, the fear of Heaven establishes priorities. "Without fear of Heaven, ... (everything else) is nothing." The halakhically disciplined *Yire Shamayim*, in this as in manifold other cases, gives in, having been educated by the law to distinguish between the sacred and the profane, between the ultimately important and the also but less important.

Daniel, however, insisted that there are many cases, even for such a person, in which there are no codified guidelines for giving everything. He or she has to think about it, asking what God demands in a particular situation, thereby clarifying to him/herself who s/he really is. Not everyone may wish to trust him/herself with every such decision. Yet he agreed with Carmela that what is required by the fear of Heaven, if it is everything, cannot be limited to what has been transmitted. He cited the Talmudic rule that "There cannot be a House of Study with no innovations."[15] Daniel also found support for his position in the writings of one of the leading ultra-traditional thinkers of this century, Rabbi Eliyahu Dessler, in a passage which he insisted we study together. The passage interprets the law of the Torah that two loaves be placed on the altar on the festival of *Shavuot*, "the time of the giving of our Torah."

13. *Pesahim* 22b.
14. Esther's text here was *Song of Songs Rabbah* 7:7 on the words, "a hedge of roses" (Song of Songs, 7:3).
15. *Hagigah* 3a. However, this is mentioned in the context of a discussion as to whether unity or plurality of opinion is the ideal state of affairs.

... And the two loaves (that the Torah commanded be offered on the festival of Shavuot) are called "a new offering" because the achievement of every level (of Torah) is completely new—actually a different world—from that beneath it. With regard to matters of this world, it is written, "There is nothing new under the sun" ... (but) in the spiritual world, at every point of ascent, a person finds himself in a new world that is not like anything that was known to him or that is in the experience of another ... And this state is called in the Torah "a new offering" that people are privileged to achieve after the impurity is removed (from the heart) by a refined and pure service (of God).[16]

Nehemyah was annoyed. To Esther he stage-whispered that what Daniel had done was typical of the way in which post-modern liberal religionists read such passages. To him it was obvious that R. Dessler referred to an inner understanding and did not mean to sanction extra-*halakhic* behavior.

Beyond Self-Restraint and Obedience

We have seen Carmela and Daniel pointing to tensions within the conception of *Yirat Shamayim* and citing *aggadic* texts that pointed to the need for initiative and innovation in spiritual life. Nehemyah and Esther, as representative of religiously traditional communities, forced us to examine this issue from within the halakhic, as well as through the aggadic tradition. Our presenting problem was: since *Yirat Shamayim* implies a total commitment, demanding everything, how can it be saved from inauthenticity if the individual, with his or her particularity, is discounted? Conversely, how can it be considered "fear" if the individual's subjectivity sets the agenda for "service"? Can one bring all of oneself to fear of Heaven when the self may be the problem? Yet Esther and Nehemyah themselves led us in the study of sources that did not limit *Yirat Shamayim* to self-restraint and obedience.

In these sources, *Yirat Shamayim* is shown to be more than adherence to publicly observable norms. In some, an emphasis is placed on private and uncommunicated intention; another teaches that diverse moral situations and environments require new applications of moral principles. And yet others intimate that the community and its leaders, while the transmitters of norms, cannot be simply identified with the norm itself. After all, what the fearer of Heaven fears is Heaven. We examined these three inward aspects of *Yirat Shamayim*:

(1) The private and inward character of *Yirat Shamayim*, which makes it more than a societal norm, is taught by our sages in connection with several commandments that conclude with the words, "and

16. R. Eliyahu E. Dessler, *Mikhtav M'Eliyahu* II, p. 24.

you shall fear your God." In the words of our teacher, Nehama Leibowitz, this norm "refers to something entrusted to the conscience of the individual. It refers to those acts which are beyond the jurisdiction of an earthly court, for the simple reason that witnesses cannot be produced to testify to wrongdoing. Only the individual conscience can know whether the action was committed in good or bad faith."[17]

The commandment, "You shall not put a stumbling block before the blind, but you shall fear your God" (Lev.19:14) is an excellent example of how the individual is referred to inward intention for "fear" in good faith. As Rashi puts it, one may not put a stumbling block before the blind in a certain respect. Thus:

> Whoever misleads an innocent party (who is 'blind' in a certain matter) and gives him dishonest advice, or strengthens the hand of a transgressor, who is blind since the desires of his heart blind him from seeing the true path, violates a negative precept, as it is stated, 'You shall not put a stumbling block before the blind'.[18]

Now, of course, with regard to commandments which are referred to the heart, the offender may publicly defend himself by saying that s/he thought s/he was giving good advice. Or that s/he forgot that s/he should not have offered wine at dinner to a former alcoholic. This may or may not be true; we cannot look it up. But we do expect that the ultimate commitment of the *Yire Shamayim* will be reflected in his/her inner integrity and moral truthfulness. To say that a person fears Heaven is to trust that person's intentions.

The Talmud teaches this in a positive sense through the example of Rav Safra, an *Amora* (i.e., later Talmudic sage) of Babylon who was also a man of commerce. Of Rav Safra it is told that he was offered a price for merchandise that was acceptable to him. However, he could not reply to the potential buyer who was making the offer because he was in the middle of his prayers. The buyer, misunderstanding his silence as lack of consent, raised his offer. Nevertheless Rav Safra was willing to accept only the originally offered amount. In this, say the sages, he fulfilled the dictum, 'And he (the fearer of Heaven) speaks the truth in his heart.'[19]

(2) That diverse situations require innovation in order to maintain the accessibility of moral principle may be considered an underlying principle of the Oral Torah itself, as the planting of trees and orchards

---

17. Nehama Leibowitz, *Studies in Vayikra* (Leviticus) (Jerusalem: World Zionist Organization, Dept. for Torah Education and Culture in the Diaspora, 1980), pp. 173-74.
18. Rashi on *Leviticus* 19:2; Maimonides, *Mishneh Torah*, *"Rozeach U'shemirat Ha'nefesh"* 12, 14. Cited in Leibowitz, *Studies in Vayikra*, p. 175.
19. Commentary of Shragai Abramson who cites the relevant sources, to *Babba Batra* 88, l. 832 in *Babba Batra*, translation and commentary by S. Abramson, edited by Y. N. Epstein (Tel Aviv: Dvir and Massada, 1958), p. 108.

that delights the king. Nachmanides, the medieval scholar and exegete, derives this principle from a specific commandment of the Torah:

> And you shall do what is do that which is right and good in the sight of the Lord ... (Deut. 6:18)
>
> (This means that) even in those matters where He has not specifically commanded, give careful consideration to what is good and just in His eyes, for He loves the good and the just. And this is a weighty matter, for it is impossible to make mention in the Torah of all behaviours of a person with his neighbours and friends and all his business dealings and social and political arrangements, but after He (i.e., God) mentioned many of these, such as not to engage in talebearing, and not to take vengeance ... and so forth, He went on to say that one should do what is good and just in everything ... [20]

(3) Finally, though the standards for serving and fearing God are, as noted, negotiated by and through the community, the community is not invariably right; social order and propriety can never exhaust the meaning of *Yirat Shamayim*. The Torah itself records a fascinating case, wherein two men, Eldad and Medad, "prophesized in the camp" without having received inspiration or authorization from Moses "and the spirit rested upon them."

> And Joshua, the son of Nun, the minister of Moses from his youth ... said: My lord Moses, imprison them. And Moses said to him: Are you jealous for my sake? Would that all the Lord's people were prophets, that the Lord would put His spirit upon them. (Numbers 11:28-29)

If unauthorized prophesying is legitimate in a community led by Moses, this is certainly the case in less richly endowed ones. Most communities may be only partially trusted, some hardly at all. If the community is always and automatically and even arbitrary trusted, then the individual loses trustworthiness; he/she has become a person who does not fear Heaven, but rather public opinion or civic certainties.

Paradoxically, therefore, *Yirat Shamayim* requires a measure of autonomy. Subservience is not enough because the trustworthiness of the *Yire Shamayim* and the integrity of that person is reflected in his/her conscience, in his/her ability to decide what circumstances demand, and in the exercise of responsibility where it would be wrong to hide beyond societal conditions or mores. The *Yire Shamayim* is accountable to the community in which God is served, but s/he is also accountable when wrongdoing is perpetrated by the community and its leaders.

> It is not written (Psalms:118:4), the House of the fearers of the Lord but those who fear the Lord.[21]

---

20. Nachmanides, Commentary on the Torah to Deut. 6:18.
21. *Numbers Rabbah,* 8. Here, this is said in praise of proselytes (who, of course, have left their communities).

Rabbi Abba examines this principle through the case of Obadiah, a prophet who lived in the Kingdom of Israel during the reign of King Ahab and Queen Jezebel:

> What is said of Obadiah is more than what is said of Abraham. For of Abraham it is not written that he feared God very much but of Obadiah it is so written. Said R. Yizhak, And why did Obadiah deserve the gift of prophecy? Because he hid one hundred prophets in the cave, as it is said, 'For it was, when Jezebel cut off the prophets of the Lord, that Obadiah took a hundred prophets and hid them fifty to a cave, and fed them with bread and water.'(I Kings 18:4)
>
> And why was Obadiah sent to prophesy to Edom? Said R. Yizhak: The Holy One, blessed be He said, let Obadiah who dwelt between two wicked people (Ahab and Jezebel) and did not learn from their deeds, prophesy against Esau who dwelt among two righteous people (Isaac and Rebecca) and did not learn from their deeds.
>
> *Sanhedrin* 39b

Obadiah is rewarded for not accepting authority when it is illicit. The fearer of God speaks the truth [22] and acts truthfully and does not act arbitrarily, even if others do. Rather, s/he is responsible towards others, towards the world, and his/her self-discernment. S/he flees from actions that, at the expense of others, constitute a service of the self, whether that self is personal or collective.

> And (Pharaoh) said to the (midwives), When you deliver the Hebrew women ... if the child is male, you shall kill it and if female, you shall let it live. But the midwives feared God and did not do as the king of Egypt spoke to them, and they let the children live. [23]
>
> Exodus 1:17

A fearer of God does not obey arbitrary authority. Conversely, those in authority may not do whatever they want, cannot act arbitrarily. Avimelech, in indignantly refuting Abraham's suspicion that "there is no fear of God in this place" seems to be saying to him: the fact that I have power doesn't mean that I can do anything, that I can be unjust. For I recognize the power of God and His standards of justice oblige me.[24] Hence the rabbinic warning:

22. In the morning prayer, the first passage read after the initial blessings is one from *Tanna Debe Eliyahu*, "A person should always be a fearer of God in secret, admit to the truth and speak the truth in his heart."
23. The idea of civil disobedience emerges more forcefully from this passage if we conjecture that the midwives are themselves Egyptians, as suggested by Cassuto, not Hebrews. See Umberto Cassuto, *A Commentary on the Book of Exodus,* 3rd ed. (Jerusalem: Magnes Press, Hebrew University, 1959), p. 5. There Cassuto places the instructions to the midwives in the category of secret directives issued by Pharaoh to diminish the Israelites before he went public with his malicious plans.
24. On this, see Robert Alter, "Sodom as Nexus; the Web of Design in Biblical Narrative," *Tikkun* 1, no. 1, pp. 30-38. There he discusses Abraham's image of Gentile cities and his learning to distinguish between cities in which there is fear of God and those that lack it.

Fear not a politician or a ruler but fear one who has no fear of Heaven.[25]

Hesed and the Virtuous Person

The fear of Heaven is thus closely related to the concept of *hesed*, of acts of loving-kindness, whether performed by Jews or non-Jews.[26] The one who does deeds of love and kindness, who also invites occasions for such deeds, is a fearer of God. The sages, remarking on the converse, state,

> When one raises a vicious dog in his house, *hesed* leaves his house and that person shakes off *Yirat Shamayim*.[27]

The reason for *hesed* leaving the house is that no poor person will approach it for help and the person who raises such a dog cannot be identified with moral and spiritual reliability. Such a person will be judgmental and cruel even when formally right, in contradistinction to those who "fear God in giving judgement and (who) seek compromises."[28]

The following Talmudic exchange examines the relationships between *hesed* (loving-kindness) and *Yirat Shamayim*, and concludes that fear of Heaven refers to a certain type of person rather than merely to certain responses or actions.

> R. Elazar said, "Every person who does righteousness and justice (*zedkah* and *mishpat*), it is as if he/she filled the entire world with loving-kindness *(hesed)*, for it is said, 'He loves *zedakah* and *mishpat*, the earth is full of the loving-kindness of the Lord.' (Psalms 33:5) Lest you say that everyone who 'wishes to leap can do so' (i.e., that every person is given the opportunity to perform genuine *hesed*), Scripture teaches us, 'How precious (i.e., scarce) is Thy loving-kindness, O Lord' (Psalms 36:8). One might think that this applies to a fearer of Heaven as well (i.e., that s/he is also not enabled to do *zedakah* and *mishpat*, thus filling the world with *hesed*) yet Scripture teaches us: 'But the loving-kindness of the Lord is from everlasting to everlasting upon them that fear Him.'" (Psalms 108:17)

25. *Pirkai d'Rabbi Eliezer*, 37. In his commentary to the Torah, *Ha'amek Davar*, R. Naftali Zvi Yehudah Berlin, dealing with the verse, "And now, Israel, what does the Lord your God ask of you but ..." (Deut. 10:12) develops the organic social conception that this and the following verse, that seem to demand everything, are actually addressed to different sections of the community. *Yirat Shamayim* is particularly demanded of the leaders of the community, who deal with public needs, are vulnerable to self-deception, bribery, and a sense of self-importance that may corrupt them. They, especially, have to keep the fear of Heaven constantly in mind.

26. On Maimonides's distinction between the Abrahamic ("universal") versus the Mosaic ("national") community in this regard, see Lawrence Kaplan, "Maimonides on the Singularity of the Jewish People," *Daat* 15, pp. v–xxvii

27. *Shabbat* 63a. Rashi comments that such a person in fact does not allow poor people to come to his door for aid.

28. *Mekhilta, Mesekhta D'Amalek*, on Exodus 18:21.

Said R. Hama bar Papa, "Each person who is endowed with grace *(hen)* is without doubt a God-fearing person, as it is written, 'But the loving-kindness of the Lord is from everlasting to everlasting upon them that fear Him.'"

Sukkah 49b

At this point in our discussion, Amir noted that God's loving-kind-ness is apparently synonymous with human acts of *hesed,* so that divine loving-kindness being "perpetually upon those that fear Him" is simply a description of an ideal character. Quite clearly, Amir declared, the discussion is not about God's loving-kindness to human beings, but about their ability to perform acts of *hesed.* This comment called forth heated responses from Nehemyah, who declared that R. Hama bar Papa's comment makes it crystal clear that we are to understand the verses to teach that human beings cannot do acts of *hesed* without *siyata deshmaya,* without God's help. M., fearing that the forum was on the verge of war or walkouts, asked the five participants to simply note the similarity between the Talmudic idea, that only a certain kind of person can be expected to have the opportunity to do loving and just actions in a way that indeed fills the world with *hesed,* to the passage from Aristotle's *Nicomachean Ethics* that also states that only the acts of justice done by a just person can truly be termed just.[29] It appears, said M., that we are dealing, here too, with a full blown character ideal. It describes a person who may be conceived as a model, or, in the terms of our discussion, the ideal educator.

And so, it was agreed that our study was bringing us to the con-tours of a comprehensive conception of personality and virtue. In stating what we had learned of the ideal in a manner that might make it a formative ideal for diversely believing educators, we had to proceed with our ever-dangerous but vital partial translation. The *Yire Shamayim,* we could now state, is committed to a normative sys-tem, is restrained and sees virtue in self-limitation. At the same time s/he is not a conformist, but an individually responsible person. Such a person is devoid of hubris and yet endowed with spiritual author-ity. S/he is a person who can be trusted by other people. In pristine religious terms we note that only such a person is completely trusted by God. "The secret things of God (He will only reveal) to those who fear Him."(Psalms 25:14)[30]

And yet we reminded ourselves not to lose sight of the converse disposition of the *Yire Shamayim,* one that also flows directly from what we have called the sense of Presence. We recalled from the

---

29. Aristotle, *Nichomachean Ethics,* Book 2:4.
30. Compare the *midrashic* description of the punishment meted out to the angels for revealing to Lot that they were about to destroy the wicked city of Sodom (*Gene-sis Rabbah* 3:9) with God's informing Abraham of what He intended to do, i.e., destroy the wicked cities of the Jordan plain. (Genesis 17:19).

deathbed scene of Rabban Yohanan ben Zakkai how the sense of Presence evoked the fear of retribution in him. We noted that the sense of Presence instills reverence and makes the fearer of God carefully observe the commandments and accept their hierarchy of value. In this mode, Presence points to the puny, the dependent, the creaturely dimension of human existence. This, we found in several texts, goes even beyond the dread expressed by Rabban Yohanan in the moments before his death; "creatureliness" or trust *(bitahon)* is an ultimate acceptance of what others might consider the unjust slings of fortune, and it expects no reward, at least in this world, for virtue.

> The Holy One, blessed be He, said to him (Moses): In this world I shall not show you the rewards of those who fear Me, but only in the world to come.[31]

The *Yire Shamayim* is thus a person who can deal with sorrow, almost stoically, for s/he places it in the same perspective as worldly achievements and riches. Thus, King David, man of action and far removed from ascetic postures of piety, could inform his courtiers that inordinate mourning for his dead son was wrong: "I shall go to him and he shall not come back to me."[32] The one who fears God learns, sometimes through bitter experience, to be concerned only with his or her response to circumstances and not with the question whether the circumstances themselves seem just or even comprehensible.

Thomas Mann has well captured this aspect of *Yirat Shamayim* in his novel, *The Tales of Jacob,* specifically in his description of Jacob's response to the death of his beloved Rachel. In the hours of her death as Benjamin struggles to be born, he asks: "Lord, what dost Thou?" And the narrator comments:

> To such questions there is no answer. Yet it is the glory of the human spirit that in this silence it does not depart from God, but rather learns to grasp the majesty of the ungraspable and to thrive thereon. Beside him the Chaldean women and slaves chanted their litanies and invocations, thinking to bind to human wishes the unreasoning powers. But Jacob had never yet so clearly understood as in this hour, why all that was false and why Abram had left Ur to escape it.[33]

That this sense of creatureliness, resignation, and trust is in genuine tension with responsibility, reliability, and trustworthiness is perhaps nowhere more blatant than in Abraham's readiness to sacrifice his son. It is for this readiness, we have seen, that he is called "a fearer of the Lord." And yet, Daniel asked, doesn't it cast doubt

---

31. *Tanhuma Ki Tisa* 27.
32. Samuel II 12:23. It is significant that David is not obsessed with self-centered guilt and immediately goes to comfort his wife, Bat-Sheva. (v. 24)
33. Thomas Mann, *Joseph and His Brothers,* vol. I, *The Tales of Jacob* (London: Sphere Books, 1968), p. 316.

on Abraham's character? Is this the way a father acts, or for that matter, any person who "fills the world with *hesed*?" For the Danish Christian theologian, Soren Kierkegaard, who enthusiastically endorses Abraham as "a knight of faith," the paradox is only apparent, for the moral dimension of commitment is more of a stumbling block to fear of Heaven than a crucial element of it.[34] But in the Jewish tradition, this distinction cannot be made, for *Yirat Shamayim* is a moral as well as a religious ideal and, in fact, this distinction is in itself problematic. Daniel mentioned that the *midrash* itself poses the problem in a straightforward manner, by having Satan say to Abraham: "Today he tells you to sacrifice your son and tomorrow he will call you a murderer."[35] You seem, Satan suggests, to have been untrustworthy, not reliable. Abraham's dilemma is that the source of reliability is also that which tested him.

Esther responded that indeed, in some situations, *Yirat Shamayim* creates weighty problems. But that did not permit dismissing or even suspending it. In a sense, what made the binding of Isaac a litmus test of fear was that it was utterly devoid of reward or even humanly understandable sense. Carmela agreed. She often, in her classes, compared Abraham's situation to the tragic dilemma of a father who, as commander of an Israeli military unit, had faced the horrific situation of sending a soldier on a mission from which he would almost certainly not return. The commanding officer discovered shortly after issuing the order that the volunteer was his own son, who happened to be on hand at the front when the task had to be assigned. Since the mission was still some hours in the future, he had the possibility of finding an excuse to release his son and sending someone else instead. Was he a bad father by making the agonizing decision not to exploit that possibility and thereby sending another mother's and father's son?

Esther was not comfortable with Carmela's example, and returned to the case of Abraham. To Daniel she remarked that God's command to Abraham is not a norm but a test. The ideal is that responsibility, creatureliness, and obedience blend together to soften the hues of human existence and of human relationships. As we have seen, David, the monarch, discusses the nature of human existence with his courtiers; Rabban Yohanan ben Zakkai, the master, admits to the fears attendant on mortality. If, in the case of Abraham, the fear of God appears harsh, it may be because one element in a complex character ideal is here so starkly dominant. But that, states the

34. Soren Kierkegaard, *Fear and Trembling* (Garden City, N.Y.: Doubleday-Anchor, 1941 and Princeton, N.J.: Princeton University Press, 1954), pp. 39-132.

35. *Tanhuma, Vayera* 22. For various understandings of this trial in philosophical and exegetic writings see, Nehama Leibowitz, *Studies in the Book of Genesis,* (Jerusalem: World Zionist Organization, Department for Torah Education and Culture, 1972) pp. 188-206.

midrash, is what God's purposes required, that one time. It was not a rule; it was only a trial.[36]

We summed up our study by agreeing that *Yirat Shamayim*, as a normative ideal, is many things. It would be a distortion to see it as only self-control or individuality or responsibility. For self-control alone as a habit is loveless, suspicious of individual authenticity; non-conformism can become cynical and lazy. And responsibility, if untempered, may turn into dangerous conceit.

Yirat Shamayim:
Representing a Morally Reliable World

The composite of the character ideal we have been considering is of a human being who, because of his or her being and acting within the world, makes the world seem more reliable, kinder, and hopeful. A *Yire Shamayim* is one whom one dares to approach without fear that something frightening about the world will be learned or re-learned in the encounter. S/he is a focus of trustworthiness. This goes together with a certain realization on the part of those who come into contact with him/her that, without such people and their way in the world that testify to what God asks of human beings the world would be rather grim. As for the fearers of God, they perceive themselves as striving to carry out this character ideal not because they fear punishment, but for fear of letting down God, and failure to demonstrate what the human world can be and would become if human beings were to serve God. Such fearers of the Lord look for fellow subjects of God's kingdom where they are to be found but are prepared for loneliness, animosity, and deprivation. The *Yire Shamayim* expects no reward in this world and sometimes becomes uneasy when he finds life treating him or her too well.[37] He or she is a person for all seasons.[38]

36. *Genesis Rabbah* 55:1
37. According to the opinion that the wicked are rewarded for their (few) good deeds in this world and the reward of the righteous is in the world-to-come. This view is picturesquely described by R. Elazar, son of R. Zadok (*Kedushin* 40b). Urbach points out, however, that such views were in a state of tension with those that did anticipate this worldly reward for good deeds (*The Sages,* pp. 384–92). In this post-Holocaust generation, it seems especially appropriate to adopt the former view, just as in the Hadrianic generation, with its martyrs, the view of Rabbi Akiva became widespread that suffering should not be seen as punishment but as arising in situations which demand the response of love "with all your soul." On this, see Urbach, *The Sages,* pp. 391-92.
38. A *midrash* (*Numbers Rabbah* 22:1) on the verse 'The Lord your God ye shall fear' (Deut. 6:13) comments: Be like those who are called fearers of God—Abraham, Job and Joseph. The *midrash* connects this to the verse in Jeremiah 4:2: "And (if) you

Conversely, where there is no fear of Heaven the world is handed over to forces and people who make one distrust and fear it. Encountering such people is to come face-to-face with the human world's potential for chaos, meaninglessness, and evil. Just as the *Yire Shamayim* is someone to depend on, someone who testifies to what being here should be, the person who lacks *Yirat Shamayim* can never be trusted. Even his or her occasional and arbitrary acts of justice fail to bring loving-kindness, *hesed,* into the world. Persons like that, or nations that fall into their clutches, spell out the worst possibilities of existence; one realizes that they take joy in disillusioning the trustful and in undermining hope; and they make their point by being cruel, destructive, and bestial.

> Remember what Amalek did to you by the way as you came out of Egypt. How he met you by the way, and smote the hindmost of you, all those in the rear who were weak, when you were faint and weary. And he did not fear God (Deut. 25:17).

From Amalek to Hitler, those who do not fear God work hard, ideologically and practically, to have that established as natural and inevitable. One should never rely upon them even, perhaps especially, when they seem "all right" or surprisingly nice.

We have worked at drawing a character ideal from sources on *Yirat Shamayim,* but throughout our discussions we have been translating, by bracketing, often implicitly, the religious dimensions of the ideal. This made Nehemyah, Esther, and sometimes even Daniel uncomfortable. They declared that it is a distortion of the fear of Heaven ideal to conclude that, in the tradition of Judaism, the texts we have considered can be summed up as moral reliability, existential courage, and loving relationship. Nehemyah and Esther especially oppose the use of expressions such as Presence of God to allude to mere humility or even existential anxiety. For religious Jews, they insist, the bottom line that is always in the background is the religious character of the ideal; the *Yire Shamayim* is one who makes the world

---

shall swear 'as the Lord liveth' (i.e., by His name and not by the name of idols) in truth, in justice and in righteousness, then shall the nations bless themselves by Him, and in Him shall they glory.' The *midrash,* like the Talmudic passage (*Sukkah* 49b) discussed above, interprets this to mean that those who do not have these qualities—of truth, justice, and righteousness, may not swear by God's name. R. Naftali Zvi Berlin, in his already referred to Biblical commentary *Ha'amek Davar,* states in this context that "the truth is fear of God that stands firm and will not waver with the change of times ... from bad (times) to good (times) or the reverse. And this is like Abraham, Job, and Joseph, who in every change of situation (lit., 'time') maintained their fear of God (Deut. 10:20). It should be noted that of three, Job is generally considered to have been a Gentile.

more reliable and trustworthy within the parameters of the Torah and its commandments and through them. And though the non-Jew is not obligated by the commandments of Judaism, the ideal here, too, remains a religious one: s/he is bound by the seven *Noahide* commandments.[39] Whether Jew or Gentile, the *Yire Shamayim* is in a very actual sense, in the Presence of God and in His service.

Nevertheless, Esther agrees, and Daniel emphatically so, that partial translation from religious and normative categories to moral-philosophical ones is necessary for there to be educational conversation among Jewish educators of various convictions who desire some common spiritual and cultural identity. Daniel, particularly, is easily persuaded that such a conversation raises the possibility of at least a limited reappropriation of traditional concepts by those who feel uneasy about them and have rebelled against them. Such a partial reappropriation, he agrees, may enable non-religious educators to help pupils acquire a sense of ownership of such concepts and of the texts which present them. Even Esther concedes that in the kind of discussion we have been having religious educators must refrain from using their convictions as slogans, and that they must endeavor to be communicative and plausible. M. insisted that the religious educators in the group also consider what such a translation can do for them in constructing their own theory of moral education. Nehemya, on both counts, remained unconvinced.

Without a doubt, Carmela has felt most comfortable with the proceedings. She has always believed that Judaism will be restored to its rightful state as a living civilization only after being translated from its former religious vocabulary and context into a contemporary cultural and moral one.

It is her position that troubles Nehemyah most. His critique is that such translation is reductionistic. It converts, he says, religious teachings into ethical ideas, claiming that that is what the texts really mean. Its thrust is to make the inherent religious teaching redundant, a mere historical curiosity.

Esther, during the conversation and study session, has often reminded Carmela and Amir that the texts of our tradition do indeed have the power to suggest educational-philosophical guidelines, but that they, like all scriptural and rabbinic writings, are religious in character. Amir, perhaps surprisingly, has expressed sympathy for this viewpoint. He has argued that unless the texts are seen in their forthrightly religious framework, the secular educator will lose his or her unique perspective. If that happens, the radically secular educa-

---

39. Maimonides, *Mishneh Torah, Hilkhot Melachim* (Laws of Kings), 8:11, where he rules that only one who accepts these laws because they are revealed is called a pious and wise person.

tor will forget how removed s/he is from the tradition, even when s/he seeks to understand it and perhaps even to learn from it.

Additional Comments by M.

What may we hope our partial translation to have achieved thus far? In terms of the educational-philosophical concepts of principle and ideal which we have been using, we may suppose that, in a rather abstract manner, considerable consensus about ideals has been discovered. All of our discussants can agree that an educated Jew will not be arbitrary and should be accountable. Amir cringes at at the word obedience, preferring strength of character and discipline, but he can tolerate "creatureliness" if it is understood as unabashed being-in-the-world. And the character-ideal of justice and *hesed* as well as disdain for hubris is certainly congenial to all. The ideal of the reflective and responsible person who has a hierarchy of values and who is therefore not carried away by what is trivial and undeserving of ultimate concern is not very controversial. We also find much agreement about the importance of membership in community, membership that yet does not infer evasion of personal accountability. Nehemyah, though, cannot conceive of such dichotomies ever applying to any but sinful (i.e., not his) communities. The ideal of an educated Jew who will make the world a more congenial place through kindness and trustworthiness and who can be counted on to combat the forces of deceit and evil is undisputed.

Thus far, our forum has enjoyed studying texts, moving within them. Nehemyah, Esther, Daniel, Carmela, and Amir feel more comfortable now with one another than they did and they have learned to see texts differently, as educators.

At times, nevertheless, our negotiation has seemed to degenerate into a political negotiation, yielding no more than moral platitudes. Therefore, we have often had to forcefully forgo congeniality to confront significant and deep-seated controversies.

Amir was frequently impatient with the entire process. He was not convinced of the need to mediate between the contemporary consciousness and the tradition through "translation." His vision of the educated Jew patently does not include an a-priori commitment to a language: to texts, traditions, and sanctified terms. Also, Nehemyah and Esther have insisted, in contradistinction even to Daniel, that the ideal of the educated Jew must be located within the parameters of the *halakhah*. For them, obedience, self-control and Presence are very concrete, given to specific formulation, visible within clearly structured and authoritative communities. In the final analysis, the ideal of *Yirat Shamayim* for them refers to a cluster of norms and what is generated by the halakhic dynamic around them. These norms may be made congenial to educational theoretical discussions by partial translation into a cultural character ideal, but the life-style and world view they teach do not depend on such translation for their very existence, as they do for Carmela. After all, Nehemyah and Esther believe that the power of Jewish teaching comes from texts and exemplary teachers, from commandments and faithful representatives of the ideal community.

And so, while we have learned to talk and even to study together, our agreement about operative ideals remains limited. Nevertheless we have discovered that it is possible, through studying and talking together, to argue coherently about a Jewish character ideal that can be examined through—and perhaps partially rooted in—the world of *Yirat Shamayim.*

But what about that world itself? Can there be a character-ideal that ignores the philosophical context of *Yirat Shamayim*, of the grim, theologically charged reality of human existence that underlies it? What can Amir, who articulately doesn't believe in that world picture do with it? Can even Esther, in whose school there are music appreciation classes and a high level of achievement in the sciences, be comfortable with it?

In our final sessions, we considered the belief structure, the principled world of *Yirat Shamayim.*

8

LOOK AT IT THIS WAY:
A *MIDRASH*
ON *YIRAT SHAMAYIM*

Translating from Theology into Philosophical Principle

*A*s we have seen, our group was able to sketch out a character ideal on the basis of texts and traditions of *Yirat Shamayim*. But we realized that commonality would become more elusive as we moved to an attempt at understanding the world of religious faith in which this character-ideal arises, and which nourishes it. Our original *midrashic* tale on *Yirat Shamayim* and its stark portrait of the hapless human soul seemed especially unpalatable to modern Jewish educators. Yet our study sessions indicated that that story, while undoubtedly blunt and disturbing, seemed well to point to the world view in which *Yirat Shamayim* as a character ideal is at home. Therefore, we thought it appropriate to examine whether, in conjunction with other relevant sources, we could understand it in a way that enhances Jewish education on a philosophical level.

Amir, not for the first time, registered reservations. He considered it farfetched to "tendentiously defend" an ancient folktale. The other roundtable discussants disagreed. They insisted that the story seemed to represent something that is inherent in the tradition, and that it ought to be examined. Amir, with his usual patience and good humor, consented to put his objections on hold.

Our *midrash,* we recall, has a view of reality that puts almost everything in the hands of Heaven. Like so many sources on fear of Heaven, the world into which we are placed by this tale is harsh, and the prospects are uncertain at best, often grim. God alone rules, in all His inscrutability, and we are here only to demonstrate our willingness to be ruled. God is all majesty but our existence is pathetically confined and determined. Who today, we have already asked, can consider that a platform for education? Even those whose principled world is one in which there is a Creator to whom we are responsible, and who reserves the right of retribution, are unlikely to believe that. And yet, if the ideal of *Yirat Shamayim* is actually anchored in that world, might not our two secular educators argue (and even two of our religious educators suspect) that *Yirat Shamayim* is indeed superfluous as a character ideal, that it belongs to a different world? (Amir has already said that!)

Here, at the beginning of our philosophical discussion on *Yirat Shamayim,* M. suggested that we have another look at Maimonides's "Introduction to *Perek Helek"* a text that we had come across in our study (Chapter Three). There we found the Rambam criticizing and even denouncing those who understand the words of the sages literally, whether in blind acceptance or in rebellious rejection. Wise people, he states, seek to fathom the exceedingly profound truths that lie in their words.

> They know that the sages did not speak nonsense, and it is clear to them that the words of the sages contain both an obvious and a hidden meaning.

Moreover, continues Maimonides,

> It is often difficult for us to interpret words and to educe their true meaning from the form in which they are contained so that their inner meaning conforms to reason and corresponds to truth.
>
> This is the case even with Holy Scriptures. The sages themselves interpreted Scriptural passages in such a way as to educe their inner meaning from literal sense, correctly considering these passages to be figures of speech just as we do.
>
> "Introduction to *Perek Helek"*

What is Maimonides doing here? He is insisting that just as the sages interpreted scripture, so must we interpret the sages. Moreover we are to do so in a manner that conforms to reason and corresponds with truth. In other words, he envisions the ideal Jew to be both loyal to the principles of tradition and to the commandments of the Torah and, at the same time, to understand and formulate them in a manner that educes their true meaning.

In terms suggested by Rawidowicz and already alluded to above,[1] Maimonides is responding to his sense of being alienated from the

---

1. Simon Rawidowicz, "On Interpretation," p. 47. Rawidowicz himself speaks of

received meaning of tradition against the backdrop of his absolute loyalty to that tradition. He here embarks upon interpretation of the tradition in order to maintain its accessibility. He is required to make it accessible for he, as a Jew and teacher-leader, sees himself commanded to live by the truth that is the Torah, and to give proper instruction in it. But this truth must be seen in a plausible manner before it can be maturely believed, practiced, and taught. However, he believes that it can be seen that way on the basis of faith in it.

M. pointed out that, in having recourse to Rawidowicz, we are applying to Maimonides the rule that he applied to the sages, who, in turn he tells us, applied it to scripture. We learn from him, even though that he did not necessarily read himself that way, that a faithful orientation to the text that demands response involves asking two questions, one *aggadic* and one *halakhic:* (a) How can we understand this text so that we may continue to learn from it? and (b) How can we read this text so that the prescriptions it makes, which claim to obligate us a-priori, will continue to do so effectively?

Answering such questions requires that we translate from the language of tradition to another idiom that will make it comprehensible to us. But this translation, as we have already said, must be a partial one. Otherwise, we shall simply be reductionistic, making the text say whatever we want it to. Were we to do that, we would in effect be making it redundant for it would merely tell us what we already know anyway. Partial translation makes it possible for us to speak about the text in our own *literature* even while asking that it speak to us in its own *language.*

We now return to our *midrash.*

M.'s Lecture on *Yirat Shamayim* and Situation

In the *midrash* with which we began our discussions, as we have seen, the notion of *Yirat Shamayim* (which we have already partially translated into a moral-existential ideal of the educated Jew) is anchored in a deterministic principle according to which the human being is thrown into a world against his/her will. We may at least suspect that without what that principle points to the scriptural and rabbinic conception of fear will be both impoverished and distorted. We have already noted that an educational ideal that combines *Yirat Shamayim* with aspirations for worldly achievement, on the assumption that such achievement is good in itself, is likely to introduce

Maimonides as one of Judaism's greatest interpreters, of those who neither accept the tradition literally nor reject it due to a literal understanding of it. (pp. 61-64)

changes into the ideal. It will make fear of Heaven seem relevant only to the religious side of curriculum.

How may we understand the principled world of our *midrash* in a way that does not impoverish and/or distort it?

Let us look again at the reality it portrays. We may summarize it as follows: human existence in this world is necessary for human self-actualization. Self-actualization is defined as resisting the temptation to be wicked, and this is the only world in which human beings can be either righteous or wicked. Yet, this existence is confining, for the conception of self-actualization is narrowly normative and human existence is coerced.

There seems to be some justice in Amir's earlier comment that this story portrays not only a principle but a particular social environment. Yet Amir apparently assumes that the value of the principle is completely dependent on the form of the narrative, or in other words that religious and theological world views cannot be seriously considered as true because they are conveyed in such peculiar (to him) stories. But that is a world view too. It, too, like other world views, may legitimately be questioned. And a good method for questioning it is to see whether there are ways of at least partially expressing that principle from within another literary framework and social context without destroying its pristine meaning.

I should like to suggest that there are such ways and I shall give one example that might help us to see the world of *Yirat Shamayim* more clearly and in a way that might make it more useful for Jewish education. The way of looking at it I am proposing may permit us to learn from our *midrash* without taking on the social world of the narrator. It is one suggested to me by categories and conceptions used by the contemporary Jewish thinker Emil L. Fackenheim in his early essay, *Metaphysics and Historicity*. In this work, Fackenheim examines the concept of historicity as it is employed by some modern thinkers, especially existentialist ones. These thinkers have posited that human being is a self-making or self-constituting process. While analyzing these thinkers' conceptions of historicity and human self-making, he describes and develops the concept of "situation" as it is used in modern, again, specifically existentialistic thinkers.[2]

Our sense of situation is understood to refer to our awareness that we are finite beings. We are limited in manifold ways by the world into which we have been thrown without our consent or knowledge and which we are destined to leave, also without our consent. But the situ-

---

2. Emil L. Fackenheim, *Metaphysics and Historicity* (Milwaukee: Marquette University Press, 1961).

ation in which we find ourselves seems to demand something of us and even to somehow define and challenge us.

In more detached terms: to say that we are situated means that we are in a framework that is other than we, that confines us. At the same time, this situation also enters into the fabric of human life, thereby losing some of its otherness.[3] Situation is not only a space and time in which we exist, but it is something that we partially take ownership of by using the opportunities it places before us and by understanding ourselves as constituted by these contexts and opportunities. Thus, for example, we may to some extent conquer space, and we try to make good use of our time. Indeed, being the people we are, in modernity, we seem to have no choice about that.

Fackenheim distinguishes between three kinds of situations in which we find ourselves, which we cannot escape without ceasing to be, for they are the ground on which we exist; they situate us. He calls them the natural, the historical, and the human situations. I shall try to partially describe them, to comment on them, and to expand upon them for the purpose of partial philosophic translation of our *Midrash Tanhuma's* world of *Yirat Shamayim.*

The natural situation sets my location and confinement within the world as a human being with a body that is placed in an environment. I did not choose my body and did not program its functioning. Because of my natural situation, I am a mammal and Homo sapien. This situation, of being the kind of creature that I am, on this planet, with these genes, makes it possible for me to develop and to express myself in certain ways but essentially it limits me; I cannot be someone else, I cannot escape age and deterioration and death.[4] With regard to this situation I am free only to the extent that I accept it.[5] Being a biological organism, I must eat, expel waste products, face the natural dangers which cause disease and injury, grow old (perhaps) and die (certainly). I can live only within a certain range of temperature, can train myself to stand on my head only for a very limited time; I require the atmosphere of the earth in order to breathe.

If one looks for references to Fackenheim's "natural situation" in the Bible, the story of Adam and Eve immediately comes to mind. They ate of the Tree of Knowledge. In Heaven, we are told, it was feared that they would stretch out their hands to the Tree of Life,

---

3. *Ibid.,* p. 45. Martin Buber and Karl Jaspers are among the existentialist thinkers who have carefully examined the concept of situation as it is here developed by Fackenheim.

4. I can, of course, escape these by commiting suicide, but in doing that, I not only end my confinement to situation but my earthly being and self-making.

5. Fackenheim, *Metaphysics and Historicity,* p. 53.

which would grant them immortality. And so, God, the creator of the world, or, we might say, the author of the natural situation, expelled them. Eating of the Tree of Life would have made them more than human. But that is impossible, a contradiction in terms. Humans cannot escape death or any aspect of the situation in which they have been placed. Only God is beyond situation; "He is The Place of the world but the world is not His place."[6] Man cannot become God. The Bible mocks persons who think they are beyond the natural situation, who think they are divine. Pharaoh is a midrashic laughingstock because he attended to the call of nature in the Nile so that his servants would consider him more than human. God put him in his human place by turning the Nile to blood.[7]

Yet this is no laughing matter. Idolatry, on a fundamental level, is rooted in the urge and desire to conquer or to be above the natural situation. O'Brian, the inquisitor, torturer, and re-educator in George Orwell's fascinatingly horrendous novel, *1984*, thinks that he could touch the stars if he decided that he wanted to, even as he thinks that the meaning of his existence is in his ability to torture human beings just for the sake of torturing and destroying them.[8]

Fackenheim terms the second realm in which we exist "the historical situation," the framework of culture, history, and human action, my own and that of others. This situation also places and confines me. I live in a certain epoch and cannot leave it. I am not only a no-longer-young male Homo sapien, but also, a twentieth-century person. I am tied to particular cultural mores and assumptions and can explore others that are currently available only because the circumstances of my situation permit this. (In the twentieth century, one can explore more than in most historical situations, and this is especially true for people in professions who can afford—or get bank credit for—plane tickets.)

Every historical situation creates its unique opportunities but also signifies lost ones. In the words of Fackenheim, "Mozart has created possibilities of experience which but for his work would not exist. And citizenship in a Greek city-state is a possibility lost to men of this century."[9] Being in a historical situation means that I cannot, without taking leave of my sanity, overcome my inability to enjoy twenty-second-century music, just as a seventeenth-century person cannot claim that it is unfair having to live before Mozart. I am the child of a particular set of parents who give birth to me in a particular coun-

6. *Genesis Rabbah* 68:8
7. *Exodus Rabbah* 9:8.
8. George Orwell, *1984* (New York: Signet Classic, 1949), part III. Compare Isaiah 14, on the hubris of Nebuchadnezzar: "You said in your heart, I will ascend into Heaven, above the stars of God will I exalt my house ... Yet you shall be brought down to the netherworld, to the uttermost parts of the pit ..." (v. 13, 15).
9. Fackenheim, *Metaphysics and Historicity*, p. 51.

try at a particular time and educated me by the lights of their cultural values. I can rebel against all that, or simply try to ignore it, but even the opportunity to engage in that particular rebellion or to cultivate studied indifference is part of my situation.

The historical situation not only constricts me but accords me opportunities for self-making. Because of my natural situation, I must eventually die, but medical technology may cure my illnesses and postpone my death. The particular historical situation in which we find ourselves gives us, as Rabbi J.B. Soloveitchik has noted, a community of dignity and majesty:

> Man of old who could not fight disease and succumbed in multitudes to yellow fever or any other plague with degrading helplessness could not lay claim to dignity. Only the man who builds hospitals, discovers therapeutic techniques and saves lives is blessed with dignity. Man of the 17th and 18th centuries who needed several days to travel from Boston and New York was less dignified than modern man who attempts to conquer space, boards a plane at the New York Airport at midnight and takes several hours later a leisurely walk along the streets of London.[10]

Of course, when Soloveitchik wrote, it was not yet so obvious that human activity in the historical situation designed for maximal conquest of the natural situation is problematic and often self-defeating. Even a partial and apparent overcoming of the natural situation exacts a heavy ecological price. Our historical situation, because of our self-making within it, leaves us thick deposits of pollution, toxic wastes, slimy rivers, a plundered planet. There is a limit to what can be done within the confines of a situation, and it cannot be transcended. When the early people of Babel tried to reach Heaven by building a tower, God confounded their tongues. Human beings can build skyscrapers but they cannot reach Heaven, at least not that way.

In theological terms, we may say that when humans are allowed to influence the natural situation or to somehow bypass it, God has miraculously given them that power. When God Himself disrupts His order for persons, we call it a miracle. For example, to save Israel, He turned sea into dry land. As for the historical situation, the miraculous act of redemption occurs when God works within the historical situation that we normally ascribe to cumulative human effort. When we religiously experience great events we are reminded that human beings do not make their situations but are located within them. In the language of the Jewish tradition: it is He who brought us out of Egypt, extended His Providence over us in the desert, protecting us with earthly and heavenly tabernacles;[11] He

10. Joseph B. Soloveitchik, *The Lonely Man of Faith* (New York: Doubleday, 1992), p. 17.
11. According to the view of Rabbi Eliezer, the tabernacles with which God provided Israel in the desert were clouds of glory; Rabbi Akiva says that the reference is to

gave us Eretz Yisrael, expelled us from our land, and accompanied us throughout our exile.

To the extent that we understand Torah as our historical culture, we may also say that he gave us not only the framework of our historical situation, i.e., what happens in history, for he is King and gives power to whom He wills, but its fundamental cultural contents. But, since we have free will and therefore are partners in the making of our history, the historical situation allows for much human self-making within it, so much so that it sometimes appears that God has nothing to do with it at all. Only when one recalls that we are situated by our historically conditioned culture, that it is a situation, does the theological imagery of God judging history come to mind. He is not only the creator of the natural situation but also the Ruler of the historical world and the Judge of human activity within the historical situation.[12]

What Fackenheim terms "the human situation" derives from a person's understanding of "the natural and historical situations … radically, as specific manifestations of a universal condition. And this leads to a new insight."

> A person discovers his natural situation when he comes upon such individual limits as his lost childhood, a disease which afflicts him, or the frailties of old age. He discovers his human situation when he sees, in the foundering attempt at radical self-transcendence, that temporality and mortality are universally part of the human lot. Again, a person discovers his historical situation when he faces up, say, to the unique historical limitations and opportunities of the nuclear age. He comes upon his human situation when he recognizes that all history is a conjunction of compulsion and freedom, and that to be subject to the one and to be challenged to realize the other is universally part of the human condition.[13]

As a result of this philosophic understanding, I come to realize that I must decide how to respond to the situations in which I find myself. I recognize that neither I nor any human being *qua* human being made the situation, that it cannot in principle be overcome. I must decide, like all human beings must, what to do in it and how to relate to that or Him that situates me. This situation philosophically points to what religious life offers as a framework for choice within the human situation–the world of the divine commandments, to be accepted or rejected. And I am at liberty to educate towards this. For

---

actual booths the Israelites built. (*Sukkah* 11b and *Sifra* 207). The controversy may be viewed as dealing with the degree of human activity and "selfmaking" in the historical situation. See Nehama Leibowitz, *Studies in Leviticus (Vayikra)*, pp. 232–38.

12. This may be considered to be the thrust of the *Malkhuyot and Zikhronot* liturgy of the Rosh Hashanah *Musaf* service. These celebrate God's sovereignty and Providence, while *Shofarot*, revelation, points to the human situation to be discussed below.

13. Fackenheim, *Metaphysics and Historicity*, pp. 76–77.

the human situation informs me that not only I, but all people, are born into this blend of coercion and choice.

Thus, as a scientist, I can understand the natural situation, for example, the needs and mechanism of nourishment. But whether to make a blessing over food, whether to feed the needy who are within the same natural situation as myself and whose vulnerability I therefore know to be universal and also mine [14] is a philosophically understood choice within the human situation. In this situation I am a partner in determining who I am, but I understand that I, as others in my situation, have no option but to make a choice. Or as a sociologist and historian I may understand how society functioned and how power was used in the Egypt of Joseph, what the historical situation was, and what the possibilities and limitations within it were. But only Joseph, within the human situation that confronted him with "the Other that situat(ed) him," could decide whether to be considerate, to honor his father, to love his brothers. At the junction of compulsion and freedom, he was challenged. At that junction, the reliable acts of *Yirat Shamayim* became an option, indeed, a realm of choice he could not escape. He had to decide on being a certain person, one with or without *Yirat Shamayim.* This decision faces, throughout the diversity of human circumstances, every human soul.

Let us look at our *midrash* this way: God throws human beings into the world. The situatedness, and thus the determined quality of human life, is far-reaching. We must be born, die, be short or tall, beautiful or ugly. While in our historical situation of Western modernity, there is a greater element of self-making than in most previous cultures, including that of our sages, so that perhaps being rich or poor is more than a matter of luck, fate or birth, we are nevertheless bound by forces beyond our control. So, for example, the contemporary therapist of the child with Downs Syndrome may heroically refuse to let genes have the last word[15] though s/he knows that the genes do have a great deal to say. But this does not vitiate the option to do all that can be done! The choice of righteousness, of *Yirat Shamayim,* is there. Who can deny that suffering is part of the natural and historical situation into which we are placed? But *hesed* done by

14. Thus, following Moriel, we may understanding the view of Rabbi Akiva that the commandment to "Love thy neighbor as thyself," is "the great principle of the Torah." S/he is *kamokha,* like yourself. We are to put ourselves in the place of our neighbor. Cf. Yehuda Moriel, *B'derekh Tovim (The Way of the Good)* (Jerusalem: Dept. of Torah Education and Culture in the Diaspora, World Zionist Organization, 1976), p. 16.

15. Oral presentation of Dr. Reuven Feuerstein, leading child psychologist and therapist, Jerusalem, 1991. For Feuerstein's approach of teaching children to go beyond themselves in growth and rehabilitation, see Mark F. Goldberg, "Portrait of Reuven Feuerstein," *Educational Leadership* (September 1991), pp. 37–40.

the fearer of Heaven for the sufferer is a way of understanding it, a choice within the human situation.[16]

The circumstances that produced the Holocaust were, for the individual caught up in it, overwhelmingly determined. No more severe crucible for *Yirat Shamayim*, for freedom within the human situation, can be imagined. Yet there were many individual Jews who responded to the Holocaust by trying to save themselves and their dignity. When Jews or Gentiles attempted to save others and when, all else having failed, they died in God's Presence, they testified that martrydom, like courage, determines who one is. In testifying, they knew that the human situation both creates the compulsion to make the choice and the freedom to make it. And they made the choice of *Yirat Shamayim*. The life of *Yirat Shamayim*, leading up to and including this moment of choice, may be considered the meaning of those peoples' lives.

Frankel has stated this point in more general and perhaps secularized fashion:

> The experiences of camp life show that man does have a choice of action ... We who lived in concentration camps can remember the men who walked through the huts comforting others, giving away their last piece of bread. They may have been few in number, but they offer sufficient proof that everything can be taken from a man but one thing: the last of the human freedoms—to choose one's attitude in any given set of circumstances, to choose one's own way ... Every day, every hour, offered the opportunity to make a decision, a decision that determined whether you would or would not submit to those powers which threatened to rob you of your very self, your inner freedom.[17]

The real and omnipresent choices people have are in the human situation. For these has s/he been sent here; this determines his or her share in the eternal world, however we understand that. On this, the *midrash* says, will s/he be judged. For in the world view that our *midrash* represents and illuminates, death, while the end of the natural and historical situations, is not an escape from the human situation. And so, even Rabban Yohanan ben Zakkai was afraid.[18]

In the human situation, there is real freedom, but, being a situation, it also invites philosophic understanding of the compulsion within it. For one is compelled to choose. Elijah the prophet stated this causti-

---

16. Recall our discussion in Chapter 7, pp 121–25. For a concise statement of *hesed* as theological wisdom and religious action, specifically as exemplified in the Book of Ruth, see Reuven Hammer, "Two Approaches to the Problem of Suffering," *Judaism* 35 (1986), pp. 300–5.

17. Viktor E. Frankel, *Man's Search for Meaning; an Introduction to Logotherapy* (New York: A Touchstone Book, Simon and Schuster, 1984), pp. 74–75.

18. Rabbi Yohanan might well find it is difficult to understand the secular argument that religious people invent a future world for themselves to conquer their fear of the unknown. At the moment of his death, one might well imagine him wishing there were no future life.

cally and dramatically when he initiated a contest on Mt. Carmel, millenia ago, between the God of Israel and the Canaanite *baal*:

> How long will you halt between two opinions? If the Lord be God, follow Him; but if Baal, follow him (I Kings 18:21).

We should note that when he mocks the *baal*, he does so by placing him within the natural situation and describing the god as bound by it: "... either he is musing or he is gone aside (to attend the call of nature), or he is on a journey or perhaps sleeps and must be awakened." (I Kings 18:27)

Whether to acknowledge God as Creator and oneself as creature is not decided in advance. Whether to choose the Kingdom of Heaven in a life of obedience, reflection, and responsibility depends on the individual. Our *midrash* suggests, boldly, that every natural and historical situation presents equally significant human situational encounters. Anyone in any natural circumstance and any historical and cultural season may be righteous, may fear Heaven or may be wicked. For wherever there is a *mitzvah,* codified or not, halakhically worked out or inchoate, there one finds oneself in the human situation, both coerced and free. In classic terms, it is in this world of natural and historical situations alone that we can be righteous or wicked. It is for this choice that God put us here.

In looking at it this way, we have, of course, translated the midrashic principled world in which the character-ideal of *Yirat Shamayim* appears into an idiom that may make that world accessible for modern thought and for contemporary Jewish education. As *Yirat Shamayim* may be seen as a particular ideal of character and character education, so the principled world in which it is anchored can be viewed as one of situation, which makes human beings conscious of creatureliness, aware of limitations, yet understanding that this is the best possible world for them because only where there is natural and historical situation can there be human situation, and only where there is human situation can we know who we are!

Here, then, is one way of understanding the world of our *midrash.* This should not be seen as an exhaustive or authoritative statement of what the various texts that describe the world of *Yirat Shamayim* mean. This is not a total translation of rabbinic theology into existential philosophy. Rather, it is itself a *midrash.* The richness of the text and, for the religious educator, its demand to be taken seriously as language, intimates that there are many ways of seeing it and understanding it better. This is one, but there are others. In *aggadah,* as in *halakhah,* there are many levels of Torah. Translations must remain partial; otherwise, the gates of commentary will be closed. Then, instead of varied exegetes standing guard over the text, we shall get definitive treatises. That would be the end of the culture of *Mikraot Gedolot,* with numerous and diverse commentaries hovering around the text. It would be the death of Jewish teaching that invites discussion, discussion that is necessary not despite the authority of the text but *because* of it.

Philosophies may and perhaps should be transcended, but to the extent that they mediate between our tradition and the way we think and understand things in our historical situation, they offer us hope of making our tradition accessible. Philosophical interpretations of texts are therefore potential building blocks for educational theory—for the Jewish world and hopefully beyond.

Educational Translation—For Whom?

Two participants in our group remain suspicious of our educational-philosophical exercise.

Nehemyah still wonders whether it is necessary and innocuous. He firmly believes that without the regimen of the tradition as transmitted by rabbinic authorities translation into educational philosophical terms invites corruption. Partial translations, seemingly designed to clarify basic principles and develop congenial educational theory and practice even among the pious, are always threatening. He fears that they will inevitably lead to total translations, to philosophical reductionism. Such translation will legitimate a way of thinking that is totally foreign to the world of Torah. The result, he believes, will be to give license to heresy and allow non-commitment to hide under the cloak of openness. There can be, he maintains, no *Yirat Shamayim* without obedience, and there is no need to look at God and His decrees through philosophical categories. He finds that such categories, in their very plausibility and communicability, blur the lines between the faithful and the non-believers.

While this view has much integrity, it may nevertheless be self-defeating. For if Nehemyah and his community insist on distancing themselves from philosophical deliberation, the riches of their religious experience will be lost for most Jews. And, paradoxically, the inability to use it for the making of educational *midrash* will make his circle of believers appear to be spiritually impoverished. This is unfortunate because it is his community more than most that insists on the wholeness of the tradition and on the unfathomable value of the texts. It is this community that, in its principled disdain for what goes by the name of success in this world, may have important lessons to teach about the spiritual danger of banality and escapism: of seeing the natural and historical situations as all there is, without a human situation at all. But to teach that, Nehemyah's community will have to take the natural and historical situation with utmost seriousness as the place of the human situation. If they attempt to escape from those, why should others not suspect that their spirituality is too cheaply bought, or bogus?

Amir enjoyed himself. He even got into the spirit of halakhic and theological debates. After all, the Bible and the world of the sages are his history and he wants, as a man of culture and curiosity, to understand his origins and the soil of Jewish beginnings and historical development. In fact, what the sages of the Talmud made out of the highly variegated documents of the Bible fascinates him.

Nevertheless, like Nehemyah, he is not sure he belongs at this particular educational roundtable. He remains suspicious of translations, not because he wants to read the texts with the reverent eyes of tradition, but because he questions the usefulness of ancient texts in solving modern problems. He is perhaps impressed by this exercise in interpretation motivated by loyalty but he still wonders whether there is not a mystification here, and whether the loyalty is not misplaced—to past books rather than to present people and their insights and concerns. He agrees that texts may be worthy of study as paradigms of social conscience or ancient debunking of even more primitive beliefs, or, simply, as windows into our past.

But Amir suspects translation as attempted demythologizing and perhaps remythologizing.[19] He has been taught that educational and intellectual honesty requires teachers to investigate, not re-enhance, ancient texts. This is not because he and his colleagues are disloyal to the Jewish people; as they see it, even debunking clears the field for an intelligent and creative Jewish future. Defending texts, by translation or any other means, seems to them to stand in the way of clear-headed thinking and decision-making. So, they have distanced themselves from the cultural compulsion to link character education with *Yirat Shamayim* and they see no reason why situation should evoke God-talk. They believe that the translation from religious tradition to contemporary thought is in fact, and legitimately, comprehensive, for it totally leaves behind that which has been translated.

19. Amir is at least partly right about this. Where there is translation of tradition into philosophical, psychological or educational categories there is demythologizing. As for remythologizing, it is, in effect, to tell a new *midrash,* which emphasizes that every genuine translation of religious ideas is only partial and that one must also try to express that which cannot be translated. For these distinctions, see Rudolf Bultmann, "The Problem of Demythologizing," in *The Hermeneutics Reader;* pp. 248-255 and Emil L. Fackenheim, "Demythologizing and Remythologizing in Jewish Experience, pp. 16–27.

Linking modern insight to tradition they view as sentimental and educationally deceptive or, at the very least, wasteful.

Yet it would be unfortunate if Amir were to decide to dismiss the experience and to walk out on the discussion. For the existential concerns he represents have played a major role in the modern thrust to re-think tradition. His group's alienation from tradition has often borne the stamp of spiritual authenticity, and the problems his mentors have raised were often recognized as cogent even by those who disagreed with their solutions.

Esther maintains that the philosophical translation was particularly useful to her. She has long been troubled by the normative comprehensiveness of the religious ideal and the consequent difficulty of placing scientific and cultural achievement within her educational ethos. Our partial philosophical translation suggests to her a previously unconsidered theory of curricular integration. It indicates that the choice of *Yirat Shamayim* demanded by the human situation is not undermined by knowing what the natural and historical situations are. Learning them in a framework of *Yirat Shamayim* is as conducive to understanding limits as it is to discovering opportunities. Carmela, as already noted in the minutes recorded above, has been extremely comfortable with the translation of principle; she and her colleagues have always tended to view religious outlooks as philosophical ones and religious norms as simply morality. She now suggests that the discussion and the insistence on partial translation may help her to conceive the ideal as having an irreducible religious dimension that cannot be simply secularized and that must, at the very least, be confronted.

Daniel has come face-to-face with a problem which is almost the converse of Carmela's. His personal and educational religious commitment, he now discovers, is so thoroughly anchored in a theological-philosophical translation of the texts and of the tradition that he has difficulty relating seriously to what is not readily translated, what doesn't easily fit into the structure of a congenial theological, moral, and philosophical system and position. Unlike Carmela, whose position is that Jewish culture is salvaged for modern Jews through translation, Daniel thinks that it is religious faith that is thereby redeemed. In this he seems close to some medieval Jewish thinkers, and even to Maimonides in the passage cited at the beginning of this chapter. But Maimonides was committed to the *halakhah* as the irreducible norm of Jewish communal existence, even when it did not exactly fit his philosophical translation.[20] Daniel, unlike the Rambam, can decide that certain matters do not speak to him. They are thereby removed

---

20. Thus, in the *Mishneh Torah* he elaborates the laws of sacrifice, though he puts them into an historical context in the *Guide to the Perplexed.*

from the realm of interpretation, of rootedness and growth. His educational path is likely to be more integrative than Nehemyah's, or even Esther's, but it may also be less rich. Where there is less language, there is likely to be correspondingly less literature.

What may we hope for from this discussion for all participants? Perhaps a discovery by each that the basic value terms of the Jewish tradition are not simply slogans, verbal fetishes or, conversely, taboos. Rather, they can be focuses of Jewish educational thinking, a set of guidelines to character education that, in the specific case of *Yirat Shamayim*, is much more than good behavior, obedience, and timidity. Educators deliberating about the value concepts that inform the literature of Torah may even come to agree that the Jewish tradition has patterns of reflection that, while different from the rhetoric and rules of Greco-Western philosophy, are a distinctive way of discourse on education and culture, a Jewish *Paideia*. It is a challenge to be discovered and explored.

Moreover, if it is true that Jewish philosophy of education does not arise in the casual conversation of thinkers, no matter how penetrating and analytic, but in the *Bet Midrash,* in the house of study, then, before philosophy, and even before teaching, there will have to be learning. Only then may the tradition be applied in the classroom, youth group or summer camp or retreat. This application may be of a kind never envisioned before the books were opened, before the texts were invited to speak in the conversation of study.

JEWISH VALUES:
THE EVIL INCLINATION AND BEYOND

9

WHY ANGELS
NEED NO TORAH

I recall, many years ago, hearing my Hebrew school teacher, a pious and devoted man, proudly telling his class of twelve-year-olds that, unlike what they thought and taught in a more liberal Jewish school down the street, we didn't believe in Jewish values and were not learning any. "We don't have Jewish values here, boys, we have *mitzvot.*"

This was my first encounter with a controversial educational issue, namely, whether it is possible to speak of education without referring to values. Much later, I was to discover that there are many ways of defining values, and that a veritable library has been written about values in education. I learned that there are those who say that all education is value education (seemingly rendering the word "value" in that phrase altogether superfluous), and others who insist that one cannot and should not teach values if one wishes to avoid indoctrination. I came upon a great variety of understandings and definitions of value and values. In Plato I found the classic philosopher for whom what we call values are metaphysically and even mystically grounded obligations to live in accordance with eternal ideas; in Dewey, the mystery and metaphysics had been taken out of it. There, a value became simply something one values as a result of a process of valuating.[1]

Here our task is not to negotiate these philosophical controversies but to explore what educators who talk about Jewish values may

---

1. John Dewey, "Theory of Valuation," *International Encyclopedia of United Science* 2 (1939). Selections from this are found in "Ends and Values," *John Dewey on Education: Selected Writings,* edited and with an introduction by Reginald D. Archambault (New York: Random House Modern Library, 1964), pp. 89–96.

plausibly and coherently mean by this, and what they can learn from Jewish, specifically, rabbinic, sources to clarify their thinking. For the purpose of this exploration, we shall refer to the term "value," at least to begin with, in a metaphysically neutral fashion. We are going to see values as connoting that something is judged to be valuable. We shall assume that the word value is relevant for education whenever we are trying to make up our minds whether a certain course of action or certain subject matter is worthwhile, or good or important. We can be more precise if, following Rescher,[2] we say that values provide us with rationales for certain courses of action that are chosen over or against others.

Seen this way, values are obviously behind all philosophical-educational discourse, whether abstract or down to earth. My Hebrew school teacher, in speaking out against values, was making a valuative statement. He was expressing his conviction that it is better and more worthwhile to teach *mitzvot* than to talk about values, which he, I think, associated with moral and philosophical ideas about religion. His reason, I assume, was that he considered the traditional Judaism to which he was committed, to provide a persuasive rationale for teaching what and as he did. He taught the observance of *mitzvot*, including the commandment of Torah study, which he valued as important and good. And he wanted us to adopt for ourselves the same rationale for the same observances.

Value Decisions and Curriculum

My Hebrew school teacher made a curricular decision on the basis of a valuative position. Needless to say, what he did is done all the time, in all realms of learning. To illustrate this: we often hear that every person, no matter what his or her future vocation or type of life, should learn about the foundations of our civilization. Those who defend this position are not comfortable with the argument that basketball players don't need it or that budding engineers have no time for it. They want athletes and engineers to live consciously and amply within that civilization, to understand it and take an active part in it. They want all adequately endowed members of our society to have the skills and sensibilities that will make them competent to benefit from its goods, and able to handle some of the problems that arise within it. These educational thinkers maintain that all citizens should have a firm base of knowledge about our civilization, our society, and

2. Nicholas Rescher, *Introduction to Value Theory* (Englewood Cliffs, N.J., Prentice-Hall Inc., 1969), pp. 8–10.

community; only thus can they intelligently identify with it, criticize, and help correct it. All this is because we think our civilization valuable; we believe in it. It gives, from our perspective, good rationales for action; it informs us to a large extent about what acting well means. We are part of the valuative world of our civilization.

We realize, of course, that there are others who are strangers to many of the cultural goods that we value. They have other values, which we sometimes consider, from our perspective, negative ones. Yet we realize that they often refer in that same way to our values. Many of them do not think highly of our civilization, believing that it is inferior, degenerate, or even wicked.

If, then, education is based on decisions about what is worthwhile, good, and important, how can there be philosophers of education who oppose value education? Is it possible for anyone not to agree that educational institutions, including schools, should teach what is deemed valuable? Is it possible to have no point of view about these things and yet to educate?

Generally, the adherents of this anti-value position mean that educators have no right to dictate to pupils what is morally or religiously right or wrong. They have no right to inculcate doctrines. They should not teach particular values, for example, that it is good to observe the commandments of a particular "true" religion, or that good people are sexually restrained. They have no right to teach that such convictions are obviously true or objective facts. Some of these philosophers of education believe that religion as such is an illusion, and that sexual self-control is a neurosis; others do value religion and restraint but do not feel comfortable imposing these values on others in the educational process. For these philosophers, such value decisions are personal and subjective matters that should be left to the individual unless a particular course of action can be demonstrated to be useful or self-evident or blatantly harmful to others. They believe that values, unlike facts or skills, are choices. Education should impart the knowledge and the skills necessary to make informed choices and the capability to carry out a large range of options, but it should not force choices upon children. In their view, that would be indoctrination.[3]

Opponents of the anti-value approach to education often point out that it, too, is based upon clear though not clearly acknowledged views of what is good and bad. To be against "value education" is to be in favor of a different curriculum that teaches a different idea of

---

3. On the perceived danger of indoctrination in education for values, see, for example, Brian S. Crittenden, "Teaching, Educating and Indoctrination," *Educational Theory* 18, no. 3 (Summer 1968), pp. 237–52; Anthony Flew, "What is 'Indoctrination'?" *Studies in Philosophy and Education* 4, no. 3 (Spring 1966), pp 281–306.

what is important (i.e., skills of doing and thinking) and good (e.g., the freedom of the individual to choose from within presumably numerous notions of good and bad). Conversely, those who speak for value education maintain that educators do wish for the next generation to continue a particular tradition with regard to what is culturally valuable and morally good. Furthermore, they claim that every human being is indeed born into a tradition and will learn to articulate his/her desires, aspirations, and potentialities within it. In opposition to those who claim that there is no innate human nature to be appropriated or objective reality to which we must be attuned, they are also likely to declare that certain questions of good and bad are indeed clear-cut, anchored in the nature of human life, potentiality and vulnerability.[4]

So, to those educational thinkers who espouse values, it seems not only irresponsible but impossible to not transmit, through education, that which a particular society values most highly. These values reflect the way they understand not only the child and what is beneficial for him or her within a specific cultural heritage but also the way they understand the human condition as a whole. And yet, the adherents of value-free education pose a telling question: by what right do we transmit and how do we really know what is good and deserving of loyalty?

There are, of course, many ways of answering that question, in line with diverse philosophical and cultural traditions. Some will say that what is important and good is known through the cumulative experience of the human race about the human condition and how best to deal with it. For example, it may be said to be known that all people are vulnerable to suffering and capable of some well-being, and that it is good to empathize with these conditions of human existence, to minimize suffering, and to enhance the well-being of others. (While most people will assent to the first part of this statement, there are, alas, some who will take issue with the second part.) Another position is that the rationale for good action is to be found in the canons of reason, for example, in systematically constructed conceptions of justice or of the human essence, its potential and its realization. Yet others, realizing that ideas of universal justice and human nature also rest on valuative decisions, will seek more modest criteria. They may say that various cultures have different historical traditions and paradigms of how to act that are in themselves generally adequate to delineate values. But many who hold this opinion will nevertheless look for some universal moral criteria that

4. See John Kekes, *Moral Tradition and Individuality* (Princeton, N.J.:Princeton University Press, 1989), Chap. 8–9.

set parameters of legitimacy and warn us when our cultural norms are, or have gone, beyond universally acceptable limits.[5]

Locating Values in Jewish Sources

In the Jewish tradition, we find echoes of all the above-mentioned conceptions of value. In previous chapters we have already suggested that an important element of "fear of God" is morally reliable behavior that does not take advantage of others' weaknesses and vulnerabilities. Empathy for others is understood by many Jewish exegetes and thinkers to underlie the value-ideal, i.e., commandment, to "Love thy neighbor as thyself." They take *kamokha* ("as thyself") to mean "for s/he is as thyself."[6] In the history of Jewish thought, from the Bible and *midrash* through systematic formulations in medieval Jewish philosophy, we come upon reasoned statements and arguments, often exegetical in nature, about what is good and reasonable.[7] And, last but not least, Judaism has a central element, in its *halakhic* tradition, of correct action that, on a day-to-day level, seems to get along even without explicit theological or moral rationales. One hears it said among traditional Jews, in the classroom and out, that "that's the *halakhah.*" In other words, that's the way it is, that's the way we are commanded to do it. At the same time, even this historical-halakhic tradition, though not always overt, can be shown to relate to universal moral criteria.[8]

Nevertheless, behind and above all of these justifications of what are important, true, and good rationales for attitude, belief, and behavior, the prophets, teachers, sages, and thinkers of Judaism have based their fundamental conceptions of value on remembered events in the history of Israel, of being told, and hearing what God, who had sought them out and loved them, wanted of them. They passed on to their children what God did for the fathers and moth-

---

5. For an important discussion of this, see Stuart Hampshire, *Morality and Conflict* (Oxford: Basil Blackwell, 1983).

6. For example, Martin M. Buber, *Darko shel Mikra (The Way of Scripture)* (Jerusalem: Mossad Bialik, 1964), pp. 103–5.

7. A classic exegetical example is Moses Nachmanides's (The Ramban's) interpretation of Lev. 19:2 ("Ye shall be holy …") in which he warns against corrupted observance of the Torah by those whom he terms "vile persons within the domain of the Torah." In his commentary on Deut. 6:18, which demands doing "what is just and good in the sight of God," he understand it to demand moral uprightness in all spheres of life. For discussion of this and other texts that suggest reliance on moral sense, see Chap. 7, pp 117–21.

8. For various aspects of the relationship between the Jewish religious and legal tradition and moral-philosophical considerations, see Ze'ev W. Falk, *Law and Religion; the Jewish Experience* (Jerusalem: Mesharim Publishers, 1981).

ers, in Egypt and at Sinai, how they had crossed the Red Sea and the Jordan. This, they said, was the history of the covenant between God and Israel, and it was this covenant that required them to cleave to God and to live by His commandments.[9]

These experiences, of seeing the great events and hearing God's voice, were recorded in the Torah. They were the rationale for the *halakhah* and the thrust behind the endless interpretation of what had been spoken by God. Moreover, the details of every law and the richness of interpretations themselves bore witness to His continued Presence and, thus, were also His word. Through the *halakhah* and the careful re-reading of every word of Torah, He could still be heard and answered, too. Therefore, while human experience, reason or cultural tradition were important, they were subsumed under God's love for Israel and His demands upon Israel. This, congealed in the Torah, were the first and in a sense also the last word about reality and goodness. And these words were entrusted to the community of Jacob which, in its life, bore witness to them.

In light of this, it seems simple to articulate what a classic philosophy of Jewish value education ought to be. We would expect it to consist of teaching what is right because it has been revealed to us, justifying it whenever necessary by reference to the holy community that lives by it and that vitalizes it by anchoring it firmly in sacred memories. ("This is what God wants, this is how it happened. That is why Jews do it, and this is the way we do it.") In light of such a philosophy, the teacher's task seems merely to be impressing what is right upon the pupils. In order to make this value education most likely of success, he or she should find ways to store reserves of meaningful experiences in learners while they are doing what is right, to make them loyal to the community and identified with its formative theo-historical narratives. As for the gifted, it seems appropriate, in due course, to guide them toward philosophical verifications of the world of Torah and/or mystic understandings of it.

No less important than teaching the right values in an unredeemed world is for pupils to be insulated against belief systems that propagate falsehood and evil. These systems are best bunched together, with as little differentiation as possible, as idolatrous; they are *avodah zarah,* which the Torah warns us against.[10]

9. The perhaps classic expression of this view is that of the medieval poet and thinker, R. Yehuda Halevi, *The Kuzari.* It should be noted that Halevi's approach is very dissimilar to that of Maimonides. Halevi finds his basic principles not in the intellect but in a prophetic faculty that is beyond (normal) human intelligence and provides the basis for genuine love and significant experience. A comparison between these two thinkers for the purposes of educational thought has much to offer.

10. Rokeach points out that there is a tendency to distinguish not only between our belief system and our disbelief systems (the world of our values and of our "anti-

It is in the spirit of such value education that Joseph Haim Kara, in his nineteenth-century commentary on *Pirkai Avot,* understands the following well-known *mishnah:*

> Rabbi Yaakov said: He who stops his study of the Torah and says, how beautiful is this tree, how beautiful is this furrow, Scripture regards him as though he deserved to lose his life. (*Avot* III:9)

As Hertz, in his commentary, summarizes Kara's *Solet Laminchah:*

> He who turns away from the Torah, i.e., gives up his belief in Revelation, and seeks his religious inspiration from Nature, that man sins against his own soul."[11]

That is, someone who deserts the value system of the Torah and turns to nature (represented by "this tree") or to faith in human technological inventiveness ("this furrow") has moved from positive to negative values and deserves to die.

Conquering the Evil Inclination

Within this simple and clear-cut conception of good and evil, we may readily locate the doctrine that human beings have an evil impulse, a *yetzer hara,* that urges them to act naturally (yet wickedly), and that this *yetzer* must be "conquered." This is to be done through obedience to Torah, the divinely revealed locale of all positive values and the book of value actions (commandments). Because the *yetzer,* the evil inclination, is the target of values, those who do not have this evil inclination do not require the corrective of good values. They need no rationales for good behavior because they are naturally good. It doesn't make sense, therefore, to speak of values with regard to angels, who have no nature to conquer. The following rabbinic story well expresses this principle:

> Rabbi Joshua ben Levi said: When Moses ascended to heaven, the ministering angels said to the Holy One, blessed be He: What is a man born of woman doing here? He said to them: He has come to receive the Torah. They said to Him: is it the precious treasure which first you hid

---

values," respectively) but also to deny differentiations within our value system and what we consider anti-values systems. Certainly, the closed person will consider all other value systems and all parts of them as equally bad and all aspects of his or her value system equally good. Conversely, an open person is more likely to make differentiations within the value system, not to value everything in his or her system to the same degree, and to distinguish between degrees of non-acceptance of elements within other systems. Milton Rokeach, *The Open and Closed Mind; Investigations into the Nature of Belief Systems and Personality Systems* (New York: Basic Books, Inc., l960), Chap. 2–3.

11. *Solet Laminhah* is found in the book *Sefer Minhat Shabbat* (Vilna: Widow and Brothers Re'em, 5668), pp. 28–29. Hertz's formulation is found in Joseph H. Hertz, *Commentary on Pirkai Avot* (New York: Behrman House Inc., 5705), pp. 53–54. I am grateful to my colleague, Shimon Oren, for drawing my attention to this commentary.

nine hundred and seventy four generations before the world was created that you seek to give to flesh and blood? 'What is man that Thou art mindful of him? And the son of man that Thou thinkest of him? O Lord, our Lord, How glorious is thy name in all the earth! Whose majesty is rehearsed above the heavens' (Psalms 8:5–2).

The Holy One, blessed be He, said to Moses: Reply to them ...

Moses said to Him: Master of the universe, what is written in this Torah which You are about to give me? 'I am the Lord thy God who brought thee out of the land of Egypt' (Ex. 20:2). Moses said to the angels: Did you go down to Egypt? Were you enslaved to Pharaoh? Then what is the Torah to you? What else is written in it? 'Thou shalt have no other gods ...' (Ex. 20:3) Are you surrounded by nations that worship other gods? What else is written in it? 'Remember the Sabbath day to keep it holy' (Ex. 20:8). Do you do any labor, that you need to rest? What else ...? 'Thou shalt not take the name of the Lord thy God in vain' (Ex. 20:7). Is there any commerce, any give or take among you? What else ...? 'Honor thy father and thy mother' (Ex. 20:12). Do you have fathers and mothers? What else ...? 'Thou shalt not murder. Thou shalt not commit adultery. Thou shalt not steal' (Ex. 20:13). Is there any jealousy in your midst? Is there any will to evil in your midst?

At once they conceded to the Holy One, blessed be He. As it is written: 'O Lord, our Lord, How glorious is Thy name in all the earth' (Ps. 8:2).

Shabbat 88b

This *midrash* on a verse in Psalms 8, in which the emphasis is placed first on the word "heavens" and then on "earth," examines, as we see, the Ten Commandments. The angels believe that the Torah belongs in Heaven, and Moses demonstrates that it is needed only on earth, where mortals have human experiences (e.g., slavery, wrong value systems exemplified by idolatry). These human experiences must be placed in a context of commandment and redemption. They must be seen as calling for value teachings. From such bitter experience as human bondage, Moses then moves to situations that are both natural and worthy in themselves but in which people are tempted to do what is wrong and unworthy, such as the life of commerce and relationships with parents. And finally, he shows that the commandments against murder, adultery, and stealing are value actions based on the rationale that one should not do "what comes naturally," that is, what the *yetzer* suggests. Angels, having no evil inclination, have no need of the value-giving Torah. It is needed only on earth, not in heaven.

This *midrash* seems congenial to the clear-cut educational model for values that we have been describing. In this model, there are difficult (apparently meaningless or at least tempting) situations and there are evil inclinations. Given that reality, one should teach what these situations mean and what the right responses to them are. We should strengthen pupils to withstand temptation and to shun wrong behavior. It is helpful, too, to make wrong, i.e. anti-value systems, look as much alike one another as possible. For if we differentiate between the worst anti-values and those only relatively bad, pupils may be seduced into tolerance of the less bad and thus slide into behavior favoured by the evil inclination.[12]

This approach which we somewhat deviously described as flowing from the classic theology of covenant has the apparent virtue of simplicity. If this value education is successful, pupils will not only know what is worthy but will always strive to resist temptation.

According to this conception, occasions of moral conflict are not really about values at all, but only about one's present ability to implement what they unambiguously demand. Living by values is exclusively a matter of overcoming weakness, laziness or wickedness. And to the extent that one is successful in this, one may (albeit with fear and trembling!) enjoy the virtuous sense of becoming constantly stronger and progressing towards greater goodness. There is an on-going struggle against the *yetzer,* and the culture of Torah enables people to enter the fray well armed, with guidelines and with hope.[13]

This message seems clearly transmitted in the Talmudic story of Rabbi Elazar ben Shimon's temptation and transgression during a chance meeting with an ugly man. The story comes up in the context of a *halakhic* discussion concerning the implements to be used for transcribing sacred writings and the decision that reeds should be used because of their yielding nature. The Talmud relates:

> Our Rabbis have taught: A man should always be gentle as the reed and not unyielding as the cedar. Once R. Elazar son of R. Shimon was coming from Migdal Gedor, from the house of his teacher, and he was riding leisurely on his ass, feeling happy and elated because he had studied much Torah. There chanced to meet him an exceedingly ugly man who greeted him, 'Peace be upon you, sir.' He, however, did not return the salutation but instead said to him, 'Good for nothing, how ugly you are.

12. See n. l0, above.
13. In the Greek philosophical tradition, the distinction may be drawn between a dualistic conception that posits a necessary conflict between the higher (rational) and lower (passion, imagination, etc.) forces in the human personality, and between a monistic view that sees human personality as having diverse factions, with the highest being reason, which is also the form of the soul, hence, ideally, guiding all actions of the soul (personality). In the former, dualistic conception, goodness (i.e., reason) must defeat the inclination; in the latter, it must inform the lower features of personality. The Platonic metaphor for the victory of reason is escape from the cave; the Aristotelian speaks of "sickness of the soul" and cure. See David Carr, *Educating the Virtues; an essay on the philosophical psychology of moral development and education* (London and New York: Routledge, 1991), Chap. 1–2. I shall maintain through the distinction between inclinational opposites (described in this chapter) and valuative opposites (dealt with in the following chapter), that, through the prism of the Jewish textual tradition, these should be seen as complementary and sequential.

Are all your fellow citizens (in this place) as ugly as you are?' The man replied, 'I do not know, but go and tell the craftsman who made me, How ugly is the vessel that You have made.'

Rabbi Elazar was caught off guard by his *yetzer,* which took advantage of his feeling good at having studied much Torah. His satisfaction with himself made him happy and elated, but actually, overbearing, insensitive, and insulting. The ugly man gives a piercing answer that makes the sage realize his sin. In insulting me, says the ugly man, you have insulted my Maker.

> When R. Elazar realized that he had done wrong, he dismounted from the ass and prostrated himself before the man and said to him, "I submit myself to you, forgive me." The man replied, "I will not forgive you until you go to the craftsman who made me and say to Him, How ugly is the vessel that You have made."

The words are identical with those used by the man previously, but we sense that something has changed. What was at first a pithy and moving rebuke, has become cynical, hard, unforgiving. Now it is the ugly man whose behavior is beginning to follow his "inclination."

> He (R. Elazar) walked behind him until he reached his native city. When his fellow-citizens came out to meet him, greeting him with the words, 'Peace be upon you, Teacher, Master,' the (ugly) man asked them, 'Whom are you addressing thus?' They replied, 'The man who is walking behind you.' Thereupon he exclaimed: 'If this man is a teacher, may there not be any more like him in Israel.' The people asked him, 'Why?' He replied, "Such and such a thing has he done to me.' They said to him, 'Nevertheless forgive him, for he is a man greatly learned in the Torah.' The man replied, 'For your sakes I will forgive him, but only on condition that he does not act in the same manner in the future.'

The ugly man is here the arrogant and offensive one; he publicly shames R. Elazar, and forgives him grudgingly and conditionally. Now it is he who, led astray by his *yetzer,* is ugly.

> Soon thereafter, R. Elazar, son of R. Shimon entered (the *Bet Midrash*) and expounded: A person should always be gentle as the reed and let him never be unyielding as the cedar. And for this reason the reed merited that it should be made a pen for the writing of the Torah, *tefilin,* and *mezzuzot.*
>
> *Ta'anit* 20a-b

We see here that every *mitzvah* is dense with reminders that one should not give in to the evil impulse which lurks in every situation, even the one of feeling good at learning Torah. And the *yetzer* can transform even a legitimate hurt, like that of the ugly man, into an anti-value, a rationale for acting wrongfully.

According to the model illustrated in our story, values are prescriptions for overcoming the evil inclination. Graphically, the problem and its solution looks like this:

Values	*Yetzer* (Inclinations)
(requirement to act for)	(inclination to act with)
truth	falsehood
peace	aggressiveness
kindness	brutality
justice	injustice
courage	fear
consideration	selfishness
observance of *mitzvot*	sinfulness
service of God	idolatry
(That is) Good	Bad

It must, of course, be kept in mind that what one person or group considers good may be seen by others as bad. A philosopher who believes that the problems of humanity are due to a repression of our natural inclinations, which are to be viewed as good, will consider all rationales for such repression evil. Moses, arguing with the angels, clearly thinks otherwise; he argues that the Torah and its commandments are good and needed for mortals precisely because natural inclinations must be restrained or even conquered. Or, returning to our *mishnah* in *Pirkai Avot,* there are indeed those who believe that "the tree", i.e., nature, is a better source of value than the Torah, but Rabbi Yaakov, according to the interpretation we have cited, vehemently disagrees and considers them worthy of death.

Were he thinking in modern philosophical categories, Rabbi Yaakov might say that the Jewish value system is first and foremost de-ontological, telling us that good actions are worthy, to begin with, not because of their good consequences but because they are simply right. In the language of the Torah, they are commanded. That God commanded them is all we need to know, at least for a start, about their worth. We shall return to this conception and its educational ramifications in a later chapter.

Inclinational Opposites: An Adequate Value Theory?

Is this an adequate model for Jewish value education? Certain doubts and objections present themselves:

If value education is concerned only with the conquest of the evil inclination, which, pietists tell us,[14] notoriously presents itself within

---

14. See, for example, Rabbi Eliyahu E. Dessler, *Strive for Truth,* translated by Aryeh Carmell (Jerusalem and N.Y.: Feldheim, 5745/1985), ("How 'Good' Can be Used by 'Bad'"), pp. 95–96.

each individual as a good inclination in the form of rationalizations for evil acts, then some authority must unequivocably determine what good acts are. This means that the intentions of the actor are held to be of little worth; obedience to those in authority becomes the primary and sometimes the sole and absolute virtue. Worthy individuals are then those who have squelched all desire for critique, who are "well-behaved." Such individuals have learned not to weigh value alternatives because they know that their own judgement is not to be trusted. They must always have the authority figure within calling distance, and the authority must be beyond criticism, automatically right, very much like God!

Values that simply dictate set actions which, in turn, are not to be reflected upon, are usually going to become, as Frankenstein understands this term, inauthentic.[15] That is, people who are, say, polite and soft-spoken with others are unlikely to be aware how much of their being nice is motivated by a fear of being disliked or a need to be appreciated or approved of. Similarly, the father who maintains a strict regimen among his children to assure their proper behavior is going to forget how much of his value-ideal is dictated by an unacknowledged tendency to bully others. Paradoxically, therefore, the insistence on obedience and conformity at the expense of self-awareness reopens the door to the very evil inclination that was supposedly brought under control. For, in fact, the inclination is not being controlled. It is simply not being faced!

A more extreme case of inauthenticity has to do with the person who seems to have no evil impulse with respect to a certain value-ideal. For example, a person may always appear to be patient but the reason is his or her inability to express anger. We would hardly say that such a person exemplifies the value-ideal of patience. We think of a valuative act as being authentic when it is represents a victory of some kind over the natural inclination. Similarly, we are likely to value a person who is courageous. We think that such a person deserves admiration and trust for having overcome the *yetzer* to fear. However if that person for some psychological or physiological reason is devoid of the impulse of fear we cannot call him or her courageous. S/he seems to be defying fear but, actually, in that person's case, there is nothing to defy. Acting bravely, like in the case of the patient person who dares not for some deep-seated reason to be impatient, is here not a virtue based on a value. Rather it is a quirk of character and probably a symptom of neurosis.

15. Carl Frankenstein, *Ha'amiti Vehamizuyaf* (The Authentic and the Inauthentic), *Al Amitut Ha'arakhim V'hahora'ah (On the Authenticity of Values and Instruction) Kenut V'shivayon; Hirhurum al Psychologia V'hinukh (Sincerity and Equality; Thoughts on Psychology and Education)* (Tel Aviv: Sifriat HaPoalim, 1977).

Isn't a value education based solely on obedience likely to be an invitation to such repression, so that the alleged conquest of the *yetzer* becomes, simply, its denial?

Understanding value education as a simple determination of right as against wrong, presents learners, willingly or not, with a straightforward choice: to accept the norm being presented or to reject it, perhaps in favor of what the teacher presents as an anti-value, as something wrong. This insistence that pupils take or leave the proffered set of values, while appearing to have a kind of rugged heroism about it, is unlikely to succeed where the value system being taught represents a cognitive minority within an open society, a society that ostensibly tolerates many valuative options but in fact subtly urges the acceptance of the norms and values of the majority. The cognitive minority's values are much more likely than the majority's to appear merely to be a set of dogmas. In such a situation, pupils may well see themselves being asked to value loyalty alone, rather than what the value-ideals really represent and what they teach to be good and important.

The perceptive pupil is also likely to notice that the system he or she is being asked to accept discourages all reflection, is incapable of self-correction, shuns appropriate confrontation with new situations, and seems immune to even internally legitimated change. The only way to assure reasonable success with such value education would seem to be social segregation, in which the cognitive majority is absent and the appearance can be maintained that "everybody who is anybody thinks and acts the way we do." In such a state of segregation, everybody allegedly knows that this system requires no self-correction, has a ready answer for every seemingly new situation, and, being Platonically perfect, considers every imaginable change a change for the worse.

Now, if the sources of our tradition proposed this valuative approach unequivocally, then a plausible argument could be made that at least traditional Jewish education should mobilize its best forces to formulate feasible ways to defend this position and to show how our description is tendentious. For example, a philosophy of Jewish education might be constructed that examines how "Torah authority" is both absolutely binding and self-correcting. It must then be persuasively argued that a Jewish educational system is ideally structured in such a manner that learners not only accept authority but may themselves become authorities through a requisite self-development and as a result of certain educational regimes and achievements. Second, ways would have to be found to convincingly counter and refute the psychological presuppositions of such hostile conceptions as valuative authenticity and neurosis. Third, a strategy for effective segregation that permitted rich, though restricted, cultural life and economic viability would have to be effectively presented and pursued.

In fact, these approaches, both as philosophy and as policy, do exist in modern Jewish life, especially in *haredi* (ultra-Orthodox) writings. The question, however, is not only whether they are successful but what price their proponents are ready to pay for such success in terms of intellectual closed-mindedness, simplistic paradigms of plausibility and the cultivation of authoritarian personality. And one should mention the actual loss of the many pupils who go to glean in other fields of existential significance.

Without a doubt, the valuative approach we have been discussing is an aspect of the classic philosophy of Jewish education. The question is whether the *midrash* on Moses and the angels and the many other passages we might cite that have the same explicit thrust[16] exhaust the teachings of our sources on the question of values. Does the entire world of Jewish values revolve around the axis of "right is what God commanded and no more need be said"? Or is there an additional dimension, a consequential one, that invites us to examine in which ways the commanded values of the Torah can best be implemented in given circumstances? And if there is such a consequential dimension, doesn't applying the values of the Torah wisely require deliberation and weighing alternatives?

Even the following story, seemingly a straightforward narrative about wrongdoing and punishment, will raise doubts in our minds about the assumption that all values are simply about warring on the evil inclination, about being righteous rather than wicked. This story opens with the declaration of Rabbi Yohanan that Jerusalem was destroyed by the Romans "because of Kamza and Bar Kamza." What transpired, we are told, is the following:

> It happened that a man had a friend named Kamza and an enemy named Bar Kamza. He made a feast and said to his servant: "Go bring me (i.e., invite) Kamza." He (the servant) brought him Bar Kamza. When the host found Bar Kamza sitting (at his feast) he said to him: "What are you doing here? You are my enemy. Get up and leave." He (Bar Kamza) said "Since I'm here, let me stay and I'll pay for all I eat and drink." He (the host) said: "No." Bar Kamza: "I'll pay for half your feast." The host: "No!" Bar

16. Often cited in this context is Rashi's commentary on Deut. 17:11, based on the Tannaic midrash, *Sifre.* The verse states that "You shall not depart from the word that they (the judges) tell you, either to the right or to the left." Rashi: "even if he (the judge) tells you of the right that it is left and of the left that it is right ..." But it may be noted that the original in the Siphre is milder. "Even if it seems to you that the left is right ..." Various ways in which this may be understood are noted by Zvi Zinger, *"Ba'ayat Ha'hachra-a v'Hasamchut B'Halakahah"* ("The Problem of Decision-Making and Authority in *Halakhah"*) in *Turai Yeshurun* I:2 (Jerusalem: the Yeshurun Organization, 1966), pp. 8–14.

Kamza: "I'll pay for the entire banquet." The host: "No!" He took him by the hand, stood him up and threw him out.

Said Bar Kamza (to himself): Since Sages were sitting there and did not protest, apparently they were comfortable (with the host's action). I'll go and give them a bad name with the king. He went and told Caesar: "The Jews have rebelled against you." Caesar asked: "Who said so (How do you know)?" He said: "Send them a sacrificial animal and see if they will offer it (upon the Temple altar)."

He (Caesar) sent a (sacrificial) calf with him. As he was travelling, Bar Kamza made a blemish in the animal on his lips, which according to our laws is considered a blemish (making the animal unfit for sacrifice) but not according to their (Roman) laws.

The Sages wished to make the offering for the sake of (political) peace. But Rabbi Zechariah ben Avkulai said: "If (we do) so, people will say that blemished animals may be sacrificed on the altar." (Then) they wanted to put Bar Kamza to death so that he would not be able to inform against them to the king. But Rabbi Zechariah said: "People will say, 'One who blemishes a sacrificial animal is to be put to death (but that is not the *halakhah*!)'."

Said Rabbi Yohanan: "The humility of Rabbi Zechariah destroyed our Temple, burned our sanctuary and exiled us from our land."

Gittin 55b

At first glance, this *aggadic* narrative is about "the evil inclination" and a spiral of sinful (i.e., anti-valuative) behavior that leads, as the Bible had warned, to destruction and exile. Because his servant brought the wrong man to his banquet, the host wantonly humiliated that man and threw him out. He was aggressive, mean, and, ultimately, violent. The host must have been an important man, certainly a dignitary, perhaps a leading priest or member of the Sanhedrin, the High Court. That would explain the presence of sages at the dinner and also why they would not wish to speak up in defense of the humiliated Bar Kamza. Yet, it seems that in not defending the hapless guest, they gave in to their *yetzer*; they wanted to stay on the host's good side. Surely the sages knew that embarrassing someone is enough to deny a person a share in the world-to-come. The idea, after all, originated with them![17]

We can't be surprised at Bar Kamza's reaction. He was very offended; perhaps what in calmer moments he would have recognized as a treasonable act looked like a clever move in a vendetta. He gave in to his *yetzer*, not knowing what terrible consequences it would have.

That is one way of understanding the story.

But there is another possible way. Perhaps the host was right in not wanting Bar Kamza at his feast. Perhaps Bar Kamza was an evil per-

17. *Avot* 3:11; *Sanhedrin* 99a.

son for whom giving the Jews "a bad name with the king" was exactly the kind of thing one might expect. Imagine the host having to decide whether he would do the careful thing and let Bar Kamza stay, or doing the courageous thing and not eating and drinking with a *rasha,* a wicked person.

In this scenario, the situation of the sages is complicated. They may have felt that it was a mistake on the part of the host to throw out Bar Kamza, but they may also have understood his action as a valuative one. Then, we might have Bar Kamza saying to himself, "They agree that I am wicked. Well, I will show them that they are right." In any case, we cannot be certain whether the host and the sages followed their inclinations against the values of hospitality and protest, respectively, or whether the host decided on the value-ideal of keeping far from the wicked rather than on other value-ideals, namely, not to embarrass a person and not to endanger the community. Similarly with the sages: they may have decided that it was more important in that situation to put a wicked man in his place than not to passively witness another person's humiliation.

If Bar Kamza was truly wronged, his action can only be judged hasty, childish, wrong. We may then surmise that he must have been eventually shocked by the consequences of his action. But if he was wicked, then we both understand the host and the sages and yet wonder whether they chose the right course of action.

In any case, in the situation that developed, the sages had to make a decision, and we are told that there was a controversy about it. Moreover, we are sensitive to the irony in Rabbi Yohanan's conclusion: he tells us that it was "the humility of Rabbi Zechariah that destroyed our Temple ..." Is humility a sin, an act of surrender to the *yetzer hara?*

That we are dealing here with several valuative possibilities becomes clear from the argument between R. Zechariah and the sages. The sages thought that the important thing to do was to get rid of the danger posed by Bar Kamza; this could have been done most easily by sacrificing the animal. They argued for the value of "the welfare of the public." R. Zechariah was not ready to consider that to be more valuable than the *halakhah* that relates to blemishes, though he realized that this was what the other sages thought. The sages then in a sense had no choice but to suggest that Bar Kamza be killed to keep him from reporting back, from endangering the community. Again R. Zechariah declares that this value, of safeguarding the community, cannot be preferred over the obvious *halakhic* rule: one is not killed for blemishing a sacrificial animal!

Surely the sages, too, knew the *halakhot* of blemishes and capital punishment. But they were ready to choose another value of the Torah itself, the welfare of the public, over the one that determined the culpability of persons who offered blemished sacrificial animals. Even Rabbi Zechariah did not say that his colleagues were sinful in saying that; he just pointed that that such a valuative decision might have unacceptable social consequences. "People will say ..." He had too much "humility"; he was too careful. He refused to entertain the thought that a change in circumstances mandated a rethinking of priorities. Rabbi Yohanan, as we see, is very critical of R. Zecharyah's humility, of his tendency to see the right way as clearly set.

Our story examines the need to consider various valuative alternatives that appear to arise in certain critical situations. But is the need for such consideration really limited to such situations? Is valuative deliberation, even where it does arise, suitable only for leaders and thus irrelevant to most educational situations? Or is it an intrinsic aspect of valuative life and value education?

To this question we turn in the following chapter.

10

PURSUING PEACE AND LOVING TRUTH

"Gentlemen," (declared the rabbi), "this is not an easy piece of *Gemara*. We must struggle to give it meaning ..."

Rabbi Rotenbush read aloud the wisdom of the great sage Rabbi Yohanan: "Anyone who grasps the Torah without its mantle will be buried without his mantle." The Rav (rabbi) said, "Let us enter into the heart of the idea, gentlemen. We know that the Master of the Universe made a covenant with us at Sinai. The Talmud tells us ... that the covenant was not simply what we read in the Scriptures but included as well the Oral Tradition. The Scriptures are not so easily understood, gentlemen. They are abbreviated, packed with hints and secret meanings. But the Oral Tradition ... is the mantle of the Torah .... .

"When God gave us the Torah at Sinai He held the mountain over our heads ... But (why) ... as a threat over our heads? We know that we accepted the Torah willingly. (We said,) 'We shall do and we shall listen ... We shall do before we listen.' So how can our Sages tell us that God held the mountain over our heads, warning us that if we did not accept His Torah He would bury us there at Sinai? ... Shmulik, can you give us the answer?"

I plunged into the commentary. "The commentaries of the *Tosphot* explain that he who does not learn the Oral Tradition will be buried by the dense weight of Scripture ... If we listen only to the condensed words of the written Torah, if we do not surround it with the mantle of the Oral Tradition ... here shall we be buried. We cannot comprehend the full meanings of each verse of the Bible, we cannot fathom its depths without the light of the Talmud. Without it we are ... as good as buried. That, gentlemen, is what is meant when Rabbi Yohanan says that if we try to grasp the Torah without its mantle we shall be buried without our mantle." 'Terrific!' Ian whispered to me ... 'A scholar,' Shlomo said, chuckling, 'he can lern'."[1]

1. Samuel Heilman, *The Gate Behind the Wall; a Pilgrimage to Jerusalem* (New York: Summit Books, 1984), pp. 176–82.

Valuative Opposites

*I*n the story of Moses, who comes to receive the Torah against the objections of the ministering angels, we see the concept of value identified with the rationale of confronting and, to the extent possible, conquering the *yetzer*. The lure of the evil impulse amidst the tribulations of earthly existence is best combated by way of the clear-cut prescriptions of the Torah. A life of value, of worth, is one in which people observe the commandments and believe in their rationale. Namely, these commandments tell us what is good and what is evil, what is important and what is trivial, what is and is not in accordance with God's will. The commandments and the rationale together comprise the content of Torah. If children are educated to cleave to what the Torah commands, they will serve God rather than idols, be righteous and not wicked, live meaningful and not empty lives.

But, in fact, as we have suggested above, it is highly problematic to view the world of value and value education as confined to that. In the world of values, there are not only postulates and doctrines but also dialectics and deliberation. The reason for this is that every value-based attribute or act that we are bidden to adopt in order to be good brings to mind another one that appears to compete with it, that claims, at least in particular situations, to be better. This valuative tension is particularly pronounced in the Jewish classic tradition and its study, for within it the concept of *mahloket*, controversy, is pervasive and perhaps fundamental.[2]

Let us begin our discussion of "opposing values," each claiming priority and demanding implementation, with a classic rabbinic example. It is a story about Aaron the High Priest who, we are told by the sages, "loved peace and pursued peace."

> When two people had quarreled with each other, Aaron would go and sit with one of them and say to him, "My son, look what your friend is saying. He beats his breast and tears his clothing, saying, 'Woe is me! How can I face my friend? I am ashamed before him, for it is I who treated him wrongly'." And he would sit with him until he had removed all rancor from his heart. Then Aaron would go and sit with the other one and say to him, "My son, look what your friend is saying. He beats his breast and tears his clothing saying, 'Woe to me! How can I face my friend? I am ashamed before him, for it is I who treated him badly'." And he would sit with him until he removed all rancor from his heart. And when the two met, they would embrace and kiss each other (*Avot D'Rabbi Natan* 12:3).

On the face of it, this is simply an inspiring, perhaps even overly sweet story, an anecdote about a saintly man. The message appears

2. For a study of this concept and relevant texts for instruction, see David Dishon, *Tarbut Hamahloket B'Yisrael (The Culture of Controversy in Israel)* (Tel Aviv: Schocken Publishing House Ltd., 1984).

to be that Aaron was good, he loved peace, and he got people to live peaceably. Since peace is indisputably a good thing and Aaron was a model of peacemaking, we should all strive to be like Aaron, "loving peace and pursuing it."[3]

But what is really involved in being devoted to the value-ideal of peace? What is the price of such devotion? When we look at the story a second time, we realize that the inspiring story of Aaron presents a dilemma. Aaron did not tell the truth and he made no attempt to get at the truth. He did not ask himself who was right, whether one of the men had been treated unjustly by his fellow. He did not try to find out which one of them, if either, deserved an apology from the other.

Aaron seems to have felt that such an approach was simply a recipe for more anger and conflict. He chose peace over truth, that is, one value over another. No doubt the one he chose endeared him to many people. In fact, this is the way it is understood in the *midrashic* work, *Avot D'Rabbi Natan.* Immediately following the story related above, we read:

> Therefore it is written: 'And they mourned Aaron thirty days, the entire House of Israel (Numbers 20:29) ... But about Moses, who chastized them with harsh words, it is written, 'And the children of Israel (i.e., the worthy among them) wept for Moses'(Deut. 34:8).

When Aaron chose one value over another, many of Aaron's acquaintances, even those who respected him, may yet have felt that he was mistaken in choosing peace over truth. But some, who disliked him or who thought about values in a one-dimensional manner, may have declared that Aaron was not motivated by the value of peace at all, which he claimed to favor over the value of truth, but by his natural inclination, his *yetzer,* to be well-liked or to avoid confrontations. These people may simply have given expression to our natural tendency to devalue the valuative decisions of our opponents. But such a reaction does force us to acknowledge the problematic nature of any value decision. Aaron's preference for peace can lead to unfavorable consequences, to injustice. And so we have to ask: When should peace be chosen over truth? When should it be set aside? Why?

---

3. If we analyze the story with care we can learn from Aaron that resolving conflict requires not only having the right values but having the psychological astuteness to carry them out. Aaron not only knew that he had to do something about the aggressive *yetzer* (evil impulse) of the two men in question; he knew what had to be done. He deflected the anger of each of the men by making up the story that the other was angry at himself. Thus he defused the aggressive feelings of both and made these feelings superfluous and unjustified. Neither could continue to harbor hatred against his fellow by imagining that the other was laughing at him, accusing him, planning revenge against him. Aaron was a man of peace and a superb psychologist. For this insight into the story, I am grateful to my colleague, Dr. Jonathan Cohen.

Once we look at the story this way, we see that the value idea of peace is not only a good thing. It is also one horn of a dilemma! Showing what the dilemma entails makes the story of Aaron—like all descriptions of value issues in our tradition—no longer dull and banal. He is not simply a person who does the right thing rather than the wrong thing. His action cannot be juxtaposed only to its anti-value opposite, namely, not making peace or cultivating enmity (which is bad and represents the passions and temptations of the evil inclination), but also to its valuative opposite. Aaron is no longer a plaster saint. He is not simply a simplistic embodiment "of what Judaism says," something that the pupil can either accept or reject. The matter is too complicated for that. If we read this story only as a case of inclinational opposites, pitting the world of value against the inclination, the *yetzer,* then Aaron is clearly a paragon of virtue. But through the prism of valuative opposites the tradition appears as a tapestry of controversy, in which "these and those are the words of the living God" (*Erubin* 13b). And then the question may legitimately arise: why did Aaron not speak the truth? What made him decide on this course of action?

This question, how one decides such matters and what are valid criteria for decision-making, often arises in Talmudic discussions. An interesting example is found in the tractate *Sanhedrin* (6b), in which sages deliberate as to whether it is better to arbitrate in disputes or to render judgement. Here, as in the story of Aaron, we seem to have a valuative conflict between truth and peace. Let us look at the discussion initiated by R. Eliezer, the son of R. Yose the Galilean:

> R. Eliezer ... says: It is forbidden to arbitrate (to make compromises) in a dispute and he who arbitrates offends, and whoever praises such an arbitration scorns the Lord, for it is written, 'He that blesses an arbitrator *(bozea)* despises the Lord'(Psalms 10:3). But rather, 'let the law cut through the mountain' (i.e., let justice be done, no matter what, even if it is difficult to get at the truth) for it is written, 'For the judgement is God's' (Deut. 1:17).

R. Eliezer is for truth at all costs and, further on in the discussion, will cite Moses himself as a representative of this view. He understands the word *bozea* as arbitration or compromise, though, as we shall see, it need not be read as meaning that. And we find R. Meir restricting R. Eliezer's idea to only a very particular kind of arbitration.

> R. Meir says: This text refers to none but Judah, for it is written, "And Judah said to his brothers, 'What profit *(bezah)* is it if we slay our brother'?"(Genesis 37:26) And whoever praises Judah for this act of compromise despises the Lord.

R. Meir reminds us that in the case of the sale of Joseph, *bezah* means illicitly gained profit. Here we have a particular instance—and kind!—of arbitration. Here, Judah, brother of Joseph, convinced his other brothers that there was no profit *(beza)* in killing him and that it was more profitable to sell him. R. Meir seems to be condemning compromises that have already made their peace with evil.

If this is what bad arbitration means, then we need have no compunctions about lauding good arbitration. Thus, R. Joshua b. Korha says:

> Settlement by arbitration-compromise is a meritorious act, as it is written, 'Execute the judgement of truth and peace in your gates'(Zechariah 8:16). (This seems impossible for) Surely when there is strict justice there is no peace, and where there is peace there is no strict justice! And what is the kind of justice with which peace abides? We must say: Arbitration!

And yet the sages attempt to limit this so that arbitration will not be devious or unjust. Thus R. Simon b. Mansya declares that "if you have already heard the case and know in whose favor the verdict inclines, then you are not at liberty to suggest a settlement."

Which value is to be favored in a particular case is not, therefore, simply a matter of temperament or whim. One should reason about it, trying to understand what various verses tell us about it, trying to fathom to which circumstances and cases they are referring.

Inclinational Opposites and Valuative Opposites

To make clear how valuative opposites differ from inclinational opposites, let us examine another case.

> Our sages taught: those who visit stadiums ... and witness there (the performance of) sorcerers and enchanters, lo, this is 'the seat of the scornful' and against those (who) visit them, Scripture says, 'Happy is the man that has not walked in the counsel of the wicked ... nor sat in the seat of the scornful, but his delight is in the Torah of the Lord' (Psalms 1:1-2). From here you can infer that such things cause one to neglect the Torah. (Yet) the following was cited as contradicting the above: 'It is permitted to go to stadiums, because by shouting one may save (the victim).' There is thus a contradiction between (the laws relating to) stadiums ... !
>
> No! They represent the opinions of (two) different *Tannaim*. For it has been taught: one should not go to stadiums because (they are) 'the seat of the scornful,' but Rabbi Natan permits it for two reasons: first, because by shouting one may save (the victim); second, because one might be able to give evidence (of death) for the wife (of the victim) and so enable her to remarry.
>
> *Avodah Zarah* 18b

At first sight, the *halakhah* with regard to stadiums appears clear-cut. The stadium, a place of sorcerers, idolatry, and gladitorial contests in which people are forced to kill each other for the amusement of vicious crowds is obviously no place for a God-fearing Jew or indeed for any decent human being. At best, the performances there are sorcery, idolatrous nonsense, leading people to neglect the Torah. At worst, it is a place of murder masquerading as spectator sport. Anyone enchanted or amused by such evil has "sat in the seat of the scornful," exchanged the "delight of the Torah" for "the counsel of the wicked." Such a person has succumbed to the evil inclination. By going to such a terrible place, whether in Rome or in Bet-Sha'an, that person celebrates cruelty, cultivates a taste for stupidity and viciousness. It seems to be a simple case: there is the Jewish value, and its evil anti-value. The scornful prefer the *yetzer* and go to stadiums; the righteous take delight in the Torah—and keep away.

But Rabbi Natan points out that even the value-ideal of not going to stadiums is not so simple, and he is thinking specifically of the worst case, the most evil stadium scene. For if the righteous stay away when the life of a victim is at stake, they are not available to shout that he be spared, they cannot point thumbs up rather than down when the winner of the contest holds a sword to his throat and awaits the verdict of the crowd. A good person should go and shout against the evil of the stadium and, if the Jewish victim is killed, should be in a position to testify to his death so that his wife be spared the status of *agunah.* Otherwise she will remain a bound wife who cannot remarry because there are no witnesses to her husband's death.[4]

Which is the better value, not sitting in the seat of the scornful or taking the risk of being corrupted but enabled perhaps to save a human life or enable a widow's re-marriage? Obviously, the answer is not clear or obvious; it depends on many circumstances. Perhaps Rabbi Natan would agree that if it is only an arena of sorcerers, one should stay away, but not where lives are at stake. Certainly, some people will be more influenced by evil companions than others; perhaps they should be directed to stay away. Otherwise they, too, might, God forbid, learn to shout for the victim's murder. There is no simple formula and there are many factors to discuss. Before that discussion commences one can distinguish the good from the bad thing (i.e., the Torah and the stadium) but one cannot as yet decide what is *good* and what is *better* to do.

And the discussions we may have about peace and truth (Aaron), arbitration or judgement (R. Eliezer or R. Simon) or protection against corruption versus responsibility and involvement (Rabbi Natan) appear applicable in every situation of value. When we begin to think about it, it becomes startling clear that there is no operative value-ideal that does not have a valuative opposite. And therefore, in

4. For a moving treatment of this Talmudic passage, see Abraham Karp, "Go Forth and Shout," *Conservative Judaism* 20, no. 4 (Summer 1966), pp. 20–28.

addition to dichotomies between values and anti-values, which create which we are calling "inclinational opposites," there are dichotomies between values and value-ideals, that is, between conflicting rationales for good behavior and patterns of good actions. This means that, in addition to the chart in our last chapter, we require an additional one, which will illustrate our dilemma:

Value	Value
peace	truth
mercy	justice
loyalty	impartiality
shunning evil	involvement and concern
observing the Sabbath	saving human life
courage	caution

In short: Good (better?)   Good (better?)

It may be objected that valuative opposition does not apply to the really important values and value-ideals. In those cases, one might say, we know what's right, even without discussion.

This is only partly true. It is true in the sense that a religious tradition, through the medium of a community, imposes itself on the individual and socializes him or her, demanding cultural habit before there can be cultural deliberation. In this sense, "we in our community," know what is true and teach it. Here, the most important things are self-understood.

Yet, at the same time, when we analyze the most important values, which seem to have no valuative opposite, we discover that they lack one precisely because they do not specifically tell us how to act but only function as synonyms for right and wrong.

Take, for example, such a central Jewish value-ideal as *avodat HaShem* (service of God). To this concept there is a clear inclinational opposite, *avodah zarah* (idolatry), but there is no value within the tradition of Judaism that can possibly stand opposite it. For the person who accepts *avodat HaShem* as a value, it is all-inclusive and therefore synonymous with the good. No value within classic Judaism can compete with *avodat HaShem*.

But the point is that, having no valuative opposite, the term *avodat HaShem* mandates no specific action. It delineates what I may not do, i.e., serve idols, and provides me with a label of identity ("I belong to those who ...") but it supplies no positive prescriptions with regard to particular actions. Shall I insist on truth in every case, because "the seal of the Holy One, blessed be He, is truth?" (*Yoma* 69b) Or shall I sometimes choose the path of peace because "even the Almighty changed (the facts) to make peace between a man and his wife?"[5] It is only when valuative opposites present themselves within the framework of *avodat HaShem* that I can consider what to do, or, in the language of Jewish tradition, to study or decide[6] what the *halakhah* is. Only when these alternatives do present themselves do we discover that without its valuative opposite(s) a value is more like a slogan than a rationale for a particular course of action. In other words it is banal; it is true in general and thus not helpful in specific circumstances. A value without a valuative opposite, even one as sublime as *avodat HaShem,* fails to recommend or mandate any particular behavior. It simply delineates the world of value from the world of anti-value. It does no more than say within the language of the Jewish tradition: do what is right and refrain from wrongdoing. To discover what is actually mandates, we have to break it down and be more specific.

Valuative Opposites and Controversy

A well known *halakhic* example: it is obvious that observing the Sabbath constitutes part of what Jewish tradition means by *avodat HaShem.* But saving human life is also the service of God. Which takes precedence? The Talmudic sages set the rule that *pikuah nefesh doheh shabbat,* saving a life, takes precedence over the Sabbath (*Shabbat* 150-51). They had to choose between valuative opposites.[7]

However, in deciding that one takes operative precedence over the other, they are not denying the truth of the value-ideal being, as it were, shunted aside. Their decision is not a devaluation of Sabbath observance. The sages took the Sabbath and the minutae of its observance extremely seriously. They were convinced that both clusters of values and value-ideals, the Sabbath and the sanctity of human life, respectively, are valid; both are on the scene, making claims. They

5. In the school of Rabbi Yishmael it was taught: great is peace, for even the Holy One, blessed be He, misreported for its sake. At the beginning (of the episode of the three men coming to Abraham to notify him that Sarah would have a son), it is written that Sarah said, "And my lord (husband) is old" (Genesis 18:12) (so how can we have a son)? And at the end (18:13) it is written that God said to Abraham, "Why did Sarah laugh saying: 'And I (Sarah) am old?'" (in order not to create strife between husband and wife). *Yevamot* 65b and Rashi on Genesis 18:12). For additional examples of misreporting for the sake of peace, see Nehama Leibowitz, *Studies in Bereshit (Genesis),* translated and adapted from the Hebrew by Aryeh Newman, 2nd revised ed. (Jerusalem: World Zionist Organization, Department for Torah Education and Culture in the Diaspora, 1974), pp. 563–70.

6. This will depend on whether I am authorized because of my expertise in the language of the *halakhah* and its previous literature or whether I am in the process of learning them. What constitutes being authorized and expert will, of course, differ from community to community.

7. For a contemporary compendium of the traditional *halakhah* concerning the priority of saving life to the observance of the Sabbath, see Yehoshua Y. Neuwirth, *Shmirath Shabbath; A Guide to the Practical Observance of the Sabbath* (Jerusalem: Feldheim Books Ltd., 1989), Chap. 19.

also knew that the Bible itself recorded a case of capital punishment for no more than "gathering sticks on the Sabbath!" (Numbers 15:32-36) Yet, they came to the conclusion that where the two options, of saving life or observing the Sabbath, conflicted, the proper and commanded way of serving God was, at least under most circumstances, to desecrate the Sabbath and not endanger life.

And, of course, numerous questions arise for deliberation and decision-making within the sphere of these opposing values. For example: how do we know when human life is really in danger? Who should decide? The patient? The doctor? Both? Assuming that saving human life takes preference, who should carry out the (otherwise, but not in this case) forbidden activity? Should it be a child, who is not yet commanded to observe the Sabbath, or an adult, who is? Also: may one save the life of an idolator on the Sabbath? After all, s/he doesn't believe that human beings are created in God's image, and we are bidden to save lives so that God's image not be diminished! Indeed, the existence of such idolators, like those who organize the above-mentioned gladitorial contests, may be construed as a menace to society and an affront to God's "kingdom"! So why save them, on the Sabbath or any other day? On the other hand, will not saving the idolator provoke emnity towards Israel? And what about *hillul HaShem,* a desecration of God's name, caused by people saying that Judaism and its God are oblivious to the welfare of others? Isn't Israel commanded to sanctify God's name, so that people, even those now enslaved to false gods, will be drawn to His service?

In the disputes between the Houses of Hillel and Shammai, leading Tannaic sages of the first century before the Common Era, we see numerous examples of disputes about valuative opposites. Each school stood within the valuative framework of the Torah. Both, the Talmud declares, expressed "the words of the living God," but they often took their stands on conflicting values. Here is one illustration:

> Our sages taught: how does (i.e., should) one dance before a bride (to delight her and her bridegroom) on her wedding day? The House of Shammai says, Delight her with what she is (that is, praise her by mentioning traits that she actually possesses. If she is beautiful, say so; if not, don't mention it.) And the House of Hillel says, Call her a seemly and charming bride. Said the students of the House of Shammai to the students of the House of Hillel: what if she is lame or blind—do you call her a seemly and charming bride? The Torah (Exodus 32:7) instructs us to distance ourselves from falsehood.! Said the House of Hillel to the House of Shammai: in your opinion, when a person has made a bad deal in the marketplace, should one speak well of the transaction or put it down (since the person is not asking for your advice and has already made the transaction)?[8]

Ketubot 16b-17a

8. The comment on the bridegroom's transaction has more than an intimation that the bride is an object of purchase. This aspect of rabbinic literature will not go away by

Here, then, is the dilemma. Is it more important to tell the bride the truth about herself (and the bridegroom about his "transaction") or to make them feel good on their festive day? Because both inclinational opposites and valuative opposites are always on the scene, that is, people must both choose good rather than bad and decide what is better in given circumstances, the argument, like any dispute about values, can in principle be viewed on two levels. On one level, we might imagine each house doubting the sincerity of the other, intimating that the other is not prepared to do the right thing because of the natural inclination of the *yetzer*. In that case, each would say that it is acting on the basis of a value while its opponent has neither the inclination nor the strength to do so, and that this explains and underlines the disagreement. For example, the House of Hillel could accuse the House of Shammai of stingy spirit, of not really caring whether a given bride will feel happy on her happy day. The Hillelites might say that the Shammaites are insensitive; they care more about preserving and parading their honesty than about the real needs of other people.

Conversely, the House of Shammai could accuse the House of Hillel of not eschewing falsehood, clearly a sin (i.e., an inclinational opposite of truth) since the Torah instructs us to distance yourselves from falsehood. The Shammaites might say that the Hillelites have a need to be well-liked, that self-love and not virtue dictates their seemingly valuative choice. Their *yetzer* has permitted them to rationalize their disregard for truth, making falsehood seem to be kind.

On a second level, we can understand the controversy as one that involves valuative opposites. We can consider the two houses to both represent, as in fact the Talmud tells us they do, "the words of the living God." There is here, then, no conflict between my good and your evil, but a disagreement about which value should predominate in making a general rule for, say, praising brides. Both values are obviously good ones; both originate in the Torah and both come supplied with proof texts. Both opinions must be preserved, for one can learn Torah through each of them.

The question is: in most cases, or in those cases that we can presently envision, which value takes precedence? Causing the bride to rejoice is a great *mitzvah*, but we are also commanded not to speak falsely. Does one have to choose one or the other, or can some strategy assure that both will be protected? The House of Hillel appears to opt for choosing between them; the House of Shammai declares that one can be both truthful and kind, thus preserving both values. It recommends both praising the bride and dancing before her, yet doing this without

---

being ignored or deleted from citations. Modern Jewish thought and *halakhic* theology may justifiably see in it a central challenge.

untruthful flattery. The House of Hillel feels that not lying to an ugly bride is, in fact, to offend her, for she knows that more attractive brides are praised for their beauty, even by disciples of the House of Shammai. The offense, they argue, is in the omission of this praise. They think that at weddings it is better to tell white lies than to offend.[9]

Once again: the tactics of argumentation may lead one to present the favored valuative choice as obvious, as challenged only by an anti-value opposite. For example, it is easier to claim that the alternative to telling the truth is no more and no less than lying, forgetting to state that people of good will and sound moral judgement may validly argue for white lies, in the case of homely brides, for example. It is easier to think that your opponent is bad rather than to think of him or her as only mistaken, and having the right to consider you mistaken. It is psychologically more comfortable to think that those who disagree with you are unprincipled and lacking values than to think of them as upholding legitimate values, values that also make an appeal to you!

Traditional Jewish theology and education assumed that disputes among the sages are motivated by valuative disagreement; controversies between sages like Hillel and Shammai, unlike those provoked by "Korah and his congregation," are always "for the sake of Heaven."[10] They are about different values, which all remain on the scene even after a particular dispute is resolved. This tradition also maintains that everything that the Torah states to be a Word of God is a value (a rationale for correct behavior) and that every commandment is, therefore, a value-ideal. Not every person or every action depicted by Scripture is laudable; even heroes can sin. But whether their actions are commendable depends on the degree of their loyalty and obedience to the Torah's norms. So, in the traditional approach, one cannot ask whether a particular Word or commandment is good or not, only what it means and when it must or may be applied. We shall shortly have occasion to explore some philosophical-educational ramifications of that.

Mahloket (Controversy) and Value Clarification

It is important to bear in mind that valuative opposites that invite deliberation are not presented as replacing inclinational opposites.

9. The custom now prevalent, especially in religious-Zionist circles in Israel, for those who dance before the bride to sing *kaitzad merakdim lifnai ha'kalah* (How does one dance before the bride) and to continue the melody without words, seems to me to be a simple but not unsophisticated solution to the controversy.

10. *Avot* 5:17. Note that the controversy that is not for the sake of Heaven involves no interchange. Thus, it is not a controversy between Moses and Korah, but simply, "of Korah and his entire congregation."

Rather, they are built upon them. There is a *yetzer hara* that we are commanded to fight through adherence to the values and command-ments of the Torah. Yet these values, and the actions they mandate, are manifold, often in seeming competition with one another and sometimes incompatable for specific circumstances. Thus, the educa-tional significance of valuative opposites in our sources is not to trans-form Jewish education into value clarifications that begin with what the individual considers right. Such an educational procedure denies the moral unreliability of the *yetzer,* of human nature, and is based philosophically on the superfluity of Moses wresting the Torah from the angels. For if children, in principle, are angels, they, like the celes-tial ones, do not require the Torah, and value clarification is enough.

An adequate educational theory of valuative opposites, rather than encouraging vacuous value deliberation, will help pupils grasp how our sources ponder the problem of implementing the values of the Torah and allow them to participate in this deliberation.

To what degree will learners be encouraged to participate in the valuative deliberation of the tradition? This depends, of course, on the religious world view of the school, on what the school considers to be the explicit vis-à-vis the implicit dimensions of Judaism. The explicit aspect of religious teaching, as I have suggested elsewhere,[11] sets parameters for what is imposed by a religious or cultural tradi-tion; what defines the community and obliges it; what is, therefore, considered the legitimate thrust and contents of socialization. The implicit dimension, I have argued, addresses the individual who, on the basis of his/her experience, search, and spirituality, is called upon to appropriate the goods of community and tradition, but without loss of personal integrity or identity. In a religious educational framework, the explicit features of tradition are taught as religious truth. Never-theless, the explicit aspects of religion must ultimately be understood by people who have not only accepted them but have thought about them. They have to some extent struggled with the normative tradi-tion; they have had the experience of being both enhanced by the tra-dition and of taking a measure of responsibility for it.

I am now suggesting that the relationship between the explicitly imposed and the implicitly discovered corresponds to the bond between truth and art: in Judaism, the truth of the Torah and the art of *midrash*. The truth cannot be known in terms of what it means and demands for a given individual in a given generation without the art, but there can be no *midrashic* art were it not for the truth of the Torah. The position being taken here is that the dichotomies that character-ize much of Western philosophy, between metaphysics on the one

11. Rosenak, *Commandments and Concerns,* Chap. 6.

hand and self-making and "cultural redescribing" on the other, is not adequate for an understanding of the Jewish tradition. Similarly, the Greek notion of perfection as aesthetic changelessness fails to encompass what the psalmist means when he states that "The Torah of the Lord is perfect."[12] Certainly there is human creativity in the tradition, but it is based on what Torah imposes; there is timeless truth in the language of Judaism, but it is exposed to view only through literature. Fishbane well captures the dialectic between revelation and renewal when he examines the rabbinic notion that God studies Torah.

> The well-known Talmudic image of God studying and interpreting His own Torah is nothing if not that tradition's realization that there is no authoritative teaching which is not also the source of its own renewal, that revealed teachings are a dead letter unless revitalized in the mouth of those who study them."[13]

In the words of a *midrash* on Leviticus 26:3:

> If you walk in My ordinances and keep My commandments and do them ... *(v'asetem otam).* Said Rabbi Hama ben R. Hanina, If you keep the Torah, I shall consider it as though you made them (the commandments) (as though it were written) *v'asitem atem.* Said R. Hanina bar Pappa, If you keep the Torah, I shall consider it as though you had made yourselves ...
>
> *Leviticus Rabbah* 35:8

Now, the explicit dimension of religious education is always at least the imposed system of values vis-à-vis its anti-value (inclinational) opposite. But it invariably includes as well a cultural language for dealing with problems and dilemmas, and a history of recognizable predispositions towards discrete accommodations and solutions. In our tradition, *halakhah* and Torah study have been the keys to that language and the universal ways of speaking it. In the traditional Jewish life and classroom, therefore, *halakhah* and its fundamental meta-*halakhic* (theological) presuppositions represent the focus of explicit religion, and *halakhic* traditions are the subject of deliberation within a culturally imposed and normative framework.

Hence, in no religiously oriented Jewish classroom will pupils be asked whether they think it is meaningful to desist from idolatry, in its ancient or modern forms. Nor, in a traditional classroom will they be invited to deliberate whether they find the laws of *kashrut* and the prohibition against cheeseburgers archaic or foolish. The laws of *kashrut,*

---

12. For the first dichotomy, see Richard Rorty, *Contingency, Irony and Solidarity* (Cambridge: Cambridge University Press, 1989); for the second, Leo Baeck, "Two World Views Compared," *The Pharisees and Other Essays* (New York: Schocken Books, 1947), pp. 125–48.

13. Michael Fishbane, "Inner Biblical Exegesis: Types and Strategies of Interpretation in Ancient Israel," in *Midrash and Literature,* edited by Geoffrey H. Hartman and Sanford Budick (New Haven and London: Yale University Press, 1986), p. 19. In the same volume, see also Betty Roitman, "Sacred Language and Open Text," pp. 159–75.

like the *halakhah*, however interpreted, will be presented as part of the explicit part of religion, as part of the valuative world Judaism imposes, as what God commands, as language. However, they will sooner or later have to discover that even that which is imposed shares the world of valuative opposites, inviting discussion of how to wisely apply it. Idolatry as an anti-value is only a slogan unless it is specified what that entails for ourselves in our world, as well as for the sages in theirs. Similarly, in a traditional school pupils may find themselves discussing and learning whether there are situations in which cheeseburgers may or should be eaten: for example, whether they may be eaten by someone whose life is in danger and for whom no other nourishment is available. In the world of commandments too, consequences matter, even if the *mitzvot* are first divine decrees.

In any case, the sages considered the values of the Torah to be binding, brought down from Heaven in order to make human life a service of God and not of the *yetzer,* nor of its diverse personifications, idols.

The sages never entertained the notion that anything in the Torah could not represent a value, that any commandment could be anything but good. For example, when the Torah prescribes capital punishment on such a large scale, they assumed that in principle it must be a good thing, pointing to the commanded meaning of human life, intimating the ability of persons to forfeit their right to it, and protecting the right of society to take action against evil-doers. At the same time, they were aware of the irreversibility of execution and the uncertainty of human judgement. They also noted that the Torah made only the intentional crime worthy of capital punishment and so they had to determine when a crime could be declared unmistakably intentional. The plethora of problems they found raised by the Torah itself occasioned the following discussion:

> A Sanhedrin which executes (a criminal) once in seven years is called a cruel Sanhedrin. Rabbi Eliezer ben Azaraiah says: a Sanhedrin which executes once in seventy years is called a cruel Sanhedrin.
>
> Rabbi Tarfon and Rabbi Akiva say: if we were in the Sanhedrin, no one would ever be killed (i.e., executed). Rabbi Shimon ben Gamliel says: actually, they (Rabbi Tarfon and Rabbi Akiva) would increase the shedders of blood in Israel.

Makkot 1:10

Because the values that militate against those underlying execution make such powerful claims, the sages deduce that it should in practice be extremely difficult to put anyone to death. Rabbis Tarfon and Akiva come to more extreme conclusions. They state that in practice the values behind execution will always have to give in to those that oppose it. They suggest questioning the witnesses until some discrepancy is found in their testimony that will disqualify them.

(Maybe their thinking was along the following lines: is it because of the fallibility of human judgement that the Torah requires a thorough investigation of witnesses? And, given the irreversibility of capital punishment, can the investigation ever be too thorough?) But Rabbi Shimon ben Gamliel points out that to say that a value confronted with a valuative opposite will never be applicable is to negate it, and to forget what it teaches. It seems to suggest that a value of the Torah (which is the rationale for execution) is immoral. But how can a value of the Torah be immoral? [14]

This valuative problem is sharply addressed in a Talmudic discussion on two of the most problematic laws of the Torah, that of the stubborn and rebellious son and that of the idolatrous city. About the former, the Torah states:

> If a man have a stubborn and rebellious son, who will not hearken to the voice of his father, or the voice of his mother, and though they chasten him, will not hearken unto them, then shall his father and his mother lay hold on him, and bring him out unto the elders of his city, and unto the gate of his place; and they shall say unto the elders of his city: 'This our son is stubborn and rebellious, he does not hearken to our voice; he is a glutton and a drunkard.' And all the men of his city shall stone him with stones, that he die; so shall thou put away the evil from the midst of thee; and all Israel shall hear, and fear.
>
> Deut. 21:18-21

As for "the condemned (idolatrous) city," we are taught:

> If thou shalt hear tell concerning one of thy cities, which the Lord thy God gives you to dwell there, saying, Certain base fellows are gone out from the midst of thee, and have drawn away the inhabitants of their city, saying, Let us go and serve other gods, which thou hast not known, then shall ye inquire and make search, and ask diligently; and behold, if it be truth, and the thing certain, that such abomination is wrought in the midst of ye, thou shalt surely smite the inhabitants of that city with the edge of the sword, destroying it utterly, and all that is therein and the cattle thereof, with the edge of the sword. And thou shalt gather all the spoil of it into the midst of the broad place thereof, and shall burn the city with fire, and all the spoil thereof completely, unto the Lord your God, and it shall be a heap forever, it shall not be built again.
>
> Deut. 13:13-17

All who are acquainted with traditional Jewish education know that these passages occasion no little embarrassment and evasion. It is possible, of course, never to refer to them. However they regrettably make an appearance every year in the cycle of Torah reading. I have myself witnessed excellent teachers in good schools warding

14. See David Weiss-Halivni, "Can a Religious Law Be Immoral?" in *Perspectives on Jews and Judaism: Essays in Honor of Wolfe Kelman* (New York: The Rabbinical Assembly, 1978), pp. 165–70.

off questions about these passages (Isn't this immoral? Primitive? Against the spirit of Judaism?) with the remarks that "there is no time now" to discuss them, or that "we can't understand" these laws but know that everything in the Torah is profound and right, even if we can't understand it.

In the first case, the teacher is giving the message that s/he indeed would like to question these laws but doesn't dare to or even explicitly disapproves of them but is not authorized to express his or her disapproval. In the second case, the teacher intimates that it doesn't matter what we consider immoral or not, and it is not for us to question why. The latter is, in a sense, true to the tradition and part of the explicit dimension of religion; it may be said to create reverence for Torah and to suggest the depth of religious teaching. But, unfortunately, it may also educate to the abdication of moral judgement and perhaps even lead to compliance with totalitarian fanaticism. When the entire Jewish people lived a powerless *Galut* (exilic) existence, this was not a real problem, since Jews had neither courts authorized to execute nor cities of their own. Today, with and in the state of Israel, there are other possibilities–and there is a distinct danger of ethical fundamentalism.[15]

Ethical fundamentalism is here understood as the belief that all values are confronted only by their inclinational opposites and never, at least not for the ordinary person, by a valuative opposite. This means that in every case of seeming conflict there is merely weakness and temptation and the *yetzer* trying to make sin look good. To the extent that there are valuative opposites, only authorities need to know about them and deal with them. After having done so, they will tell us which is the right way, so that we are smoothly brought back to the inclinational value vs. anti-value distinction, which is the only level on which most people should be allowed to function.

To the above-mentioned educational notion and tactics, there are two obvious alternatives.

One is to teach in a straightforward manner that these are ancient texts and laws, reflecting archaic ideas about society, imbued with the cruelty that was so self-understood throughout the ancient world.

15. I have discussed such possible and actual developments in Rosenak, "Jewish Fundamentalism in Israeli Education," *Fundamentalisms and Society* 2 (Chicago: American Academy of Arts and Sciences, 1992), pp. 372–412. It should be noted here that the stricture against the position of we can't understand it is not meant to be applied to those ritual laws of Judaism that are often referred to in the tradition as *Hukim* (statutes), which have their lack of explanation as a distinguishing mark. (See *Yoma* 67b and Rashi on Numbers 19:1); yet compare Maimonides, *Guide to the Perplexed* III:26, where the lack of reasons for the *Hukkim* is meant for "the multitude." The problem of ethical fundamentalism arises in the case of the Torah's social legislation which, if considered "language," requires thoughtful and appropriate application.

This text describes the circumstances and mindset of our ancestors. We need not be ashamed of them, for they lived and struggled with moral issues in the childhood of humanity, and we can neither blame them nor be surprised at them for being childish. Since the text merely describes a given historical reality it does not prescribe for us, and we can learn no values from it. A good teacher might even express the opinion that we may even be somewhat proud of the authors, for they instituted improvements in ancient barbaric practices. They insisted on both father and mother being responsible for the child's fate; they took the power of execution from the father and gave it to elders and courts. And they insisted on diligently investigating all rumours of wrongdoing. This pedagogical approach certainly constitutes a break with traditional Jewish education. But for many it is required by intellectual and moral integrity.

The second possibility is *midrashic*. This approach is based on the premise that the Torah instructs us truthfully about the world of value, but that this truth is exposed to view only through the art of valuative deliberation. The valuative deliberation may be sparked by a dissonance between two explicitly commanded value-ideals, such as truth and peace, both of which are ideally operative. It may result from changing moral perceptions about one or several values that now conflict with other values in a new way. For example, the value-ideal of *tzaar baalei haim* (the prohibition against causing pain to living creatures) now appears to conflict with the value-ideal of divine worship through animal sacrifices. Or the dissonance may be the result of some fundamental change in the perception of what is valuatively possible. The rule of *lo dibrah Torah ela keneged yetzer hara* ("The Torah spoke with due regard to the evil impulse")[16] implies that if and when people change, a particular value-ideal will no longer be mandatory or even perhaps permissible. Finally, it is possible that the situation in which we find ourselves is not specifically addressed by the Torah and we must glean guidelines from the paradigms that the Torah does provide.

The *midrashic* option is based on the traditional assumption that the art of interpretation is applicable to every sentence and word of the Torah, and that we cannot know in advance what we shall learn from any word. Thus we may understand the seemingly radical Talmudic statement, "One who says the entire Torah is from God but for one word, of him/her it is said, He/she has despised the Lord's Torah." (*Sanhedrin* 99a) That is, such a person gives up midrashically speaking, on one verse or word as Torah; he or she seeks and/or makes no *midrash* on it, for it is not considered worthy of valuative probing.

16. Rashi on Deut. 21:11. The reference here is to the law of the woman taken in captivity who, after a certain "cooling off" period in which which she mourns her parents, may be taken in marriage by her captor.

Now, let us return to our paradigmatic difficult texts. The Talmud in one passage discusses the stubborn and rebellious son together with the condemned city. Our *mishnah* teaches:

> If his father desires (to have him punished) but not his mother, or the reverse, he is not treated as a stubborn and rebellious son, unless they both desire it. R. Yehudah says: if his mother is not fit for his father, he does not become a stubborn and rebellious son.

> *Sanhedrin* 8:4

The *Gemara* begins its discussion by asking what is meant by "not fit" and immediately dismisses the idea that this simply means that the marriage of the parents is an illicit or forbidden one; after all, "his father is his father and his mother is his mother"—their marital status is irrelevant. The conclusion:

> But he (the Mishnaic teacher) means not physically like his father. It has been taught likewise: R. Yehudah said, If his mother is not like his father in voice, appearance and stature, he does not become a rebellious son. Why so? Scripture says, he will not obey our voice (in the singular), and since they must be alike in voice, they must be also in appearance and stature. With whom does the following *baraita* agree (and to whom may it be attributed):

>> There never has been and never will be a rebellious son. Then why was the law written? That you may study it and receive reward (for studying Torah).

> This *baraita* agrees with R. Yehudah. Alternatively, you may say it agrees with Rabbi Shimon. For it has been taught: R. Shimon said, Because one eats a *tartemar* (measure corresponding to two portions) of meat and drinks half a *log* of Italian wine, shall his father and mother have him stoned? But it never happened and never will happen.

> Rabbi Yonatan said, 'I saw him and sat on his grave.'

> *Sanhedrin* 71a

In prior discussions, the sages have already asked when and to whom the law of the stubborn and rebellious son could apply. It appears to the student that the thrust of these questions is to limit the law's scope, and the sages may be assumed to have moral considerations in mind. But their explicit concern is with the apparent conflict between this value-ideal and other values in the Torah. Specifically, the rebellious son is executed for crimes that he is sure to commit in the future, since stealing meat and wine from his parents and eating and drinking in bad company is hardly a crime deserving such punishment; it is preventive punishment. But this is a very problematic category![17] On the other hand, this law, no mat-

---

17. The law of the thief who breaks into a house at night (Exodus 22:1–2) shares this problematic. Since the thief is presumed to harbor hostile intentions, the owner is considered to be acting in self-defence when s/he kills the thief. S/he is not liable

ter how rarely applicable it can be understood to be, is Torah! It represents a value. But when can this value be applied, if at all?

Rabbi Yehudah discovers in the text the word *kolainu* ("our voice" in the singular, without a *yod*), a clue that the Torah does not intend that value to ever be applied; the conditions are impossible to meet, for no two parents have the same voice and appearance and stature. Therefore, he declares, we have here a value from which we can "learn Torah" but which cannot be literally applied.

What, for example, might we learn from it? Perhaps that parents should educate their children with great care, seeing in this figuratively a matter of life and death; that parents are both responsible for their children's upbringing or that they must speak with the same voice in education. The principle that the delinquent is a threat to society and that neither parents nor society can assume indifference to that is also taught to us by the Torah. But it cannot ever be translated into practice; the opposing values to the one mandating the execution of the rebellious son will, in each conceivable case, have the upper hand. Rabbi Shimon states this explicitly. If the *halakhah* posits that eating a certain measure of meat and wine makes one a rebellious son, this is certainly not all that the Torah meant. There are so many others features of rebellion and factors to be taken into consideration that carrying out this value-ideal is surely impossible; all we can do is study it for its theoretical teaching.[18]

Rabbi Yonatan disagrees. We shall come back to him after looking at the continuation of our Talmudic discussion:

> With whom does the (following) *baraita* agree (to whom may be it attributed)?
>
>> There never was and never will be a condemned city. Why then was it written? That you may study it and receive reward (for studying Torah).
>
> It agrees with R. Eliezer. For it has been taught (that) Rabbi Eliezer said: no city containing even a single *mezzuzah* can be condemned. Why so? Because the Bible says (in reference thereto) 'And you shall gather all the spoil of it in the midst of the broad place thereof and shall burn (them).' But if it contains a single *mezzuzah* this is impossible, because it is written 'And you shall destroy the names of them,' i.e., the idols, but 'Ye shall not do so unto the Lord your God' (Deut. 12:31).
>
> Rabbi Yonatan said: I saw it (a condemned city) and sat upon its ruins.
>
> *Ibid.*

---

because of what the thief is likely to do, i.e., kill him or her. Yet, see the Talmudic discussion that seeks to limit the owner's right to do so, especially *Sanhedrin 72*.

18. David Weiss-Halivni, "Can a Religious Law Be Immoral?", footnote, p. 170. It should here be noted that the *halakhah* does not follow the opinion of R. Yehudah that father and mother must have not only identical voices but also identical appearances and stature. See Pinchas Kahati, *Mishnayot M'vuarot, Seder Nezekin* I, p. 422. For some of the possible teachings of these laws, see R. Adin Steinsaltz's commentary on *Sanhedrin* 71a in his *Talmud Bavli, Masekhet Sanhedrin* II, 1977, p. 315.

As is the case of the "rebellious son," the "condemned city" appears to fly in the face of every sacred value. What about the innocent within the city? What about a trial for the allegedly guilty? What possible justification can there be for the purge of an entire community? Rabbi Eliezer declares that there never was such a city. The Torah, he says, teaches the careful student that it is prohibited to destroy anything associated with or containing the name of God. Since one cannot imagine an entire city of Jews without a single *mezzuzah,* this means that the commandment to burn everything within the city would have to include the burning of a parchment mentioning God's name. But that, we see, is forbidden. And so a "condemned city never was and never will be."

Again, we need not doubt that there are many values that R. Eliezer associates with this law that must be studied as Torah. The idea that a community that deserts the ways of God and turns to idolatry has lost its right to exist, both theo-politically, because it denies the Kingship of God, and morally, for turning to idols which sanction the basest human passions, to this R. Eliezer, were we to engage him in conversation, would no doubt assent. There is much that can be learned from the law of the condemned city about communal responsibility, leadership, and the consequences for the entire public of a community be led by base fellows. But yet he teaches the law itself, though it must always be kept in mind, cannot ever be applied. Is it not written, "Ye shall not do so unto the Lord your God?"

Rabbi Yonatan disagrees. It is reasonable to assume that he was speaking metaphorically in saying that he had sat on the grave of the son and the ruins of the city. If there had been such a dramatic event as the destruction of a condemned city, surely the other sages would have known about it; it would have been recorded. What Rabbi Yonatan appears to be doing in both of our cases is arguing for the principle that where there are opposite values it is not enough for the deliberation to assume that both are legitimate only in principle. A principle that can never be applied, we may hear him saying, stops being serious. "I sat on his grave" or "I sat on its ruins" invites us to imagine the circumstances under which this value-ideal would deserve application.

We can envision a latter-day R. Yonatan wondering under which circumstances the execution of, say, a homicidial psychopath of thirteen, could be defended.[19] Would it have to refer to a son who has already attempted parricide? Most probably. Would it have to take

---

19. These conjectural comments are based on the assumption of Weiss-Halivni that R. Shimon maintained that the meat and wine consumed by the rebellious son are not the whole story, that there must have been something else.

place in a society which has not yet discovered therapeutic detention and care? Almost certainly.

Similarly, we can imagine him asking at which moment the destruction of Hitler's Berlin would have been a proper application of the Torah's values, even if there was still a *mezzuzah* in the city. The moment he and his base fellows came into power? When they invaded Poland? Decided on "the final solution"? Would such an action, he might say, not have been a boon to Germany and to humanity, sparing the victims of the Holocaust, as well as the tens of millions of all nations who died because of the war, from Stalingrad to Hiroshima? Isn't this what the Torah is teaching us?

In this connection, we can imagine Rabbi Yonatan annoyed at the question why God permitted the Holocaust and even "misunderstanding" the question. He might angrily retort that God did not permit it, but in fact expressly forbade it in the law of the condemned city, a law later to be made accessible to the entire Western world through Christianity and Islam. These world religions are expected to understand that the Bible is ruthless about idolatry because idolatry is the greatest menace humanity ever–and always–faces, especially when idolators are the powerful tyrants who strut the stage of history. R. Yonatan might say that the theological question, "why did God let it happen?" is mistakenly phrased. God told us not to let it happen. We did. The law of the condemned city was ignored, causing untold suffering.

Rabbis Yehudah, Shimon, and Eliezer we assume would agree, but only in principle. They would say that the conditions cannot be made congenial to the punishing act (R. Yehudah), that we do not have enough facts to be unequivocal in making such a decision (R. Shimon) or that there is an opposing valuative factor that is paramount (R. Eliezer). And R. Yonatan, apparently a somewhat dour and realistic man who calls a spade a spade, might say that a value that is never true except in principle is really not held to be true at all.

Most of us most of the time would prefer for Rabbis Yehudah, Shimon, and Eliezer to have the upper hand in the discussion, but I suspect that a person who has seen something of what goes on in the world and studied at least a little Torah would want R. Yonatan on the scene too, to speak his piece and to be overruled.

We have seen teaching values to take in doctrines and deliberation, truth and art, texts and their valuative clarification. What is required is a language within which to choose. We need the Torah and its mantle.

But a fundamental question presents itself for educational theory. In terms of the subject-matter of education, how much *language* is required to make good *literature?* With reference to teachers and learners, how much commitment must there be for openness to remain within the language? And, in the environment of modern education, can there actually be education for commitment in an open society without indoctrination?

In our next exploration, we shall examine whether Talmudic rabbis can be helpful in resolving this issue.

Section V:

BECOMING AN INSIDER:
INITIATION AND COMMITMENT

11

HILLEL CONVERTS THREE STRANGERS

(The proselyte) came before Hillel and said to him, 'O gentle Hillel, may blessings rest upon your head, for bringing me under the wings of the Divine Presence.'

Shabbat 25

*W*e have seen that having values and even having been given them involves a measure of decision-making and choice. In our examination of some rabbinic texts, we have seen them assuming both commitment to a language of norms and the ability to use that language in determining our attitudes and actions in concrete circumstances. But how does a young person get inside such a language in the first place so that s/he necessarily encounters such decisions and choices? How does s/he become committed to it? In principle, can learners be initiated in a manner that does not stifle openness and even honest controversy? And specifically, in our generation, can commitment in an open society be congruent with open minds?

My discussion of this issue makes three controversial assumptions.

(1) If education is about values, then it is legitimate to initiate learners into a culture. Therefore, teachers may legitimately envision educated persons who have been brought into a community that speaks

the same language. They have the right to anticipate that pupils, in the course of the process of learning and growing, will become loyal, identified, culturally reliable. They will have membership of participation.

(2) Commitment does not imply lack of criticism on the part of the educated person or closed-mindedness. On the contrary, real commitment involves maintaining standards, controversy for the sake of what is valued, openness for the enrichment of one's own collective, and individual identity.

(3) The focus on texts in Jewish education reflects an educational norm, namely, that Jews be initiated through them into the language of Judaism.

It is not easy to dismiss the arguments against teaching commitment, especially within the context of sources. For within the classroom and in the wider community, the authority of texts as such, and sacred ones all the more so, has largely dissipated, and many look askance at the very educational ideal that such authority represents. Doesn't commitment to sacred communities, bound to holy books, invite the cultivation of closed minds? How can a youthful spirit be taught to fly when the aim is to bring it "under the wings of the Divine Presence"? These problems and others, considered from an educational-philosophical point of view, will be the focus of our discussion and our learning of a Talmudic short story.

"We Shall Do and We Shall Hear"

The special status of commitment is illustrated for the Talmudic sages in their understanding of Israel's declaration at Mount Sinai: "We shall do and we shall hear." (Exodus 24:7) This declaration, "we shall do and we shall hear" *(Na'ase v'Nishma)* and a *midrashic* discussion of it is the subject of a Talmud lesson by Emanuel Levinas, the great contemporary Jewish-French thinker.[1] His text *(Shabbat* 88) commences with the remarkable imagery of God holding Mount Sinai over the heads of the Israelites and saying to them, "If you accept the Torah, all is well, if not, here will your graves be." The discussion proceeds to an examination of the willingness of the Israelites to do (obey) the Torah even before hearing (understanding) it, and the subsequent appearance of six hundred thousand angels who came down and attached crowns to the head of each Israelite, one for the doing and the other for the hearing. Levinas comments:

1. Emmanuel Levinas, "The Temptation of Temptation," *Nine Talmudic Readings,* translated and with an introduction by Annette Aronowicz (Bloomington and Indianapolis: Indiana University Press, 1990), pp. 30–50.

'We shall do and we shall hear.' The Talmudists kept on being astonished by it. The ... paragraph ... which follow(s) forcefully underline(s) the importance of this sequence and also show(s) how concerned the Talmudists were to distinguish the inversion of order from the expression of the simplicity of childish souls.

Rabbi Eleazer has said: when the Israelites committed (themselves) to doing before hearing, a voice from heaven cried out, "Who has revealed to My children this secret, that angels make use of, for it is written, 'Bless the Lord, O His angels, you mighty ones, who do His word, hearkening to the voice of His word'" (Psalms 103:20).

They do before hearing. It is a secret of angels which is in question here, not the consciousness of children ... 'We shall do and we shall hear,' which seemed to us contrary to logic, is the order of angelic existence.[2]

Aronowicz, commenting on Levinas's interpretation of Talmudic sources, notes that his Talmud lessons make the Rabbinic story "a source of standards for measuring the present" and that this requires that authority be given to the text even before we know its contents. "One of the most striking features of (the Israelites') ... acceptance is that they agreed to accept the commandments before they had even heard what they were ... The authority given to the Torah and to the standards embedded in it must precede the actual discovery of these standards, if they are to come to light at all." Allowing himself to interpret and apply the text to modern times and submitting to its power to teach means that Levinas, like the ancient Israelites, "does not bow to the superiority of the text, its power to teach and judge, after the fact of reading but before the fact of reading. There is a certain prerequisite attitude in which the text must be interpreted."[3]

That such an undertaking is plausible when God is believed to "hold the mountain over their heads" requires scant argument. But we shall have to deal with the question whether those who do not have that certainty can be expected to teach—and learn—what Levinas suggests, and if so, on what basis.

Who's Interested? Why Not?

The Talmudic passage that lies at the center of our discussion describes encounters between the sages Shammai and Hillel and three heathens who wish to be proselytes. But before we come to that, let us formulate more precisely what our problem is.

We have spoken of Jewish education as the enterprise whereby people, usually young, are initiated into a language of Judaism as well

2. *Ibid.*, p. 45.
3. Annette Aronowicz, Introduction to *Nine Talmudic Readings*, (Bloomington and Indianapolis: Indiana Universty Press, 1990), p. xxvi.

as the history of prior literature in that language. Success, then, may be measured by the extent to which educated persons know the language and internalize it, so that they can learn excellent dispositions from it and mold wholesome Jewish identities through it. In short, Jewish education should make people fine human beings within the framework of Judaism. Educated Jews will know much of previous literature (i.e., what Jews have said and done in the language) and will themselves use it, perhaps even to make literature of their own.

Yet, many modern educators, even those who are not simply against commitment, would remind us that in this venture of acculturation, much care is required. The educator intent on educating rather than indoctrinating should not program or otherwise stifle the learner. Ultimately, the optimally educated person is the one who "acts well" on the basis of reflection and understanding, not simply the "well-behaved" one who does what s/he is told .[4] In teaching language, one may never forget that it is the medium for the creation of variegated literature.

At the same time, certainly for traditional Jewish educators, knowing the language involves trusting it, using it conventionally even before being genuinely creative in it. It means finding oneself and the source of one's being within it. Otherwise, succor and salvation will come from another place, from a strange culture and other gods. In the final analysis, therefore, commitment cannot be less than both loyalty and freedom. Whether this is possible, and if so how will become clearer later, when we negotiate the use of our text for modern Jewish education through a general philosophical theory.

But the entire dialectical problem of being Jewishly educated, thus committed and yet not indoctrinated, may strike many Jewish teachers as highly theoretical. Their experience all too often is that no such problem arises in their classrooms, for the children have no intention of becoming committed. Indeed, these pupils and their parents often assume that Jewish learning has no power to educate them. And so, many contemporary Jewish educators have the exasperating experience of trying to teach a language that no one wants to learn, that seems locked against transmission.

In exasperation, they are likely to conclude that all they can do is to make some Jewishly focused literature in the non-Jewish languages their students speak. For example, they may present the Exodus from Egypt as an early and dramatic example of national self-determination; creation they portray as a myth rather than as a teaching, and *mitzvot* are rituals, not commandments. Yet they know that this total translation into a non-Jewish language is tantamount to denying that

4. Thomas F. Green, "Acting and Behaving," in *Philosophy and Education,* edited by Israel Scheffler (Boston: Allyn and Bacon, Inc., 1966), p. 115–35.

Judaism has educative power. For it to have such power it must be both a distinctive way to say universal things, and a universe of its own which says distinctive (particularistic) things. It must, as a language, be learned and appreciated on its own terms. And the problem of these teachers is that this seems unlikely to happen and perhaps impossible to achieve.

In reflecting upon this problem, educators may begin by asking themselves the following questions:

(a) How might one describe and evaluate a state of affairs in which young people are inside such a language? What are the outer limits of belonging and how does one achieve both a state of fellowship based on a common language and at the same time wide and pluralistic parameters that accommodate diverse understandings, circumstances, and temperaments?

(b) Conversely, what is really meant by being outside a tradition or language, even when one is somehow attached to it? Specifically, what characterizes a Jew who is an alien to Jewish tradition and language?

(c) Is it possible to get learners who are outside the language of Judaism to become insiders or does one have to be partially within it to begin with in order to make sense of it? If it is possible to initiate genuine outsiders, what may we consider sound and legitimate educational ways of getting people into Jewish tradition and fostering a commitment to it?

Two Stories

As already mentioned, we shall approach these issues of educational initiation and commitment by examining a classic Talmudic story, which features disparate dialogues of sorts between a sage and three heathens who are thinking about becoming insiders but aren't at all clear about what that entails. In each case, as we shall learn, the sage Hillel indeed converted the non-Jew after his more severe colleague, Shammai, refused to have any truck with these inquisitive and, to him, annoying persons.

But before coming to that, we shall take a look at a modern story, having to do with people who express modern doubts about Jewish commitment. These people have fallen or are falling into non-commitment; they are turning their backs on Jewish language and perhaps are beginning to forget it. Unlike Hillel's proselytes, these young people are wavering insiders wanting out rather than curious outsiders looking for a way to enter. As G.N. Schlesinger relates the story:[5]

5. G. N. Schlesinger, "The Problem of Skepticism," *Tradition* 10, no. 3 (1969), pp. 87–88.

There was, once, in the days of the Yeshiva of Volozhin, a group of Jewish students in Berlin. They were severely affected by the Enlightenment and were troubled with great religious doubts, which, of course, they discussed with great vehemence. Finding themselves unable to resolve the questions of Jewish faith to their satisfaction, they decided, in the interest of fairness, to send one of their group to the Yeshiva in Volozhin for two years. Perhaps he, after studying the sources and sitting at the feet of great scholars and authorities, would come up with satisfactory solutions to their problems. And so, an intelligent and studious young man went to the Yeshiva for two years and immersed himself completely in that life. Upon his return to Berlin, his friends greeted him eagerly and asked: "Well, how was it?" "It was wonderful," he replied. "These two years have probably been the best of my life." "Do you now have answers to all the questions we had?" "No, I have answers to none of those questions." "Then what was this all for?" "But I have no more questions left, either ... ."

This apparently apocryphal story is in line with the thesis suggested by D.Z. Phillips in his *Religion Without Explanation*. Phillips denies that religious beliefs are hypotheses that might turn out to be false, or that there are questions to which such beliefs are the right or wrong answers. Rather:

> We are held by them, (i.e., our religious beliefs) captivated by the picture they present ... No contradiction is involved between the believer and the unbeliever; they just have different pictures, different perspectives. The atheist who denies the existence of God does not contradict the theist who puts his trust in God. He is rejecting a whole mode of discourse rather than expressing an opposite view within the same one. And so, we cannot stand outside a religion to judge it ... our beliefs are not so much propositions about reality, they are part and parcel of a way of life which involves such things as prayer, worship, praise and penitence.[6]

In Phillips's sense, we might say that the former *maskil* but now *yeshiva* man turned from non-commitment to commitment when an already known language of belief and commitment reasserted itself over one of non-belief vis-à-vis his Jewish religion or culture. What we have here is a conversion of return[7] in which one leaves the world of one enticing, comprehensive language for that of another familiar one.

The model intimated by this story clearly has certain attractions: it offers a simple and straightforward prescription for initiation: don't let him or her get near, or get him/her out of the wrong language environment! Moreover, under the right circumstances, this educational prescription often works.

But, understood in this Phillips mode, it is theologically problematic. Is the only difference between the world of the Enlightenment

---

6. D.Z. Phillips, *Religion Without Explanation*, pp. 183, 226.
7. This phenomenon is impressively described in Peter L. Berger, *The Heretical Imperative; Contemporary Possibilities of Religious Affirmation* (Garden City, N.Y.: Anchor Books, 1980), Chap. 3.

and that of Volozhin one of picture and perspective? Isn't truth-seeking and truth a dimension of the Berliners' bewilderment and the *yeshiva* student's happiness? Doesn't he now believe that he is plugged into God's language once again? In other words, isn't believing that something is the truth an essential feature of all commitment? Isn't it on the basis of such an acknowledged truth, even though one may be wrong, that one carries out valuative acts that testify to belief?[8]

Furthermore, this model raises a number of moral and educational problems. Though sundry institutions and teachers dedicated to leading their students towards repentance, to *hazarah b'teshuvah,* do what the model requires gladly and effectively, we are not sure whether, once its philosophical ramifications are understood, the model will be considered acceptable by most committed Jews. Certainly it reflects neither the wealth nor the complexity of modern Jewish commitments nor, given the variety of human potential and personality, does it point in the direction of pedagogically fair practice.

In other words, we may have some suspicions about an educational product lacking all questions. We have the feeling that having no questions testifies to an overly simple conception of the Jewish language that the student has come to accept. We may also fear that the young man who has all the answers but no questions will misrepresent Judaism. In his teaching, he is liable to cast doubt in the minds of his perhaps sophisticated listeners as to the adequacy of the Jewish language itself to comprehensively describe reality and to prescribe for worthy action within it. The young man now reminds us too much of those the Rambam calls "the first group of those who expound the words of our sages," those who are adolescently philosophical and far removed from the wisdom of irony.[9] Yet we should not write off our young man from Volozhin and we shall come back to him shortly.

Before that, let us look at our second, impeccably classic story, our text from *Shabbat* 25. The Talmudic tale begins as follows:

> A certain heathen came before Shammai and asked him, "How many *Torot* do you have" "Two," he replied, "the Written Torah and the Oral Torah." Said the heathen, "I believe you with regard to the Written one, but I do not believe you concerning the Oral one. I want you to make me a proselyte on condition that you teach me the Written Torah." Shammai rebuked him and threw him out in a rage. He came before Hillel who converted him. The first day (of instruction) Hillel said to him, *"aleph, bet, gimmel, daled."* The next day, he reversed it (calling an *aleph* a *daled*, etc.). He (the proselyte) said to him, "But yesterday you did not say it so to me." Hillel said to him, "Are you not relying on me (for which letter should be called an *aleph*)? Then for the Oral Torah you may also rely on me."

8. For an important discussion of this point, see Roger Trigg, *Reason and Commitment* (Cambridge and London: Cambridge University Press, 1973), esp. Chap. 3, 5.
9. See Chapter 5.

From this first incident, several things characteristic of the entire narrative are already evident. Shammai seems not to look kindly on wrong questions and refuses to provide answers to them. A wrong question is one that shows a basic ignorance of ground rules, basic cultural assumptions, in short, of the language. The heathen does not know that Judaism, at least for such Pharisaic teachers as Shammai, requires a-priori allegiance to both the Written and Oral law. In Shammai's language, that is what Torah means. Therefore, one cannot be converted to a Judaism of only Written Torah. Shammai seems to be saying: when you know enough to ask the right question, and therefore will not make foolish stipulations that show your basic ignorance of our language's syntax, then and only then come back.

Hillel, on the other hand, is not surprised at the inability of the heathen to formulate an insider's question. He looks behind the question, rather than at it; he asks himself what the questioner is saying in his language and he translates it.[10] He wonders why the person standing in front of him wishes to convert, not whether his concrete question makes internal sense. And so, the fact that the heathen obviously does not realize that he has come to a Pharisaic rabbi who cannot possibly accept his condition does not unduly disturb him. In fact, Hillel promptly converts him, and then begins to teach him Torah, beginning with the Hebrew alphabet. And while teaching him, he demonstrates that written symbols, for example, the Hebrew letters themselves, do not transmit their own meanings or even their own names. A teacher must orally convey these, and if the student is to learn anything the teacher must be trusted. By calling the letters by different names on different days he has shown that the meaning even of what is clearly written depends on oral communication and recognition of the teacher as reliable. He is saying to the proselyte, "What is it like to believe in the Oral Torah? Isn't it like believing that there are people who can tell you what the written letters really mean?"

Meanwhile, or some time before or thereafter, another Gentile appears on the scene and comes before Shammai.

> He said to him, "Make me a proselyte on condition that you teach me the entire Torah while I am standing on one foot." He drove him away with the builder's measuring-stick which was in his hand. He came before Hillel, who converted him. Hillel said to him, "That which is hateful to you, do not do unto your fellow. This is the entire Torah; the rest is comment ary—go learn it."

Once again, Shammai sticks to principle. A person wishing to learn the entire Torah while standing on one foot may be tuned into Roman

---

10. This point is made by Gershfield in his enlightening analysis of this and the following stories; see Edward M. Gershfield, "Hillel, Shammai and the Three Proselytes," *Conservative Judaism* XXI, no. 3 (Spring 1967), pp. 29–39.

tastes for brevity and conciseness in intellectual formulations[11] but he has no idea of how complex Torah is; therefore he cannot be taught. And once again, Hillel reacts differently. Just as he answered the first heathen's ideological question with an epistemological answer (where there is no common language, there are no clear rules of dialogue) so he takes what appears to be a philosophical insistence on the essence of Judaism and answers with a *halakhic* rule. The Biblical commandment to love thy neighbour as thyself means in the normative sense that one should first of all not do unto others what one would not wish done to oneself. And while expounding this legal regulation, Hillel, as we have already seen him do, is initiating a process of study for his fresh convert. "Here," he says, " is your first lesson. Now go and study for yourself."

And finally, there is a third fellow, at first sight the most unlikely candidate for initiation into Judaism.

> On another occasion, a heathen was walking behind a schoolhouse and heard the voice of the teacher saying, "And these are the garments which they shall make: a breastplate and an ephod" (Exodus 28:4). He said, "For whom are these?" They said to him, "For the High Priest." Said the heathen to himself, "I will go and become a proselyte in order that they should make me a High Priest." He came before Shammai and said to him, "Make me a proselyte on condition that you make me a High Priest." He drove him away with the measuring stick which was in his hand.

Having already read of his impatience with two previous would-be proselytes, we are well prepared for Shammai's response. But we wonder whether Hillel will not admit, faced with this outlandish person, that this time Shammai has a point. And yet:

> He came before Hillel, who converted him. Hillel said to him, "Is a king ever appointed who does not know the strategies of kingship? Go now and study the strategies of kingship" (i.e., in your case, of priesthood). He went and began to study Scripture. When he came to the verse, "And the stranger that comes nigh shall be put to death," (Numbers 1:51) he said to Hillel, "About whom is this verse said?" He answered, "It includes even David, king of Israel." Whereupon the heathen reasoned a fortiori concerning himself, "If with regard to Israel, who are called children of the Almighty, who in His love for them has called them 'Israel, my son, my first-born' (Exodus 4:22) the verse says, 'And the stranger that draws nigh shall be put to death,' I, a mere proselyte, who comes with his wallet and stick, so much the more so!" He came before Shammai and said to him, "Am I then capable of becoming a High Priest? Is it not written in the Torah, 'And the stranger that draws nigh shall be put to death'?"

Reading this episode of a person who, as a result of studying Torah, moves so easily from stupidity to sophistication, we wonder whether what we have here is a real heathen or simply a metaphoric story of a child who moves through stages of development. Indeed, the begin-

11. *Ibid.*, p. 33

ning of the episode reminds us of Maimonides's parable of the childish learner who studies Torah in order to be given nuts and raisins.[12] For it seems ridiculous that any adult would engage in such wild fantasies. Can our heathen really wish to change his entire life, learn to speak in an entirely new language, just in order to receive fine garments? And what's the sense of it? Has he never seen fellow-heathens with fine garments, or Jews without them? Can he be so foolish as to expect that, as a Jew, he will be handed the high priesthood on a silver platter?

In any case, Hillel sticks with his method. He converts him, leads the heathen to the study of Torah for the man's own extrinsic reasons, and is rewarded with a person who not only has studied Scripture, but is able to relinquish his childish desires when forced to do so by the application of Talmudic rules of reasoning that he has now mastered. (With a bit of anachronistic imagination, one can even imagine him singsonging the a fortiori, the *kal vahomer,* with the intonation of a Lithuanian yeshiva student.) Moreover, he has no inhibitions about criticizing Shammai for not pointing out the truth to him! (To which claim Shammai probably have responded that, in their previous meeting, it would have been futile; the heathen would not have understood the truth.)

We are told that this proselyte not only scolded Shammai but lavishly praised Hillel:

> He came before Hillel and said to him: "O gentle Hillel, may blessings rest upon your head for bringing me under the wings of the Divine Presence."

In conclusion, the Talmudic narrator tells us:

> After some time, the three of them met in one place. They said, "The impatience *(kapdanut)* of Shammai sought to drive us from the world; the gentleness *(anvetanut)* of Hillel brought us under the wings of the Divine Presence."

In some ways, the Talmudic text about Hillel and the proselytes is similar to the tale of the Berliner who went to Volozhin. In both, the non-committed person doesn't understand; he or she doesn't know or is in the process of forgetting how the system works and therefore asks "stupid" questions. Also, both stories introduce us to learners who have a certain interest and are somehow open; the non-committed in these stories, even when asking the wrong question, is asking some question. And in both narratives someone who was an outsider ultimately realizes and articulates that he has become an insider. In the first case, he no longer has any questions; in the second case, he shows an ability to solve his problems in the language of the tradition.

However there are significant differences as well. Let us look at some of the distinctive features of the Talmudic story:

12. See Chapter 3, p. 45.

(a) A person who asks wrong questions can be dealt with, we are shown, in at least two distinct ways: s/he can be answered honestly, that is, told the way it really is with reverent regard for the integrity of the subject matter (i. e., Judaism) under consideration. In such a case, s/he will be literally or figuratively chased away. Or, s/he may have matters explained to him or her in a manner that clearly does not represent the ways insiders understand things, yet is conducive to growth and prepares the learner to confront the subject matter when he or she is ready for it and has grown into it. The person being initiated is enabled to make sense of Torah and Judaism through associations and nomenclature that are familiar and comprehensible. Hence, one is invited to consider the regulation that is "the entire Torah"; another is sent to study the strategy of kingship, and another is allowed to entertain the notion of Judaism as Written Torah alone. (We can readily picture Shammai scoffing, with great authenticity, at the very idea of an essence of Judaism, or at the notion of teaching the High Priestly trade.)

(b) Each proselyte is encouraged to go and learn and then discovers for himself, as Hillel thought would happen, that learning Torah is surprising and enhancing.

(c) Concluding the three individual stories of three very diverse people, we are told that there was a meeting, and a meeting of minds, among them. The individual development of the three, quite startlingly, has a group aspect. The three proselytes get together "in one place." Perhaps it is at a *minyan,* at the *shuk* scouting for a beautiful *etrog,* or in a *Bet Midrash.* Wherever it was, it must have been somewhere in the sphere of Torah for them to strike up a conversation about their experiences with Hillel. It is here that they find themselves speaking the same language. When they note that Shammai "sought to drive them from the world," the reference is obviously not to our planet, Earth, but to the world or language of Torah. Now speaking the language and sharing it, they fondly recall how Hillel brought them "under the wings of the divine Presence." Plainly, they have become insiders, committed, each in his own way, yet sharing the good fortune of a common teacher who understood that some quest was hiding behind their disparate and somewhat bizarre questions and demands.

Three Conceptions of Commitment

In order to gain maximum educational illumination from our two stories of initiation and commitment, three clusters of concepts, which we have already discussed, will prove useful.

Let us once again recall the distinction between language and literature. Language we have understood to refer to the basic assumptions, structures, and patterns of a culture and its vocabulary, while literature connotes the ways in which individuals express matters and themselves within the language-culture. The Jewish tradition, we have insisted, may well be seen as having–or rather, being–a language in which certain words, actions, and attitudes make distinctive sense, inviting and facilitating the specific fellowship of Jewishness by building particular modes of communication. The language, as we previously noted, says distinctive things and states universal sentiments and ideas in its own way. In that language, there is a *Tanakh* but no Old Testament; there is an aspiration that children attain to Torah and *maassim tovim* rather than simply success, and that they be *Yire Shamayim* and not just mature. And of course, there are many ways of doing Torah and growing in it–many literatures, ranging from philosophy, *halakhic* responsa, kabbalistic mysticism and literary exegesis. In each, individuals within fellowships of the like-minded give discrete articulation to the language, through which they re-affirm it and buttress its foundations. At the same time, through the literature they use and make, they test the language's limits and stretch its parameters in line with their experience of what is true and what has to be said.

Within the language, we may differentiate between underlying principles of education and operative ideals by which we live and to which we educate. The former refer to basic beliefs about the nature of reality, knowledge, and value; the latter may be described as patterns of aspiration and behavior, as social and personal modes that translate principled assumptions about reality and value into concrete forms of human life. That is, wherever there are given specific principles (basic assumptions and beliefs), the question arises: which ideal life, of characteristics and actions, is mandated by these principles and flows from them.

Finally, and consequentially, we must be cognizant of the fact that every culture and every educational enterprise that socializes children into a language thereby presents them, on the basis of cultural ideals, with specific hero-types, or models of virtue and self-actualization. These are persons who represent the culture at its best and who are therefore considered worthy of admiration and emulation.

These conceptual frames help us to identify and delineate diverse yet overlapping types of non-commitment among modern Jews.

One way of thinking about the non-committed is to see them as persons who do not accept the principles of the tradition as expressed and taught in its sacred texts. That is, what we may call the theology of classical Judaism does not mark the principled world in which they live. Their principles are, rather, the ostensibly self-understood ones of their non-Jewish cultural environment; they see no meaningful or even possible connection between these received and accepted (Greek, Christian, secular, pagan) principles and those underlying the Jewish tradition. They may possibly be well acquainted with the principled world of classical Judaism, but they find the beliefs of Torah, Talmud, and *midrash* to be quaint or dull, primitive or exotic. In any case, they refuse to consider this Jewish cluster of principle a genuine option for thinking about things, as a possible way of seeing reality, knowledge, and value; they do not accept them as philosophical foundations for a good life.

The non-committed may also be those who don't accept the ideals that have been drawn out of these principles, or are declared in the texts of Judaism to naturally follow from them. That is, they are not committed to a life of Judaism of which, for example, study of Torah is an integral part. These non-committed persons are perhaps ready to accept some or all of the principles (e.g., belief in God, in the possibility of a better [Messianic] world) but they see no way or reason to carry these beliefs and principles into the realm of operative Jewish ideals.[13]

In both of these categories, therefore, there are non-committed persons who know the language, or some of it, but who refuse to trust it. This means that they do not believe that the language of Judaism can be utilized to generate worthwhile literature. This non-committed view implies that while the texts and traditions may be worth researching, they are not or no longer inherently enhancing and educative.

A third way of viewing the non-committed is to regard them simply as persons who don't know the language. Thus, when they hear it spoken, they don't understand what is being said. So they are not even aware of what Jewish commitment entails.[14]

As a result of the above, singly or in the composite, the non-committed do not consider the hero-types of the Jewish tradition worthy of study or emulation; they do not see them as paradigms of noble living.

Conversely, we may portray the committed person as inside the principles, however interpreted. He or she views the good life and society within the framework of the ideals, though they may be diversely understood and applied. S/he therefore may be said to

---

13. If the meaning of our principles is that they are the philosophical ground of the ideal actions, then not to be committed to the ideal action is tantamount to not having the relevant principle. See R. M. Hare, *The Language of Morals* (Oxford and New York: Oxford University Press, 1964), p. 1. But this understanding of principle is synonymous with the conception of value as we have used it in Section IV. We are assuming that people can have certain ideas about what is true, knowable, and worthy without making the connection between these beliefs and the way they act.

14. This way of viewing the matter often seems all too comfortable. For non-commitment thus understood seems easy to deal with. All that is apparently required is to immerse the noncommitted in the language! Indeed, such immersion often works even for those who think they have rejected it. (Isn't that what happened to the young man at Volozhin?)

"speak the language" of the Jewish tradition, to trust it, and to make literature, at least to the extent that he or she has a personal understanding of the significance of his/her life in that language. In doing so, the committed person walks in the footsteps of masters, who are viewed as paradigms of self-actualization within the language.

Between Jerusalem and Volozhin

The similarities between the young man at Volozhin and the proselytes of Hillel, as well as the differences between them, should now be somewhat clearer. We may assume that the Berlin band of enlightened young people had been raised in the language of Judaism, but had become acquainted with new principles and ideals that led them to question their Jewish ones, to raise doubts about whether the Jewish language was still worth speaking, still deserved their loyalty. The one of their group who went to Volozhin found there that the Jewish language was vital and all-pervasive, and functioned as the natural medium of everybody's literature. This strengthened his bond to that language to such an extent that he had no more questions. The thrust of the story is that the problem of principles arises not when other principles become more cogent, but when another language, in which foreign principles and ideals reside, becomes more powerful, pervasive and, thus, attractive. The yeshiva man became committed, not because he had grappled with and thought through some abstract or culturally neutral problems, but because he had joined another fellowship in which the language and problems were those of Jewish tradition and not those of Berlin high society.

As for the proselytes, they spoke the wrong language. Thus, quite naturally, they articulated confused notions about Jewish principles and ideals. This exasperated Shammai, who threw them out. Hillel, on the other hand, related to the principled requirements of the first two, responding to them (somewhat deviously) in the idiom of the Roman-heathen language they understood. He then sent them on the way mandated by his ideal which, to him, justified the deviousness. They were told to study Torah. The third proselyte cannot be accused of having principled requirements, but he, too, was told to learn Torah. This learning led him to discover that his personal aspiration, in his new language, was ludicrous.[15]

15. Frankel remarks on the literary significance of the juxtaposition of the simple former-heathen, with his staff and wallet, and the exalted King David, with regard to

And so, all three found themselves in Hillel's world of language and literature. Having started with their questions, whatever they were, they were sent by Hillel onto a journey of development and discourse. He took the questions of the first two seekers seriously, as inquiries about what is true, and he did not dismiss the expressed needs of the third person. We can imagine him happy to find that their journey led them to a meeting of minds, to a common language and fellowship.

So far, so good. Or perhaps, too good.

Educators who may even have participated in enrichment seminars in which such stories are used to bolster their own commitments may well ask how they can utilize them, how they may guide and perhaps change their educational practice. The educator is likely to have a number of questions and is not certain that Hillel, as presented so far, can be helpful.

For example, what shall the teacher do with this teaching in the contemporary context in which:

(a) most people have many commitments and some appear to have none;

(b) there is serious controversy even among committed Jews as to what commitment actually entails, and which commitments are currently worthy or viable;

(c) it is not clear which distinct commitments are compatible;

(d) there are principled disagreements about how one decides these matters; and

(e) teachers themselves often wonder what their own specific commitments are, what they require, and what they have the right to teach.

A concrete instance of one of these issues: there are contemporary Jewish commitments that would have been totally incomprehensible to both Hillel and Shammai, such as those secular ones that deny the authority of all texts. Can one call maintaining an interest in these texts, and even declaring ownership of them, to be commitment? What about people who consider them irrelevant to Jewish identity and commitment, but declare themselves to be nevertheless Jewishly committed?

---

the High Priestly role. Both of them constituted strangers who could not draw nigh. Our proselyte also learns that despite the fact that most Jews are "strangers" in the sense and context of high priesthood, they are called God's "first-born and His beloved." See Yonah Frankel, *"Tzurot Hizoniot L'umat Arakhim P'nimi'im"* ("External Forms As Against Internal Values"), in *Mikhtam L'David (Memorial Volume for R. David Ochs),* edited by Yitzchak D. Gilat and Eliezer Stern (Ramat Gan, Israel: Bar Ilan University, 1977), pp. 123–24.

And that is not all. With the exception of the latter group, all affirm that Jewish texts are educative and capable of fostering Jewish personalities when they are studied seriously. Therefore, in almost all Jewish schools, great attention is given to Bible instruction. But given the pluralism in contemporary Judaism, what makes a reading "serious"?

Teachers who raise these questions seem to be asking for a handle to such a source as the one we have just examined, which will help them to look at it as educators. They wish to know how to think about initiation in a manner that corresponds with everything else they do as educators, in a mode that sets them thinking about the processes, and not only the purposes. This is especially true because many of the purposes come with a theological language that some teachers find problematic. The experience of teachers is that spiritual matters such as commitment to Judaism are often presented in ways too edifying, exalted and imprecise to be of practical help. And when theology is presented to them as educational theory, the frequent backlash is classroom activity that is demonstratively down to earth, utterly practical. The unfortunate consequence of that, as I have noted elsewhere,[16] is that the theory that is incorporated in teaching is only haphazardly congenial to Jewish education. The theories that are used have a no-nonsense aura about them, but they suggest only the skimpiest criteria of success, such as "the kids seem to like it." (In this case motivation is identified with achievement, which is totally unrelated to consideration of Jewish excellence.)

Will recourse to general philosophical discourse help us to discover criteria for *serious* study, *genuine* initiation, and *real* commitment in Jewish education? Will it help us identify criteria that can be utilized even in an age of valuative pluralism and cultural change? Can we suggest a philosophical approach that is congenial to Jewish tradition and therefore can illuminate what Hillel was doing and show the modern teacher what Hillel meant in terms of what s/he actually does or could be doing?

To these questions we turn in the following chapter.

---

16. Rosenak, *Commandments and Concerns,* pp. 193–94.

12

A THEORY FOR A SAGE

Looking for a Theory

*A*t first sight, it looks easy to locate a general conception that can draw out the meanings and uses of our story for education. All that seems to be required is to do the following three things:

(a) to examine any one of a number of theories of commitment that coherently offers a description of what commitment is, in which contexts it arises, and how it works;

(b) to see how the proposed theory explicitly relates to education or has been applied to educational theory; and

(c) to spell out what Hillel is saying in terms of that theory.

But, in fact, it is not that simple, for our task is not to show how the story of Hillel and his proselytes illustrate commitment in general, but to show which conception of commitment helps us to understand them. Our aim is not to show how our Talmudic tale is the same as any other story of initiation we might find in the pages of Western civilization, but to show which general conceptions, which wisdom from anywhere, is congenial to it, illuminating it, and drawing out what it is saying for educational discourse.

The theory we are looking for will not necessarily be drawn from Jewish theology or based on it; it may even, philosophically, say something else, something with which Jewish educators, in defending the language of Judaism, may wish to take issue. (For example, it may, like Emile Durkheim, view society as the ultimate locus of authority, unlike the Jewish language, which sees God in this role. Or the writer, in discussing religious education, may, like Paul Tillich, be explicitly thinking of church education.)[1] But if it describes commitment in a way that points to the way Judaism "works" the theory may still be useful when partially translated.

On the other hand, we are unlikely to consider a theory congenial that is totally and obviously opposed in its assumptions and ramifications to what the Jewish tradition upholds as true principles and normative ideals. We cannot, for example, address ourselves to the problem of authority in Jewish education with the aid of fascistic theories of commitment, nor can we solve the problem of pluralism in contemporary Jewry by pretending that relativistic notions of being committed to one's freely chosen values are one way of understanding Hillel as an educator. Hillel was not a totalitarian idolator and he believed in revelation.

Moreover, we require a theory that relates to the present situation and problems of Jewish education, that encourages us to focus on the concrete challenges facing Jewish educators. For example, while a sociological theory of commitment, such as that of Emile Durkheim, illuminates the ways society educates by socializing to its perceived needs,[2] and while this tells us important things about the ways Judaism and Jewish education work, it will not necessarily be useful to Jewish educators. These educators often sense that their students are all-too-well socialized into a general society, and that the problem is the perceived dearth of Jewish society available to complement or counter, or at least temper, the pupils' commitment to that general society. The problem of educating for Jewish commitment outside of Israel or in very traditional and self-segregating communities in the Diaspora, seems not optimally treated by such sociological theories. Those who wish to educate Jewishly in open but non-Jewish societies (to which the Jewish school and community are also committed) will require a theory capable of clearly distinguishing between society and community.

Furthermore, we seem to be looking for a theory that addresses teachers directly. Teachers are usually men and women who strive to be loyal to Jewish tradition, who have achieved some degree of mastery in this cultural and/or religious enterprise, and who wish to bring young people into it because they deem it valuable. However,

1. For example, Emile Durkheim, *Education and Sociology,* translated by Sherwood D. Fox (New York and London: The Free Press and Collier-Macmillan Ltd., 1956); Paul Tillich, "A Theology of Education," *Theology of Culture,* edited by Robert C. Kimball (London and Oxford: Oxford University Press, 1959), pp. 146–57.

2. See Emil Durkheim, *Moral Education: A Study in the Theory and Application of the Sociology of Education* (New York and London: The Free Press and Collier-Macmillan Ltd., 1961).

due to circumstance and conviction, these educators often feel more comfortable and honest fostering commitment that does not hinge on explicit ideological affirmations and does not necessarily encourage existential leaps of faith.

A good theory must shed light on commitment as an educational aim, and help teachers understand what educating toward commitment might imply and require. It may be expected to suggest pedagogic guidelines and perhaps even syllabi. In our classic Jewish idiom, we suggest that teachers who are armed with such a theory may more concretely think about what educators should understand by the Talmudic praise accorded to "doing before hearing" and how they may, as teachers, grapple with Hillel's technique of converting people in order to teach them.

A good example of a general theory that meets these criteria and that can be used to coax a philosophical conception of initiation into the world of Torah out of our sources is found in Alisdair MacIntrye's lengthy discourse on virtue and practice. We shall summarize this and examine what an educational translation of MacIntyre's conceptions might look like.

Practice and Virtue

In *After Virtue*,[3] MacIntrye proposes three stages in the logical development of the concept of virtue, each of which has its own conceptual background.

> The first stage requires a background account of what I shall call a practice, the second an account of ... the narrative order of a single human life and the third an account ... of what constitutes a moral tradition. Each earlier stage is both modified by and reinterpreted in the light of, but also provides an essential constituent of each later stage ...[4]

A key concept, then, is *practice*. MacIntrye's definition of practice is complex. In his words, it is:

> a coherent and complex form of socially established cooperative human activity through which goods internal to that form of activity are realized in the course of trying to achieve those standards of excellence which are appropriate to, and partially definitive of, that form of activity, with the result that human powers to achieve excellence, and human conceptions of the ends and means involved, are systematically extended.[5]

Following Larmore, we may state this more simply as "a cooperative human activity having shared standards of excellence that deter-

3. Alasdair MacIntrye, *After Virtue,* 2nd ed. (Notre Dame, Indiana: University of Notre Dame Press, 1984).
4. *Ibid.,* pp. 186–87.
5. *Ibid.,* p. 187.

mine a form of success that is instrinsically related to the activity itself."[6] Thus, all fields of organized endeavor in which the highest rewards are intrinsic ones qualify as practices, while specific, even skilled, activities in isolation from their field do not. The work of an historian is a practice, as is that of the musician and architect, but reading a history book or bricklaying or listening to a symphony aren't. Doing the dishes or tossing a ball back and forth with a child would not qualify, but such complex social, standard-bearing, and intrinsically rewarding endeavors as educating, maintaining a household, building a family, and playing football do.

It should be clear from the above that the ultimate aim of practices is to attain to the good that the community of practitioners declare to be inherent in them, which can be attained in no other way. For example, the real purpose of playing chess, we are told by those on the inside of this practice, is to master the game, to enjoy playing, to achieve excellence in it, to sense what possibilities for achievement and enjoyment are hidden within it.

However, it is likely that before one reaches intrinsic enjoyment, mastery and self-expression through the game, there will be chess-playing for such extrinsic awards as candy (for children), or prestige, status and money (for adults). What characterizes the extrinsic rewards is that they have no necessary relationship to chess whatsoever, whereas the internal reward cannot be gained through any other activity or practice. It follows that extrinsic rewards are scarce; few can win prizes in chess competitions. Intrinsic rewards, on the other hand, are potentially available to all who involve themselves in the practice and excel in it.

However, one cannot hope to gain these intrinsic rewards before one understands and becomes proficient in the practice and even sits at the feet of masters.

> A practice involves standards of excellence and obedience to rules as well as the achievement of goods. To enter into a practice is to accept the authority of those standards and the inadequacy of my own performance as judged by them.

Thus, one must subject one's own "attitudes, choices and preferences and tastes to the standards which currently and partially define the practice." This is not to say that practices are immune to criticism; they are not, both because they have a history and because they are subject to development. Yet "we cannot be initiated into a practice without accepting the authority of the best standards realized so far."

> If, on starting to listen to music, I do not accept my own inability to judge correctly, I will never learn to hear, let alone appreciate, Bartok's last

6. Charles E. Larmore, *Patterns of Moral Complexity* (Cambridge: Cambridge University Press, 1987), p. 36.

quartets. If, on starting to play baseball, I do not accept that others know better than I when to throw a fast ball and when not, I will never learn to appreciate good pitching, let alone to pitch.[7]

Thus it is clear that practices involve communities comprising all those who engage in a practice. The community includes those who are learning how to do it from others and those who teach it. Naturally, it also takes in those who have done it in the past, who brought the practice to its present state. We may now understand how MacIntrye defines virtue in a way that relates it to practice.

A virtue is an acquired human quality the possession and exercise of which tends to enable us to achieve those goods which are internal to practice and the lack of which effectively prevents us from achieving any such goods.[8]

One can thus hardly conceive of virtues outside the context of practices, for virtues arise for appropriation within practices. We may surmise that the more comprehensive the practice, the richer and more complex the funds of virtues within it. But, in fact, no community of practice can function without its inherent virtues. For example, chess, like most practices, requires honesty; almost all practices require some humility; few can do without courage. Every practice also needs people who are committed to acquiring knowledge and who consider shoddy performance to be lacking in virtue. And since practices do have histories, the people presently involved in them in a serious way require some relationship to past practitioners and a sense of continuity with them.

A second stage of virtue is what MacIntrye calls "the unity of a human life." We cannot, he claims, understand any activity without having an idea in which context it should be seen, what its setting is. Each of us, if he or she lives a life of sense and cumulative meaning, sees her/his life as having a beginning and an end. We wish for our acts and attitudes to constitute a whole story as free as possible from the discontinuities that rob us of our identities and which, at the least, make us capricious. Thus, "the unity of a virtue in someone's life is intelligible only as a characteristic of a unitary life, a life which can be conceived and calculated as a whole." In part, I am the author of my story, but since the tapestry of my life is woven with the threads of practices and virtues that have communities and histories, I am also a character in various stories. Part of the meaning of "the unity of life" is that "I can answer the question 'What am I to do?' only if I can answer the prior question, 'of what story or stories do I find myself a part?'"[9]

7. MacIntrye, *After Virtue*, p.190.
8. *Ibid.*, p. 191.
9. *Ibid.*, p. 216.

I am part of a story of others and they, of mine. The good for me is "how best I might live out that unity—bring it to completion." It follows that "to be the subject of a narrative that runs from one's birth to one's death is ... to be accountable for the actions and experiences that compose a narratable life."[10] Yet, once again, the narrative of my life is intertwined with that of others; like any rich plot, the story of my life has more than one character.

Now, therefore, with the aid of the concept of practice we come upon the idea of the unity of life as signifying a good life. The good life is a whole and worthy "story," given its unity by steadfast adherence to the virtues that inform the practices in which one is involved, to which one, in a sense, belongs. We may now note that it is to the practices and their internal virtues, and to the story that a person is telling, with others, to which he or she can be viewed as being committed.

This brings us to the third stage, which constitutes the consciousness not only of striving for a unified life, a meaningful personal story, but a history. "... I inherit from the past of my family, my city, my tribe, my nation, a variety of debts, inheritances, rightful expectations and obligations. These constitute the given of my life, my moral starting point."

> What I am, therefore, is in key part what I inherit, a specific past that is present to some degree in my present. I find myself part of a history and ... whether I like it or not, whether I recognize it or not, one of the bearers of a tradition.[11]

And yet, to bear a tradition is not all reverence or sweetness and light. Traditions, when vital, embody "continuities of conflict." "A living tradition ... is an historically extended, socially embodied argument, and an argument precisely about the goods which constitute that tradition." Since they "continue a not-yet-completed narrative," living traditions "confront a future whose determinate and determinable character ... derives from the past."[12] And it is in this tradition that practices develop and the individual's story is told.

This, in brief, sums up MacIntrye's conception. Like every such conception, of course, it occasions controversy among philosophers. I have surveyed it as a congenial illustration of the possible uses of general theory in Jewish educational thought.

Unified Lives: From Berlin to Jerusalem

Now, before returning to Hillel and Shammai, a final glance at our friend from Volozhin. If one may say that the language of a culture

---

10. *Ibid.*, p. 217.
11. *Ibid.*, p. 223.
12. For example, Larmore, *Patterns of Moral Complexity*, pp. 22–39.

is the ground of its various practices and that its most comprehensive and central practices describe and place the language, then it will be correct to say that our Volozhin student, formerly of Berlin, moved back into the Jewish language by anchoring himself in one of its focal and paradigmatic practices, *limmud Torah* (study of Torah), and becoming, at least for a time, a yeshiva man.

His Berlin friends were probably annoyed at him. They must have found it difficult to put up with such a facile dismissal of the questions that had previously perturbed him. The new certitude he displayed seemed unreliable on his part; it was a break in the unity of his life, an irresponsible indifference to a previous chapter in his story. This was perhaps especially exasperating to his friends, for they were very much a part of that previous chapter, of the Jewish Enlightenment, and probably felt that a character in the common narrative had walked out on them. The yeshiva man could, and perhaps did, reply that he had recovered his moral tradition, and was again plugged into a greater narrative than that of his personal life. But, anachronistically citing MacIntyre, his friends might have retorted that the third stage of a moral tradition cannot be divorced from the second stage (the unity of a life). Their former fellow had rediscovered the old way of speaking the language, but they had sent him to Volozhin to discover whether people like them, in their actual story, could still speak it, make literature in it. They had wanted to know whether these practices were still recognizably worthy, the locus of recognizable virtues.

We can only hope that his experience in Volozhin enabled him to answer that question!

Now let us return to Hillel and his proselytes. It seems plausible to say that the first two outsiders who asked principled questions about revelation and regulations were asking about the unity of life, about the organizing principles of the good life. Hillel, in MacIntrye's terms, may have been saying to them:

"I should like to say to you, 'First things first.' We do not begin in our culture with theological questions or even with moral philosophy. Rather, on the basis of the experiences we have had with God, our fellow humans, and other nations, we begin with practices and the virtues that attend and sustain them. We believe that these practices are divine in origin and that they make sublime human virtue possible. You obviously don't understand this; that is why the conscientious but severe Shammai sent you on your way.

"But I shall give you some answers to your questions, answers garnered from the reflective world of the practices. I do this not because you understand them or have earned them; after all you are not yet within the practices. But I, unlike Shammai, feel that you do deserve some response because you are adults and you have narrative needs dictated by the stories in which you have lived until now, as authors and characters.

"I assume that you have come to me because no matter how you articulate it you find something faulty with the story lines in which you find yourselves. Indeed, you seem to feel, as authors and characters, that you are in the wrong stories. Behind your questions is the desire to enter our story. That is a weighty decision, for it means cutting yourself off from other characters and other authors and it means learning a new set of practices, from the beginning, like children.

"I shall perform a formal act that places you within our story, within our community, in this and in past generations. I shall convert you. But then, having joined our story, you must enter the practices, and I shall teach you how to start. Afterwards, you'll catch the story line and understand the moral tradition within which we write the chapters and the virtues that hold them together. That story line, as you will discover, is held together by the Torah, and a central practice of that story, for all of us who write and live it, is *limmud Torah*. Go and learn."

The situation of the proselyte who wished to become a high priest was in principle no different from that of the other heathens, though he described it most ludicrously. Uninhibited by the sophistication of the others, he declared that the narrative of his life would be different and better if he switched stories. In learning how to do so, he discovered King David, a prominent nonpriest of the historical story. No less important, he learned how to criticize Shammai–a teacher who refused to initiate him into the practice of Judaism or to explain the grammar of its language to him. Note his outcry, "Am I then capable of being a high priest? Is it not written ...?"

Commitments and Certainties

Hillel, as previously noted, had greater confidence than most moderns have in the stability of the moral tradition and in the unity of the story which, after all, was held together by the Creator of all characters. Hillel also knew how the practices and virtues were linked to the innermost meaning of the plot, namely, the will of God. Can there be commitment to Jewish practice, unity of life, and moral tradition without such certainty?

In approaching this question, let us operate upon the assumption that the issue of educational initiation and subsequent commitment can, for those who find it congenial and useful, be plausibly and handled through the conception of practice and all it entails with regard to virtue, the unity of an individual life and fellowship with other practitioners. Through the prism of this conception, Hillel and Shammai are seen to disagree about whether one can teach the "practice" of Judaism to outsiders, but they can be assumed to share the view that the Jewish people attain their identity and purpose through the comprehensive practice of Torah.

Hillel, unlike Shammai, seems to be saying that everyone can enter this practice through *limmud Torah*. Moreover he, a master of practice, is ready to give an introductory lesson to all who ask, after which he will send them to study by themselves. He does not think that one has to know a good deal about the practice in order to be taught it. Any question about the practice of Judaism that testifies to good faith, even if it betrays total ignorance of the "coherent and complex … activity through which goods internal to that activity are realized," no matter how ludicrous, ignorant or childish, should be welcomed as a willingness to learn. In the course of study, through which he or she appropriates the practice of *limmud Torah,* the learner will discover the virtues within Judaism that are made accessible through *limmud Torah*. For *limmud Torah* is itself a kind of avenue of access, that is, an initiation into the comprehensive practice, i.e., language, of Torah. Having discovered the rules, methods, and virtues of the practice, the learner will then continue to study, ask pertinent insiders' questions, join the world of Jewish fellowship. We may then say that he or she has been initiated, competent in the practice, committed to its virtues, and a member of its community. The conversion that began the process not only introduced the heathens to the practice, it anticipated their belonging to it and understanding it—just as the learning of the child bears the promise of adult ownership of culture and society. That that would happen is the chance Shammai was not ready to take.

Yet, relating does not, for Hillel, mean acquiescence to the learner's terms but only a readiness to understand his or her situation. Learning a practice, as our proselytes discover, means accepting the discipline of initiation. Practices require mastery, and mastery implies effort and discipline. It requires a measure of trust. Those who wish to acquire a practice have to "do" even before they "hear."

Recall our first proselyte. Apparently he had matters worked out ideologically and even theologically. It made innate sense to him on the basis of his experience in his own heathen world that there were sacred, revealed books, but not revealed discussions. So he could believe Hillel about the Written Torah, that it was divinely revealed, normative, a legitimate source of authority. But he didn't believe him about the Oral Torah.

Neither Shammai nor Hillel understood the practice of Torah thus; furthermore, since they were masters of the practice, we have reason to trust their understanding, despite—and perhaps because of—their controversies. Yet Hillel relates seriously to the man standing in front of him. He is ready to move him into the practice but begins by pointing out to him that he is a novice. (The ingenuity of converting him first becomes apparent. Had he not been taken in he would have been be an outsider rather than a novice, and outsiders have no motivation to learn, except to satisfy noncommittal curiosity.) As a novice, he doesn't know the rules yet. In order to get to know them, to really become a practitioner, he has to trust representatives and masters of the historical community. It is they who know what the words mean. Later, when he has mastered the practice, he may engage in controversy about the Oral Tradition. But at this stage, not to believe it is not to be able to learn it. If he or she doesn't "do" it, s/he won't "hear" it.

The second proselyte, despite his apparent sophistication, is also a stranger to the language. Shammai is so furious that he cannot even bring himself to say that the practice of Judaism hardly employs the idiom of an essence that can be stated on one foot, or in one overarching regulation. What Shammai could have said to him but didn't is the following:

"I understand your wish to be told what Judaism is in 'ten words or less.' This is difficult to do in our language, not only because there are varying opinions of what is most important, but also, because in this language we have both embellished ideas, called *aggadah*, and legal norms, called *halakhah.* In both cases, though, we keep away from generalizations and abstractions; we proceed from particular stories, incidents, cases, and specific norms of behavior. Even when we have a general rule, like 'Love thy neighbour as thyself,' we apply an *halakhic* method to it. We ask what it actually means in diverse cases and what are its minimal and its several more expansive requirements, both positive (i.e., what to do) and negative (what not to do). In fact, when we have a problem, like "from which time to recite the *Shema* on the evening," we prefer to answer with another *halakhah,* such as "from the time that the priests enter to eat of their tithes,"[13] rather than simply to say, "when the stars appear in the heavens," even though in terms of the time these answers are identical. The world of our practices is studded with *halakhot* just as the world of our stories resides in an elaborate medley of *aggadot.* This will make the practice of Torah or Judaism more difficult to get into but with perseverance you'll learn how it's done."

13. *Berakhot* 1:1 and the insightful discussion of Judah Goldin dealing with this and kindred features of rabbinic literature. See *The Living Talmud; the Wisdom of the Fathers and its Classical Commentaries,* selected and translated by Judah Goldin (New York: New American Library, 1957), pp. 13–17.

The man who liked high priestly garments began, like most beginning practitioners, with motives so extrinsic as to be laughable, and, to Shammai, infuriating. Hillel had to ask himself: how does one pass from practice for the sake of extrinsic reward to engaging in the practice for its own sake, committed to the virtues it exposes to view and finding significance in them? This is a question that we found Maimonides raising in his "Introduction to *Perek Helek*." Every educator comes upon it whenever s/he is faced with a child who is now, here, sitting in the third row on the left, a cognitive alien who will hopefully become an adult, but who even now has every right to learn, just as he or she is.

In fact, if we think of the simple man who is the third proselyte in our series as a metaphor for every learner, we can understand Shammai as a person who simply has no use for education as initiation, but only for teaching those who, fundamentally, already know. Shammai can be imagined as a brilliant university professor or as an outstanding teacher in an excellent classically oriented high school. But one cannot picture him teaching the first grades of school where a child may freely imagine how nice it must have been to walk through the streets of Jerusalem in the beautiful clothes of the High Priest, who wishes "that I were the High Priest."

And now, we may address our question of commitment as it relates to religious faith and/or certainties. We have had to approach it indirectly because in entering a practice one can hardly expect the masters to spell out its intrinsic demands, pleasures, and potentialities. True, novices can, in some hazy fashion, anticipate them, and for those entering a practice that anticipation is itself a kind of faith. Yet it is hardly the understanding shared by members of the fellowship nor the certainty that expresses true at-homeness in a story. And so it is noteworthy and clearly sensible that Hillel, in initiating the proselytes into the practice and language of Judaism, says little or nothing about God, Whom, we may assume, he considered the authority behind the practice and the source of its worth, its demands, and the promise or reward inherent in it. Believing appears in the initial Hillel-heathen interchanges only when the first man "believes" him about the Written, but not about the Oral Torah.

But our proselytes, while in the process of mastering the practice, fathoming its tradition, and perceiving the contours and possibilities of a unified life within it, had the experience of becoming committed to it. Apparently, the practice and its community conferred significance upon their lives and bestowed upon them the possibility of and demand for unified life within it. Moreover, in reflective moments, they must have asked themselves where the virtues discovered within the practice really came from, and whether the practice that they were now entering through learning didn't seem like more than a socially established human activity.

We find evidence of such reflection in the meeting of the proselytes in one place. Discovering that they belong together, having been initiated by the same careful teacher, they find themselves "under the wings of the Divine Presence." They are now ready to articulate their conviction that this practice, of Torah, is a "world" that gives them a more-than-human moral tradition, an opportunity to write a coherent narrative in which there is, in addition to themselves, a senior Author. Hillel, being gentle, knew that the less he said about that, the better. He understood that one may enter a language by learning ideals of action even if the principles of belief remain discomforting; indeed, that principles are better come upon than explicitly taught.

All three of his pupils, having had a gentle teacher, learned that within the practice of Judaism, within the community of those who spoke this language, there were masters who could be trusted. Hillel taught them that even the signification of the letters of the alphabet depended on a reliable community, that even ethics required *halakhic* rules and that the study of Torah was an ever surprising adventure. For example, what is more surprising than to discover such exalted personages as King David in the context of their *halakhic* limitations? Imagine, the man must have thought, King David is called with regard to priesthood "the stranger ..."!

Through this master of practice they eventually found themselves to be members of the community "in one place." But this master, representing this community, did not expect everyone within it to be the same; each had a different story to write. He made no demands on them except that they do what getting into the paradigm required, to enter the language of Judaism through study. He felt at ease with learners of different temperaments and needs. He expected them to arrive at the principles differently and he knew that they would bring their own inclinations and experiences to the expression of the ideals. This he knew because they asked different questions and though he answered them deviously, in terms of an anticipated future understanding on the part of each pupil, he did answer them.

Hillel's Strategy Today

Many Jews today reject Hillel's educational approach, both because it seems like a mere tactic ("study Torah and through it you will arrive at the comprehensive practice of my Judaism") and because they are uncomfortable with the idea that belonging requires the mastery of a holy literary tradition. In other words, they reject the idea that the language has a foundational literature only through which one becomes literate in that language. They may even feel that the Jewish people merely has a literature within the common language of Western civilization. In either case, they are not satisfied with the kind of pluralism that MacIntrye's model suggests with regard to Hillel's teaching: that once one is within a language, a tradition, and a community, each life within it will have its own unity, and that it will participate in "an historically extended, socially embodied argument." Suspicious of those who set the rules of this argument, they claim that it is initiation enough to cultivate Jewish identity, commitment enough to shoulder the fate of the Jewish people and wisdom enough to be actively involved in the solution of Jewish problems.

I think that here, even the patient Hillel might demur. Had he studied MacIntrye's concept, he might have said that Jewish identity is not in itself the name of a practice, as, for example, learning is. Membership in the community of Jewish fate, when actively confronted or embraced, may indeed be a practice, when it goes together with the acquisition of cultural goods, historically transmitted and appropriated. But that, Hillel, might point out, requires learning. For without history, community, and the narrative of a unitary life, identity may be no more of a practice than, for instance, a stoically borne but joyless social responsibility. Or, it may be like an uninformed love of music, a sense of guilt for every concert not attended and a compelling but irritating need to contribute to the musicians' fund.

As for the solution of problems: it is true, of course, that every educated human being is bound to apply him/herself to this and that every human group, the Jewish included, is well-advised to devote large efforts and resources of intelligence to the modes and means of understanding, using, and not misusing our natural and cultural environments. There can also be no doubt that the location and solution of problems involve manifold practices that every educational system must teach. For example, every modern educated person must be enabled to bring a knowledge of various applied sciences and skills of systematic reflection to contemporary problems. And these, too, are practices. They, too, have histories, invite practitioners to fellowship, and require cultivation of discrete virtues. One can hardly deal with problems effectively without such virtues as courage, persistence, competence, and honesty in inquiry.

Yet it is not these practices that in themselves systematically extend Jewish conceptions of means and ends as the study of Torah did for our would-be High Priest. They do not mandate specifically Jewish ways to narrate a human life nor do they require the understanding, maintanence, and extension of a Jewish moral tradition. None of them in themselves teach Jewish language or necessarily express themselves in a Jewish literature. That is, the skills of problem-solving need not reflect the Jewish historical community and its story. All modern people share an idiom of problem-solving and in every modern individual life the practices of modern science and technology should be part of things, part of the person's internal unity and of the ongoing narrative of his or her life. Indeed, Zionists have always demanded, justly, I think, that problem-solving and its relevant practices be placed on the agenda of the Jewish people as a people, and that Zionism should be promoted and publicly recognized as contemporary Jewish literature *par excellence.* Indeed, it is a literature that draws on crucial features of the language, on much Jewish experience, and on the *hokhmah* of many peoples.

So to say that these general practices do not in themselves teach the language of Judaism is not a stricture on them , nor a suggestion that one should not be committed to them. For these now-universal practices are indeed intrisically valuable; they demand knowledge and educated sensibility, expose to view and teach distinctive virtues, bestow membership and responsibility within widespread communities of practitioners. Modern Jews should be aware that without these practices there could have been no Zionism and no state of Israel, which required state-building, road-building, and many fields of competence that life in *Galut* had deceptively made to appear insignificant or trivial for Jews.

Therefore, to maintain that these practices do not teach the language merely refers to their universality in principle and thus, their human insufficiency. For human beings live in distinct languages that reflect actual, responsible, and intimate experiences with Transcendence. These experiences are re-enacted and replenished with the help of reason and custom, together with people and texts, in solitude and celebration. At their highest, these experiences are individual and collective self-discernments, setting moral and existential limits on problem-solving practices.

Problem-solving practices do not in themselves tell a comprehensive life story that relates which problems are worthy of great attention—and why. Judaism is about such a total story; Jewish education for commitment initiates learners into the story and lays down ground rules for composing the book of one's life, together with others. That is why it may bring one "under the wings of the divine Presence."

Though he didn't mention it to the proselytes who had to discover what that meant for themselves, and in their own ways, I imagine that Hillel believed that, ultimately, their questions and his answers were really about that. As a teacher of Torah, who also thought that "coming under the wings of the divine Presence," was the ultimately important thing, he was ready to tolerate some outlandish questions. He knew that the greater the practice, the greater the difficulty in entering it.

For this reason, he might have said, great practices require empathetic—and patient—teachers.

THE JEWISH EDUCATOR AND JEWISH SOURCES

13

A LEXICON FOR
JEWISH EDUCATION

*W*e began this book by noting that a fruitful way of focusing on philosophical issues in education is to ask which excellences should be transmitted to the young and why these rather than others constitute the moral qualities, habits, funds of knowledge, and competences to be fostered by the educator. We suggested that the Jewish educator turn to the sources of Judaism to examine whether they point to a comprehensive view of culture and education in which the issues of educational philosophy are addressed. Through the study of selected sources we wished to explore the textual tradition of Judaism, its language and its continuing literature. Our explorations in this book were intended to demonstrate that this tradition indeed has a genuine and rich language that invites us to do educational thinking from within it.

A brief reminder on the way we introduced and used such terms as language, literature, and educational thought: language, we suggested, might be understood as the store of basic assumptions, problems, aspirations, forms of rhetoric, methods of inquiry, patterns of community, symbolic expressions and paradigms of order, coherence, and norm of a culture. Literature is what can be articulated in the language; it explores its actual and possible uses, its vistas of meaning and its interactions with other languages. We defined sacred literature as that corpus of writings that presents the language, as the basic and formative way the language is put before us. The "excellences" of Judaism are thus to be understood as what the language posits for ideal life as these ideals are articulated in sacred literature and subsequently recaptured and reworked in an ongoing literature of commentary and interpretation. The literature protects the language, testifies to its potential and scope, enlarges it.

On the foundations of these working concepts, we proposed that the task of Jewish education be understood as the transmission of the language of Judaism through its sacred literature as well as the teaching of representative literature. Excellence would consist in this scheme of knowledge of the language, competence in using it, and loyalty to it and to the communities that speak it. Excellence would include a widespread knowledge of its diverse literatures, the possession of defensible criteria for what good literature is, and the capability to make literature according to standards and procedures deemed congenial by masters of the practice of Judaism.

Several Crucial Features of the Language

Let us recall what we have done in our brief and all-too-fragmentary study of the language of Judaism and some of the ways literature emerges from it.

(1) First, (Section I) we explored aspects of how the language "thinks" and how several of its metaphors suggest modes of making literature. We then surveyed some views of the relationship between its internal contents *(Torah)* and the wisdom *(hokhmah)* that is useful and sometimes crucial in creating new Jewish literature even when this *hokhmah* arises in other languages, as it often does. The links to be found in Jewish history between *Torah* and *hokhmah* as well as the controversies occasioned by these links indicated that there are diverse literatures as to what that relationship should be.

(2) We then looked at several features of one literature project, that of Maimonides (Section II). We saw it exemplifying literature both in the way it drew norms and insights out of the tradition and in the way it poured *hokhmah* into it. We found the Rambam's philosophical literature of Judaism to be a paradigm for translation of the non-philosophical language of Torah into philosophical-educational categories. And we drew the Rambam into several discussions with contemporary educational *hokhmah*.

(3) We then investigated through a study of mostly *midrashic* texts a central character ideal of Jewish language, *Yirat Shamayim* (Section III). We partially translated it into moral philosophy in order to clarify and make its character ideal more generally communicable. We then commented and enlarged upon one contemporary philosophical *midrash*, Emil Fackenheim's, that points to a possible understanding of the prin-

cipled world of *Yirat Shamayim.* This study was conducted together with five archetypical educators whose roundtable discussion showed how joint study with a view towards partial translation might be useful to teachers of various world-views.

(4) Our next exploration (Section IV) showed us two tiers of value in the language. We found that "value talk" was readily coaxed out of the world of the Talmudic sages once *hokhmah* was mobilized to give us Jewishly congenial uses of the term value itself.

(5) Our final text study (Section V) was designed to examine how initiation and commitment, as done and taught by the sage Hillel, could be better understood for educational purposes through a contemporary philosophical discussion of practice.

In our study, we have come upon seven operative assumptions and aspirations within the language, i.e., within the sacred literature of Torah, that are crucial for educational philosophy. (Two of these have to do with the relationship of the language itself to other languages.) These statements within the language may be formulated as follows:

(a) The language requires literature. This is the case both because it must be diversely explored in order to be understood and because the language must be protected and enhanced in changing circumstances. Stating this differently: being religiously "deep," its inherent wisdom must constantly be mined anew; being culturally and even nationally concrete, it authorizes the use of general wisdom to make it communicable and accessible from different cultural perspectives and in different cultural climes. Conservative interpreters of the tradition tend to claim that even this general wisdom was always within the language of Torah. But they agree with liberal interpreters that it has to be there to make Torah (the language's term for the language itself) comprehensive and present.

(b) The language, like any framework of cultural and religious life, is particularistic, but a principled universalism is part of its content. On the one hand it may be enhanced by all human languages, through new Jewish literature. On the other hand, the language itself envisions that all human beings will be partially within it. Thus, the righteous of all nations "have a share in the world-to-come." Some of these, like our proselytes, may wish to convert, to join others, like Job, or Bitya, Moses' adopted mother and the daughter of Pharaoh, exemplify *Yirat Shamayim* outside the community of Israel. On the one hand, therefore, the language of Torah is people-specific, arising in God's redemptive and revelatory acts with Israel. In this sense, the language is national; it is culture as well as commandment. But on the other hand, it is universal. It sets criteria for normative truth and ideal human life through the *Noahide* commandments and the insights, the knowledge of God, that is to be learned through them.[1]

(c) Commitment and acceptance precede deliberation and discernment. This is the principle of *Na'ase v'Nishmah* (we shall do and we shall hear) that we found attributed to the angelic hosts themselves.[2]

(d) Closely related but developmentally beyond *Na'ase v'Nishma* is *Torah l'shmah*, knowing and doing for their own sake. This ideal spells out the potentialities of persons to achieve self-realization within the language. It is what Maimonides described as walking toward the palace, reaching it, and entering it.[3]

(e) The vocabulary of the language of Judaism favors the concrete over the abstract. It prefers paradigms to definitions, the action to the disembodied theory.[4] In speaking of the nature of Providence, it relates historical disputes about what kind of tabernacles Israel sat in or under on the festival of *Sukkot* in the desert rather than refining theological abstractions. What in some languages are theoretical formulations on civic involvement and moral responsibility are here embedded in discussions of, for example, going to the stadium and shouting there.[5]

However, this concreteness is not merely national-cultural, as might be expected, but also religious-covenantal. The sacred literature beginning with the Garden of Eden assumes that God wants and humans need personal relationships and these are, by their very nature, concrete and specific. These relationships, and their all-too-frequent breakdown, are between people and God, between the man and the woman, between brothers. Without these relationships, there is alienation, wandering, killing. Relationships are concrete not only within families but also between God and the family of Abraham and Sarah. And this covenant sets a paradigm for personal relationships between people, and the "families of the earth" to one another.

(f) The language posits a moral ideal that is rooted in God's will, His commandments. The morality it envisions for ideal persons and communities is, therefore, to begin with, de-ontological, declaring actions to be either good or evil on the basis of an external and authoritative source. Yet this morality of obedience is, even within the sacred (language-presenting) texts themselves, generally legiti-

---

1. I have previously discussed this in Michael Rosenak, "The Religious Person and Religious Pluralism," *The Meaning and Limits of Religious Pluralism in the World Today,* edited by Allen R. Brockway and Jean Halperin (Geneva: World Council of Churches, 1987), pp. 7–22.
2. See Chap. 11, pp. 190–91.
3. See Chap. 3, pp. 36–38.
4. See Chap. 1 and n. 22.
5. See Chap. 10, pp. 168–69.

mated on consequential grounds and it generates ethical deliberation. That is, while one must do what is good because God said so,
what God says is (but not always evidently!) justified by the favorable
consequences it will have for society and the individual. Here, the
language clearly spells out a theological principle (God's will) and a
moral ideal: to accept the yoke of Heaven and to act according to
God's promise so that the moral promise will be realized.

(g) An ideal human being fears Heaven. Existentially, such a person
stands in the Presence of God. S/he is conscious of his/her limits, creatureliness, and dependence. Conversely, on the level of observable
moral ideal, such a person is reliable, making the world a more trustworthy habitat. He or she is a harbinger of redemption, of Messianic
days when the kingship of God will be visible through the knowledge
and fear of God that will cover it "as the waters cover the sea."

Needless to say, these assumptions and ideals of the language of
Judaism do not exhaust the vocabulary of the language nor do they
adequately disclose what the various literatures of Judaism tell us
about the potentialities and controversies within the language. Because
they are not the entire dictionary nor the building blocks of all significant sentences within sacred texts, one could certainly draw a more
comprehensive portrait of Jewish *Paideia* after careful, educationally
oriented analysis of additional sacred texts and ensuent bodies of literature. For example, studies of *halakhic* exegesis, mystical doctrine,
theodicies in times of catastrophe, and problem-solving in radically
new situations would flesh out the contours of Jewish educational
thought. We obviously have not, in this one volume, conducted these
studies nor are we competent to do so. We have merely invited them.

Yet, though these seven clusters of lexicon are not the sum total of
what Judaism "says," they do indicate that it does say a great deal that
is relevant to philosophy of Jewish education. We dare to maintain
this despite the cogent argument, often advanced by scholars, that
not everything in the language of Torah is compatible and that it is
ignorant or archaic for modern students of Torah to pontificate on
what Judaism says.[6] We suggest, however, that it is one of the mandates of literature to create Jewish theologies and philosophies that
present reasoned positions about what is fundamental to Judaism,
that suggest hierarchies of value within it, and that argue for a congruent Jewish world view despite apparent incompatabilities, despite
valuative opposites and undeniable difficulties within the sources.

6. This point has been cogently argued by Arnold Eisen, "How Can We Speak of Jewish Values Today?" *Forum* 42–43 (Winter 1981), pp. 69–81.

Let us look again at the five statements that do not explicitly deal with the relationships between language and literature, to further explore their educational-philosophical uses. (We shall deal with the first two in the following chapter.) In doing so, we shall use the terminology of the language itself. Our five topics of language and literature are:

(1) *Na'aseh v'Nishma;*
(2) *Torah l'shmah,*
(3) "What's the *halakhah?*"–"What happened?"–"What is this like?"
(4) *Hatov V'Hayashar,* "the good and the upright," and, in conjunction with this,
(5) *Yirat Shamayim.*

"We Shall Do and We Shall Hear"

A fascinating *midrash* on Exodus 21:1 relates the following exchange between the Emperor Hadrian and his brother-in-law, Aquilas, a renowned second-century proselyte:

> Now these are the ordinances (which you shall place before them) (Exodus 21:1). It is written, "He declareth His word unto Jacob ..." (Psalms 147:19) Aquilas once said to the Emperor Hadrian, "I wish to be converted and become an Israelite." He replied: "... After this people do you hanker? See how I have degraded it, and how many of them I have slain (after the war of Betar and the defeat of Bar Kokhba). You wish to ally yourself to the lowliest of peoples; what do you see in them that you now wish to be converted?"
>
> He (Aquilas) replied: "The least among them knows how God created the world and what was created on the first and second day and how long it is since the world was created and on what the world is founded. Moreover their law is one of truth." He then said to him, "Go and study their law but do not be circumcised." To which he retorted, "Unless he be circumcised, even the wisest in thy kingdom and even a grey-beard of a hundred years old cannot study their Torah for so it is written: 'He declareth His word unto Jacob, His statutes and His ordinances unto Israel, He hath not dealt so with any (other) nation and has not made known His ordinances to them ...'"
>
> *Exodus Rabbah* 30:12

This is an amazing story in several ways. Hadrian has warred against the Jews and brutally subdued them because they revolted against him and his decree forbidding circumcision. He cannot understand why a Roman nobleman would wish to join the vanquished and humiliated enemy of Rome. Aquilas's answer is that not only do they have a moral law of truth, but, and this he mentions first, they possess philosophical truth. They know, he says, "on what the world is founded."

The emperor is doubly perplexed. He cannot understand why one has to join them in order to acquire their philosophical wisdom. Moreover, if their law involves such irrational prescriptions as circumcision, what philosophical wisdom can they possibly have? The rational person acts according to the nature of things, accepting nature as it is, not trying to improve upon it.[7] He therefore implores Aquilas not to be circumcised. Aquilas responds that one cannot know what they know, one cannot study their Torah without accepting it. And for this strange and seemingly irrational view, he gives no argument but, in line with his position, that "He declareth His word unto Jacob," simply cites Scripture. The knowledge that doing must come before understanding is a gift that God has bestowed upon them alone among the nations. It is an internal part of their language, though the case of Aquilas himself shows that non-Jews can learn it. This knowledge is not only the divine *hok*, an inscrutable statute, but also God's *mishpat* (ordinance), that is, the appropriate way to proceed when carrying out mandated or desired actions.[8]

Aquilas is explaining *na'aseh v'nishma* to the emperor. He is telling him that one cannot know and understand morality without being inside it. In fact, one cannot even understand philosophical truths objectively. Aquilas might have mentioned that for this reason Hillel, several generations before, had had to convert his confused heathens before sending them to study Torah.

Aquilas, Hillel, and the expression of Exodus they are interpreting suggests a particular form of educational initiation and socialization, giving children what the English philosopher Michael Oakeshott has called "habits of affection and conduct."[9] Before children are encouraged to engage in reflective morality, states Oakshott, they must learn "the unreflective following of a tradition of conduct in which we have been brought up." The habits of conduct we acquire in this behavioral

---

7. Hadrian, according to many scholars, prohibited circumcision as part of his legislation against castration. A well-known example of the polemic between Romans and Jewish sages on this issue is the discussion between the Roman governor Tineius Rufus and Rabbi Akiva whether divine creation or human art were superior. Rufus asked R. Akiva why the Jews "insist on attempting to improve God's creation through circumcision," to which the sage replied that while ears of grain are God's creation, yet the loaves of bread manufactured by humans are more useful. *Midrash Tanhuma, Tazrea* 8. For a discussion of these conversations, see Louis Finkelstein, *Akiba: Scholar, Saint and Martyr* (Cleveland and Philadelphia: Meridian Books and Jewish Publication Society of America, 1962), pp. 244–46.

8. On the concept of *mishpat* as a cosmic principle of appropriateness, see the study by Eliezer Berkovits, "The Biblical Meaning of Justice," *Judaism*, 18, no. 2 (Spring 1969), pp. 188–209.

9. Oakeshott, "The Tower of Babel" in *Rationalism in Politics and Other Essays* (London: Methuen 2nd Co. Ltd., 1962), p. 61, and see discussion throughout this essay, pp. 59–79.

mode we learn before we discover why they are excellences. Personal discovery of the worth of the excellences is commendable, but this discovery must be built on the foundation of a tradition of virtuous action.

The ideal suggested by *na'aseh v'nishma* creates, within the language of Judaism, a hierarchy: initiation and habit come first, reflection follows. Thus, for example, in the realm of values, inclinational opposites should be internalized before there is explicit treatment of valuative opposites. The "perfection of the body" precedes "perfection of the soul"; sitting at the feet of masters and carrying out their prescriptions (even when the master is as gentle as Hillel) precedes arguing with them.[10] Of course, children will not be asked to be obedient always and in all things because that will cause them to break rather than to grow. It is a truism that children are cognitively and emotionally different from adults. We found Egan explaining this perhaps better than Maimonides, but we know it from within the language, too. Human beings are concrete manifestations of humanity; neither adults nor children are an abstraction. And each person does and hears "with his or her own strength." (We shall return to this point below.)

Nevertheless, in a school in which *na'aseh v'nishma* is intrinsic to the language being taught, there is what Tillich has called "inducting education," in which children learn the acts and the contexts of "the tradition, symbols and demands of the family" and community. "Its aim is not development of the potentialities of the individual, but induction into the actuality of a group, the life and spirit of community, family, tribe, town, nation, church. Such an induction happens spontaneously through the participation of the individual in the life of the group."[11] In Jewish community, children who receive inducting education act out Jewish norms because they are part of the order of things. They confer identity and security, a sense of order, a ground to life. Later, one will learn various matters from and through them. The adult community will eventually explain them, and give intellectual guidance to those who live by these traditions and do the requisite acts. "Induction precedes interpretation, but interpretation makes the induction complete."[12] Hopefully, one will eventually come to see the depth of the norms and traditions–and understand them diversely. From commitments, discernments will follow. And on the basis of varied discernments, garnered through diverse life experiences, there will be controversy, new literature–and new learning.

Yet because of the competition of rival languages in the environment of the modern Jewish child, contemporary Jewish education that takes

10. See Chap. 11–12.
11. Paul Tillich, "A Theology of Education," p. 147.
12. *Ibid.*

itself seriously is always prey to the temptation to restrict itself to the behavorial mode, to choose systematic segregation from the threatening world as the best protection for their pupils. This temptation, to sever *nishma* from *na'aseh,* should be resisted. Total segregation can only keep wisdom and literature out, and we have learned that language without literature buries one;[13] the making of literature requires openness to wisdom wherever it may be found. An education based on segregation will produce only uncomprehending conformity or rebellion. These, we recall, correspond precisely to Maimonides's 'two lamentable types of those who misunderstand the teachings of the Sages![14]

While induction is the *alef-bet* of the language's educational foundations, it is not its goal. It is the beginning of wisdom but not its end. Certainly in modern and free societies inducting education must be for the sake of the wisdom, joy, and meaning it points to. And children must receive an inkling of that, even while learning to do, if for no other reason than that they possess the happy talent to acquire discernments and commitments that are not given them by teachers.[15]

Moreover, if initiation is for the sake of what they can eventually learn to say in the language, then those who are learning it must be able to trust those who teach them. These teachers must be, in Heschel's apt phrase, text people, not merely presenters of text books.[16] Children realize very quickly, though they are not yet insiders enough to express it that way, who sanctifies God's name and who profanes it. Or in somewhat prosaic terms: who makes the language look good and who doesn't.

Nor is this simply a modern concession to a brute cultural reality; it is embodied in the language itself. The Children of Israel, we recall, accepted the Torah only after the splitting of the Red Sea, after God and His servant Moses had proven themselves trustworthy. Why should children of Israel today, or for that matter children as such, be different?

Torah L'shmah

Norman Lamm's study, *Torah l'shmah,* deals mainly with the educational-philosophical approach and activity of Rabbi Hayyim of Volozhin, disciple of the renowned Rabbi Eliyahu, the "Gaon of

---

13. Recall the Talmud lesson described by Heilman (Chap. 10, p. 164). The *halakhah* mandates making a blessing upon seeing a wise person, even if s/he is from "the nations of the world." (*Berakhot* 58a). But if one has no access to wisdom, how may one recognize it, and bless God for it?
14. See the discussion on his "Introduction to *Perek Helek,*" Chap. 3.
15. See discussion in Chap. 4.
16. Abraham Joshua Heschel, "Jewish Education," in *The Insecurity of Freedom: Essays on Human Existence* (New York: Schocken Books, 1972), p. 237.

Vilna," and founder of the famed nineteenth-century Yeshiva of Volzhin. In discussing Rabbi Hayyim's view of Torah study, he cites the following passage:

> One must study with powerful exertion to attain the true meanings of Torah, each according to his capacity. The more one learns, the more he wants to learn ... for by means of the light which we have already attained we can see that there is yet more light, and we hope to attain that too.[17]

These sentences succinctly distinguish *Torah l'shmah* from *na'ase v'nishmah*. The former focuses on the beginning of the cultural-educational process, demanding that one be firmly and socially situated before proceeding to higher stages of self-realization, while the latter gives a perspective on where one may go from there. We have briefly noted how this concept arises in biblical narrative and wisdom, from Abraham, who obeys God without question and extrinsic motivation at the *Akedah* (the binding of Isaac), to Joseph and Job, fearers of God "for all seasons." There "for its own sake" is close to an exalted, perhaps even fearsome and disinterested *Yirat Shamayim*. And this theme is developed by the *mishnaic* teacher as well:

> Antigonos of Socho ... used to say, "Be not like servants who minister to their master upon the condition of receiving a reward; but be like servants who minister for their master without the condition of receiving a reward; and let the fear of Heaven be upon you."
>
> *Avot* I3

In the Talmudic passage from the Tractate *Pesahim* discussed in an earlier chapter, *l'shmah* refers to the study of Torah: "A person ought always to labor in the Torah even if not for its own sake. For, doing it not for its own sake, he may come to do it for its own sake." Maimonides's rationalistic literature develops this theme to signify an intellectual and intrinsic understanding that has learned to lay aside all interest in extrinsic or instrumental considerations. For kabbalistically oriented literature, this conception of learning Torah for its own sake goes beyond the joys of intellectual understanding, and produces an ineffable change not only in the learner but in "the higher worlds" of the divine emanations *(sefirot)* as well. The Torah is in a sense one with the divine itself, and Torah study enhances, as it were, God's unity. "The Holy One and Torah are a unity, and he who is attached to His Torah is attached to Him." Furthermore:

> all his studies are (considered) for the sake of the unification of the Holy One. And when he exercises his mind in matters of *Halakhah*, exoterically, certainly the *Shekhinah* dwells upon him at the very time of his

17. Norman Lamm, *Torah Lishmah; Torah for Torah's Sake In the Works of Rabbi Hayyim of Volozhin and his Contemporaries* (Hoboken, N.J.: Ktav Publishing House, Inc., 1989), p. 244.

study, as the sages said, "The Holy One has in His world but the four ells of *Halakhah*."[18]

In the mystically oriented world of learning, there is, as in the Rambam, testimony to reaching the inner sanctum of the king through the road that God has provided for inner achievement and self-transformation. Moreover, what individuals may become affects what all the worlds and the divine within them may become! And, as one reaches the ever-new goal that comes into view with previous achievement, one becomes aware of the uniqueness of the inner experience, the wealth of transfiguring experience that awaits individuals with persistence and courage. R. Hayyim of Volozhin states it thus:

> It may be compared to one who enters a room in the treasure house of the king, which is filled with all kinds of precious objects. There he finds a door leading to an inner chamber, and in there he finds yet another door to other inner chambers; and the closer one comes to the chamber of the king himself, the more precious and beautiful it is than the one before it. Had he not entered the outermost chamber, he would have known nothing of other, inner chambers. So it is with Torah: by means of the light he attains at first, one sees that there is yet greater light, and so on. Thus does one desire to understand and attain more, until one has attained all the mysteries of the world and its fullness.[19]

For both the Rambam and for R. Hayyim, the challenge and the achievement are, albeit in different ways, intellectual. Yet *l'shmah,* for its own sake, is not only an intellectual goal, even for Maimonides and R. Hayyim. Both are describing a personal and ineffable spiritual yearning; for both there is a palace, and a profound desire to be "where the king is."

Moreover, just as *na'ase v'nishmah* need not be understood only in terms of study but as action and existential commitment, so has *l'shmah,* the ultimate goal, been viewed as a way of observing the commandments.[20] For *l'shmah* is a total way of being in the world. It is to be within the most sublime practice of the language, for its own sake, for the doors that it opens to the human potential of the individual who is masterfully within it. To do something *l'shmah* is to have entered the gate of self-actualization through the practice that is designed for that. The *Yire Shamayim,* we recall, is generally taught to expect no extrinsic reward in this world for the way s/he is.[21]

Torah l'shmah is thus on the individual level what *na'ase v'nishmah* is on the social level of life. But it is a different rung on the ladder.

18. *Ibid.,* p. 243.
19. *Ibid.,* p. 244.
20. See discussion of such medieval thinkers as Yehuda Halevi, Crescas and Albo in *ibid.,* pp. 142–43.
21. Yet, there are those who disagree. See Urbach, *The Sages,* pp. 269–71.

Since there is no value clarification before there is commandment, and no perfection of the soul before perfection of the body, there can be no *l'shmah* without *na'ase v'nishmah!*

Torah l'shmah evokes the recognition that the ultimately important things, the intrinsic end-goals of social assumptions and behavior, cannot be taught. Students can only be prepared to learn them on their own later. In other words, the highest and most significant accomplishments of education come to light through what people do by themselves on the basis of what they have learned as children. Nevertheless, just as there must be intimations of *nishmah* (understanding) in the *na'ase* (doing), so must there be "rumors of angels," intimations of *Torah l'shmah,* of self-actualization, in the regimen of *na'ase v'nishmah.*

For otherwise why should modern Jewish children embark on the road that leads through the fundamentals of language for everyone and that, for the talented, may seem dull? This is a particularly acute dilemma for modern educators, for there are so many things going on elsewhere. But it is not only a modern problem: we have seen the Rambam grappling with it, too. One element that seems particularly important: those who teach, especially those who teach children too young for higher stage understanding, i.e., those who are learning *lo l'shmah,* must be trustworthy examples of what can be done in the language, and at the same time, people who love teaching the language, even to small children.

Egan, we recall, expressed it well: "If one has a distaste for the immature and their various modes of expression and kinds of interest, then there is no point trying to teach ... We might wisely be equally wary of those who seem ashamed of having been young and those who see childhood as the best life has to offer."[22]

What is the Halakhah?
What Happened? What is This Like?

Benno Jacob, the modern Bible scholar and commentator, writes on the first of the Ten Commandments:

"I am the Lord ... who has brought you out of the Land of Egypt ..." In saying 'I' he taught them the personal character of their God, who is not an idea that one speaks about or in which one believes but 'a living God' who confronts with 'I' the 'you' of the hearer who can therefore turn to Him with 'you.' And 'I', whose name is the Tetragrammaton ('the Lord') is your God in that He took you out ... in this taking out, in this inter-

22. Egan, *Individual Development and Curriculum,* p. 156, and our discussion above, Chap. 5, pp. 78–79.

vention in your life, in this guidance that He gave you, in leading you
from Egypt till this day, in that is He your God ... [23]

In the first section of this book, we discussed the concrete and down
to earth character of Jewish language. There we considered the implications of this concreteness for philosophy of Jewish education. We
proposed that aspects of its embedded theory be coaxed out of its concrete, often mundane, particularity by the *hokhmah* of all nations if this
wisdom can be shown, though study of the texts, to be congenial to it.

This concreteness is an inherent trait of Judaism and its sacred literature; it is unmistakably part of what the language says as well as how
it is spoken. For note: when translations from Judaism are more than
partial, but comprehensive, then the Jewish language becomes redundant; Judaism is left with nothing more to say. The scandal of Jewish
memory, practice, aspiration, and faith is its very particularity, namely,
its concreteness within the historical situation. In this language, the
God of all humankind makes a covenant with a particular people. The
language, instead of speaking of a universally true faith, speaks of an
elected people, which is a culturally concrete and particular way of saying much the same thing but perhaps more modestly. (There can be
only one universally true faith but covenants can be made with more
than one people and such covenants are prophetically envisioned for
the future.) In this language there is a land upon which one people is to
live by the Torah which in many respects obligates it alone.

This is not a language that lends itself to transmission by cate-
chism or theological treatises. It is about experience, but also events.
It touches often on collective hopes, but also on memory. It is conveyed by stories. These stories can be shared within communities,
celebrated. Only after having been appropriated by learners and
listeners can the ideas in them be picked out for the philosophical
understanding that will allow educated Jews to bear the scandal of
their particularity comfortably.

In this language, there are *halakhic* cases that invariably seem to
remind one of other cases—and to pinpoint the resemblances and the
distinctions. There are many things to remember and many things to
remember them by: ten plagues, ten commandments, four categories of guardians of borrowed, leased or simply taken-care-of
property, thirty-nine types of forbidden labor on the Sabbath. Because Judaism's concreteness is a scandal in the eyes of some other

---

23. Benno Jacob's commentary is cited in Nehama Leibowitz, *Studies in Exodus (Shemot),* translated and adapted from the Hebrew by Aryeh Newman (Jerusalem:
The World Zionist Organization, 1976), pp. 307–8.

religions, all this can be made to appear legalistic and trivial. In fact, Talmud-studying insiders may also have experienced concreteness as sometimes picayune, earthy or even crude. And yet they know that each detail opens up avenues of discourse: about Providence, revelation, social relations, sanctity. In our brief explorations into Torah study we have seen what kinds of valuative questions are raised when the prescribed praise of brides is treated with religious-moral seriousness, or what spiritual concerns should be evoked by the soft and gentle writing instruments mandated for Torah scrolls, *mezzuzot* and *tefilin* (phylacteries).[24]

Not only laws deal with concrete things or stories with concrete happenings on earth, or between heaven and earth. Beauty is concrete, in a beautiful *etrog* picked up on *Sukkot*, in a beautiful tree or a beautiful creature, the sight of which requires one to recite a blessing to the One "Who has such (things) in His world." You have to see it to bless God for it; it is not an idea. Even wisdom is to be praised only upon seeing a wise person.[25]

Finally, just as Israel is a concrete and singular people, just as laws deal with concrete matters, as stories relate to particular happenings, and as even aethetics is concerned with beautiful things, so are human beings concrete and different. The relationships between individual people, especially relationships of love, reflect the love between God and Israel. Thus it is that R. Akiva called the Song of Songs "the holy of holies" in sacred literature.[26] And individuals experience things diversely.

> "I am the Lord your God ..." (Exodus 20:2) R. Simlai (explained to his disciples): Why does the Torah state (Deut. 4:33) "Has a people (ever before) heard the voice of God ...?" How is this possible (to hear it as it really is)?" If Scripture said 'The voice of the Lord is in His strength' the world could not endure, but rather (Psalms 29:4) 'The voice of the Lord is in strength'–(not His strength but) the strength (capacity) of each and every one, the young (robust) people according to their capacity and the little ones according to theirs ... (*Exodus Rabbah* 29:1)

Each person is a world in him/herself "for which the entire world was created."[27] In the language of Judaism, the specificity of human existence takes in both the community and the individual. But they are not the same. The community imposes itself upon the individual in education and will always need him or her but the individual cannot be anonymously collapsed into it. The individual moves ahead

---

24. See above, Chap. 9, pp. 155–56.
25. On this, already referred to in n. 13 above, see our discussion in Chap. 15, p. 258. A clear exception to this rule is Biblical wisdom literature, most especially the book of Proverbs, which does praise wisdom as such.
26. *Megillah* 7a.
27. *Sanhedrin* 4:5

in the adventure of life, finding what is intrinsically valuable to him or her, even though the community continues to demand his or her presence and commitment.

How shall children be brought into it in the general culture that considers such concreteness, such personal binding, and such religious specificity a scandal? Clearly it requires communities, stories, personal experiences. But communities, stories, and experiences, for children and perhaps for adults, are only as compelling as those who represent, tell, and guide. Just as Benno Jacob portrays God speaking personally to the Israelites, reminding them of divine trustworthiness, so teachers have to be personally believable on behalf of communities and their stories. Despite what others are saying about this language, with its trivial laws, its naive tales and its historical conceits, teachers have to communicate that the language can be trusted, that it teaches concrete things because human beings and human communities are that way. Justice, joy, and love are possible only in the specific situations of people. When we make them abstract, we dehumanize them, we become attuned to ignoring actual people. From there the way to callousness and cruelty is all too short.

Hatov V'hayashar: What is Good and Right

Throughout our study we have seen a central concern with what is good and right. The midwives in Egypt cannot agree to do what is wicked and arbitrary; this is because they fear God. Those who have intellectual knowledge of God must "walk in His ways," which are righteous and merciful. Discussions on the laws of the Torah by the sages are based on the conviction that they are moral and upright and thus they tend to assume that laws concerning the execution of criminals or rebellious sons must mean something different from the plain and literal meaning of the Biblical injunctions. The heathen who wishes to learn all of Judaism while standing on one foot is simply told that the whole Torah is "not doing to your neighbor what you would not have him/her doing to you."[28] Summing up these lessons, we might well surmise that the language of Judaism is essentially one of universal morality with the addition of particularistic cultural folkways that illustrate this core vocabulary of morality but add nothing to it in principle and may, in some cases and through some particulars, actually detract from it. At best, it could be concluded that Jewish education is simply a case of moral education. At worst, due to its historical, cultural, and national specificity, couldn't it often be less than that?

28. See Chap. 11, pp. 203.

Yet, there is something suspect about both best case and worst case formulations of Judaism and Jewish education. With regard to the best case: we recall some morally dubious data in the background of our study. Take, for example, Elijah on Mount Carmel standing up to the prophets of Baal: didn't he, after that, massacre them? Why should a stranger, even King David, be put to death for drawing nigh to the holy of holies? Why would God demand the sacrifice of a son and a father acquiesce? Why capital punishment for gathering sticks on the Sabbath?! And then there are, as we have found in our study, the *Hukim,* the statutes for which the Torah gives no reason. So much for the Torah as simply a case of universal morality.

But the worst case is also problematic. Don't the sacred texts maintain that the commandments come from the God who is merciful and just and who demands justice and mercy? Don't the Talmudic sages constantly deduce ethical teachings from historically-specific laws? Recall that Deuteronomy itself mandates Sabbath rest for "thy servant and maidservant" in conjunction with the historical (particular, national) experience of slavery in Egypt! Doesn't the Torah say that the commandments are wisdom, that they are "for your good always," close to us "in our mouths and hearts"?[29] How about Rabbi Natan in the Roman stadium? What about R. Akiva and R. Tarfon, who incessantly question witnesses to deliver defendants from execution? And the love of peace that makes Aaron lie and even God misreport?

What are we to learn from this seeming paradox? Of course, it is quite possible and even conventional not to take the teachings of the Bible and the Talmud seriously—and not to learn anything from them, to decide that modern people cannot go to them for wisdom. Where that decision is made, the question whether there are gems of morality in sacred literature or not becomes pedagogically irrelevant. For in such a case, what we like about their morality we already knew!

But let us assume, as Jewish tradition does, that there is a real language in these writings and authentic teaching, that the texts require close reading, and that teachers, as learners, may learn new and unexpected things from them. With this assumption, let us go back and study.

The very first source cited in this book was the commandment given to Noah and his family:

> "S/he who sheds the blood of a person, by humans shall his/her blood be shed, for in the image of God He made the human being. (Genesis 9:7)

29. Deut. 4:6 describes the commandments as "your wisdom and understanding in the eyes of the peoples." Also, Deut. 4:9 and Deut. 30:14.

This is an example of what the Talmudic tradition terms a *mitzvah bain adam l'havero,* a "commandment between people," but God plays an important part in it. After all, it is God Who commands, and gives a reason for it, seemingly more related to the Almighty than to one's fellow human being. Namely, that humans are created in the divine image. So, on the one hand, the law is not arbitrary; after all, we are supplied with a reason for it. On the other hand, the reason itself seems odd. Does this divine fiat translate plausibly into what we may call morality?

Let's look at it this way and take it step by step:

(1) When the Torah makes principled statements about reality and value, we are to learn from them how to understand things so that we shall know what to do. This means that the principle of the divine image in humans is directly related to ideal behavior. We are beings in the divine image.[30] Hence, we are not to kill one another and we must punish killers. The ideal (commanded) behavior flows from the principled truth-statement. Usually, we learn about things from the opposite direction. Usually, the Torah tells us what to do and that will teach us to understand. However this case is different.

(2) Through certain commandments of God we are to acquire the most important discernments about ourselves, to discover who we are. These are called *mitzvot bein adam laMakom,* commandments between humans and God. They inform us, in a primary fashion, who we are, what our "situation is," as individuals, as creatures. We are then bidden to express this self-knowledge in our commanded relationships to our fellow humans.[31] The latter are termed commandments between a person and his/her fellow *(bain adam l'havero).* These relationships are also commanded because we learn who we are as members of the the human community, hence, as humans, from them as well.

A concrete and primordial example: Adam and Eve were to learn who they were from the arbitrary decree not to eat of the tree of

---

30. This way of looking at it is partially suggested to me by R. Akiva's well-known teaching: "Beloved is the human person, for s/he was created in the image of God; but it was by a special love that it was made known to him/her that s/he was created in the image of God …"*Avot* 3:18.

31. Using Ramsey's frame of conceptualization, (see Chap. 4) the commitment to commandments between humans and God *(bain adam laMakom)* creates discernments that, in turn, generate the commitment that help us to understand the wisdom expressed in commandments between human beings *(bain adam l'havero).* But these commandments, too, precede our understanding of their wisdom; as commandments they also teach us who we are, in this case through our commanded relationships with our fellow humans.

knowledge of good and evil. This commandment was to teach them
to see themselves as children of God, to tend the garden together, to
educate their children "in one voice," to love each other. But they did-
n't obey God's commandment, and so they lost—or failed to learn—
basic discernments. They became alienated from each other, from
nature, from their children, and from God. They separated from each
other for one hundred and thirty years, states a *midrash*.[32] They were
expelled from Eden, one son was killed, and the other killed him!

(3) Because there are divine commandments between people and
God and between people, our relationship to our fellow human
beings has two aspects. We are obliged to this relationship because we
are given commandments between people and through these ethical
commandments we learn who we are through the prism of who our
neighbor is. Here, commitment to our neighbor and our community
comes first and leads us to discernment about ourselves. Second, we
are able to carry out these commandments in a good and upright
manner because we have been told that our fellow humans are "like
yourself," and we have been taught about ourselves through the
commandments between God and humans (and/or Israel). We know
who they are because we know who we are. In this sense, self-discernment enables us to be committed to others, to have empathy for
them. After all, we were slaves in Egypt, and we remember being
redeemed. And so we must carefully observe the consequences of
what we do and how we do it. We may not do to our neighbors what
we would not want done to us. This, we recall, was Hillel's formulation of the entire Torah.

(4) Thus, moral actions, too, always remain rooted in commandment. As commandments, and not merely nice ways to act, they
reflect what God knows about us and what we are to learn about ourselves through our relationships with the Almighty and with our fellows. At the same time, we must apply the commandments in the
light of what we already know about ourselves and our neighbor.
The ritual commandments between humans and God are designed
to refine us, telling us not only to love thy neighbor as thyself, but to
make thyself lovable and possessed of justifiable self-esteem. (History has had its full of ignoble and self-hating persons who treated
their neighbors as they themselves deserved to be treated, with a
hate they felt towards the self.)

(5) If we fail to keep in mind that ethics remains commanded, we
shall forget who we are and then we shall no longer be trustworthy
in what we do, even if we mean well. We also continue to be obliged
by commandments that have no obvious moral reasons, because

32. *Tanhuma* Genesis 11.

without them we will forget how we are situated, what our identity is. Then our morality, too, will be unreliable, rootless, lacking humility, often irresponsible and arbitrary.

Looking at it this way, we may now understand why the *Yire Shamayim* is coerced and fearful before s/he is responsible. Before daring to be all that God has in this world, s/he knows him/herself as limited. For this reason too, values opposed to inclinational opposites are the basis of goodness. We are told what is good before being invited to consider valuative opposites and to weigh what is good and what is better in specific circumstances. Thus, also, *na'ase* comes before *nishmah*.

We are taught by what we must do before God what we are, in ourselves and to our fellows. But we never completely learn this. Therefore, one must study Torah "till the day of death"; we are always dependent on God's *hesed* to help us learn more about ourselves. The reason that some commandments have no reason, no meaning for us is that we never completely know about ourselves all that God does. As long as we are situated in this world, God is teaching us, "enlightening us in (His) ... Torah."[33]

This, I believe, explains why, on the one hand, the morality of Jewish language always insists in being rooted in God's will, and why, on the other hand, we are always being promised that obedience to His commandments will bring us benefits.

To begin with, therefore, the good and the upright is what moral philosophers call a de-ontological morality. You must do it simply because it is right. This means that you have been told that it is right. You do not do it because you have reflected on the consequences that this particular action would have vis-à-vis other possible actions and their consequences but because it is God's commandment.

The *hukim,* laws for which we can discover no reason, represent such human limitation in self-knowledge and the transcendent aspect of knowing who you are, or, rather, never entirely knowing that. Here, then, we are back at *na'ase v'nishmah,* with no guarantee that we shall ever completely understand.

But that is only one side of the coin. For at the same time that the Torah is imposed, and the hearers treated as yet too uneducated to argue, it also pleads for acceptance and demands responsibility! Hence, if we shall do the the commandments "it shall be well with us": our days will be lengthened and "the land shall not vomit us out." Moreover, Moses, in pleading for obedience to the divine commandments and loyalty to the covenant, tells Israel that carrying out these statutes and ordinances "is your wisdom and your understand-

33. See discussion above, Chap. 7, pp. 124–26.

ing in the sight of the peoples that, when they hear all these statutes, shall say, 'Surely this great nation is a wise and understanding people.'" (Deut. 4:6) That is no de-ontological argument. Moses is not saying that one should observe these laws simply because God said so but rather because they are so good that even the Gentiles recognize this to be a good system. Living by the Torah will be clearly seen to have good consequences.

Since the commandments "between God and people" always maintain an unknown and transcendental quality, for we never completely know ourselves, they are observed with fear, or at least reverence; they always maintain an alien and coerced quality (Why can't I listen to music this Sabbath afternoon? Whose business is it if I drink myself to death?) But in good character education, the "commandments between people" are to become second nature. How, otherwise, will the fearer of God be reliable? For this reason, only a person who is a *Yire Shamayim,* Jew or Gentile, is permitted to do acts of *zedakah* and *mishpat.*[34] One who fears God is one who may be depended upon: this requires good character as well as good deeds.

Furthermore, if, as we have seen, the *Yire Shamayim* makes the world more reliable, then s/he shares in the divine promise that what begins as de-ontological will eventually be seen to be consequential. If God wants the world to be the Kingdom of God, "He has nothing in this world but the *Yire Shamayim.*" In much the same way as the modern welfare state promises its citizens basic necessities and physical protection against foreign foes and then proceeds to draft them into the army and collect taxes from them, so is God's loving-kindness largely in the acts of those who fear Heaven. For example: in the

---

34. The first example is obviously *halakhic.* The second example is intended to allow non-*halakhic* persons to relate to this coerced character, which is not, strictly speaking, moral. They may speak, with Charles Taylor, of "moral and spiritual intuitions," that involve discriminations not only of strictly moral issues but "our sense of what underlies our own dignity ... what makes our lives meaningful and fulfilling." In this sense, "while it may not be judged a moral lapse that I am living a life that is not really worthwhile or fulfilling, to describe me in these terms is nevertheless to condemn me in the name of a standard, independent of my own tastes and desires, which I ought to acknowledge." Charles Taylor, *Sources of the Self: The Making of the Modern Identity* (Cambridge: Cambridge University Press, 1989), p. 4. Here, then, is a kind of secular translation of the conception of commandments between God and individuals. The idea that commandments between people and God maintain a coerced quality is stressed by Maimonides in his discussion *(Shmoneh Perakim* [Eight Chapters]), Chap. 6. There he argues that the statement in the *Sifra* in the name of Elazar ben Azariah that a person should not say "I do not wish to commit (particular transgressions) ... (Rather) I do, but what can I do given that my Father in Heaven forbids it" applies only to such commandments that are not strictly speaking *bein adam l'havero* and do not necessarily cause harm to others. With regard to what we may call moral commandments, he agrees with the philosophers (i.e., Aristotle) that the doing of them must be ingrained in the character of the doer.

blessing after meals, we are first bidden to praise God Who "supplies food to all." Then, in the concluding paragraph we say: "I have been young and grown old but never have I looked on when the righteous were forsaken and their children sought bread."[35]

The educational issues that arise here are fundamentally those raised by the ideal of *Yirat Shamayim,* of the education of the good person. For *Yirat Shamayim* is a consequence dimension of the various language clusters we have been looking at, and of their diverse literatures. By this we mean that the fearer of Heaven has been initiated into a community of deeds, has been introduced to literatures, has sought his or her potential, and has consequently learned to be caring and just. The *Yire Shamayim* is a dedicated observer of the commandments, but if s/he is a Gentile s/he has another identity than the one that situates the people of Israel. So, s/he may never have heard of separating meat and milk or of *sha'atnez* or of any of the commandments imposed specifically upon the Jewish people, informing Israel of God's relationship to it.[36]

But in any case, s/he is both loyal to the educating community and yet seeks, through the love that is the highest stage of fear, to be him/herself, to live within the language uniquely, intrinsically, *l'shmah.* That person is morally reliable and beloved, in the specific circumstances of life, vis-à-vis God and other people. His or her morality is, in the first instance, de-ontological, but God fulfills His consequential promises, at least partly, through such a person.

The world, we have learned, exists only for the sake of those who fear God.

---

35. I am indebted to one of my teachers, the late Rabbi Leo Jung, for the insight that the word *ra'iti,* generally translated as "I have seen," should here be understood as "I have looked on," (i.e., without doing anything) as it is used in Esther 8:6.

36. Righteous Gentiles, of course, have reference to the language only in its universal aspects but in these aspects they are considered to be within the language. On this point, see Isa Aron and David Ellenson, "The Dilemma of Jewish Education: To Learn and To Do," *Judaism* 33, no. 2 (1984), pp. 213–15. Here the authors discuss whether a Gentile child who is not obligated by the commandments of Judaism may study them in a Jewish school, since s/he is therefore not learning in order to do. Faced by this question, a leading nineteenth-century *halakhic* authority, Rabbi David Zvi Hoffmann of Germany, ruled that the child may participate in those classes in which the commandments also incumbent upon Gentiles are taught. In Jewish sources we have examined, we have found that Gentiles are obligated to observe the seven *Noahide* commandments. God, we may say, teaches them who they are through them, and through their experiences, which yield their discrete religious doctrines. If, as I believe, the diverse experiences of people with God are only partially describable to and for the benefit of others, then a Christian philosophy of education might find some of my categories useful but will suggest other contents. The commonality, from a Jewish point of view, is in the shared universe of *Yirat Shamayim.* Creatureliness and moral responsibility can be recognized even in those who seem culturally and doctrinally quite different.

The education of a *Yire Shamayim* in the modern world raises new problems.

This is so, first of all, because the convictions characterizing our times are in many ways unrecognizably altered vis-à-vis previous speakers of the language. They could hardly have imagined the present situation: of secular humanism and bureaucratic dehumanization, of text criticism, of an expanding universe and overwhelmingly expanded—and expanding—funds of knowledge. Can it be maintained, in our present historical situation, that only one who speaks the language in the same way as our ancestors did can be a *Yire Shamayim*? Can modern people agree that such sameness is ever more than a historical illusion? And what can and do modern Jews believe the language to be? And what about those who think of any cultural heritage as no more than cumulative literature, with no substance demanding loyalty, who deny that it must be protected at all costs?

Secondly, since the funds of knowledge at our disposal are radically different from those available in the past, old literature is unlikely to suffice for us in understanding the language. Can we consider a person morally reliable in this epoch who knows very little of what educated people in the twentieth century generally do know, including what they know in the field of Jewish studies? What are we to learn from modern *hokhmah* about making literature? Or, given the weakened state and status of language, and of the communities on which it largely depends, is it perhaps wise to be wary of making literature altogether? If we dare make new literature, as seems demanded by our times, what assurance have we that it will not demolish the language?

In our final two chapters, we turn to those questions and then make a curricular proposal.

14

LANGUAGE
AND LITERATURE

*I*n one sense, we have now completed the task we set ourselves. Having begun with the question whether the Jewish textual tradition has the power to relate to crucial educational-philosophical issues, namely, what should be taught and for which reasons, we could now stop, leaving on the educational counter a partial yet hopefully representative lexicon of Jewish language and a selection of Jewish literature. We could solemnly conclude that the language of Torah provides firm foundations for educational philosophy and a wide range of literary options for further development. We might now simply suggest that scholars on *halakhic* and other modes of the language and literature, together with educational thinkers, undertake to further investigate aspects of Jewish *Paideia* and thereupon discover together how the subject matter of Judaism can be used to establish guidelines for teaching.

But our reader, unless all that s/he wished to know was whether the Jewish tradition is maligned when it is denied a historical *Paideia* of its own, deserves more. For while it is edifying and perhaps comforting to have discovered that there has been a Jewish language, and that its vitality, accessibility, and relevance have always been secured by ongoing literature, the reader cannot simply translate this into educational theory and practice. S/he has to cope with the facts that contemporary Jews differ about what the language really is; many are uncertain what they themselves wish it were; and many others are not at all sure that the language, Jewish literature, and literature-making really interest and concern them. Why, then, use this language and these funds of literature for the re-evaluation of other dictionaries of culture that are significant to them?

Moreover, the readers know that languages are spoken in communities, and that it is in communities, too, that the need for literature-making arises. Literature has no power where the language has no authority. Yet most Jews today cannot honestly say that they live in communities, even when they have joined them and are members of them. The community does not function as an authority for them; they don't hear the collective norm imposed on them by Torah, thus ultimately by God through it. And they may well consider our task unfinished if they find us evading these issues.

Finally, they may feel let down if, even after some ground-clearing on the above, we loftily refrain from suggesting a possible direction for all this philosophy of Jewish education to take us.

Language and Literature: Three Positions

Were we to ask those Jews who think about such matters today, and who are ready to think in terms of the categories we have suggested what they think about Jewish language and literature in these times and for their lives, we may expect the three following types of response.

The first, quite Jewishly, answers our question with two questions: (1) What still remains for modern Jews as language?; and (2) How much ground does it cover, or may be allotted to it, given the other significant languages Jews are expected to know and are committed to speaking? Despite their disagreements we might expect three of the five educators who joined us for a discussion of *Yirat Shamayim,* Esther, Daniel, and Carmela, to respond in this manner, anxious to locate the language and discover its scope for modern Jewish education.[1]

A second type of response articulates a principled discomfort with all languages and with those who insist on bringing them into the cultural conversation. The idea of protecting a corpus of culture, deemed to be authoritative and somehow perennial is here dismissed as medieval and obscurantist. Those expressing this view may have considerable sympathy for historical memories, for problems and achievements, for longstanding social affiliations and allegiances—in short, for previous literatures upon which we build our cultural enterprise. But nothing in the past is inviolable and sacred simply by virtue of having been in the past. Judaism, too, is best understood by modern people as that which Jews do, and decide to remember, as the dilemmas and challenges they face rather than the

1. See Section III and our roundtable of Jewish educators.

loyalties they owe. Thus, if the sacred literature of Judaism takes its meaning from the language it alleges to present and represent, then it behooves the modern Jew to de-sacralize it, to read it for pleasure and insight rather than to study it. A modern Jew need not look up in texts or practices of tradition what his or her life allegedly means. Among our colleagues in the *Yirat Shamayim* sessions, Amir defended this point of view.

A third kind of respondent takes exception to our categories but may grudgingly agree to use them for the moment. This respondent is convinced that the very conception of language and literature undermines Judaism and invites shaking off the yoke of Torah. Admittedly, there are new challenges and problems in Jewish life, but they are to be negotiated by the authoritative interpreters of the language. And the resulting interpretations and applications, at least as far as the community is concerned, are themselves language. Or, to state this in more internal language, a *da'at Torah* (a Torah opinion, even without proof-texts) is itself Torah. Of those at our *Yirat Shamayim* roundtable, Nehemyah identifies with this position.

If the second and third opinions take us to the heart of the controversy in modern education between normative and deliberative orientations, the first approach exposes the crisis within the inner life of Judaism in our age. It is because of the varying viewpoints among those in the first group (e.g., Esther, Daniel, Carmela) that we cannot be sure what other Jews understand by Judaism. Consequently, we cannot be sure whether we ourselves are speaking of it descriptively or normatively. And we are aware that until modern times Jews did not doubt that the descriptive (What is it, as an historical phenomenom?) and the normative (What does it mean and oblige?) were inseparable and identical. The crisis reflected in the first category of response revolves around the lack of agreement among contemporary Jews as to what the language is, and to which degree it can be considered more than an aspect or even fragment of culture, such as mere religion in a secular world or colorful ethnicity for universally-minded people.

Locating Jewish Language

The question: What is the Jewish language that can or must be protected in order to safeguard a Jewish identity that has specific cultural or religious content, may be understood on the plane of history, of sociology, or of philosophy and theology.

On the plane of historical research, the issue comes to this: what has Judaism really been and what has remained the same within it throughout historical change and development? Those who wish to salvage doctrines within the landscape of historical inquiry attempt to conceptualize this question in a strictly chronological-archeological manner, in terms of clearly delineated time-strata: which texts are really the sacred ones, and where does the canon stop? What was given "at Sinai"? This doctrinal approach makes language synonymous with material that is impeccably ancient and axiomatically beyond the scope of scientific inquiry.

However, historical research in the academy is not guided or limited by such theological dispositions. Professors of Jewish studies and their doctoral students do not stop at some arbitrarily drawn time line beyond which they dare not trespass. They investigate everywhere, and everywhere discover diversity, controversy, and fluidity. And they describe the sacred texts differently than adherents of language are used to or comfortable with. These scholars routinely refer to the horizons of the early or late *midrash,* the world of the Talmudic sage, the ideology (priestly, prophetic, etc.) of this or that specific Biblical writer. In other words, scientific historical research makes all language seem like varieties of literature. The landscape, viewed from the windows of the university library, appears strewn with ruins.

Actually, it is unlikely that researchers as such will hope or claim that through scientific inquiry they may discover what the perennial language is or what, if anything, modern Jews should consider normative Torah. Those wishing to protect the truth of Judaism from being undermined and corroded by scientific inquiry can no longer anticipate that the researcher will supply objective demonstrations of what that normative Torah is. Rather, s/he will espouse the position that language dwells elusively elsewhere than in the libraries and laboratories of the scientific world, that it is truly "in your mouth and in your heart to do it."

Academic study may certainly be helpful in exploring the ways in which communities and individuals have understood and used the language. One may study what Jews have been committed to, what they have written commentaries on to resolve difficulties. Historians as well as theologians can document for what Jews have been prepared to give their lives, what they have meant when they testified to living within their Judaism, what their criteria were for evaluating the education of their children as successful or unsuccessful. Academic sociological study can also document how, in modern open societies, Jews have conducted cognitive negotiation with the supposedly general language of the emancipating societies in which they lived and in which they usually aspired to full membership; how they agreed to limited accommodation with a majority, relinquishing some cultural goods in order to retain other, less obtrusive or more important ones. Questions that are open to inquiry are: what did they consider most important? Why?[2]

In this negotiation, and in the refusal of some to explicitly negotiate, philosophical and theological questions arose. It was necessary to clarify the relationship of what was retained to the general culture. It was considered important, too, to link that which was adopted from the general culture to the tradition. There was a re-thinking of language and literature for our times. Consequently, there had to be new ventures into educational philosophy. What a person considered language determined what s/he insisted on transmitting; what was considered literature set the bounds for Jewish matters to which learners would be exposed for appreciation, evaluation, and selection.

For some modern Jews, the essential language, the litmus test of authenticity and loyalty, resided in the norms of Jewish behavior, the *halakhah*. This, certainly, was the position of Western European neoorthodoxy as fashioned by Rabbi Samson Raphael Hirsch and his circle. For others more secular and cultural, like Ahad Ha'am, the language was the pristinely expressed basic character traits of the Jewish people, traits articulated in the prophetic demand for justice, and in basic cultural idioms. Others, like Leo Baeck, found the language in a fundamental world view or, like Kaufmann, in the national commitment to a monotheistic faith. In all but the most radically secular cases, modern Jewish thinkers described not only a language to be protected but also a new literature to be fashioned, often based on *hokhmah* of the nations or at least formulated in its terms.[3]

For those orthodox thinkers who agreed that historical culture legitimately made demands on the present, authorization for this innovative literature had to be in some sense located within the language and anticipated in previous literature. Language, after all, was synonymous with Torah, and contemporary Torah had to be essentially continuous with the perennial and past Torah. Therefore, these new formulations, whether wide or narrow, were usually presented, at least in part, as new exegesis on sacred and familiar texts. Orthodox thinkers had an additional reason for doing this, namely that the Judaism they advocated and defended was comprehensive in principle, and could not be

2. On limited, controlled accommodation as an option for a cognitive minority in modern society, see Peter L. Berger, *A Rumour of Angels*, (Garden City, New York: Doubleday and Co. Inc., 1967) pp. 36–37.

3. For a literary example of the writings of Samson Raphael Hirsch, see *The Nineteen Letters of Ben Uziel*, translated by Bernard Drachman (New York: Bloch Publishing Co., 1942). For examples of the writings of Ahad Ha'am, see *Selected Essays of Ahad Ha'am*, translated from the Hebrew by Leon Simon (Cleveland, New York, and Philadelphia: Meridian Books, 1962). See also Leo Baeck, *The Essence of Judaism* (New York: Schocken Books, 1948). A short and concise example of Yehezkel Kaufman's views is "The National Will to Survive," in *Sources of Contemporary Jewish Thought* II, edited by David Hardan (Jerusalem: World Zionist Organization, 1970), pp. 83–121.

bought off with a small slice of life alongside the general culture. In practice, however, they, too, often slipped into compartmentalization, speaking two languages that remained foreign to each other.

An outstanding example of the traditionalist tendency is Rabbi Joseph D. Soloveitchik's already classic essay, "The Lonely Man of Faith."[4] Here, Soloveitchik describes the Biblical story of Creation as referring to two types of humans. The differences and even contradictions between the first and the second and third chapters of Genesis he explains as if teaching a Biblical typology, which he calls Adam I and Adam II. Adam I is the majestic person who uses theoretical thought to control a world that would otherwise subjugate him/her. Creation in God's image means that humans have a capacity for achieving dignity through power over nature as well as the cultural ability to make life orderly and pleasant. Adam II seeks to escape the innate loneliness of Adam I, the achiever, by seeking and finding a community of covenant initiated by God, wherein friendship becomes possible through existential self-knowledge. In this community, the need to impress, manipulate, and control is relinquished in order to make room for existential redemption.

It is clear that Adam I represents one who speaks the language of modernity, but we should note that this mode of existence is legitimated Biblically and *halakhically* as one part of how the Torah envisions a Jewish and human ideal. After all, the story of this first Adam is in the Bible itself; the majestic community is a requirement of the Torah and Adam I implements the image of God in which s/he was created! Yet, Judaism demands that the covenant community of Adam the second guide the majestic community by establishing the sovereignty of the *halakhah* throughout an integrated life of the two Adams, who together constitute human personality.

Such comprehensiveness, even in principle, has been problematic for the non-Orthodox. They have had difficulty in defending a worldview or an educational philosophy that is completely internal to a religious Jewish language. They are too committed to what modernity offers, and too differentiated in consciousness for an exegesis that "midrashizes" traditionally.

A non-Orthodox approach that yet acknowledges the sovereignty in principle of Jewish language is suggested by the Israeli educational thinker Ernst Akiva Simon.[5] Simon describes historical Judaism as a "catholic" religious culture that encompasses all aspects of life and cul-

---

4. Soloveitchik, "The Lonely Man of Faith."
5. Ernst Akiva Simon, "Are We Israelis Still Jews? The Search for Judaism in the New Society," in *Arguments and Contexts: a Reader of Jewish Thinking in the Aftermath of the Holocaust,* selected and with an introductory essay by Arthur A. Cohen (New York, Evanton, and London: Harper and Row, 1970), pp. 388–401.

ture; everything, including relations of love, means of livelihood, nationalism, science, and philosophy are within it. As various domains liberated themselves from religion in early modern times, Protestant faiths, disengaged from culture, emerged. They were characterized by intensive faith, theological reflectivity, and existential search. They made fervent prophetic demands on culture—but alongside it.

Simon makes a cultural, ultimately educational, prognosis: if Judaism maintains its traditional totality, it will in the modern situation be distorted and corrupted by its catholic aim to control all aspects of life. It must develop a Protestant, limited yet intense, mode of believing existence. Religious Jews will testify to their belief, live within the religious tradition to the best of their ability, draw upon the sacred literature for their understanding of themselves, and build their moral-spiritual world upon its foundations. But they will be citizens of the religiously neutral cultural world as well. However, being loyal Jews who understand Judaism to be catholic (i.e., total) in principle, they anticipate the ultimate return of Judaism to its catholic character—in Messianic times. Here, the language is one of a faithful orientation, rooted in the Bible, Talmud, and *midrash*. The most important literature for the modern Jew is in the modes of accommodation, reflection, and searching out the demands of faith in this historical hour. Jews are commanded to a critical loyalty to tradition and a religious critique of secular culture. But they belong to the world of secular culture as well.

We see that those in our first category of response must ask themselves what they consider justified and essential transmission in education, which *hokhmah* they enlist for the making of new Jewish literature, and how comprehensive they see Jewish education to be. To these questions, as we have seen, there are diverse answers.

No Language or All Language?

The position that modern people should consider the concept of language as pernicious for life and education is fundamentally one that frowns on norms. Conversely, to maintain that new literature is unnecessary because everything is already covered by the language is to negate the role of deliberation and innovation in education. We have discussed this controversy at some length elsewhere,[6] but we cannot suggest curriculum guidelines without reviewing crucial features of it as they relate to language and literature.

Normative educators tend to argue that the new generation must learn—and learn to identify with—what the adult world considers to

6. Rosenak, *Commandments and Concerns*, Chap. 1.

be excellent, virtuous, cultured, and civilized. An education for norms "sees" the community before the individual, and the individual as a community member. For an education within the normative framework, the rationale for the entire enterprise lies in continuity, in transmission, in communicating trust in the existing cultural world to the young and loyalty to it. Teaching what is really educative is to achieve in the learners the desire, the need, and the ability to act as the adult world does and to have optimal understanding of the principles underlying this behavior. Then, even when new circumstances urgently require modification of previous habits, one may still be guided by the community's principles in regulating the necessary, hopefully minimal, innovations that must be made. Even in times of cultural instability, perhaps especially so, these principles are criteria of worth and legitimacy.[7]

The second, the deliberative school of educators, finds it archaic and authoritarian to chain the educational enterprise to some vision, religious teaching, philosophical doctrine or rational truth. Rather, education and reflection upon it (philosophy) should be in constant dialogue with our experimental findings on what human life, both healthy and impaired, is actually like. A healthy life is one in which people can function well, hence grow, be creative, and interact satisfactorily with others and with their total environment. They are able to resolve the problems that threaten to impede such health. They acknowledge distress and are ready to cope with the problems to which distress points. They also know how one works towards appropriate solutions to these problems. If education should make it possible to live life to the full, educators should help learners understand what they are actually doing in their lives, which changes will be beneficial, and how they may best implement them.

The norms of the past will not necessarily serve them well in understanding their lives and solving their problems. Actually, norms may be an impediment in living life well, for they are congealed and often fossilized solutions to the problems of previous generations. They are deceptively authoritative, because they have been deviously moved from earth to heaven, from the arena of unending adaptation to that of philosophical and religious perennial truth. What can such norms teach those who tread on new territory, in which human beings are presented with unanticipated dangers, challenges, and opportunities?[8]

---

7. Robert M. Hutchins, _The Conflict in Education in a Democratic Society_ (New York: Harper and Row, 1953).

8. John Dewey, _How We Think: a Restatement of the Relation of Reflective Thinking to the Educative Process_ (Boston: Heath, 1933), p. 13. "... A man traveling in an unfamiliar region comes to a branching of the road. Having no sure knowledge to fall back on, he is brought to a standstill of hesitation and suspense. Which road is right? And how shall his perplexity be resolved? There are but two alternatives: he must either

The contemporary educator has tended, at least in conviction and theory, to side with the deliberative type of educational thought. Among the good reasons for this, we may mention the following:

The normative conception of education requires stable communities; there, norms function naturally. In such communities education initiates the young into sacred stories, symbolic actions, absolute morality, and the existential rightness of what is known to be true and good. But these communities have all but disappeared in the Western world and with them the "habits of the heart"[9] that animated them and were sustained by them. The fact is that where such pristine communities still exist the normative approach remains majestically in force. But often the entire enterprise seems somehow incongruous, thus exotic; the upholders of the perennial virtues generally appear to be insecure, sometimes even panic-stricken, and consequently fanatical.

As education for induction into stable communities atrophied, education for most people became functional and technical. It was designed to train them for productive living, that is, to make a living in industrial society, perhaps to make good or at least to be useful. For the happy minority, education became heavily humanistic, centering on an aesthetic appreciation of the past and its alleged riches, which, it was suspected, were admired partly for their very uselessness. Hence it became quite plausible for the multitude to identify norms with snobbishness and superfluity. Tradition and its norms also intimated manipulation, keeping those who possessed only practical knowledge in their place. This place was, of course, considerably beneath those who knew the language.

Modernity has indeed brought with it such rapid and radical changes that traditions and the authorities that speak in their name have often seemed both ignorant and insensitive about the real problems and circumstances of modern people. It appears that everywhere we tread we are on unfamiliar territory. There are many roads and no adequate road signs.

Given such arguments, it would make sense for normative education to gracefully or otherwise made its exit. That it is still with us might be taken as an indication that it is more convenient for teachers to tell than to explore, that nostalgia is pleasant, and that normative education is simply easier to do even if it not always done honestly. But that is a polemical and one-sided presentation. The ideal of nor-

---

blindly and arbitrarily take his course, trusting to luck for the outcome, or he must discover grounds for the conclusion that a given road is right."

9. For a sociological-philosophical analysis of what constituted staples of society and what has happened to them in a major modern society, see Robert Bellah, *et. al., Habits of the Heart: Individualism and Commitment in American Life* (Berkeley: University of California Press, 1985).

mative education has hidden strengths, and, in self-defense, has succeeded in pointing to some once unsuspected weaknesses in the opposing position.

Normatively-minded educators may still and once again argue that a life without norms makes every problem in principle equally serious and all equally trivial. They will maintain that a society and an educational conception based on problem identification and solving makes for a technological view of life. Such a view, they say, is ultimately empty and insignificant, for the problem of human being cannot be solved, but only confronted. And this problem, the really crucial one in human existence, is evaded in principle by those who think that solutions are everything. Their thesis is that there are no solutions to what the totality of human life is about, to what its significance is and its fundamental obligations are. To these matters, there is only response. Hence the lives of individuals, like of civilizations, must rest on some ground, whether revealed by God and/or discovered through reason and/or distilled from wise reflection on experience.

The following philosophical conversation about the foundations of the world graphically describes their view.

> Says one: "The world cannot hover in the heavens of its own accord." (So who holds it aloft?)
>
> Replies the other: "Atlas holds it aloft,"
>
> "And how does Atlas stay in the air?" "He sits on the back of an elephant."
> "And where does the elephant stand?" "He stands on the back of a turtle."
> "And where does the turtle stand?" "I'm afraid, from there, it's turtles all the way down."[10]

This is a pristinely normative anecdote, for its point is that something has to hold the world in the heavens and that "turtles all the way down" is absurd. Down to where? And because everyone knows this intuitively, the problem-oriented society, say the norm-oriented educators, engenders fundamentalism and fanaticism. Such escape from freedom is a reaction, based on a true insight that turtles all the way down, is as ugly as it is ludicrous. Hence, a desperate dogmatism arises to deal with a pervasive skepticism. Without norms, life is a free-fall into an abyss.

A *midrash* makes the normative point in its own distinctly valuative rhetoric, and quite without recourse to turtles. The ground in this *midrash* is that of the *mitzvot* located in the Torah within which the normative world resides. Without the *mitzvot* life is a raging and hostile sea. On the verse, "Speak unto the children of Israel and say

10. Tobin Siebers, *Morals and Stories* (New York: Columbia University Press, 1992), pp. 22–23.

to them that they make themselves *tzizit* (fringes) on the corners of their garments" (Numbers 15:38) our *midrash* teaches:

> The Holy One blessed be He ... left not a thing in the world about which He did not charge Israel with some commandment. If an Israelite goes out to plough, then (s/he is charged with the commandment) "You shall not plough with an ox and an ass together" (Deut: 22:11); to sow: "You shall not sow your vineyard with two kinds of seeds" (*Ibid.,* v. 9); reap: "When you reap your harvest and have forgotten a sheaf ... you shall not go back to fetch it" (*Ibid.,* 24:19) ... If s/he builds a house: "You shall make a parapet for your roof" (*Ibid.,* 14:1) and then "shall write them (the passages of the *Shema* in the *mezzuzah*) on your doorposts" (*Ibid.,* v. 9); if he wraps himself in a cloak: "Say to them that they make themselves *tzizit* (fringes)."

> To what may this be compared? To the case of one who has been thrown into the water. The captain stretches out a rope and says: "Take hold of the rope with your hand and do not let go, for if you do you will lose your life." Similarly, the Holy One blessed be He said to Israel: As long as you adhere to the commandments then "You that did cleave to the Lord your God are alive, every one of you to this day" (Deut. 4:4). In the same vein it says: "Take fast hold of instruction, let her not go: keep her, for she is your life" (Proverbs 4:13).

> *Numbers Rabbah* 17:5

Not Drowned And Not Buried

This *midrash* reenforces what we generally believe about Judaism and, for that matter, about any religious tradition, textual or not. Such traditions, we tend to assume, are blatantly normative. Moreover, on the face of it, our explorations into Jewish sacred literature confirm our certainty that the language of Judaism, as of all institutional religious teaching, is "truth engraved on tablets of stone." What is good is the will of God who sets the norms and whose pedagogy is to point out the dire consequences of trusting human autonomy and judgment. Isn't that what Torah, the language of Judaism, is all about, beginning with Adam and Eve in the Garden of Eden? It is clear that, in the textual tradition of Torah that we have been examining, normativeness and the principles that explain it constitutes language. This language is quite comfortable with a-priori postulates (e.g., "observe the *mitzvot*" and remain alive as the Torah defines life). It mandates social behaviors, it imposes its own forms of thought and teaches that these forms are requisite for one who claims authority or strives for real communicability.

This normativeness, even more than their antiquated and unscientific world pictures, is said to account for the weakness and irrelevance of religious languages today. After all, the world in which we live is all "unfamiliar territory" (Dewey) In our society change is deemed both natural and good, and problems are recognized as inherent in change. For modern people, it is an historical fact and sociological truism that traditional communities have shown themselves to be dysfunctional. As a result of the demise of these communities we have discovered that individual rights and aspirations count for more than communal expectations and duties, that, in sociological terms, personal dignity is more cogent than communally imposed and maintained codes of honor.[11]

The person who is against an educational conception based on language will seldom admit that the modern secular approach reflected in these axioms and convictions also is a language. Yet it is. Its experimental mode of looking at the world is based on given assumptions, it promotes specific values and norms of inquiry. This language, like religious ones, seeks to transmit to children a trusted way of looking at the world, a way to which we are committed, that reflects our principles and incorporates our ideals. For example, the deliberative educator, charged with transmitting this language, might be expected to operate on the principle that it is morally right to act in accordance with what we find to be the nature of things from our scientific study of human beings and the cosmos. And that we constantly have new findings that must not be neutralized by excessive reverence for established (i.e., older) ones. And while there are old bodies of literature, like those of religious traditions, that may be learned for their historical interest and for the still-valid insights they contain, these traditions are to be recognized for what the deliberative language teaches them to be—literature.

Yet the distinctions drawn here, while useful for intellectual comprehension and clarity, are also rigid and simplistic. For, though it is true that any attempt to reflect systematically about Jewish education on the basis of its texts will begin with its normative language, this language, we have seen, not only authorizes literature but mandates it. On the verse, "And you shall keep my statutes and ordinances which a person shall do and live by them," (Leviticus 18:5), the Talmud teaches:

> From whence do we know that saving a life supersedes the observance of the Sabbath? R. Yehudah said in the name of Shmuel: "As it is written, ... that a person shall do and live by them, and not die through them."
>
> *Yoma* 85b

Nothing is more obstinately normative than statutes, yet even they are to be lived by! Torah needs commentary; it thrives on hidden but also unanticipated problems. It constantly theorizes about its vital con-

11. Peter L. Berger, Brigitte Berger, and Hansfried Kellner, *The Homeless Mind* (Harmondsworth, Middlesex, England: Penguin Books, 1973), pp. 78–89.

tacts with the literature that will grow out of it, and it does so in both liberal and conservative ways. Thus, on the one hand we have the view that the Torah (i.e., the language) was given only in general outline to Moses; on the other hand, that the last teaching to be taught by a student of the last generation was also given at Sinai. Here are two different ways of understanding the Oral Torah to be revealed together with the Written Torah, however difficult it was for our Roman heathen-proseltye to understand at first.[12] And it is through the literature that historical communities are enabled to remain loyal to "Torah" and individuals may keep faith with communities.

We have seen how contemporary Jewish thinkers, even when they consider the texts to impart and teach a language, will disagree as to where language stops and literature begins. But despite the unprecedented perplexity about this issue among modern Jews, a perplexity that cannot be evaded, all who are not radically secular or religiously fundamentalistic agree that both language and literature are inherent in Judaism. For them Jewish education remains the transmission of the former and making learners capable of recognizing the latter.

The Torah, our *midrash* told us, must be culturally pervasive: "it is your life," and without it we shall be drowned in a raging sea. But let us recall too how the medieval *Tosaphist* explains the Talmudic text that Heilman reports himself studying: if we take hold of the Torah without its mantle, we shall be buried. Just as to have only literature is a free-fall into absurdity, so to have only language is suffocating and sooner or later fatal.

Jewish education for most remains the transmission of the former and making learners capable of recognizing the latter. The educated Jewish person swims in the language, speaks in its terms, but also, lives with problems. And s/he deals with them by choosing from the options the literature presents, and building upon them.

12. See Chap. 11.

15

REALMS OF
JEWISH LEARNING

Two Conceptions of the Educated Jew

*A*mong the conceptions of the educated Jew that were proposed in the centuries bridging medieval and modern Jewish life, two come to mind that clearly distinguished between a comprehensive and a supplementary view of Jewish education.

The first is that of the sixteenth-century Rabbi Yehudah Loew, the Maharal of Prague.[1] Maharal argues for the legitimacy of teaching general or universal wisdom. Among the bases for his position is a *halakhah* that obliges one to make a blessing in the presence of "the wise of the nations of the world" no less than in the presence of a wise Jew. He reminds his readers that the *midrash* (*Lamentations Rabbah* 2) states that "if someone says to you that there is wisdom among the nations, believe it ... (but if it is said) that there is Torah among the nations, don't believe." From this we learn two things: first, that we are to cherish wisdom wherever and in whoever it is found, and, second, that we are to differentiate between Torah and wisdom insofar as the former is directly revealed and thus entirely divine and spiritual. As for the Talmudic insistence that one should not study Greek wisdom (*Menahot* 99b), the Maharal neutralizes it by distinguishing between Greek wisdom "which has no relationship to the Torah at

---

1. Rabbi Yehudah Loew (Maharal), cited from *Netivot Olam (Paths of Eternity)* in Simcha Assaf, *Mekorot B'Toldot Hahinukh B'Yisrael (Sources in the History of Jewish Education)* vol. I (Tel Aviv: Dvir Co. Ltd., 1954), pp. 51–52.

all," and general wisdom, about which we make a blessing and which is found "among the nations." Thus:

> if this is so (that He "gave of His wisdom to flesh and blood"), it seems that one should learn the wisdom of the nations, for why should one not learn the wisdom which is from God, may He be blessed? (And if this has nothing to do with the strictures against Greek wisdom, then) ... the domains of wisdom which have to do with the reality and the order of the world one may certainly learn ... for why would they (i.e., the sages) call it Greek wisdom if it were concerned with the reality of the world, since this wisdom is the wisdom of every person?

A second conception is suggested, some two hundred years later, by Naftali Herz Wessely (Weisel) in his *Divrai Shalom V'Emet (Words of Peace and Truth)*.[2] Weisel divides all knowledge and studies into two categories: *Torat Ha-adam* (the teaching of humanity) and *Torat HaShem* (the teaching of God). The former includes culturally appropriate behavior *(yediot nimusiot)*, the ways of morality and good character, civility *(derekh eretz)* and clear, graceful expression. It also takes in history, geography, astronomy, and the like. The knowledge of all these, including the moral code of "the seven *Noahide* commandments," is founded on reason. The same is true of the natural sciences "which provide genuine knowledge of all things: animals, plants, minerals, the elements, meteorology, botany, anatomy, medicine, chemistry, etc. It is in man's power to study all these phenomena by means of his senses and reason: he does not need anything divine to comprehend them."

Weisel notes the *midrashic* teaching that there were twenty-six generations between Adam and Moses (*Leviticus Rabbah* 9), which he takes to mean that *Torat Ha-adam* preceded *Torat HaShem* by these twenty-six generations. Thus, from the creation of humankind until the revelation at Mount Sinai, people acted according to the teaching of humanity alone. This means that they concerned themselves with the *Noahide* laws and with the etiquette, arts and science that constitute worldly affairs. Moreover, even now, *Torat Ha-adam,* being anterior to the exalted divine laws, should be learned well to prepare the heart for learning the teachings of God. Weisel intimates that *Torat HaShem,* despite its sublimity, is practically useless in isolation from *Torat Ha-adam.* For it is the latter alone that "benefits the commonweal."

> Therefore he who lacks *Torat Ha-adam,* even though he has learned the laws and teachings of God and lives according to them, gives no pleasure to others ... his fellowship is burdensome ... his speech in worldly affairs will not be in conformity ... with reason, and his actions worse than use-

2. Naphtali Herz (Hartwig) Wessely (Weisel), "Words of Peace and Truth," in *The Jew in the Modern World: a Documentary History,* edited by Paul R. Mendes-Flohr and Jehuda Reinharz (New York and Oxford: Oxford University Press, 1980), pp. 62–63.

less … . (Also) … even though the laws and teachings of God are far superior to *Torat Ha-adam,* they are closely correlated with it: where *Torat Ha-
adam* ends, the divine teaching begins, instructing us on what is beyond
man's power of reason. Therefore, he who is ignorant of the laws of God
but is versed in *Torat Ha-adam,* even though the sages of Israel will not
benefit from his light in the study of the Torah, will give benefit to the
remainder of humanity. But he who is ignorant of *Torat Ha-adam,* though
he knows the laws of God, gladdens neither the wise of his people nor the
rest of humanity.

The differences between the two orientations is obvious. For Maharal,
study of general wisdom is advised because "it is from God, may He
be blessed." The justification for all studies is based on *halakhic* and
aggadic sources in the Talmud and *midrash.* It is internal to the language. Maharal is also careful to keep his educational literature
securely within the bounds of the language. Thus, he distinguishes
between Greek wisdom and general wisdom, for the strictures of the
sages with regard to Greek wisdom must be respected, interpreted,
and thus protected, even in an open approach such as his. Note that
the distinction between Greek wisdom and the wisdom of every
person is not a formal nod in the direction of tradition, but normative. It informs us that certain studies have no place in the curriculum and that others, even if not exclusively Jewish, do. Purely
Greek wisdom is outside the pale of true, thus divine, wisdom.[3] The
wisdom of every person does belong, because it, as genuine wisdom, comes from God.

Weisel, on the other hand, makes the language of Judaism to be
transmitted in education largely perfunctory, and certainly supplementary. The important, useful, and even the moral features of life
belong to a universal language called *Torat Ha-adam.*[4] *Torat HaShem*
may be sublime and exalted, but its language is largely pre-empted
by the universal one of *Torat Ha-adam. Torat HaShem* is something
religious that Jews ought to study in addition to what they learn from
their "real" education. One may assume that Weisel, having put Jewish language into a particularistic niche, will have no strong urge to
create literature in it but will, in new circumstances, simply restrict it
still further. The action is elsewhere.

3. Maharal states that Greek wisdom consists of ways of speech and Greek language,
   hence specific features of Greek culture that are of no use in understanding any
   aspect of the Torah. *Netivot Olam* (Bnai Brak, Israel: Yahadut Pub., 1980), p. 60.
4. Weisel here follows his master, Moses Mendelsohn, who considered the seven
   Noahide commandments to follow from reason and not to require revelation for
   their authoritative status. See discussion of this in Jacob Katz, *Exclusiveness and Tolerance: Jewish-Gentile Relations in Medieval and Modern Times* (New York: Schocken
   Books, 1962), pp. 174–77.

The guidelines of Weisel are not likely to be helpful if we envision a Jewish education based upon a comprehensive and inherently valuable language which has given rise to a variegated, complex, and ongoing literature, though they undoubtedly inform much of Jewish education today.

Realms of Meaning

Let us rather follow the train of thought of Maharal and of those who enlarged upon it in the contemporary world and so to suggest curricular guidelines for the transmission of a comprehensive Jewish language, seen through the prism of a rich literature that incorporates universal *hokhmah*. We shall do this by looking at Jewish education through the conceptual frame of six domains or realms of meaning. These are intended to indicate what might, in line with our study throughout this book, constitute goals for the educated Jew: which Jewish excellences s/he will possess, what kinds of experiences s/he will have undergone, what s/he will know, what s/he considers germane to cultural life, and the kind of things s/he will engage in to enlarge knowledge, understanding, experience, and virtue. These six realms of meaning are hopefully fruitful forms for the guidance of teaching and learning. They are intended to constitute a way of envisioning what an educated modern Jew will be like as a person who has acquired Jewish language and has sufficient familiarity with literature to understand, appreciate, and use it responsibly, imaginatively and in an open fashion.

The concept of "realms of meaning" I have taken from Philip H. Phenix's book by that name.[5] Phenix is a structure-of-knowledge educational theorist who posits that "knowledge in the disciplines has patterns or structures and that an understanding of these typical forms is essential for the guidance of teaching and learning." In his view, "the various patterns of knowledge are varieties of meaning and the learning of these patterns is the clue to the effective realization of essential humanness." His thesis "grows out of a concept of human nature as rooted in meaning and of human life as directed towards the fulfillment of meaning."[6]

We shall not follow Phenix's specific division of knowledge into his realms of meaning (which he terms symbolics, empirics, esthetics, synoetic or personal knowledge, ethics and synoptics) since we are concerned with the lexicon of Jewish language and the issues that arise in the "literary" use of this language. But Phenix is a modern

---

5. Philip H. Phenix, *Realms of Meaning: a Philosophy for the Curriculum for General Education* (New York: MacGraw Hill Book Co., 1964).
6. *Ibid.*, p. x.

teacher of educational *hokhmah* from whom we have much to learn. He is a theorist who reminds us that diverse aspects of curriculum are variously approached and learned, that they speak to diverse dimensions of human life in all of its cultural diversity. If, as Maharal teaches, "all wisdom comes from God," then every feature and form must be present in the teaching-learning enterprise of Jewish education; all dimensions must be represented, cultivated, and ultimately brought into contact with one another.

The six realms of Jewish education being proposed[7] are:

(1) Initiation into *Knesset Yisrael* (the community of Israel). Here we are concerned with those aspects of its language that delineate the collective life of Judaism for the educating fellowship and those aspects of literature that are seen to mark off Jewish cultural identity at the present moment. This realm depends heavily on *na'ase v'nishmah* and on learning how the language relates to its literature. It also draws on the de-ontological features of Judaism's moral code.

(2) Cultivation of the individual's uniqueness, the realm of *adam,* the human being as such. Here the development of the person who can live Judaism for its own sake, *l'shmah,* is a crucial criterion of educational practice, as well as the concreteness of individual life and relationships.

(3) Those aspects of language and literature that initiate the learner into the wider human fellowship, into what the language of Judaism calls *Bene Noah* (*Noahides,* i.e., humankind). Here the universal aspects of Jewish language comes into educational focus, as well as the consequential meaning of Jewish morality.

(4) *Hokhmah,* and understanding the created world. This requires familiarity with and competence within the "natural and historical situations" (Fackenheim), enabling the educated Jew to live comfortably and productively in "the community of majesty" (Soloveitchik). Here, too, the relationship between language and literature is central, as is *Yirat Shamayim,* for the acquisition of *hokhmah* is a prerequisite for the achievement of *da'at.* (See 6 below.)

(5) *Hiddur.* Here, we are concerned with nurturing the learners' sense of beauty, of "wisdom of the heart." In this realm, the lexicon of concreteness as well as *lishmah* are brought into play.

---

7. This general scheme was first proposed in a previous essay, Michael Rosenak, "Towards a Curriculum for the Modern Orthodox School," in *Orthodoxy Confronts Modernity,* edited by R. Jonathan Sacks (London: Ktav Publishing House in Association with Jews College, 1991), pp. 62–80.

(6) *Da'at,* the achievement of understanding. *Da'at* allows one to draw distinctions, to make connections, and to integrate knowledge without shortcuts or reductionism. The comprehended and admitted limits of *da'at,* in principle and for any given individual, as well as the reliability and moral power of the person who has *da'at,* link this realm to the character ideal of *Yirat Shamayim.*

Let us now briefly outline some foci of each realm:

The realm of *Knesset Yisrael* initiates the young person into the communal life of the Jewish people. In a traditional-religious community, this requires teaching the language of the *halakhah,* though not even all traditionally religious Jews will agree what that entails for the contemporary Jew.

We may expect that in such a community, children from an early age are invited to wash (and to make the blessing for hand-washing and bread) rather than to simply sit down and eat. In the realm of *Knesset Yisrael,* they will learn the skills and rhythms of prayer, and in general how one lives within the language when it is seen as a self-understood medium of cultural and spiritual life. Belonging to the community of Israel in a broad sense invites at-homeness in the Hebrew language, in the text-cycle of Torah reading, in the life-cycle of the Jewish people and in its land, *Eretz Yisrael.* Within the structure of *Knesset Yisrael* pupils develop habits of learning Torah, a readiness to take it seriously and to represent it. They learn to formulate questions in the language, such as: what does Rashi say (on this verse)? When is candle-lighting (for the Sabbath)? Is this a Jewish thing to do (morally)? They learn to mourn catastrophes of the Jewish past and to dance on happy occasions. They have no compunctions about asking whether a given development or policy of Jews or Gentiles is "good for the Jews." They enjoy the companionship of fellow Jews and the inner life of Judaism and they are capable of deliberating about Jewish problems.

Of course, each community of Jewish educators in the modern world will have to think through its conception of Jewish socialization, its working definition of *Knesset Yisrael.* For non-*halakhic* Jews, teaching the language cannot include the initiation of children into the world of the *halakhah;* they believe that *halakhah* is merely one species of Jewish literature, one option for understanding the national or prophetic or civilizational language.

One community of modern Jewish people will understand this realm to mandate intensive and enthusiastic study of texts, designed to inculcate a uniquely Jewish existential orientation of non-normative faith. In such learning communities, the study of the textual classical tradition will foster comprehensive knowledge of Jewish origins and of how early generations grappled with the perennial problems of spiritual and national collective life. Yet others may demand an emphasis on the teaching of Jewish history (how did our present literature grow out of our language or our ancient literature?). For yet another group, induction into *Knesset Yisrael* focuses on prophetic teachings of a good society and a perfected world and the ways we should interpret these teachings here and now, in our own Jewish communities, and in our own Jewish commonwealth.

No matter how diverse educators understand the language of Torah and its literatures, the teaching under the aegesis of this realm is culturally and/or religiously explicit. This means that it appears as a normative and perhaps self-understood reality that preceded the learners into the world and now confronts them and imposes itself upon them. For religious educators, it signifies bringing the child under the wings of the *Shekhinah* (the divine Presence). For all, it is making him or her a *ben/bat bayit* (i.e., an insider) in the inner world of the Jewish people. This is done, whether admitted or not, upon the assumption of *na'ase v'nishmah*. The child does even before understanding; s/he acts, and therein discovers his or her identity. The school, camp or other educational framework, through its *Knesset Yisrael* dimension, embodies but also builds community. For through this realm, educators convey the message that they, who tell him or her what to do, know what they are doing, that they may be trusted when they say that the language being taught is worthy and excellent.

Part of the trust that the child is asked to give the educator is implicitly based on the assumption that s/he will be part of the community and, in fact, already is. As already noted, this means not only that the child is promised that s/he will eventually understand, but that the child has the right to demand intimations of understanding even now, while being socialized. Hillel realized this and therefore converted his heathens before they began to study Torah. He understood that one cannot get people into a community-defining practice such as *limmud Torah* unless they have an inkling that it is more than a skill learned by rote, leading nowhere.

What was true of the proselytes is at least partially true of modern children. To become insiders, they must eventually learn to intuit how the language works and not only what it says. And the working of the language of Torah will not be understood, but only dogmatically affirmed, if there is no learning of how it functions, how it stimulates the making of literature, how it deliberates on variegated concrete circumstances, how it enlists *hokhmah* to preserve its own health, relevance, and trustworthiness. Where there is *na'ase* there must also be intimations of *nishmah*.

Given the dependence of the *Knesset Yisrael* realm on community, contemporary educators have to examine the extent to which they speak for living Jewish communities and what they can do to make the school, the summer camp, the fellowship of educators themselves elements for the strengthening and rehabilitation of community. We have mentioned the element of trust, and of the school, center or camp community as trustworthy. Communities do have cognitive learning experiences that distinguish them, but they are more than cognition, competence, and scholarship. Communities act together, they allow and encourage sub-communities that belong but have their own agendas (such as youth movements within the educational framework but independent of it) and they establish standards (of commitment and behavior) that obligate those in the learning community. They also invite, but cautiously; they know that good things ought to be shared and the ranks of community need be replenished, but also that indiscriminatory outreach may undermine fellowship by diluting shared commitments and experiences and compromising standards of "practice mastery."

Finally, the syllabus must incorporate subject matter that highlights paradigms of Jewish fellowship, in which cultural goods are both taken for granted and argued about. The arguments are as important as the taken-for-granted; practice is both community and controversy, and respect for language is reenforced and rendered plausible by bold literature-making.

Two subjects that are central educational tools for this are the study of Bible with commentators and the study of Talmud. The former has been made into a pedagogic art by Nehama Leibowitz in her various "studies in the portion of the week." As for the latter, it involves enormous difficulties with regard to skills and selection, but we suggest that there is no better place to see how the Bible and the Tannaic literature of *Mishnah, Tosephta* and *Baraita* serve the later *(Amoraic)* teachers of the *Gemara* as language that must be mined for meaning, and that does not inhibit teachers from shaping these works to the demands of valuative dilemmas, of reason, and of new situations. The language to which they are committed does not keep them from making literature. In fact the literature they make, that the language invites them to make, reenforces their devotion to the language.[8]

The realm of *Adam,* the human being as such, may appear to some traditionalists to embody an unexamined negotiation with other languages, or even an acknowledgement that the particularistic should yield to the

8. This is true both in biblical commentary and in Talmud. In the first case, it is the Biblical text that is believed and then expanded. In the second case, the Tannaic literature is similarly the ground of interpretation and expansion.

universal, that commitment to community is at best a stage. It seems to
be based on the assumption that before one speaks philosophically of
Jewish education, one should speak about education as such.

That assumption is, in fact, quite reasonable in itself. For it is true
that the Jewish child, like the Protestant Danish and the Shinto Japanese one, has certain needs and innate interests and that s/he has them
in common with the Dane and the Japanese. For this reason, when we
today speak about the rights of the child we condemn invidious distinctions between those who allegedly deserve more or expect more,
and those whose circumstances ostensibly make them naturally content with less. It is generally agreed that all children should have an
education that makes them capable of knowing themselves, that gives
them the abilities to use the world beneficiently, to build trusting and
warm relationships, to learn how to use the tools that can put them in
control of their emotions, their environments, and their lives to the
greatest extent possible. All children, we hope, will also be enabled by
their education to live realistically, but with some genuine joy. There
are unhappily all too few children who live in societies that believe in
that and/or can afford that, but most people in free societies believe
that it ought to be an universal aspiration. It is also an aspect of Jewish
messianic literature and is articulated in the lives of *Yir'ai Shamayim.*

And this literature brings us back to the language itself. The realm
of *Adam,* while intimating something envisioned for children as such,
is introduced here as a requirement of the language of Torah for
Jews. The assumption being made is that no person who does not
know him/herself and his/her potential, can reach the palace of
Torah l'shmah or speak the language masterfully enough to know
where the palace is and which roads lead to it.

It may be objected here that this self-knowledge is part and parcel
of *na'ase,* of the commanded existence to be discovered in *Knesset
Yisrael.* Have we not ourselves argued that the de-ontological will of
God teaches people who they are through what they must do in the
commanded life?

However, this objection proceeds from the assumption that everything we have to learn about ourselves is contained in the life of
community. This, I would argue, is not true to the language. Each
individual is not only part of a covenantal collective but is unique,
created in God's image. Each, in the words of one *mishnah,* is "an
entire world"; each must say "for me was the world created." Like
Eldad and Meidad in the wilderness, each may eventually prophesy
"in the camp," declaring in the name of God what Moses himself
does not know, what he has never heard.[9]

9. My reference is to the story of the two men of whom it is told that "they prophesied

The realm of *Adam,* therefore, portrays the road a Jewish child will travel towards individual self-discernment. One cannot know what one will eventually do *lishmah* without knowing who one is as an individual, what one's unique potential is. This takes place within a supportive teaching community but it is not merely a matter of proper socialization and initiation. It has to do with personal discernments that arise in many and often surprising contexts and unanticipated experiences.

My late friend, the historian Uriel Tal, liked to tell the story of the *hasid* who came to visit his *rebbe* (rabbi-teacher).

> When he knocked on the door of the *rebbe's* room, a voice from within called out, "Who's there?" To which the *hasid* answered, "Yankele." But there followed no invitation to enter. The young man woefully left. When he returned the next day, the same thing happened. Yankele knocked on the door, the *rebbe* asked who it was, Yankele repeated his name, and the door to the *rebbe's* study remained closed. Before coming back on the third day, the *hasid* mulled over the matter carefully and came to a decision. After knocking on the door this time, and hearing the *rebbe's* question who it was, he remained silent. Whereupon the *rebbe* called out: "Come in." The *hasid* thought he understood what had transpired but, nevertheless, asked the *rebbe* to explain. "Simple," said the *rebbe,* "If you know who you are, you don't need a *rebbe.*"

In the realm of *Adam* one discovers who one is without a *rebbe.*

It was Abraham Joshua Heschel who pointed out that a way of life that is perceived exclusively as a set of answers to questions that have themselves been forgotten becomes a rote, incomprehensible, and lifeless matter. He insisted that the child be helped to rediscover the questions to which the tradition of Judaism gives certain answers. Thus, one who has never been astonished at the fact that there is food when there might also not be any cannot understand why one should make a blessing upon eating. Heschel considered such questions, rooted in wonder, as God's "search for man."[10] It is only when His search is successful, when we have been found, that we can be addressed with the specific answers (commandments) of the Torah. Where there is no realm of *Adam* in principle, *Knesset Yisrael* ceases to be educative. It invites dullness, conformism and indoctrination.

And so, the realm of *Adam* is more focused on the questions that children ask than on the answers they are given; the curriculum of *Adam* is geared to arouse these questions. In this realm, therefore, the existential aspects of Torah are emphasized. First, there are stories of

---

in the camp" (without the authorization of Moses) (Numbers 11:26). When Joshua suggests that Moses imprison them, Moses responds: "Would that all the Lord's people be prophets!" (v. 29). That what they prophesied was unknown to Moses is suggested in the Talmud, *Sanhedrin* 17a.

10. Abraham Joshua Heschel, *God in Search of Man; a Philosophy of Judaism* (New York: Farrar, Strauss and Cudahy, 1955), Section I.

interesting heroes who raise questions and who turn out to be complex; eventually, Psalms, Job, and Kohelet (Ecclesiastes) should be studied. If the realm of *Knesset Yisrael* seems to focus on *halakhah* or on explicit cultural norms, *Adam* more generally speaks the language of *aggadah* and the questions the *aggadist* raised after reading the more normative texts. Thus, the realm of *Adam* not only anticipates a time when the child will be able to live the life of *Knesset Yisrael* for its own sake but teaches him the existential features of Jewish language through some of its literature. It anticipates the child's readiness for religious and/or cultural maturity, for literature-making.

In order for that to become possible, the child must of course have recourse to raw materials, to *hokhmah* that has no specific Jewish label on it, that is "the wisdom of every person." This wisdom must be congenial with Torah to the extent that it doesn't alienate the child from it; it should not be, at least for the immature child, Greek wisdom. But the wisdom of every person takes in a great deal of territory. It includes everything with which Jewish literature can be made.

Thus, poetry from everywhere releases the power to muse and reflect, and unlocks stores of empathy; children must think and dream, and express themselves in sundry ways. There must be opportunities to listen to music at leisure; for making things to learn about the fun of handling materials. The child discovers his/her concrete existence when s/he dreams not only about goals to achieve but intentions to strive for; not only what one hopes to get but what one hopes to become.

In this realm, the guiding principle of education is what I have called the implicit-religious one,[11] the search of the individual for God, addressing God in her/his life through an idiom that, hopefully, is that of *Knesset Yisrael* but that expresses something irreducible to the norms of the community. For each person is a world for whom, alongside commandments, there are concerns. These concerns are also at home in the language and they engender a more intimate literature than *halakhic* responsa and festival traditions. This is a literature of palaces, of doors waiting to be reached and opened, of the joy of the *mitzvah* and not only its "yoke." This literature grows out of *Torah l'shmah*, the language of individual potential and spiritual accomplishment. The person who knows who s/he is through an education in which there is adequate attention paid to the realm of *Adam* may not often need a *rebbe* but has the spiritual capacity to become one.

The realm of *Bene Noah* is that which brings children to see themselves as members of the human family, sharing a planet, a physical and psychic structure, a common fate, common createdness in God's image.

---

11. Rosenak, *Commandments and Concerns,* Chap. 6.

In the realm of *Bene Noah* we teach ethics but also ecology. We reach towards an understanding of humanity through social studies, but also teach foreign languages and world literature. We do this to expand horizons but also to make it clear that while there are dimensions of our lives in which distinctiveness and particularity, (i.e., those things we learn about in the realm of *Knesset Yisrael*) are of cardinal importance, there are also moments and dimensions in which the loving, suffering, and striving of people create human kinships that make these differences insignificant. This reflects the existential aspect of *Bene Noah.*

There are also two normative aspects of *Bene Noah.* Looking outward, this realm highlights the seven *Noahide* commandments, that is, universal norms of civilized behavior: a decent, morally reliable life and *Yirat Shamayim* for all human beings and all peoples. Looking within, it brings into focus what is to be learned from human experience as such, and how *hokhmah* is a hammer on the rock of Torah. Both of these normative features of *Bene Noah* are messianic, in that they anticipate a different and better world and they are part of making the world that way, of building bridges and trust between people. Building such bridges is directly opposed to a Jewish education in which the *Bene Noah* element is ignored because it is deemed to belong to something external entitled *Torat Ha-adam* or because it is deliberately excluded. In the latter case, there is nothing to be expected from the nations. They simply hate us, for "Esau hates Jacob" and can never be trusted. Consequently, there is nothing to be learned from them.

A Jewish education that deliberately excludes the dimension of *Bene Noah* has never seemed more realistic and less naive than in this post-Holocaust generation. But such exclusion denies a fundamental feature of the language, that which makes commandments between people an expression of divine Providence, that which makes the *Yire Shamayim* one who prepares the way for the kingdom of God. In other words, without the realm of *Bene Noah,* Jewish education is denied its redemptive dimension. For *Bene Noah* intimates redemption and anticipates it and teaches commitment and involvement. Children who have been educated into the condition of mankind within the framework of Torah will not be able to feel that they have nothing to do with the suffering of others and that this is, no matter how bad, the best of all possible worlds. The person whose education incorporated *Bene Noah* knows not only that it is perverse to attend the gladiatorial stadiums that reflect much of the true state of the world, but that, if at all possible, one has to go there and shout, hoping to meet there other Jews, and the righteous of all nations.

While *Knesset Yisrael* signifies commandments between people and God, *Bene Noah* points to the consequential feature of Jewish morality, to what "commandments between people" are all about. Indeed, these commandments have both a partial or particularistic aspect, when they relate to the relationships between Jews, and a universal one, which is fundamentally Messianic and redemptive. Which of these is more important? Which is more authentic?

A *midrash* tells us of the disagreement between Rabbi Akiva and Ben Azzai as to which statement in the Torah is its "great principle." R. Akiva declared that it is, "Love thy neighbor as thyself." But Ben Azzai found the great principle of the Torah in the verse, "These are the generations of man (all people!) ... for in the image of God He created him."[12] If R. Akiva's principle refers to fellow Jews (as most interpretations have it), Ben Azzai most defintely refers to *Bene Noah.* Adam and Eve, after all, were the parents of everyone.

I suggest that the two approaches may be viewed sequentially. What it means to be a *Noahide,* a member of the human family, is arrived at through the avenue of *Knesset Yisrael.* And the way this road is travelled and traversed requires the wisdom of *adam,* engaged in a lifelong exploration of what it means to be created in God's image.

In the realm of *hokhmah* we are concerned with what can be known about the world and everything within it. It can make us see intelligently what the Torah teaches about how the world was founded and how we may sensibly carry out the commandment: "Fill the earth and conquer it." For modern people, the realm of *hokhmah* is primarily that of science, in both its theoretical and practical aspects. The grounding of this realm within the language is both clear and problematic.

Let us dwell briefly on the problems first. As noted, activities in this realm of meaning are properly guided by and based upon scientific modes of thinking throughout the various disciplines. They involve the creation of hypotheses on the basis of the perceived inadequacy of prior ways of understanding, experimentation and other problem-appropriate forms of inquiry, and the positing of tentative solutions. They therefore raise serious questions for normative educational philosophy. A crucial one is: how shall one educate to normative commitments of the kind characterizing *Knesset Yisrael,* and at the same time initiate into a culture of authentic inquiry and deliberation? How are children to negotiate between truths and testing, commitment and open minds?

For both religious and culturally committed secular educators, the issue is how to assure commitments, how to protect language against a mode of life that is nothing but literature, how to combat a technocratic and relativistic world view.

12. *Sifra, Kedoshim* 4:12.

Religious educators see the problem to be doctrinal as well. This often tempts them to minimize the teaching of science, reducing it to its mechanical and technological aspects, attempting thereby to hide the philosophical problems. In other cases, religious teachers will compartmentalize religion and science as Jewish and general, *Torat HaShem* and *Torat Ha-adam*. Yet the theology of either approach raises more problems than it solves. The former undermines wholeness in the name of wholeness and the latter creates precisely the differentiation that leads to a radically secular orientation, disputed by cultural secularists no less than by religious thinkers, in which it is assumed that all real problems have scientific solutions. It is a theology that denies the comprehensiveness of the language in order to get away from the need to make literature.

A possible avenue of solution lies in a religious conception of humankind's relationship to the created world and its place both within that world, situated by it, and yet in a sense, through understanding, also above it. The conception of a "community of dignity" or "majesty" proposed by Soloveitchik that we have briefly addressed above seems like a large step in the right direction.

In any case, ruling this realm out of Jewish education is not a plausible strategy or policy. It is paradoxical and ironic that those who frown on this realm are often enamored of technological techniques originating in the secular-scientific world, in part because they are oblivious to the philosophical-scientific hinterland of these techniques. Ignorance of *hokhmah* also leads necessarily to alienation. Berger, Berger, and Kellner have nicely described the flower person of the sixties who refuses to enter an airplane piloted by someone who looks like him/herself,[13] and Jewish analogues readily come to mind. Alienation makes people not only exotic and vaguely irresponsible but insensitive and manipulative.

But quite irrespective of such dangers, it must be stressed that the relationship of this realm to the language is quite clear. To refer back to one of our own partial translations: one certainly cannot choose within the human situation (and fear God) if one is ignorant of the natural and historical ones. An ignorant person, say the sages, cannot not be pious. Without the realm of *hokhmah* there can be no acknowledged literature. To deny *hokhmah* is to block off the Torah from the situation in which it makes its claims. Or to be *halakhically* specific: how shall one praise God for the *hokhmah* bestowed on "flesh and blood" if one cannot recognize wisdom when one sees it?

The realm of *hiddur,* of beauty, represents the dimension of aesthetics, both appreciated and made. The knowledge gained in this

13. Berger, Berger, and Kellner, *The Homeless Mind,* pp. 193–94.

realm seems close to what Maharal described as Greek wisdom. Doesn't it deal with music, often blatantly Christian, and plastic and other arts, sometimes pagan? Yes, and there is also the ability to admire the structure of mathematical formulae and to see how a literary work or a Talmudic passage *(suggua)* is put together.

And *hokhmat lev* takes in much more. In and through this realm children learn to enjoy playing, not as something childish to be outgrown but as an enlightening activity in which one learns to know oneself better, where one tests and expands one's powers within the rules of the game. In the realm of *hokhmat lev* one gets the sense of how things out in the world connect to the inner light and life of individuals who then give back into the world by good performance.

The connection with the language of Judaism may seem tenuous, until we look more carefully at the scandal of concreteness and particularity that characterizes this language. Note how much of literature has been generated by the chapters of Exodus elaborating the building of the tabernacle in the desert. How, it was asked, could the Creator of the world take an interest in building construction? The late medieval exegete, Abrabanel, well formulates this question:

> Why did the Almighty command us regarding the construction of the tabernacle saying, "I shall dwell among them" as if He were a circumscribed coporeal being limited in space when this is the opposite of the truth ... it is said in Isaiah (66:1): "The heaven is My throne and the earth My footstool—where is the House that you may build for Me?" Solomon likewise said regarding the building of the Temple: "Behold the heaven and the heaven of heaven cannot contain Thee; how much less this house that I have built!" (1 Kings:8:27)

Part of his answer is: "The Divine intention behind the construction of the Tabernacle was to combat the idea that God has forsaken the earth and that His throne was in heaven and remote from humankind. To disabuse them of this erroneous belief, He commanded them to make a Tabernacle, as if to imply that He dwelt in their midst ..."[14]

Perhaps even more scandalous is the preoccupation of the Biblical text (an entire chapter!) with the high priestly garments. Why would the Bible command, "Thou shalt make holy garments ..."? What defense of such outlandish language can be put forward? Here is the commentary of one nineteenth-century commentator, Rabbi Meir Leibush Malbim:

> Now the garments ordained were evidently external ones and the text is concerned to relate how the artisans performed the work. But in reality they symbolized inner vestments. The priests were to invest themselves

---

14. Abrabanel's Commentary on the Torah, cited in Leibowitz, *Studies in Shemot (Exodus)* II, pp. 471–72

with noble qualities which are the vestments of the soul. These vestments the artisans did not make. But God commanded Moses to make these holy garments, that is to instruct them in the improvement of their souls and their characters so that their inner selves should be clothed in majesty and splendor.[15]

In both cases, the artistic work is intended, according to these commentaries, as a concrete way of evoking a state of the soul that represents something that is to be found "out there" and that ought to be shaped "in here," in the human soul. And, at the peak of its development, the beautiful and orderly construction bespeaks what is already in the soul. God gives the wisdom to construct to those who have an inner wisdom. Thus, for example, does the Talmud understand the wisdom of Bezalel, the tabernacle's chief builder. (*Berakhot* 55a).

The dimension of *hokhmat lev*, the wisdom of the heart, is not to be confined to refined spirits. The tradition instructs quite ordinary mortals in *hokhmat lev*. The *Amidah* prayer opens with the petition that God may "open our lips" so that we may praise the giver of speech. We are to learn to take the sights, sounds, and forms of the world that are given to us, to cultivate and distill, to reach an understanding of what is beautiful, for what we may be grateful, and to give back this concrete beauty through concrete commandments performed beautifully, with *hiddur*.

This realm, like that of *hokhmah*, may be seen to be close to that of *Adam*, and is thus connected to *l'shmah* and self-development. At the same time, it is linked to health and fitness, which we are "given," but have to use and express. It is clear that traditional educators will be wary of making too much of it for aspects of this realm, such as an exaggerated emphasis on the physical and on the plastic, seem situated on the very edge of Greek wisdom. And yet they may consider the point that the aesthetics of an *halakhic* life, the way it is constructed and what the individual can do within the rules of the game, is a not inconsiderable feature of its power. Through these aesthetics of spiritual life, educated persons can come to see how spontaneity and individual sight are enriched by a normative system, and how, in turn, *hokhmat lev* gives vitality to norms and helps to make them attractive and compelling.

Can *hokhmat lev* accommodate the music and the sundry arts that arise in other languages and seem to exclusively articulate their literature? On this, there are differences of opinion. What some view as Greek wisdom, others will consider general wisdom of the heart, given to all.

With regard to this issue, I have always admired the sentiment of the first-century Rabban Gamliel, who was once asked why he

15. Commentary of Malbim on the Torah, cited in *Studies in Shemot (Exodus)*, p. 532.

bathed in the Bath of Aphrodite in Acre since there were statutes of
the pagan goddess therein. His answer was:

> I came not within her domain; she came into mine. (For) People do not
> say, "Let us make a bath for Aphrodite" but "Let us make an Aphrodite
> as an ornament for the bath."... It is written, (and you shall hew down the
> graven images of) their gods (Deut. 12:3) only. Thus, what is treated as a
> god is forbidden, but what is not treated as a god is permitted.
>
> *Avodah Zarah* 3:4

Finally, the realm of *da'at,* of understanding. This, like Phenix's
synoptics, is concerned with large and comprehensive ways of seeing
the whole picture. In Phenix's scheme, it is related to the study of history, religion, and philosophy. In our conception, too, informed by
some texts we have studied and their commentaries, this realm is
meant to put things together. It should enable pupils in the later
years of their formal Jewish education to see and to make connections betwen *halakhah* and *aggadah,* a prerequisite of all valuative
deliberation. They must get to see the point of diverse activities like
scientific inquiry and literature and what constitutes the integrity of
each. For without understanding what various domains look like
from within and how they are done by competent practitioners, they
cannot be taught to perceive honest and plausible relationships
between Torah and *hokhmah.*[16] Only after getting inside the diverse
universes of discrete inquiries are students able to build conceptual
structures and insights regarding the relationship between Judaism
and other faiths, between Israel and the nations. Without that, they
will not and cannot grasp how languages are both distinct and connected, when literature is required, and how it is nourished.

In the realm of *da'at,* the sense of meaning and relationship is fostered by study, reflection, and discussion. Clearly, activities stimu-
lating young people to see the point are also designed for seeing the
problems. Before one can put realms of meaning together, one must
discover the tensions within and between them. Otherwise, *da'at* will
look like facile apologetics and pseudo-philosophizing. For example,
in our generation there is tension between the lack of agreement as
to what Torah (the language) is and between the desire to maintain
Jewish unity. This problem is within the realm of *Knesset Yisrael.*
There are also glaring tensions between realms, with regard to what

---

16. It is crucial for the achievement of non-bogus *da'at* that linkages and integration
between realms of knowledge not precede competence and care in doing the specific thing being done the way it is done by those who are acknowledged masters
of it. How corruptions of scientific study may take place in the name of the theological conception being furthered is well illustrated (in this case, for Catholic
schools) by George R. La Noue, "Religious Schools and 'Secular' Subjects,"
Harvard Educational Review 32, no. 3 (Summer 1962), pp. 255–91.

we learn from them. There is the *adam,* within teachers and students, that is uncomfortable with particular givens of *Knesset Yisrael.* And there are perceived dichotomies between the particular and the universal, between *Knesset Yisrael* and *Bene Noah.*

Thoughtful educators may envision *da'at* as moving learners towards a large measure of integration, but not too much. Represented in the curriculum by subjects such as Philosophy of Judaism, *parshanut* (exegesis), and philosophy (including issues in scientific thought) *da'at* may lead students not only to see the point of diverse activities and realms of knowledge, but to build into their personalities points of contact between them. They may discover not only the possibilities inherent in each realm but how each enriches the other and, at the same time, sets limits to the others. For example, certain kinds of art may be "non-kosher"; likewise, there are unaesthetic– therefore unpleasant and wrong–ways to perform *mitzvot.* Learning about the interrelationship between realms even while comprehending what constitutes the integrity of each is learning to be one person who can do many things, who can find him/herself in different situations. *Da'at* should move learners towards integration of themselves and of their knowledge.

The realm of *da'at* is a kind of consequence dimension of Jewish education. This means that it demonstrates what the other realms can produce in the learner when approached thoughtfully and with integrity; how these realms, individually and together, help us to become whole human beings. From *da'at* we learn that, ultimately, wholeness is not a matter of knowing about the world, or being able to explain why something is beautiful, or even knowing a great many "reasons for the *mitzvot.*" It is being in the world in a certain way, having beauty in the soul, being a Jewish person. *Da'at,* Rashi teaches us, is *ruach hakodesh,* the holy spirit.[17] It is not what schools teach, but the life experiences with God and people and things they prepare us for.

Parallel to *da'at* and informing it is the character ideal of *Yirat Shamayim.* It is itself a moral and existential consequence of the language that Jewish education is meant to transmit. It is the ideal of the educated person.

Yirat Shamayim, as we have seen, stands for reliability and trustworthiness as well as humility and self-limitation. That, the reader may recall, is the way we translated the idea that "the fearer of Heaven is all that God has in this world." That is how we explained the sense of being in the presence of God. For contemporary Jews, it is difficult to imagine reliability and trustworthiness in people who do not know

17. Commentary of Rashi on Exodus 31:3.

what educated people in today's world generally know, for moral fervor and piety should not look like blissful ignorance. To be oblivious to the complexity both of goodness and of truth makes it difficult to open doors and windows to "the world as it ought to be," to speak in the name of a vision that is the soul of Torah, of Jewish language. Those who maintain fervor and conviction even in the midst of irony, and even a measure of perplexity, seem more trustworthy than those who maintain their integrity by not knowing.

But *da'at* must also cultivate the other side of *Yirat Shamayim,* that of humility and self-limitation. Much learning and knowledge may well lead to arrogance and callousness. We have seen how Rabbi Elazar temporarily gave in to that when he met an ugly man.[18] It can lead to a facile philosophical comprehension where everything fits, or to intellectual dogmatism that transcends all doubts and scoffs at all existential situations. *Da'at* when informed by *Yirat Shamayim* has humility. The more we know, the greater the circumference of ignorance and mystery, the more choices faced in the human situation.

Ernst Akiva Simon[19] has made a valuable distinction between what he calls "initial innocence" *(hatom harishon)* in which we are "authentic but not communicable" (as little children are) and "second innocence" *(hatimmimut hash'niyah).* To reach the second innocence we must pass through the realms of knowledge that make us communicable but perhaps no longer personally authentic. Successful education leads young people to this *timmimut sh'niyah,* where they can find themselves, get to know themselves, and rediscover themselves—yet without regressing to an "authentic" incomprehensibility. They have been given a language with which to speak, and now they may make some literature of their own.

They have been educated. They are on a road to the palace.

---

18. See Chap. 9, pp. 155–56.
19. Ernst Akiva Simon, *"Az Aitam: Al Hatimmimut Hashni'ya"* ("Then I shall be Blameless: On (the Concept of) Second Innocence," in E. A. Simon, *Ha'im Od Yehudim Anahnu (Are We Still Jews?)* (Tel Aviv: Sifri'at Hapoalim, 1982) pp. 135–69.

POSTSCRIPT

*A*fter the expulsion of Adam and Eve from Eden and the death of Abel, they separated, in anger and shame, for one hundred and thirty years. Then, in an act of repentence, they came back together. Thereupon a third child, Seth, destined to become the father of all who survived the flood, was born to them. The Torah goes on to say:

> And to Seth too there was born a son, and he called his name Enosh; then people began to call upon the name of the Lord. (Genesis 4:26)

The traditional commentators are perplexed by the final phrase of this verse. Can it be that before the birth of Enosh, there was no calling upon God? After all, the Torah teaches that humankind was monotheistic from the very beginning! True, Adam and Eve hid from God in the hour of their transgression and Cain was expelled from the divine presence, and wandered. But do we not learn from rabbinic commentary that they returned?

This difficulty leads some exegetes to understand the verse differently. The word *huhal* (began) they interpret to derive from the word *hol,* meaning profane. In the generation of Enosh, they explain, people began to profane and corrupt their calling upon God. We have seen Maimonides adopt this approach when he explained that the worship of God became idolatrous through wrong religious reasoning by the people of Enosh's time. Rashi similarly states: "They began to call the profane by the name of the Lord." Others, insisting that *huhal* does signify a beginning, suggest that it was in this generation that the righteous began to educate the young, teaching them the name of God.

From my late uncle, Rabbi Felix Aber, I once learned another approach. Only where there is a real family, he said, where grandparents remember and relate, where parents hope and anxiously seek advice, where children get the measles—or worse—and grandchildren walk and talk with the old people who are the parents of their parents, is religious life a social and solid reality. Individuals may run away and return, they may experience religious moments and even hear "the voice of the Lord God walking in the garden," but tradition arises only when there are those to whom one passes it on. Then God has a name, and people get together "to call upon the name of the Lord."

My uncle, it now seems to me, was saying that the pristine place of language is the family. The family is there before we are and it itself is the heir of previous generations. If we learn to trust a language, we generally learn this first from parents and grandparents. They are our first community, enabling us to see and to hear, setting the stage for discernments and teaching us commitments. Through and within families, people learn to call upon the name of the Lord.

That the family is in deep crisis throughout the Western world is a truism. And nothing could be more banal than to sermonically lament that and preach about it. Nor is it helpful to simply scold contemporary Jews for often choosing individual self-actualization over family, or for the increasing number of parents who do not speak "in the same voice." These are issues that must be addressed; there are energies and funds that must be invested, there are policies that should be tried and tested. Simply being against the conditions of the open society that produce weak and small families, families that share no common faith and can teach no language, is futile. Total segregation is one possible policy, but those who cherish modern liberal society are justified in looking for other solutions and seeing segregation as a last, desperate resort.

The reason that I did not dwell upon the family throughout the book but preferred to speak of trustworthy teachers, schools, and communities is that I did not wish to pontificate. The reason I bring it up now is that teachers and schools should not be made scapegoats. They cannot solve every problem and they may fail even if they are doing their best, and doing it well.

And, in the meantime, teachers might remember that those who despair of their charges will find themselves, like Adam and Eve in their years of separation, without children to instruct" to call upon the name of the Lord." And those who become cynical, learning to be at ease with violence and corruption, may be tempted to teach idolatry, "calling the profane by the name of the Lord."

Apparently, in the *language* of our Enosh text, too, there are diverse *literatures* that lead from the text to *teaching*.

GLOSSARY

aggadah	the non-legal component of rabbinic literature.
ahavat Shamayim	love of Heaven, sometimes considered a higher stage of piety than "Fear of Heaven."
Amora, (pl., Amoraim)	Talmudic scholars of the later Talmudic generations (ca. 220–500 of the Common Era).
avodat HaShem	The service of God.
avodah zarah	Literally, "alien service," idolatry.
bain adam laMakom	the relationship and, specifically, the commandments that set and regulate the relationship between the human being and God.
bain adam lehavero	the relationship and the commandments between human beings and their fellows.
Bet Midrash	"house of study," the institution of rabbinic Judaism designed for study and discussion of Torah.
bene Noah	"children of Noah," a rabbinic term connotating the entire human family, generally, in reference to all those not bound by the revelation of the Torah, i.e., Gentiles.
Baraita	Tannaic (early Talmudic) teaching not incorporated into the Mishnah.
hillul HaShem	a desecration of God's Name. acting in a way that reflects badly on the religious

	tradition of Judaism and its bearers, the Jewish people. To be distinguished from kiddush HaShem, sanctifying God's name by noble behaviour.
hokhmah	"wisdom," generally distinguished from "Torah," and hence universal.
hokhmat lev	"wisdom of the heart," a category sometimes identified with moral value and/or, aesthetic insight and skill.
da'at	"knowledge"; in some exegetical writings, identified with the end-product of thought and practice.
etrog	a citron fruit used in the celebrations of the festival of Tabernacles (Sukkot).
Gehenna, Gan Eden	the locales of punishment and reward, respectively, in the future life.
Gemara	rabbinic (Amoraic) discussion, commentary and interpretation of the Mishnah. Together with the Mishnah, it constitutes the Talmud.
halakhah, (pl. halakhot)	the legal rulings of the sages, constituting thereby, traditional Jewish norm and law.
Haredi	Lit., one who fears <the Lord>; in modern usage, an ultra-Orthodox Jew.
Heaven	In rabbinic literature, a synonym for God. Hence, "Fear of Heaven".
hesed	loving-kindness.
hiddur	the quality of beauty.
Kabbalah	the corpus of Jewish mysticism, pre-eminently, the Zohar (Book of Splendor).
kashrut	the dietary laws of halakhah that stipulate which foods are kosher, how they are to be prepared and with which other foods they may be eaten.
Knesset Yisrael	the community of Israel, the Jewish people as a covenantal entity.
limmud Torah	study of Torah.
l'shmah, lo lishmah	actions, including study, done "for their own sake," i.e., for their intrinsic

	value, or "not done for their own sake," respectively.
ma'asim tovim	"good deeds", generally with the connotation of refined ethical sensibility.
mahloket	"controversy," either "for the sake of Heaven" i.e., to determine the meaning of Torah tradition, or "not for the sake of Heaven," i.e., motivated by pride, aggressiveness, etc.
mezzuzah	small scroll attached to the doorpost of the Jewish home, containing two passages of Deuteronomy exhorting to love of God and diligent observance of His commandments.
Midrash	a mode of interpreting Scripture, which homiletically expounds words and verses.
minyan	ten worshippers who constitute a quorum, a praying community.
Mishnah	the collected Oral Torah tradition by Rabbi Judah the Prince (212 C.E.). The authorities cited therein are the Tannaim (sing. Tanna). A single passage of the Mishnah is a mishnah.
mitzvah (pl., mitzvot)	commandment(s).
na'aseh v'nishma	"We shall do and (then) hear (understand)"
Noahide commandments	Moral laws incumbent upon all humanity. In Talmudic literature they are considered divinely revealed, to Adam and to Noah.
Pentateuch	The "Five Books of Moses," i.e., the Torah, as distinct from Torah, i.e., the entire written (Scriptural) and "Oral" (rabbinic) tradition.
Pirke Avot, Avot	A small tractate of the Mishnah containing only moral adages and homiletic teachings with special emphasis on the virtue of limmud Torah.
Rasha	A wicked person; the opposite of zaddik, a righteous person.

sha'atnez	A mixture of wool and linen in a garment, making that garment halakhically proscribed.
Talmud	The "Oral Torah," consisting of Mishnah and Gemara.
tanna (pl. tannaim)	"teacher," early rabbinic sage(s) in the first centuries of the Common Era (till circa. 220 C.E.)
Tanakh	"Torah, Prophets and Writings," the Bible.
Tosefta	A Tannaic collections of laws which supplements the Mishnah.
tosafot	A group of medieval commentaries on the Talmud, which are "additional" to those of Rashi, the master exegete. Their expositors are known as "Ba'alei Tosafot" or Tosafists.
tza'ar ba'ale haim	(The prohibition of) causing pain or suffering to living creatures.
yetzer	In rabbinic literature, "the created inclination." The yetzer hara, the evil inclination, is juxtaposed to the yetzer hatov, the good inclination.
zedakah u-mishpat	righteousness and morally appropriateness, the foundations of moral behaviour and of a moral society.

SUBJECT INDEX

NAME INDEX